# MANY MEXICOS

LESLEY BYRD SIMPSON

# MANY
# MEXICOS

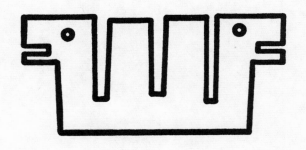

FOURTH EDITION REVISED

UNIVERSITY OF CALIFORNIA PRESS
BERKELEY AND LOS ANGELES
1967

*University of California Press*
*Berkeley and Los Angeles, California*

*Cambridge University Press*
*London, England*

*© 1941, 1946, 1952, 1966*
*by Lesley Byrd Simpson*

*Fourth Edition, Third Printing*

*Printed in the United States of America*
*Library of Congress Catalog Card Number 66-19101*

# PREFACE
# TO THE FOURTH EDITION

The gratifying acceptance that *Many Mexicos* has long enjoyed carries with it a growing sense of responsibility toward its readers. The vast deal of publication in the history of Mexico these past twenty-five years makes it possible and necessary to revise a number of chapters, enlarging some, eliminating errors from others, and in general, it is hoped, making a fuller and better book of it.

In the process I have had to make some change in method. Originally my thought was to spare the casual reader the distraction of citations and scholarly apparatus. While not abandoning that plan altogether, I now feel the need of throwing up breastworks against critics who have taken exception to some of my more challengeable comments. Where feasible, I have incorporated this defense in the text, but in a number of instances I have had recourse to footnotes. To the same end I have expanded the English reading list to include the more significant recent works. I have also compiled a glossary of the Spanish and Nahuatl terms that have no English equivalent.

To the acknowledgments made in the Preface to the Third Edition I wish to add the name of my distinguished colleague, Professor Woodrow Borah, whose suggestions for the improvement of chapters 1 to 14 have been adopted. Professor Wilbert H. Timmons, of Texas Western College, has kindly given me leave to quote from his *Morelos of Mexico*. Dr. Howard F. Cline, of the Hispanic Foundation, has been no less charitable in allowing me to quote from his *Mexico: Revolution to Evolution, 1940–1960*. Finally, during the past year I have had the stimulating experience of preparing an English translation of Dr. Robert Ricard's classic, *La*

v

*Conquête Spirituelle du Mexique,* in the course of which I found my earlier notions of the history of the Church in Mexico undergoing considerable modification.

Lesley Byrd Simpson

Berkeley, 1966


# PREFACE TO THE THIRD EDITION

Mexico as a subject of discussion seems to be charged with emotion beyond reasonable necessity. There seems to be no comfortable halfway station in which to take shelter, pleasantly remote from extremes of love and hate. If, forsaking your cherished pose of scholarly detachment, you let yourself go about this or that less amiable aspect of our charming neighbor, you are in for it. Thus I have been damned by the pious for doing wrong to Mother Church, although others, no less pious, I should judge, have cheered me for doing the contrary. I have been raked over the coals for giving too much space to such old stuff as Spanish colonial Mexico, at the expense of Independence and, especially, of the glorious Revolution of 1910. Some academic critics have registered shock at my having discarded footnotes and other learned apparatus; others suspect me of deviating toward journalism; still others, of dabbling in philosophy. In Mexico it would all quite sensibly be laid to the altitude.

Well, in this edition, in which I have taken some care to meet serious criticism, I have not changed my mind about fundamentals; that is, I still think we cannot know ourselves without knowing our past and our "cultural landscape," as it is called. Events are not the more important because they happen before our eyes or happen to us. Consider the nameless genius who invented the wheel some five thousand years ago, or that other who invented the alphabet, or that other who observed that water runs downhill and put it to work. People have been doing things for a very long time. The Chinese act like Chinese; the Russians, like Russians; the Mexicans, like Mexicans, not because of any novel departures in their current forms of government, but rather because of the immense weight of habit formed through uncounted centuries. The study of habit gives meaning to history, and history will help us to understand ourselves, and in this case that fascinating abstraction we know as Mexico.

So in my book I invite the reader to make with me a rewarding journey into Mexico's past, in the hope that it will suggest the answers to certain insistent questions that will occur to him whenever he breaks away from the paved roads and takes a look at the human landscape.

At the same time, the crowded events of the past twelve years have caused me to modify some of my tentative generalizations, which seemed valid enough in 1940. Intensive and, indeed, frantic industrialization, and a vastly increased food supply have changed the face of Mexico, and, happily, I can no longer say with such cheerless finality: "Mother Mexico is not feeding her children." Her cities have doubled and tripled in size, while shining new factories turn out every conceivable essential for urban living, from motor cars to cortisone, and an eager pride in these blessings of civilization is manifest on every hand. All these things have their price, however, and no one can hope to escape the reckoning.

Many of the technical aspects of the overwhelming changes of recent years are beyond my competence to explore, even if I had the space. Readers desiring to venture beyond my brief summing-up may consult three extraordinary books: Nathan Whetten's *Rural Mexico* (1948), Frank Tannenbaum's *Mexico: The Struggle for Peace and Bread* (1950), and Sanford Mosk's *Industrial Revolution in Mexico* (1950). For their further guidance I have included in this edition a selected list of standard English titles covering the more significant topics of Mexican history and culture.

My own comments on the contemporary scene, apart from the historical chapters, are rather the notes of a friendly observer, gathered from books, newspapers, travel, and a lot of conversation with my favorite informants, to wit: schoolteachers, college professors, and writers; bus drivers, farmers, barbers, priests, and politicians; hotel keepers, bartenders, traveling salesmen, and manufacturers; train conductors, engineers, baggage-smashers, and bootblacks. It would have been less confusing, perhaps, to have selected those of one mind; but Mexico is as far from having one mind as it is possible to get, and the reader will have to put up with this painful lack of standardization. In time he may even learn to love it, for, whatever else Mexico may be, she is never dull—for which I may add *Thank God!* and likewise *¡Viva Mexico!*

I wish most gratefully to acknowledge permission to quote from Frank Tannenbaum's and Sanford Mosk's books, just mentioned. Arturo Torres-Rioseco was equally generous in allowing me to use his valued *New World Literature,* as was John Tate Lanning in placing at my disposal his scholarly *Academic Culture in the Spanish Colonies.* No student of modern Mexico could dispense with Carleton Beals' *Porfirio Díaz, Dictator of Mexico,* which the author characteristically gave me leave to ransack.

Finally, a major part of my firsthand knowledge of Mexico was acquired during several years' residence there financed by the John Simon Guggenheim Memorial Foundation, the Rockefeller Foundation, and the University of California.

L. B. S.

January, 1952

# CONTENTS

# MAPS

*Grant me, Lord, a little light,*
*Be it no more than a glowworm giveth*
*Which goeth about by night,*
*To guide me through this life,*
*This dream which lasteth but a day,*
*Wherein are many things on which to stumble,*
*And many things at which to laugh,*
*And others like unto a stony path*
*Along which one goeth leaping.*

(L. B. S.)

Prayer of an Aztec chieftain upon his election.

(After Bernardino de Sahagún, O. F. M., *Historia General de las Cosas de Nueva España*, 5 vols. [Mexico, 1938], vol. 2, p. 81. Sahagún completed his famous book before 1569).

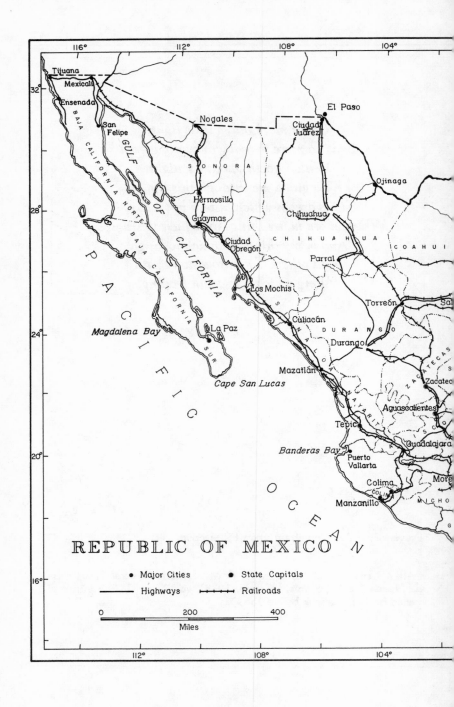

REPUBLIC OF MEXICO

- • Major Cities
- • State Capitals
- —— Highways
- ++++++ Railroads

0    200    400
Miles

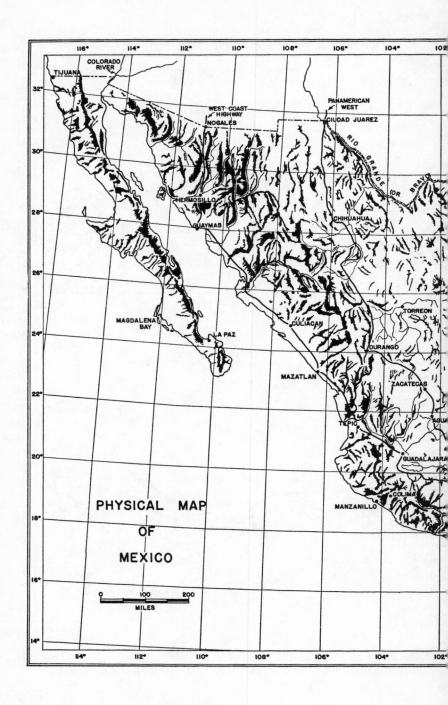

PHYSICAL MAP

OF

MEXICO

# 1

## MANY MEXICOS

Once upon a time, in the immensely remote past—so long ago that only geologists and astronomers would be interested in computing it —Mexico was split across the middle by a great rift in the earth's crust. That rift, or tectonic seam, extends from Cape Corrientes on the Pacific coast, eastward to Tuxtla San Andrés in Vera Cruz, on the Gulf of Mexico. North and south of the seam huge blocks were uptilted into what we call the Central Plateau of Mexico, which covers about two-thirds of the total area of the country. How high the blocks originally were, no one knows, but where they meet along the seam they are still about 8,000 feet above sea level, although they fall off somewhat toward the west. From the line of the seam northward the Central Plateau slopes gently downward to an average elevation of about 4,000 feet along the border of the United States.

The seam itself is a chaotic belt of broken land 100 miles wide and 800 miles long. Through it a magnificent procession of volcanoes pushed up: Colima, Sangangüey, and Ceboruco, at the Pacific end; the Nevado de Toluca, Ajusco, Popocatépetl, Ixtaccíhuatl, and Malinche, on the Plateau; and the incomparably beautiful Pico de Orizaba, or Citlaltépetl, that is, "Mountain of the Star," as the Aztecs called it, whose dazzling snow-capped cone rises more than 18,000 feet and may be seen from a hundred miles out in the Gulf of Mexico. Scores of smaller volcanoes, which in less overpowering company would be worthy of mention, dot the seam from one end to the other, while lakes and rivers and mountains of lava and volcanic ash make the region in many parts a sort of gigantic natural slag heap, called *malpaís,* or bad country. *The effects of that upheaval*

1

*were to determine (a few million years in the future) the conditions and habits of life of a great part of the Mexican people.*

The upheaval did not happen all at once; indeed, it is still going on. Frequent earthquakes, some of them very destructive of life and property, keep the pious in a continual state of bewilderment over the inscrutable ways of Providence. In February, 1943, for example, after preliminary tremors and subterranean explosions, a fissure opened in a cornfield near the village of Paricutín, Michoacán, from which an immense stream of lava poured and inundated the countryside. The neighboring village of Parangaricútiro was completely buried, and ten other villages and towns of the vicinity suffered varying degrees of damage. Up to the time of its quiet death, on March 2, 1952, it is estimated that the Volcán de Paricutín had vomited up a billion or so tons of lava, which probably did less harm than the vast amount of volcanic sand and ash that it spewed over the region, killing crops and trees, and rendering the land useless for cultivation, although in time the ashes will make a new layer of fertile soil, a process that is already well along. There is no likelihood at all that such activity has ceased.

The block of the Central Plateau south of the great seam is more violently uptilted than its northern counterpart, broken and split into a labyrinth of lesser blocks, and pitched and tumbled about in all directions, forming several thousand square miles of the wildest country imaginable. These planless mountains and deep depressions are such an effective barrier to circulation that they quite literally cut Mexico in two. The timid little railway that twists and doubles its way between Mexico City and Oaxaca emphasizes the thoroughness of that barrier, and even it had to give up before the formidable mass of the Sierra Madre del Sur. Only lately has the barrier yielded to the onslaught of modern bulldozers, and the Pan-American Highway between Oaxaca and the Guatemalan frontier is a spectacular tribute to the skill of the Mexican road builders.

The lower axis of the southern block is the Isthmus of Tehuantepec, to the east of which the land again rises into the rough limestone plateau of Chiapas, which in turn drops off northward into the steaming coastal plain of Tabasco and Campeche. The difficulty of the terrain is indicated by the lack (until recently) of communi-

2

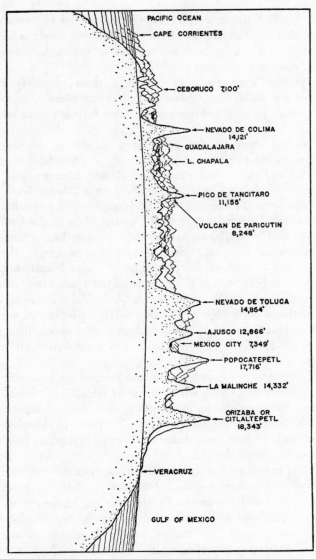

PACIFIC OCEAN

CAPE CORRIENTES

CEBORUCO 7100'

NEVADO DE COLIMA
14,121'

GUADALAJARA

L. CHAPALA

PICO DE TANCITARO
11,155'

VOLCAN DE PARICUTIN
8,248'

NEVADO DE TOLUCA
14,854'

AJUSCO 12,866'

MEXICO CITY 7,349'

POPOCATEPETL
17,716'

LA MALINCHE 14,332'

ORIZABA OR
CITLALTEPETL
18,343'

VERACRUZ

GULF OF MEXICO

Profile of the Great Seam at approximately Lat. 19° N.
(After J. L. Tamayo, *Geografía de Mexico*.)

3

cation between Chiapas and Yucatan. The railroad (Ferrocarril del Sureste) that finally traversed the region was long wryly referred to as *el ferrocarril del centenario,* because it would be running a hundred years hence.

The peninsula of Yucatan is a huge sheet of rarely broken limestone, a paradise for archaeologists, but one whose thin soil and erratic rainfall make it a very spotty paradise for the people who live there.

Along the edges of the great land masses of Mexico, and everywhere within them, the earth's crust has been further creased and folded and ripped into ranges and clusters of mountains. From the border of Arizona southward, the Sierra Madre Occidental, which is about 100 miles wide on the average and 1,200 miles long, cuts the Central Plateau off from the coastal plain of the Pacific, so effectively that it can be pierced in only three or four places in its immense length. For those who like to flirt with danger, the hair-raising stretch of highway between Durango and Mazatlán can be recommended. Southeast of the great seam these mountains continue for a thousand miles more as the Sierra Madre del Sur, which comes down to the water's edge and makes a large part of the states of Oaxaca and Guerrero a forbidding and unmapped waste. Beyond the Isthmus of Tehuantepec they form the unbroken wall of the southern escarpment of the Chiapas highlands.

Along the eastern edge of the Central Plateau the same phenomenon is repeated. Beginning with the low brown hills of Nuevo León, just across the Rio Grande, the Sierra Madre Oriental separates the highlands from the coastal plain of the Gulf of Mexico for a thousand miles, rising toward the south to a stupendous green wall nine thousand feet in height.

As if the mountain barriers and escarpments were not enough to discourage any notion of geographic unity in Mexico, nature has further complicated the matter by slashing the plateau with innumerable gullies and canyons, called *barrancas,* cut by the heavy summer downpours. The canyon of the Santiago is one such barranca, bearing comparison with the Grand Canyon of the Colorado in Arizona. This vast abyss extends from the vicinity of Guadalajara several hundred miles across the states of Jalisco and

4

Nayarit to the Pacific. Another is the 400-mile gorge of the Moctezuma, which crosses the Central Plateau through the states of Querétaro, Hidalgo, and Vera Cruz. The rivers that flow down most of these barrancas are feeble trickles during the dry season and raging brown torrents from June to November, useless for transport and too far below the surrounding country to be utilized for irrigation. In pre-Conquest times the barrancas were easily defended barriers and became the natural boundaries between the nomad tribes of the north and the agricultural peoples of the south, and today they are formidable obstacles for highways and railroads to overcome. *Most streams of any consequence in the Central Plateau run through barrancas, from hundreds to thousands of feet deep.* An important exception is the meandering Lerma River, which drains and fertilizes the rich Bajío country of Michoacán, Guanajuato, and Jalisco, before flowing into beautiful Lake Chapala. In 1951 it was tapped to supply Mexico City with water at the rate of 22,718,620 gallons a day. What effect this heavy withdrawal will have on the agricultural life of the Lerma basin is an uncomfortable problem for agronomists to ponder.

The tale is not yet told. An almost equally great barrier to human circulation in primitive times was presented by the extremes of climate at the different altitudes. A moment's reflection will make the reason clear. The mean temperature at any given place drops one degree Fahrenheit for every 300-foot increase in altitude. Thus, Mexico City, at 7,300 feet, is normally about twenty-five degrees cooler than Vera Cruz, at sea level. That might not be so bad, but the humidity drops at a corresponding rate as one approaches the higher altitudes, until the rapid evaporation on the Plateau makes the *sensible* difference in temperature much greater than the thermometer indicates. The effect on living conditions should at once be apparent. In the hot coastal plains and in the depressions of the Plateau the Indian wears few clothes, and his children none at all, and his habitation is a flimsy affair of canes and thatch, through which the winds blow and the rains splash. The higher he climbs the sturdier must be his house and the warmer his clothing, and, lacking such protection, as he frequently does, he is more than likely to fall a victim to the respiratory diseases that are the scourge of the

5

high country in winter. Also, in the lowlands his lungs are conditioned to the breathing of air rich in oxygen, and he gets along on comparatively little of it. Transfer him to the highlands, however, and he must take in a great deal more air, with a corresponding strain on his heart, as all tourists soon learn. Contrariwise, a highland Indian brought to the lowlands has more lung capacity than he needs, and the unused part of his lungs makes an excellent breeding place for assorted deadly germs. The danger of bringing men from the low country to the high, or vice versa, was so great that the Spanish government forbade it by stringent laws, not always observed, to be sure.

The rugged terrain that I have described would not necessarily make life difficult within the various isolated regions of Mexico if it were not for the fact that it also determines to a large extent the amount of rainfall in a given locality. If, for example, you live on the windward side of the eastern escarpment, you will be drenched by a regular deluge for many months of the year. Move a few miles inland over the mountains, however, and you will spend a good part of your time praying for rain.

A second and equally important fact about the climate of Mexico is that the greater part of the country lies in the wide band of stagnant air between the path of the northern cyclonic storms (the prevailing westerlies) and the tropical rain belt, famous in the days of sailing ships as the "horse latitudes." This band moves north and south with the ecliptic but extends, roughly, from Lat. 32° N. to Lat. 16° N. Rainfall in these latitudes is extremely capricious, although, generally speaking, it is very light in the far north and very heavy in the far south, and occurs only in the summer months, with occasional exceptions in the winter. *Average* precipitation means very little. Years may go by with hardly enough rain to water the maize crop, followed by a succession of disastrous floods and such high humidity that the grain sprouts in the ear. There is hardly any such thing as a "normal" season for the Mexican farmer. In the summer of 1943, for example, a severe drought destroyed a large part of the maize crop, an estimated loss of 500,000 tons, and in the late summer of 1944 floods washed away 200,000 tons more.

The farmer is further plagued in the high country by unpredictable frosts, which may kill his maize while it is sprouting, or kill it while the grain is still in the milk. Losses of 50 per cent are not uncommon, and once in a long time comes such a frightful catastrophe as the great freeze of August, 1784, which totally wiped out the maize and bean crops of the Plateau, causing the death by starvation of an estimated 300,000 people.[1]

Rainfall is of such transcendental importance in the life of Mexico that we must once again follow the map around in order to understand it. Beginning with the extreme northwest we find the long tongue of Lower California spanning the belt of greatest aridity. Its northern end, on the Pacific coast at least, comes in for a small share of the rains brought by the cyclonic storms, but the next 700 miles of it are a scorched and almost uninhabited desert, until its southern tip intrudes a little way into the fringe of the tropical rain belt. Crossing over to the east side of the Gulf of California, we come to the Sonora Desert, which for 500 miles south of the border is one of the most fearfully arid wastes on the surface of the globe, where the temperature rises to such heights as to make the desert impassable save in the relatively cool months of winter. But south of Guaymas the aspect of the coastal plain gradually changes, becoming greener and more habitable in Sinaloa, and, finally, going to the opposite extreme, becomes a dense tropical jungle north of Cape Corrientes.

East of the Sonora Desert the wide expanse of the Sierra Madre Occidental catches a fair amount of rain, and its long narrow valleys make a pleasant enough habitat for man. Continuing eastward

---

[1] I find it excessive that Ernest Gruening, in his usually thoughtful *Mexico and Its Heritage,* should inferentially attribute the mortality of that famine to Spanish indifference. "A Spanish muleteer," he writes, "who became rich enough to lend the king a million pesos was created Conde de Regla; when his son was christened the whole party walked from his home to the church on ingots of silver. But in 1784, 300,000 people perished in New Spain from famine and its consequences." This is one of the most astonishing non sequiturs I have ever come across. The fact of the matter is that in the unprecedented disaster the viceroy opened the public granaries, and Crown and Church officials and private citizens organized relief on an immense scale. The records of the great famine fill many hundreds of folios in the National Archives of Mexico (*Ramo de Indios*), and are mostly concerned with relief measures.

beyond the mountains of Sonora, we enter the immense triangle of desert that stretches far down into the Central Plateau and covers a large part of the states of Chihuahua, Coahuila, Durango, and Zacatecas. The desperately dry plains of this central desert offer poor support for the population, except where the waters of the Conchos River, the Nazas, and other streams have been diverted into great irrigation projects, such as the Laguna district of Durango. Two hundred miles eastward across the desert we come to the beginning of the Sierra Madre Oriental and sufficient rainfall to put eastern Coahuila and Nuevo León among the best farming districts of the Republic. Dropping down into the Gulf state of Tamaulipas, however, we enter the hot and relatively sterile northern end of the coastal plain of the Gulf of Mexico, which is a continuation of the topography of the southern end of Texas.

And so down to Tampico, Vera Cruz, where the great horseshoe of the coastal plain begins, appearing first as a narrow strip of land 500 miles long, lying under the shadow of the eastern escarpment of the Central Plateau and drenched by incredible quantities of water dropped by the wet winds blowing in from the Gulf. The precipitation increases as we go southward, until at the middle of the horseshoe, on the north side of the Isthmus of Tehuantepec, it reaches the staggering total of *ten feet a year*. The numerous torrents, swamps, and jungles resulting from the continual deluge make southern Vera Cruz, Tabasco, and Campeche one of the most difficult regions of Mexico to traverse. Here the heavy runoff turns the country into a network of great rivers and its people into a race of boatmen. Rain, which is precious beyond all things on the Plateau, is here one of man's worst enemies, because it leaches plant food out of the soil and makes large areas hardly more than soggy green deserts, where a few sorry-looking villages somehow manage to eke out a living, in competition with the mosquitoes.

The coastal plains are further ravaged by destructive hurricanes which blow in from the Caribbean and the Pacific. These huge masses of saturated air, thousands of cubic miles of it, get to spinning and wandering about in the most curious and unpredictable fashion. Our fun-loving Weather Bureau gives these terrifying meteorological tops appropriate feminine names, such as Moll, Betty, and

8

Dolly, and watches their career with a sharp eye. But there is nothing funny about a hurricane, which is one of the most murderous weapons in the abundant arsenal of nature. Galveston will not soon forget the 6,000 citizens who perished in the flood of 1900, and one dreadful hurricane (typhoon) in 1737 killed 300,000 people in Bengal.

One of the favorite targets of the Caribbean hurricanes is the Gulf coast of Mexico, where they beat themselves to pieces against the mountains, and in the process dump their enormous cargoes of water. The hurricane of September, 1944, wandered in over Yucatan and the Isthmus of Tehuantepec, and struck squarely in the Papaloapan basin, where it dropped somewhere around ten thousand million tons of water, *all at once.* For five days winds attaining a velocity of 120 miles an hour battered the unlucky region. The Papaloapan River covered the city of Cosamaloapan to a depth of ten feet. Vultures scrabbled in the mud for dead bodies, and the people who escaped drowning were attacked by the ferocious clouds of mosquitoes which rose like a plague of Egypt out of the steaming muck. The state of Vera Cruz suffered damages estimated at 100,000,000 pesos, and deaths from drowning and disease ran into the hundreds. In 1951 a hurricane smashed into the valley of the Pánuco and devastated the whole Huasteca region of Vera Cruz, Tamaulipas, and San Luis Potosí. The Tamesí and Pánuco scoured their basins clean of the works of man. The Lázaro Cárdenas Dam in San Luis Potosí had to be dynamited, and added its weight to the general destruction. The south coast is occasionally visited by these monsters. In the fall of 1959 an exceptionally violent hurricane raged in from the Pacific and struck in the state of Colima. The port of Manzanillo was all but wiped out, and the town of Minatitlán was totally obliterated and turned into a stinking inferno of unburied corpses. Some fifteen hundred people lost their lives, and the property damage was in the neighborhood of a billion pesos.

The moisture-laden winds from the Gulf of Mexico beat against the northern escarpment of the Chiapas plateau, and the heavy precipitation creates an all but impenetrable jungle in the depression between Chiapas and Yucatan. (This is the jungle that Cortés had to hack his way through in 1524.) The winds lose some of their

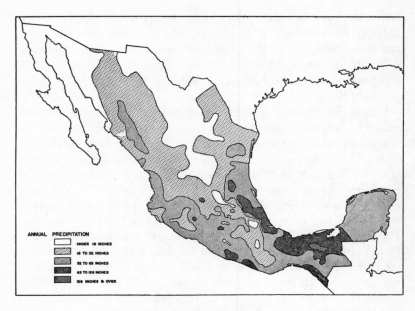

Average Annual Precipitation
(After Secretaría de la Economía Nacional)

fierceness as they pass over Chiapas and make that region one of the
best watered and pleasantest in the Republic. When, however, they
blow down over the southern escarpment they change their character
again and howl across the narrow Pacific coastal plain in a fury of
heat, dust, and flies in the dry season, which are only a shade less
unbearable than the heat, mud, and mosquitoes of the wet season.
To avoid the worst of these hazards, the Spaniards built a "summer
road" over the mountains between Oaxaca and Guatemala, and a
"winter road" along the coastal plain. The discomfort and danger of
the Tehuantepec Gale have provoked sour comment from travelers
for four hundred years. Thomas Gage, whose *New Guide to the
West Indies* I shall have occasion to quote a number of times,
negotiated the formidable pass of Macuilapa (between Oaxaca and
Chiapas) in 1626, and was obliged to wait three days for the wind to
subside enough to let him through. His pain was increased by his

having to live on green lemons the while. The Dominican historian, Francisco de Burgoa, wrote of this pass in 1670: "The other [summer road] to the east begins to climb the steep grade of Macuilapa, dangerous because of the north winds, which blow at the summit with such violence that they sometimes blow mules, together with their riders, off the precipice." A night spent in that screaming gale, or an airplane trip through it, is an experience to be enjoyed only in retrospect.

In our hasty journey around the rim of the Republic I have purposely omitted the most important part of it lying in the two sections of the Central Plateau north and south of the great seam: all the territory, roughly speaking, between Lat. 22° N. and the Isthmus of Tehuantepec, except the coastal plains. Three-fourths of the total population of Mexico live in this area. It is the essence, the very heart and kernel of Mexico, enjoying more or less similar living conditions, given differences in altitude. The reason, of course, lies in the rainfall, which, although capricious and unreliable, can usually be counted on to water the maize during the crucial early weeks of its growing season.

This rough sketch of the topography and climate of Mexico is admittedly only an approximation, since any generalization about them is likely to break down locally. Accidents of the terrain play unexpected tricks upon lovers of order in nature. A cool and well-watered valley nestles in the Sierra de San Pedro Mártir of Lower California, or an unaccountable bit of desert appears in the heart of the tropical rain belt, where it has no right to be, as on the northeastern tip of the peninsula of Yucatan. It should begin to be apparent to the reader, therefore, why there are many Mexicos—why, for example, there are some fifty distinct language groups among the Indians, and why the Maya of Yucatan are total foreigners to the Yaqui of Sonora.

# 2

## THE TYRANT

From remote antiquity the people of Mexico have had a common heritage; that is, wherever maize will grow—and it will grow everywhere save in the out-and-out deserts and the waterlogged places I have described—their staff of life is the *tortilla,* that flat, leathery, not unpleasant thin cake which is the Mexican's bread, as well as the simple instrument for conveying to his mouth such dripping and delectable messes as bean soup, fried beans, and *guacamole,* this last a paste made of *aguacate* (avocado) and chili, now happily naturalized in the U.S.A. The dry maize is prepared by soaking it overnight in a solution of lime or wood ashes, which removes the tough outer skin. It is then ground into a wet meal (*masa*) with a stone rolling pin (*mano*) on that curious three-legged washboard contraption known as a *metate.* The masa may be mixed with water and drunk as *atole,* but its principal use is in the making of tortillas, which are baked on an earthenware griddle (*comal*). From one end of Mexico to the other the grinding of the masa and the patting of tortillas is the morning song of life. It has been going on for such countless centuries, and is so thoroughly a part of immutable *costumbre,* that I suspect that the vendors of labor-saving gadgets and those kindly people who would emancipate the Indian woman from her ancient drudgery will not completely interrupt the rhythm of the *tortilleras.* It may be objected that not all Mexicans are Indians; but to most of them (67 per cent, according to the 1960 census), the tortilla is bread. In the cities, to be sure, and wherever electricity and gasoline are available, the motor-driven *molino de nixtamal* now does the work of grinding the maize, but this machine-made product has to contend with a popular superstition that the masa does not taste quite right unless it is ground with mano and metate, and the tortillas patted as God ordained.

This all-pervading heritage goes back to that distant day when the wandering seed-gatherers of the highlands of Central America (or perhaps Peru) found a luscious grass, with edible seeds growing in a single ear. No one has any idea how long ago it was, nor do we know how long the gatherers were content to collect the wild seeds, until one day the accidental sprouting of a lost kernel or two gave some forgotten scientist the idea of planting them. From that moment dates the civilization of the Western hemisphere. The Inca, the Maya, the Toltec, the Zapotec, the Mixtec, the Tarascan, the Aztec, all the numerous cultures of pre-white Middle America, in short, owed their existence to the discovery of maize. *That discovery was one of the most important achievements of mankind anywhere.*

Maize, like rice, wheat, and most other plant foods, was not merely a discovery; it was an invention. The principle of selection had to be thought of before any progress could be made toward the heavy producers we know today; but, once that principle had been established, the long evolution from the wild grass of Middle America to the stupendous cornstalks of Iowa was assured. Those early American scientists, by careful selection, got the wild maize to yield more and more seeds, until it gave a great many more than were needed for reproduction. They also learned that the seeds would keep indefinitely if guarded from moisture, and they stored them in elevated stone bins against the lean months. They brought the seed to the hot country of the coast and to the semiarid country of the Plateau, and made it grow where wild maize had never been. Maize began to take on a certain esoteric or miraculous quality in their minds and became in time the center of the tribal religion. It was the holy grain, the *teocentli* of the Aztecs. Its planting and harvest became the occasion for the most solemn sacrifices of the year, for it was the bread of life, *and it still is.*

The intelligent people of Middle America discovered and invented many other valuable things. They took the small bitter seeds of a species of lupine and from them developed the infinite variety of beans that we know. A small wild squash, under their patient hands, became the pumpkin. A morning glory with a thick root was

13

metamorphosed into the sweet potato. The "Irish" potato, tobacco, "Sea Island" cotton and the ordinary "Egyptian" cotton, a great many useful herbs, the fibers of the maguey and henequen, cochineal, a native indigo, and Tyrian purple (from sea snails), and the techniques of cultivation and manufacture of all these things were Indian discoveries and inventions. Perhaps, if they had not been disturbed, they would have got round to inventing money, interest, time payments, and gunpowder.

Their useful discoveries, however, exacted a price. They learned to depend on maize for their food supply. With the abundant yield of the new grain a larger population could be supported, and, after it had come into existence, it *had* to be supported. The Indians became the slaves of their own inventions. Maize imposed a severe discipline upon her devotees. Land had to be cleared and prepared for cultivation at one fixed season of the year; the grain had to be planted at another, harvested at another. To learn precisely when those seasons occurred forced them to study astronomy, to invent mathematics and an exact calendar. Rain had to be prayed for and gods and priests propitiated with gifts and sacrifices. One break in the eternal round and a community would be faced with starvation or the anger of the gods. No more moving about as in the old free days of hunting and seed-gathering. Surplus food meant that the Indians could now afford the luxury of parasite classes. Warriors and an elaborate hierarchy of priests, artists, poets, scientists, craftsmen, architects, and engineers lived two thousand years ago in the cities of Yucatan. The discipline of maize spread north and south, to the valleys of the Andes and the villages of the Iroquois. In time it might have reduced the people of the whole hemisphere to civilized immobility. And then came the crowning irony of maize: When the Spaniards arrived, to their amazement and delight they found a numerous agrarian population, long accustomed to the sober responsibility of raising food and, after the defeat of their rulers, not unwilling to exchange one parasite class for another.

Maize would brook no competitors. It made ancient Mexico a one-crop country. The reasons are clear. Maize was the single crop that flourished under the peculiar climatic conditions of the Plateau and the lowlands. The seasonal humidity (June to September) coincided with its growing season. It did not require irrigation. As late as 1930 three-fourths of the maize crop was raised on unirrigated land. The weight of this fact will be appreciated after what we have learned about the nature of the terrain and the rainfall pattern. The thoroughness of the tyranny of maize is best illustrated by a few figures. In 1930 more than two million metric tons of maize were produced, or, say, about sixty million bushels. The next two ranking cereal crops, wheat and rice, totaled 365,000 metric tons, and beans yielded some 87,000 tons. In other words, the production of maize was more than four times as great as that of the three other major food crops put together. To state the problem in another way: the ideal diet would include 150 grams of maize a day (under six ounces), but, according to statistics published by the Bank of Mexico in 1945, the city dweller was consuming 565 grams and the country dweller 852 grams a day.[1]

The immense shift of population to the cities, owing to the mechanization of farming, has, of course, during these past few decades changed the eating habits of the country. There are still, however, large numbers of rural folk to whom maize is the holy grain of Mexico. If the ancient gods of rain and fertility have been baptized and made over into Christian saints and virgins, their functions have not materially changed. The local *santo* is still paraded through the fields at planting time, and is vigorously scolded when the rains fail to come. The growing of maize can never be wholly a business for the peasant. *It is a way of life.*

Maize exacts another and more insidious tribute from her slaves. It is one of the most soil-exhausting of crops, and only in the great haciendas and state-operated farms is the soil's fertility kept up by massive use of chemicals. In primitive conditions, which prevail in isolated communities, a plot of land (*milpa*) is good for two or three seasons at most, after which it is abandoned for several years. The

[1] Of late years the agricultural and dietary picture has changed radically. In 1961 maize was still the ranking crop, with 5,500,000 metric tons; wheat, 1,400,000; rice, 275,000; beans, 600,000. The production of maize was still immense, but had shrunk to only twice that of the three mentioned. At the same time the Ministry of Agriculture has encouraged the planting of other food crops with notable success, until the diet of Mexico is far less top-heavy in cereals.

preparation of a new milpa is a laborious task. It is cleared usually with machetes and mattocks, and the brush is piled up to dry. Toward the end of the dry season, usually in March, the new milpas are burned over. Immense areas every spring are cleared by fire, and the country seems to be burning everywhere. The burned-over land, enriched by the potash, is plowed and planted after the first rain, and must be kept reasonably clear of weeds, especially in the more humid parts. If the rains come as they should—and they usually do—and if the frost does not destroy the crop—and it usually does not—the maize matures in ninety to a hundred and twenty days, depending upon the altitude, the grain is harvested, and the round is begun over again.

Now, the endless depletion of the soil and the destruction of its protective cover by fire have had certain obvious and disquieting effects. Recent studies have made it pretty clear that slash-and-burn agriculture and its wicked sister, erosion, have been marching side by side in Mexico for thousands of years. Leaving out of the reckoning for the moment the white man's contribution to the process (cattle, sheep, goats, the ox and the plow), and his tendency to appropriate the best lands for his own use, it is evident that, as the population increased, more and more land had to be brought under cultivation, which meant that the milpas moved farther and farther up the mountainsides and that the land was cultivated until it was exhausted beyond the point of recovery. Denuded slopes and abandoned fields were then subjected to the intense battering of the summer rains, and what little soil remained was washed down the barrancas to the sea. It is a melancholy thing to see once-cultivated and once-prosperous countryside now thrusting out its fleshless bones in unheeded protest against the vandalism of man. An example is the mountainous part of Mixteca Alta, in western Oaxaca, which four hundred years ago was a heavily populated province, renowned for its high culture and industry. It is today an almost unrelieved stretch of badlands.

The second effect, then, of the tyranny of maize has been the destruction of the soil. That this process is well along in the highlands no thoughtful person can doubt. The pitiful stands of maize growing in pocket-handkerchief milpas on the tops of mountains, or in the cracks and crevices of their naked slopes, and the undisguised poverty of the communities depending upon them, are fierce reminders that maize is a savage taskmistress. To break her iron rule will require an inventiveness, patience, and fortitude as great as those of the ancients who first harnessed her to the service of mankind.[2]

Among the theories advanced to account for the strange succession of Maya "empires" in Yucatan, the most plausible is the exhaustion of the soil. The peaks of Maya culture occurred at intervals of about five hundred years. The intervening depressions were not caused by conquest, so far as we know. The Aztec invasion during the last "empire" in the fifteenth century could hardly have been more than a raid, given the extreme difficulties of penetrating the jungle barrier. It took Cortés and his army, equipped with steel tools, six months to hack their way through, and even so they were all but defeated by starvation. There is likewise no record of an invasion by water. Yucatan seems to have been beyond the range of the Caribs, the only pre-Conquest people who might have managed it. Gradual exhaustion of the soil, and political unrest caused by the dwindling food supply, may account for the mysteriously abrupt collapse of the Maya state.

The soil of Yucatan is a thin layer of decomposed limestone. Although originally fairly rich, it will raise only two crops of maize before it begins to fail, and the farmer must clear new milpas. Available agricultural land is sharply circumscribed, and the uncontrolled birth rate must have pushed its carrying capacity to the limit within a comparatively short time. Several generations of abundance and expansion were followed by a period of falling production and depression of the subsistence level, until the bulk of the population revolted, emigrated, or died. An "empire" ended.

Centuries passed, during which the decomposition of the limestone and the accumulation of humus created a new layer of soil. Yucatan was rediscovered by its exiled population, and the cycle was

[2] Quite aware of the urgency of the problem, the government in the past thirty years has constructed vast irrigation systems, mostly in the west and north, and brought millions of new acres under cultivation, with the encouraging results already noted.

repeated. This theory is supported by evidence of massive migrations back and forth. The extensive ruins of Palenque, Copán, and the Lake Petén district, where the earliest "empire" had its beginning, are all indicative of these wanderings. At the time of the Spanish Conquest Yucatan was in the trough of one of its depressions and had been so for about two hundred years.

Maize is probably the greatest but not the only culprit in the destruction of the soil. When the Spaniards imposed new burdens upon it they accelerated the process. They introduced the ox-drawn plow, which may have done as much damage as any other single factor. In primitive times the planting stick of the Indians did not disturb the mat of roots which bound the soil together and retarded erosion. The plow, on the other hand, not only broke up the root binder but created convenient channels for the water to use in its work of destruction. The reader is reminded that a summer's downpour in the Plateau frequently attains the cloudburst rate of two inches an hour. Immediately after the Conquest, the Spaniards brought in sheep and cattle, which bred so freely that in an amazingly short time they had overrun a great part of the country. By the end of the first century of the Spanish occupation overgrazing and the cutting action of hooves, particularly those of sheep, were disastrous. A sharp competition for survival developed between livestock and the Indian population. Horned cattle discovered a taste for green corn and it was virtually impossible to keep them out of the milpas, although the Indians planted cactus fences and killed the intruders. For three hundred years the law courts were flooded with suits for damages.

In this context the story of sheep may be the most important. In Spain for several centuries before the discovery of the New World wool was a valuable article of international commerce. The sheepmen, encouraged by the government, organized themselves into a great confraternity, called a *mesta,* which operated under its own laws and enforced them in its own courts. The sheepmen became a privileged and arrogant aristocracy. It was natural, therefore, that the settlers of New Spain should go in for sheep raising on a large scale. Thousands of grants for sheep *estancias* were made by the Audiencia of Mexico, and the manufacture of woolen stuffs soon became a major industry. The Indians of the Plateau replaced their traditional cotton *manta* with the warmer and more easily manufactured woolen blanket. Indian communities and *caciques* followed the lead of the Spaniards and turned their idle lands into sheep ranges. There was an immense amount of vacated land available, because something like nine-tenths of the native population died off in the first century of the Spanish occupation. By, say, 1600, sheep and goat estancias occupied an estimated area of 36,000 square miles. The tiny province of Tlaxcala was one of the first to be exposed to European techniques of sheep raising and wool manufacture, and the Tlaxcalans soon became celebrated for their skill in weaving, as they still are. Even today, after a marked decline in the wool industry, Tlaxcala has a sheep and goat population of about 200,000 (for an area of 1,500 square miles, more or less), and the land is good for little else.

Another serious cause of erosion was (and is) deforestation. Wherever a Spanish town was built, the surrounding woods had to supply beams for the roofs and charcoal for the kitchens. The reconstruction of Mexico City after the Conquest destroyed the famous stand of cedars (*ahuehuetes*) which extended over the hills beyond Texcoco to the mountains of Tlaxcala. The Spaniards continued the tradition of the old country, which was so thoroughly denuded of trees that a popular saying has it that a bird can fly over Castile and never find a branch on which to rest. Then, every Spanish household (and soon every Mexican household) did its cooking with charcoal. Although its consumption has fallen off considerably in recent years, owing to the increasing use of petroleum products, Mexico City alone consumes some 450 tons of charcoal a day, which means that 3,000 tons of live trees must be fed into the charcoal burners' ovens.

The destruction of the forests by the cities, however, was a small affair in the early days as compared with the ravages of the mines. Shafts and drifts had to be timbered with heavy beams, and all smelting was done with charcoal. Wherever a mining community (*real de minas*) was established, a diseased spot began to appear, and it spread and spread until each mining town was in the middle of

19

something like a desert. As early as 1543 the Indians of Taxco were complaining to Viceroy Mendoza that all the forests nearby had been cut down and that they were forced to make a day's journey to get timber for the mines. The mountains of Zacatecas, the richest of the mining districts, were once covered with a heavy forest. After four centuries of cutting they are now rocky grasslands where the ubiquitous goat has to scratch for a living. The same story was repeated at all the other mining centers of New Spain: Guanajuato, Ixmiquilpan, Zimapan, Pachuca, Zacualpan, Temascaltepec, Tlalpujahua, Parral, and the rest.

Still another cause of soil destruction is the cultivation of maguey (*Agave americana,* or century plant), from the sap of which pulque, the universal tipple of the highland people, is made. The maguey plant requires a great deal of soil. The enormous consumption of pulque has made the maguey the most typical, or at least the most conspicuous, vegetation of the Plateau, where huge estates are given over to its cultivation. The plants are set out in rows, with wide alleys in between, which must be kept free of grass and weeds. The rains descend and the winds blow, and they wash and blow away the soil, until the alleys become gullies and the land is fit for little else but the growing of more maguey.[3]

Meanwhile, the pressure of population on the soil continues to

[3] William Vogt, after a visit to Tlaxacala in 1963, reported some progress there in the control of erosion. "The volcano La Malinche," he writes, "the upper part of which is one of Mexico's typically raddled national parks (pecked away at for potato patches, firewood and grazing), is the source of flash-floods that threaten downstream towns, have stripped away thousands of acres of soil, and cut ravines nearly a hundred feet deep. . . . With a minimum of machinery, and an abundance of the very cheap labor available in the Mexican countryside, the soil conservation technicians have treated a section with a series of diked trenches to hold water as it falls, long earthen dams to retard runoff, and a series of semipermeable dams in the many ravines. They report that the flash-floods virtually disappeared in the first year. . . .

"Between Tlaxcala and Mexico City there are considerable areas in two or three hundred acre farms where broad benches have been laid out, and their edges anchored with maguey. . . . Neighboring farmers had been so impressed that the terracing extended over hundreds of adjoining acres" ("Comments on a Brief Reconnaissance of Resource Use and Conservation Needs in Some Latin American Countries," Conservation Foundation, New York, August, 1963).

20

threaten the food supply. The population has tripled since 1910, and demographers see no letup in its advance.[4] The heartening success of the government in bringing more land into production, with the consequent increase in foodstuffs, has led enthusiasts to predict that technology will always keep ahead of the food crisis. But the numerous dams and irrigation systems, the much-publicized *ejido* (which was to have saved the country by breaking up the haciendas and giving the land back to the peasants), the greatly increased use of farming machinery, improved seed, and chemical fertilizers—all these intelligent measures are defeated in advance by the prodigious fertility of the Mexican mother and the virility of the Mexican male, for whom a vast family is visible proof of his manhood.[5] It looks as though the stage were being set for a Malthusian tragedy. If, as I suspect, the soil of Mexico will one day break down under the intolerable burden of feeding such a huge mass, and the people are eating themselves out of their own house, then the food problem transcends in importance all others. By comparison, the army problem, the Church problem, the school problem, democracy itself, sink into insignificance if the land rebels and the Tyrant has the last laugh.[6]

[4] The pattern of future population growth accepted as most probable by the geographer Jorge L. Tamayo (*Geografía General de México* [Mexico, 1962], 4 vols., vol. 3, p. 448) is as follows:

| | | | |
|---|---|---|---|
| 1970 | 49,699,000 | 1980 | 66,421,000 |
| 1975 | 57,689,000 | 1985 | 76,534,000 |

A simple arithmetical projection of these points gives a figure of about 100,000,000 by the end of this century.

[5] Arthur F. Corwin, "Mexico Resists the Pill," *The Nation*, May 11, 1964, pp. 477–480.

[6] The whole distressing problem of people and land in Mexico is thoroughly explored by Robert C. Cook, "Mexico: The Problem of People," in *Population Bulletin*, vol. XX, no. 7, pp. 173–203 (Washington, D.C., November, 1964). Further discussion of the problem will be found in chapter 27, below.

# 3

# HERNÁN CORTÉS

Throughout the length and breadth of Mexico one looks in vain for a town, village, hamlet, or even a street, named after her great conqueror. One of the few monuments allowed to suggest the magnificent adventurer who destroyed a nation and laid the foundations of a new one is the lonely hill called El Peñón del Marqués, which stands in solitary bleakness on the salt waste that was once Lake Texcoco. The reason for this bit of irony is not difficult to discover. Since Independence, and especially since the Revolution of 1910, it has been the fashion among liberal elements to decry all things Spanish, a fashion which of late has been carried to the absurd extreme of denying Mexico's Spanish heritage altogether. In school texts and in enthusiastic eulogies of the Mexican Revolution written by friendly commentators one reads that Mexico is fundamentally Indian, and we are invited to believe that the manifest destiny of the country is a reversion to something like the good old days before the Conquest, although no one has thus far had the hardihood to suggest the resumption of human sacrifice.

A necessary step in the establishment of such a thesis is, of course, the denial of everything that might conflict with it, and so the first objective of the campaign is the vilification of the conqueror, personified in Hernán Cortés, the destroyer. Against him it has become the fashion to play up the noble Aztec, typified by Cuauhtémoc, the last of the native rulers, whom Cortés had hanged. Mexico would not be Mexico if the conflict were not dramatized. This has been done by two discoveries that have brought on the Battle of the Bones. It seems that Cortés, in his will, bequeathed his remains to Mexico, and they were duly brought over from Spain and interred in the convent of San Francisco de Texcoco. A little more than two centuries later they were transferred to a rich tomb in the Hospital de Jesús in Mexico City—quite appropriately, because Cortés was its founder and patron. During the high feeling against the Spaniards in the War of Independence, the casket was hidden by Lucas Alamán and some pious friends in the chapel wall of that same hospital, where it was found in 1946 by a young Spaniard named Fernando Baeza. The discovery, of course, immediately took on political coloring and was the occasion for a fine burst of polemics between Left and Right. Cried the labor leader, Vicente Lombardo Toledano: "The remains of Cortés ought to be buried along with the bones of Franco!" Answered Bishop Maximino Ruiz y Flores: "The most fitting place for them would be a sacred place, that is, a Catholic temple!" The casket was, in fact, restored to the Hospital de Jesús, after Baeza's discovery had been verified.

Justice demanded that something be done to even the score. An enthusiastic Cortés-hater, Dr. Eulalia Guzmán, of the Institute of Anthropology and History, went to Europe and dug in the archives, and came up with an unconvincing portrait of the Conqueror, showing him to have been an undersized, bowlegged, chinless, and thoroughly repulsive cretin—attributes that had somehow escaped the notice of his not uncritical contemporaries. The effect of her discovery failing to be as shattering as circumstances required, Dr. Guzmán, to no one's astonishment, went to the village of Ixcateopan, Guerrero, and announced, in a tremendous burst of publicity, that she had found the bones of Cuauhtémoc reposing in a secret grave beneath the altar of the parish church, brought thither from Tabasco by his mourning people, through a thousand kilometers of wilderness. A bronze plaque identified the grave beyond a doubt, and documents bearing the signature of the saintly Father Toribio de Motolinía really clinched the matter.

Excitement was intense. The Institute of Anthropology and History immediately appointed an investigating commission of eminent men to assist Dr. Guzmán in verifying her discovery. Unfortunately, the commission's report was entirely negative. It pointed out the patent absurdities in the documentation, demonstrated that the bronze plaque was a clumsy forgery of recent manufacture, that the bones were a jumble of odds and ends from several different skeletons, and that the church at Ixcateopan was not

23

even built until 1565, that is, forty years after Cuauhtémoc's death. No matter. His bones *had* to be found, and anyone daring to doubt their authenticity was a traitor! That irrepressible cynic, Diego Rivera, long committed to the anti-Cortés school, said that regardless of the evidence the bones must be those of the hero and that it was the patriotic duty of all good Mexicans to believe in them. The Party of the Revolution decreed a Cuauhtémoc Week, and a huge demonstration was staged before his monument in the Paseo de la Reforma.

Understandably shaken by the fury of the protest, the government dismissed the commission and appointed a new one, chosen from among the most distinguished scholars and scientists of the National University. For two years they sifted the evidence with more than academic thoroughness, and then arrived at substantially the same conclusions as their predecessors. This was dangerous stuff. The commission prudently met in secret, but enough of its deliberations were announced to stir up bitter denunciations and threats of violence, so the commission wisely deferred full publication for eleven years, and even then had its report privately printed.[1]

Thus another myth was manufactured for the arsenal of the Revolution. Cuauhtémoc, who was certainly a stout fellow and an authentic hero, but who was hated by most Mexicans as the leader of the Aztecs, has been metamorphosed into the symbol of democratic resistance to the oppressor, and a pair of grim soldiers with loaded rifles guard his tomb in Ixcateopan against desecration.

---

[1] *Los Hallazgos de Ichcateopan: Actas y Dictámenes de la Comisión* (Mexico, 1962). "When our report was made public," wrote the president of the second commission, Professor Arturo Arnáiz y Freg of the National University, "the hostility of certain journalists became vociferous. They described us as a gang of traitors, and in several periodicals they went to the extreme of demanding that we be shot as such."

For risking their necks to expose this mad piece of official patriotism, the members of the two commissions deserve an honorable salute. The first was composed of Silvio Zavala, Eusebio Dávalos Hurtado, Javier Romero, Carlos Margaín, Alfredo Bishop, Luis Limón, Alfonso Ortega Martínez, and Lt. Col. Luis Tercero Urrutia and Major Roberto Tapia of the Mexican army; the second, Arturo Arnáiz y Freg, Rafael Illescas Frisbie, José Joaquín Izquierdo, Wigberto Jiménez Moreno, Alfonso Caso, Manuel Gamio, Julio Jiménez Rueda, Pablo Martínez del Río, and Manuel Toussaint.

There is an abundance of evidence to show that the conquistadores were a very rough lot, most of it supplied by the Spaniards themselves, for, if they conducted themselves like conquerors of all times, they did not escape a tremendous castigation at the hands of their articulate and powerful clergy. The most outspoken and famous of their critics was the Dominican Bartolomé de las Casas, whose writings have had a curious fascination for the enemies of Spain for four hundred years. They are an interesting example of a principle that has been effectively applied in many situations; that is, if you say a thing often enough and loud enough someone is bound to believe it. Las Casas, who had witnessed the frightful annihilation of the peoples of the Antilles, which was horribly true, applied the same story indiscriminately to all parts of the Spanish Indies, regardless of truth. He was a man possessed. He saw himself as a wrathful St. Michael, with his flaming sword, leading the celestial hosts against the minions of Satan, who, it turned out, were always his own countrymen. His *Brief Relation of the Destruction of the Indies,* from the moment of its appearance in 1552, became the indispensable handbook for those most interested in believing it. In the first century after its publication the *Brief Relation* went through forty-two foreign editions: three Italian, three Latin, four English, six French, eight German, and eighteen Dutch! And, of course, one of his chief devils was Hernán Cortés, whose secretary and biographer, Francisco López de Gómara, he hated with equal ferocity. In Las Casas and his modern followers it is the custom to place against the dark picture of the destroying Spaniard that of an innocent and unspoiled race, subject only to the rule of a kindly nature. Rousseau is outdone by Stuart Chase, whose lively *Mexico: A Study of the Two Americas* mournfully contemplates "four centuries and more of cringing abjection in a land where once civilized men walked free, fearless and masters of their destiny."

Ancient Mexico may have been such a paradise, but the evidence is not conclusive. On the contrary, it is pretty clear that Cortés was able to carry out his awe-inspiring feat only because most of the Mexican people welcomed him as their deliverer from the unbearable exactions of the Aztecs. Indeed, when Mexico–Tenochtitlán fell, on August 13, 1521, it took all his address to prevent his Indian allies from slitting the throats of the pathetic remnants of the population. In any case it is true that Cortés put an end to Aztec power. And yet, while destroying that civilization (or, rather, its political and religious structure), Cortés became the founder of modern Mexico, unless we are willing to deny all meaning to the word. For Cortés was a builder, however much we may deplore the violence that preceded the building. We do not like the connotation of the word "conquest," but we are prone to forget that Cortés was a child of the fifteenth century, the age of the Borgias, of Ferdinand misnamed "the Catholic," of Henry VIII, and of Machiavelli. He was a true son of the Renaissance. He was ruled by intelligence. He was not in the least squeamish about the means he employed. When the occasion demanded, he lied, cheated, bribed, and cajoled. Gómara relates of him that, when he scuttled his fleet at Vera Cruz in order to discourage any notion of retreat among his men (surely one of the most fantastic deeds ever recorded), he left two ships afloat. One of them he saved to carry dispatches back to Spain, and then, assembling his troops, he offered to allow all those who wished, to return to Cuba in the other. At once the partisans of his enemy, Governor Diego Velázquez of Cuba, stepped forward. Their names were taken, the ship was then scuttled, and Cortés had a blacklist of all those of doubtful loyalty. The story may be apocryphal, but it is one of those yarns that ought to be true, for Cortés preferred to gain his ends by address or trickery, but, when he had to strike, he struck so terribly that a second blow was seldom necessary. Honest grumbling he met with "honeyed words," as Bernal Díaz del Castillo calls them (in his delightful *True History of the Conquest of New Spain*), but treachery and disobedience ended on the gallows. In his absurdly small band of immortals he had to rule the toughest crowd of adventurers the Indies could produce, but his genius molded them into a disciplined, hard-hitting force, which he contrived to fill at the same time with something of his own flaming spirit and a belief in their destiny, just as later he inspired in the conquered peoples of Mexico a feeling akin to worship. Even the crusty and envious old Bernal Díaz admitted as much.

"Here in this island [of Cozumel]," he wrote, "Cortés began to command in very fact, and God gave him such grace that to whatsoever he turned his hand he did well, especially in pacifying the nations and peoples of those parts."

"One morning after Mass," he wrote later, "after having scuttled the ships in the sight of all, and having gathered together all the captains and soldiers, Cortés spoke to us of military matters. He begged us to listen to him and he discoursed in the following manner: He said that we were now in the midst of the campaign upon which we had embarked and that, with the help of Jesus Christ, we should win all our battles and encounters; but that we should prepare ourselves well for it because, if we should be defeated, which God forbid, we could not raise our heads, being so few in number; that, having no ships in which to return to Cuba, we had no help but God, our strong hearts, and our good fighting. With all this he made many comparisons with the heroic deeds of the Romans. His speech was very good and, to tell the truth, was spoken with more honeyed and eloquent words than these I have used."

The favorite thesis of the old chronicler was that Cortés never planned or made a move of importance without consulting his men beforehand. Bernal Díaz may well have believed it, being a simple soul entirely incapable of penetrating the subtle mind of his chief; but his thesis is untenable, however much one might wish to credit him, as many have. Dangerous and intricate campaigns demand the single direction of the commander, although Cortés always sought advice and utilized all the intelligence available. In spite of himself, Bernal Díaz supports my contention. It was always Cortés who made final decisions, and no detail of preparation was too small to escape his eye. The maintenance of discipline and order, the infinite precautions necessary on the march or in camp, the procuring of arms and supplies—all these were the responsibilities of Cortés alone, and it could not have been otherwise.

The greatness of Cortés as a commander was tested in defeat. Forced to fight his way out of the island stronghold of the Aztecs, into which he had rashly led his army, he lost 450 troops, some thousands of Indian "friends," all his guns, and most of his horses, while few of his men escaped unwounded. The famous treasure of Moctezuma, valued at some hundreds of thousands of ducats, disappeared in the rout. This was the retreat of the Noche Triste, which ends with the unlikely story of Cortés weeping for his dead companions under an *ahuehuete* tree. "In truth," he wrote the Emperor, "seeing the great strength of the Indians and the little resistance they found in us, because we were very tired and almost all wounded and fainting with hunger, we thought that our last day had come." Undismayed, he led the bleeding and exhausted remnants of his forces back to Tlaxcala, fighting the whole way, and there had enough of his old magic left to convince his Indian friends that he would yet prevail. A year later, with his reformed army and clouds of Indian allies, he returned to Mexico–Tenochtitlán and, in one of the bloodiest and most stubborn sieges in history, took it.

It was a terrible and sickening deed, but I cannot wholeheartedly share the tears of Bernal Díaz, who mourned over the fall of Mexico while enjoying the fruits of the conquest. Neither does it become our own romantic historians to be too scornful of the Spanish barbarians, while we are living in a land wrested from the Indians in a conquest just as ruthless and infinitely more thorough than that of Mexico. In fact, the more I read of other conquests, including those of recent years, the more I appreciate the moderation of Cortés.

The very completeness of the destruction of Aztec power had the virtue of eliminating the necessity of another blow. Posing and, indeed, accepted by the other peoples of Mexico as their deliverer, Cortés received the homage and allegiance of all the surrounding states. Once the messy business of taking the capital was over, a new Cortés appeared, Cortés the builder and statesman. He had a vision of empire much greater than the petty dynastic ambitions of his sovereign, the Emperor Charles V. "From what I have seen and learned of the similarity between this country and Spain," he wrote the Emperor, while the Aztec power was still intact, "in its fertility, its size, its climate, and in many other features of it, I thought that the most suitable name for it would be New Spain of the Ocean Sea, and thus in the name of Your Majesty I have christened it."

For three years after the fall of the capital Cortés devoted himself to the colossal task of welding the warring fragments of his conquest into a new empire, a task in which he displayed to the full his gift of "pacifying the nations and peoples of those parts." His moderation and political wisdom became at once apparent and make him almost unique among modern conquerors. "As I had always desired that the

28

city should be rebuilt," he wrote the Emperor in 1524, "because of its great and marvelous situation, I strove to collect the natives, who since the war were scattered about in many parts. I still held the ruler of it [Cuauhtémoc] a prisoner, but I charged one of his captains, whom I had known in the days of Moctezuma, to repeople it, and, in order that he might enjoy greater authority, I gave him the same office that he had held in the time of his sovereign. . . . At the same time I appointed other personages to the important offices they had formerly held. I also gave these new officers such territory and people as were necessary to maintain them, although not so much as they had held before, or enough to make them dangerous, and I always take care to honor and favor them.

"They have done very well, and now the city is peopled with about thirty thousand families and is just as orderly as before. Moreover, I have granted them such liberties and immunities that they will increase greatly. They live quite as they please, and many artisans make a living among the Spaniards, such as carpenters, masons, stonecutters, silversmiths, and the like. Merchants trade in safety; others live by fishing, and others by agriculture, for there are already many who have plantations sown with all manner of vegetables that we have procured from Spain. I assure Your Caesarean Majesty that, if we could obtain plants and seeds from Spain, . . . the ability of these natives in cultivating the soil and making plantations is such that they would shortly produce an abundance, and great profit would accrue to the imperial crown of Your Highness. . . . I beg Your Majesty to order . . . that no ship be allowed to sail without bringing a certain number of plants, which would make for the increase and prosperity of the country."

Cortés was driven by an insatiable curiosity about the vast dominions that destiny and his own genius had placed in his hands— or driven, perhaps, by greed, as his detractors would have it. However it was, he set about exploring New Spain in every direction. In the next few years his expeditions and those of his lieutenants covered the country from the Gulf of California (which he not unjustifiably named the "Red Sea of Cortés") to Guatemala, and from the Pánuco River (in northern Vera Cruz) to Honduras. His men carried careful instructions regarding the treatment of the native population, which may be summed up as a policy of conciliation, with the use of force only as a last resort. Cortés gave a vivid lesson in this policy on his first march to the capital, when he strung up one of his men for stealing a couple of turkeys from an Indian. The man was cut down at the supplication of his friends, but the lesson was not forgotten. No lieutenant of Cortés, even the rough-and-ready Pedro de Alvarado, ever disgraced himself by indulging in the senseless atrocities which made the names of Francisco Pizarro and Nuño de Guzmán infamous. Once away from the stern eye of their chief, to be sure, his men interpreted their instructions rather broadly, but by and large Cortés achieved the pacification of New Spain with extraordinarily little bloodshed. He became the idol of the Indian population. What is more important for the subsequent history of New Spain, his policy was adopted by its rulers and was more or less rigorously followed for three hundred years.

Cortés suffered the penalty of greatness. The envy and hatred of those who came too late played upon the suspicions of a jealous despot, and royal agents were soon in full cry after the vassal who dared to be greater than his lord. After six years of it, Cortés was forced to return to Spain in 1527 to defend himself; but he had hardly left Mexico when the ill-starred First Audiencia, under the presidency of his archenemy, Nuño de Guzmán, proclaimed his *residencia,* during the course of which Cortés was charged with every crime in the book. Even Charles V had not the face to support his accusers, and Cortés was vindicated. When he returned to New Spain in 1530 he was a *magnífico,* resplendent with honors and the fine title of Marqués del Valle de Oaxaca, lord of a semiautonomous feudal estate that included some of the richest land in the country. The Marquesado del Valle, even after the Second Audiencia had trimmed it down considerably from the original claims of Cortés, comprised the Valley of Toluca, the province of Cuernavaca, Coyoacán (Federal District), the provinces of Cotaxtla and Tuxtla San Andrés (Vera Cruz), and a large part of the Valley of Oaxaca and the Isthmus of Tehuantepec—an estimated 25,000 square miles. In 1569, when it was held by the Crown during the trial of the second Marqués del Valle for conspiracy, it was yielding something more than 80,000 gold pesos a year in Indian tributes alone.

The great man, now virtually a royal prince, arrived at Vera Cruz, and his arrival was the signal for an outburst of rejoicing, among Spaniards and Indians alike. "He was welcomed at Cempoala," wrote Gómara, "and wherever he passed, even though most of the country was uninhabited, he found an abundance of food and drink. Indians came to greet him from eighty leagues away, bringing presents, offering their services. . . . They showed the greatest joy at his return; they swept the road and scattered flowers before him, so beloved was he. . . ." So universal and so enthusiastic was the demonstration that the Crown authorities in Mexico City, fearing that he meant mischief, forbade him to enter the capital. Their fears may have been groundless; but Cortés was now the master of a princely estate; he still had the support of his old conquerors, who would certainly have followed him, even in rebellion; to the Indians he was king, and they would have risen at his word. The prestige and power of Cortés were truly formidable, and he had every reason to resent his treatment at the hands of the Crown officers. And yet he showed no tendency to abuse his power. The day of the conquistador was done, and Cortés may have sensed it. Thenceforth New Spain was to have a civil government, and Cortés, although he did his share of grumbling, did little to disturb it.

What the fate of New Spain would have been if Cortés had been a man of smaller stature is terribly illustrated by the history of Peru and New Galicia. Both Francisco Pizarro and Nuño de Guzmán were killers. They killed when there was no sense in killing. Pizarro raged through the most advanced culture in the New World and left it a charnel house; his inability to control his men bequeathed a legacy of violence and lawlessness from which Peru never fully recovered. Nuño de Guzmán's wasting of the western provinces of New Spain had no intelligence behind it. By comparison with his contemporaries and, I repeat, with some much later conquerors, Cortés was an angel of mercy.

During the nine years after his triumphal return from Spain in 1530, Cortés concerned himself with an amazing number of activities. He built a fleet to explore the west coast and to discover a route to the Spice Islands. His ships carried the products of the Marquesado to the markets of Peru. He erected graceful buildings, such as the Palace of Cortés at Cuernavaca, and supported churches and ecclesiastical foundations with a lavish hand—hence the understandable admiration of Mexican Catholics, who regard him as the lay founder of the Church in Mexico. He planted mulberry trees and encouraged silk culture. He brought cattle and sheep from Spain. His great slice of the Isthmus of Tehuantepec became the largest center of mule breeding in New Spain. He planted wheat, fruit trees, and sugar cane. His two sugar mills (at Tlaltenango in Morelos, and Tuxtla San Andrés in Vera Cruz) were the first on the mainland of the New World. His energy was so great and his projects were so ambitious that it was again whispered he was planning to take over the country.

Nothing is more sensitive than a despot's ear. The Crown redoubled its badgering of the old conqueror. Viceroy Mendoza skillfully maneuvered him into peevish opposition by blocking all his schemes. Finally Cortés could stomach it no longer and in 1539 returned to Spain for the last time to appeal to the Emperor. He was studiously ignored. His work was done, his glory had departed from him, and he wore out his great spirit in a vain attempt to regain his sovereign's favor. He had spent his fortune and genius in the service of his country; he had added a domain to the Spanish Empire which passes the imagination; but he died neglected, in bitterness and disillusionment, in 1547.

"Hernán Cortés," wrote Gómara, his faithful secretary, "was of a good stature, broad-shouldered and deep-chested; his color, pale; his beard, fair; his hair, long. He was very strong, courageous, and skillful at arms. As a youth he was mischievous; as a man, serene; so he was always a leader in war as well as in peace. . . . He was much given to consorting with women, and always gave himself to them. The same was true with his gaming, and he played at dice marvelously well and merrily. He loved eating, but was temperate in drink, although he did not stint himself. When necessity demanded, he could suffer hunger, as he proved on the Honduras expedition, and on the sea that he named for himself. He was a very stubborn man, as a result of which he engaged in more lawsuits than was proper to his station. . . . In his dress he was elegant rather than sumptuous, and was exceedingly neat. He took delight in a large household and family, in silver service and dignity. He bore himself nobly, with such gravity and prudence that he never gave offense or seemed unapproachable. . . . He was devout and given to praying; he knew many prayers and Psalms by heart. He was a great giver of alms and, when he lay dying, he strongly urged his son to emulate him. . . . Over his doors and on his coat of arms he had inscribed: *Judicium Domini apprehendit eos; et fortitudo ejius corroboravit brachium meum* ('The judgment of the Lord overtook them; His might lent strength to my arm')."

Such was the man who is now made into a fortune-hunting adventurer, whose vulgar ambition was to return to Spain and there lead the life of a swaggering hidalgo. I call him a builder. The Kingdom of New Spain was his vision and very largely his accomplishment.[2]

[2] This appraisal of Cortés, as might have been expected, has not escaped criticism. I should like to call to my support Dr. José María Luis Mora, the eminent Mexican philosopher and historian of the early nineteenth century, himself a Creole and a Founding Father of the Republic, whose *México y sus Revoluciones* is still the classical statement of the background of the Wars of Independence (3 vols., [Paris, 1836], ed. Agustín Yáñez, Mexico, 1950):

"In a contradiction common enough in revolutions," he wrote, "the descendants of the Spaniards, in their hatred of the conquest, . . . to which they and the Mexican Republic owe their natural and political existence, [acting] with an animosity that cannot be given a name or assigned a rational explanation, caused the disappearance of this monument [the casket of Cortés].

"Such was the end of this illustrious captain, whose fate was shared by all those of his class. Envied by his contemporaries, humiliated and ignored by the sovereign whom he had served, he became the admiration of posterity. His memory is stained by occasional acts of cruelty which can never be satisfactorily defended. It must be confessed, on the other hand, that hardly any of these acts can be charged to the ferocity of a barbarous character, or to the base passion of vengeance. . . . For the rest, the conquest of Mexico was the exclusive accomplishment of the talent, constancy, and valor of Cortés. He conceived the enterprise and carried it through, forcing all the attendant circumstances to serve his design: mutinous soldiers, whom he ruled solely by virtue of his election; populous cities; warriors jealous of their independence; and a proud absolute monarch, who had never known any curb on his will other than his own caprice. These obstacles Cortés converted into means for furthering his purpose. . . .

"Thus the great work of the conquest was achieved. It gave birth to the colony of New Spain, which in the revolution of independence was later transformed into the Mexican Republic. The name of Mexico is so intimately interwoven with the memory of Cortés that so long as that name endures, his memory cannot perish."

# 4

## GANGSTER INTERLUDE

The spectacular conquest of New Spain had attracted a swarm of adventurers, all panting for a share of the spoils and ready to use any means to get it. They were an unruly and unscrupulous lot, not essentially different from the old conquistadores of Cortés, with the very great difference, however, of having no Cortés to control them. Up to 1524 there was no government in New Spain but Cortés, the various municipal corporations he had founded, and the fiscal agents of the Crown. Cortés chose this critical moment to absent himself, leaving the country open to the hungry newcomers.

The occasion for his unlucky decision was the news that an expedition, under Andrés Niño and Gil González de Avila, duly licensed by the Crown, was slowly making its way up by land and sea from Panama to Honduras. Seeing this as a threat to his new domain, Cortés sent a force under one of his most able lieutenants, Cristóbal de Olid, to occupy Honduras in his name. But Olid had wider views. On his way down he stopped off in Cuba and made a deal with that ancient enemy of Cortés, Governor Diego Velázquez, whereby he would have Honduras to himself. Cortés was furious at this piece of treachery and sent his kinsman, Francisco de las Casas, to checkmate Olid. What ensued was one of those novelesque episodes so beloved of chroniclers.

Olid duly met and defeated Gil González, and took him prisoner; but he had hardly done so when the two caravels of Francisco de las Casas were sighted off the coast. Olid's luck held. A storm blew up and Las Casas was forced to land and join Gil González in captivity. Olid, with foolish optimism, given the nature of his prisoners, invited them to dine with him. While they were eating, Las Casas and Gil González set upon their host with their table knives. Olid, a powerful man, although badly wounded, managed to shake them off and take refuge in the woods, all to no avail, for his assailants, with the help of the Cortés men in Olid's camp, soon captured him. After some kind of trial, Olid was beheaded at Naco, and his executioners set out for Mexico to bring the joyful tidings to Cortés.

He, however, had had no word from Las Casas and feared that his kinsman had perished, so he decided to go to Honduras in person. Gathering together a large company of his veterans, 150 horse and 150 foot, with 3,000 Indian "friends," in October, 1524, he set out on his famous and disastrous march. At Coatzacoalcos he picked up, fortunately for posterity, the expedition's future chronicler, Bernal Díaz del Castillo. They marched through the trackless morasses of southern Vera Cruz, waded rivers alive with alligators, penetrated the poisonous jungles of Tabasco, Chiapas, and Guatemala, and finally emerged on the Gulf of Honduras. The starving men had to slash their way interminably through dense forests and build bridges over rivers and swamps, while their worried chief somehow managed to keep them from open mutiny. The Indian "friends" were a constant source of anxiety, for they could easily have revolted under the fierce Cuauhtémoc. That redoubtable chieftain, indeed, was reported to be plotting the destruction of the Spaniards. Whether the report was true or not, the danger was real, and reasons of state made the trial and execution of Cuauhtémoc a virtual necessity. Gómara, in one of the rare instances in which he does not approve of his hero, wrote: "Cortés, indeed, should have preserved his life as a precious jewel, for Cuauhtémoc was the triumph and glory of his victories; but Cortés did not wish to keep him alive in such a troubled land and time."

The march to Honduras was an amazing feat and one that deserves to rank with any march in history, but Cortés' two years' absence was a disaster for New Spain. The Honduras adventure is not easy to understand. I cannot account for it by laying it to blind rage and ambition. Cortés was no ingenuous soul to risk a kingdom for the sake of revenge. There were other and no less powerful motives, although they cannot be documented. Cortés' position in New Spain had been getting steadily worse. The Crown officers had repeatedly attempted to curb his dangerous power. As early as 1521 an officer, Cristóbal de Tapia, had been sent to New Spain by the Audiencia of Santo Domingo to keep an eye on him, but Cortés persuaded him (by bribery, it was whispered) to go back where he came from. The four treasury officers had been given the additional duty of spying on Cortés and reporting back to Spain, and they interpreted his actions in the worst possible light. Up to 1524 his ingenuity had been equal to all threats, but he was definitely being crowded. It may be that in the Honduras expedition he saw an opportunity to confound his enemies, for in that unknown country who knew what great cities and what new treasures lay hidden? Another stunning triumph like the conquest of Mexico would put him beyond the reach of wagging tongues and petty jealousies.

Whatever the motives of Cortés may have been, the expedition turned out to be the worst thing he could have done. Trouble began immediately. The statesmanship he had displayed in the pacification of New Spain gave way to a fumbling and short-sighted opportunism. He was in such a hurry to get away that he left the government in the weak hands of two of the treasury officers, Rodrigo de Albornoz and Alonso de Estrada. He had hardly got started when he was overtaken by the most direful news of rebellion and anarchy in the capital. He should have turned back at once, but, instead, he gave the two remaining officers, Peralmíndez Chirinos and Gonzalo de Salazar (who seem to have invented a good part of the story of the rebellion for purposes of their own) authority to take over the government. These two worthies even altered Cortés' instructions and gave themselves absolute power to act in his stead. Mexico was split into two warring camps, the men of Velázquez against the men of Cortés. In the civil war that followed, the structure of the new state came down in a heap, and, when the smoke had cleared away, the Velázquez men, with Chirinos and Salazar at their head, were in the saddle and Cortés' old conquistadores were eating dirt.

The rule of New Spain's first dictators was one of unashamed highjacking. Nothing stood in their way but the opposition of the old conquerors and the possible return of Cortés—an event which they so keenly feared that they repeatedly published stories of his death. He, however, was very much alive. After his futile expedition to Honduras he made his way by water to Vera Cruz, where he landed with a handful of rusty and scarecrow followers. He had long since been given up for dead and was so wasted by hardship that even his old companions did not at first recognize him. On the contrary, the sudden appearance of his bedraggled force caused such a panic that the guard was called out to repel the invasion. But once Cortés had made himself known, his reception turned into a triumph. The news spread like wildfire. On his progress to the capital the returning conqueror was hailed by huge crowds of Indians, who celebrated the event in their charming way by strewing his path with flowers. They had every reason to rejoice, for their oppression under the usurpers had been unbearable. Cortés' old companions in the capital were no less jubilant, and showed their elation by rising and smiting down their late masters and exposing them to derision, and other unpleasant things, in two wooden cages. Cortés at once set about repairing the damage done during his absence, removing the creatures of Chirinos and Salazar and restoring his own men.

His triumph was short-lived. He had been back only a few days when he heard that that most dread officer, a royal visitor, in the person of the Licenciado Luis Ponce de León, had landed in Vera Cruz, armed with full powers to remove him from office and take his residencia, that is, to hear any charges that might be brought against him. The visitor hastened to the city, convinced by rumors that Cortés was on the point of taking over the country, and he reduced Cortés overnight to the status of private citizen. But the conqueror had one of his usual strokes of good fortune: Ponce de León had no more than proclaimed the trial of Cortés when he was laid low with a fever and promptly died. He died so opportunely, in fact, that it was noised about at the time that Cortés had had a hand in it, although nothing was ever proved. Dying of a fever in those days was not so rare that one has to invent a murder to account for it.

Ponce de León's *visita*, however, plainly showed Cortés that he was being successfully undermined in Spain. Abandoning his plan to conquer the province of Pánuco, he resolved to go home and fight his battle in person, his resolution being hastened by a summons from the Emperor himself. So, leaving New Spain again in the hands of the treasurer, Alonso de Estrada, Cortés sailed from Vera Cruz in 1527.

Meanwhile the Crown (or rather, the Council of the Indies, which was now the responsible governing body of all the Spanish Indies), pursuing its policy of easing the old conquistadores out of power, while setting up a permanent civil government in New Spain, appointed the first Audiencia of Mexico. The Audiencia was a peculiarly Spanish institution, being a supreme court, council, and executive body (in the absence of a viceroy), with a sprinkling of legislative functions thrown in. Of this, more hereafter. The first Audiencia was originally composed of four justices (*oidores*) and a president. Two of the justices, however, died on the way over, and the two survivors, Diego Delgadillo and Juan Ortiz de Matienzo, with the president, Beltrán Nuño de Guzmán, became in their turn the undisputed dictators of New Spain. The only curb on their power was the Council of the Indies, and it was far away. Their principal and most agreeable duty was to break the power of the conquistadores, which they interpreted as applying exclusively to the Cortés party, and they gave that duty the widest possible interpretation. In fact, Nuño de Guzmán's principal qualification for his job was his fierce jealousy of Cortés, which became in time a consuming phobia.

Beltrán Nuño de Guzmán offers a problem to the historian. He has been damned so thoroughly from his day to ours that I find it hard to believe in the existence of such a monster. And yet nothing in his acts or in his sanctimonious letters (written in a beautiful clerical hand and dripping with quotations from the Scriptures), or in the sworn testimony given at his trial later, allows me to think differently. He was one of those rare characters whose exclusive function seems to have been that of destroyer. He had great personal bravery and the ability to command men, but his capacity for hatred was only equaled by an apparent delight in sadistical orgies of burning, torture, and destruction. While governor of the province of Pánuco in 1527–1528 he used his office solely for self-enrichment, enslaving as many of the natives as he could capture and shipping them off to sell in the placer mines of Española (twenty-one shiploads of them, according to Bishop Zumárraga). His ferocious slave raids almost depopulated the rich province of Huasteca, which never quite recovered from them. Two years later, hearing that he was to be removed as president of the Audiencia, he sought to avoid retribution and to repair his fortunes by leading a large force of idle Spaniards (mostly Velázquez men) and Mexican "friends" in the conquest of the unknown western provinces, which he named New Galicia. Michoacán, Jalisco, Nayarit, and Sinaloa were invaded in turn, and in each the hordes of Nuño de Guzmán pillaged, enslaved, burned, and destroyed. And yet, the influence of Nuño de Guzmán and the presumed importance of his conquest were such that the Audiencia allowed him to go unchecked for seven years. Flourishing provinces were permanently depopulated, and the hatred and despair of the victims mounted to such a pitch that they eventually rose against the Spaniards in the wild rebellion known as the Mixtón War, which broke out in 1541, when New Galicia had been stripped of its defenders to man the famous wild-goose chase of Francisco Vásquez de Coronado into the northern wilderness.

Such was the man whom the Council of the Indies, in an evil hour, chose to rule New Spain. His policy and that of his colleagues was to destroy Cortés and despoil the conquistadores, a course in which they were encouraged by the Crown. Backed by the power of the throne, the Audiencia willingly listened to every charge brought against Cortés and his men by malcontents and out-at-elbows adventurers. These charges were Guzmán's pretext for seizing the conquistadores' goods, jobs, and *encomiendas* of Indians, and distributing them among his friends. The encomienda, as will be explained more fully later on, was a kind of trusteeship, by which a conquistador was granted the power to collect tribute from the Indians, while presumably devoting himself to their protection and indoctrination in the Christian religion.

The first Audiencia's rule became a reign of terror, with confiscation, imprisonment, and the gallows freely employed. To prevent news of it from getting back to Spain they set up a rigid censorship at Vera Cruz—a device resorted to by later rulers. The result of the Audiencia's cynical disregard of law was bitterness and dissension, enslavement of the Indians, and wholesale spoliation of Indians and Spaniards alike. It may seem odd that the conquistadores did not take up the arms that they knew so well how to wield; but they were outnumbered, their old commander was in Spain, and Guzmán had

39

on his side the mysterious machinery of the law. Even so, they might have been driven to civil war but for the work of one man, Fray Juan de Zumárraga, first bishop and archbishop of Mexico.

We know very little about the origins of Zumárraga. He was born in a humble Basque family about 1468. He was admitted to the Franciscan order, we do not know when or where. He seems to have had as good an education as could be got in Spain—which meant a very good education indeed. He became known as a man of letters and an eloquent preacher, and his rigid austerity earned him a reputation for saintliness. For the rest he seems to have led a humdrum life, slowly climbing the ladder of ecclesiastical preferment in his order, and eventually achieving the dignity of the guardianship of the convent of Abrojo, in Valladolid. The Emperor happened to stop at Abrojo one day in 1527 and was so impressed by the ability of the guardian that he kept him in mind for higher things. The time was at hand for organizing the Church in New Spain, and in December, 1527, Juan de Zumárraga was nominated by the Emperor to head the diocese of Mexico. Since the time of Isabella the Catholic, it should be explained, the Spanish monarchs had the right (*real patronazgo*) of nominating men for ecclesiastical offices, secular and regular.

Zumárraga felt himself unworthy of the post and was induced to accept it only by the direct command of his superior. But once he had done so he bent his admirable energies to his new task. He did not wait for consecration, but embarked at once with his future enemies, the members of the first Audiencia of Mexico. One title given to Zumárraga was that of "protector of the Indians," which had been invented as a result of the clamor of the Dominicans over the barbarous treatment of the Indians of the Antilles. The title did not fit into any existing scheme of government; no one knew what a "protector" was or what he could do. In brief, it was an anomaly and a confusion. But in 1528 it was a fortunate thing for New Spain that such an office existed.

The machinations of Nuño de Guzmán and the Audiencia were directed, as I have said, against Cortés' old companions in arms and their goods, but, since a great part of the wealth of these men came from the tributes paid by the Indians of their encomiendas, the spoliation had an immediate and disastrous effect on native life. The

40

Indians were regarded by Guzmán's men as a source of quick wealth, and they suffered every kind of extortion and abuse as a consequence —not that Cortés' companions were guiltless in this respect, but they were not in such a hurry. Under Guzmán New Spain was threatened with the same horrible fate that had destroyed virtually the whole Indian population of the Antilles in a single generation.

Zumárraga's title as "protector of the Indians" manifestly gave him something to say in the matter—just what neither he nor anyone else knew, but something. He began by making mild remonstrances to the Audiencia and by demanding that his authority as protector be recognized. Needless to say, he was blocked by technicalities from the abundant store in those legal minds, the principal one being that Zumárraga was not a real bishop at all, since he had not been consecrated. They would be glad to recognize his authority, of course, when and if he could produce the proper documents. As it was, he would do better if he devoted himself to his religious duties and ceased his meddling in affairs of state.

The Indians, however, continued to bring in stories of abuse, and the Franciscans, possibly encouraged by Zumárraga, egged them on. Soon the bishop had, in effect, set up an independent court for the redress of Indian grievances, which multiplied beyond control, some grave, some frivolous, for the Indians soon showed considerable talent for litigation. The bishop was repeatedly admonished by the Audiencia to mind his own business and call off his friars. He retorted that he would do his duty even if he died for it.

The battle grew hotter. The Audiencia forbade both Indians and Spaniards, under heavy penalties, to go to the bishop on any matter concerning the treatment of the Indians. The bishop countered by exposing the whole situation in a sermon and by threatening to lay it before the Emperor. Guzmán, in his turn, threatened to eject the bishop from the pulpit if he should repeat the performance. He also anticipated modern usage by circulating a scurrilous libel, in which the bishop and the Franciscan order generally were accused of such shocking conduct that Zumárraga could not bring himself to quote it, saying merely that "it was full of abominations." The incident that brought the row to a disgraceful climax began with the complaint of certain Indians of Huejotzingo (Puebla), who charged that Guzmán's men were exacting such unbearably heavy tribute

41

from them that they were obliged to sell their women and children into slavery in order to pay it.

With this the bishop's wrath reached incandescence and he resolved to have it out with Guzmán. It is a pity that the dry records of the case give few details of the epic scene between the irate prelate and the violent and supercilious Guzmán, with the two oidores nervously looking on. After laying the Huejotzingo case before them, Zumárraga demanded that the tribute schedule be submitted to him for approval, so that he could protect the Indians from extortion. Guzmán replied that no one was to meddle with the schedule established by the Audiencia, and that the Indians had to obey the law, whatever the cost. The bishop's answer is not recorded, but it must have been adequate, for the scene ended by Guzmán's threatening him with the gallows.

Guzmán had badly judged the character of Zumárraga if he thought that the old Franciscan could be bulldozed into submission. The bishop called his friars together (stout Cortés men all) and mapped out a campaign. It was decided to make a public issue of Guzmán's libel. Their best preacher, one Fray Antonio Ortiz, was chosen to expose the whole affair in a sermon. The sermon and its subject were well advertised, and the church was crowded on that Whitsunday of 1529. In the congregation were Guzmán and the oidor Delgadillo, with a number of their henchmen. Fray Antonio got through the conventional part of his sermon, but had hardly begun the matter of the libel when Guzmán shouted to him to drop it. The preacher begged permission to continue, but at a signal from Delgadillo a constable and several men surrounded the pulpit and, shouting insults at the friar, seized him by the cassock and unceremoniously yanked him down.

The scandal, as Zumárraga must have anticipated, was sensational. Open war was declared between the bishop and the Audiencia, and denunciations, excommunications, and reprisals were of daily occurrence. But Guzmán had been maneuvered into an untenable position, and even his friends the Dominicans could not stomach such irreverence. The power of the Church was against him, and the bishop could now lay the quarrel before the Council of the Indies with the certainty of being heard. It was not easy, however, to get a letter past Guzmán's road block at Vera Cruz. The bishop sent his first letter by way of Pánuco, but it was intercepted by Guzmán's agents and used as a pretext for further persecutions. No one could be trusted to carry a letter to Vera Cruz, much less to Spain. So, finally, the bishop made the long journey to Vera Cruz himself and there found a Basque sailor from his own province, whom he persuaded to take the risk. Between them they hid the letter in a cake of wax, which in turn was dropped into a barrel of oil. The Basque sailor was faithful to his charge, and the letter was delivered to the Council of the Indies.

That letter, in my opinion, was one of the most important ever written from New Spain. It was a complete and damning exposition of the misgovernment of Nuño de Guzmán and the Audiencia. The letter was so circumstantial, and the bishop's reputation for integrity so well established, that Guzmán's friends at court were confounded and Guzmán himself was discredited. The evil effects of putting the direction of New Spain into the hands of corrupt and irresponsible men were tardily recognized. It was decided to raise New Spain to the category of a viceroyalty, ruled by a representative of the King's own person. It was a fortunate decision, and from that time onward the best brains and talent available were, with singularly few exceptions, chosen for the government.

The year 1530 marked the beginning of an orderly and civilizing régime in New Spain (always excepting the unhappy territory where Nuño de Guzmán was allowed to complete the destruction known as the conquest of New Galicia). A large share of the credit for the change must be given to Fray Juan de Zumárraga, whose championship of Cortés and support of the conqueror's policy of conciliating the natives shaped the thinking of the Council of the Indies, to the very great benefit of New Spain.

Among the builders of Mexico, then, we must include Don Fray Juan de Zumárraga, who is commonly referred to as an ignorant and superstitious zealot, the destroyer of the art and literature of the Aztecs.[1]

---

[1] It is a curious commentary on the power of repetition that Juan de Zumárraga should be famous principally as the destroyer of the great Aztec library of Texcoco. At times it is a positive misfortune to be gifted with

eloquence. In the luminous pages of Prescott the fact of the burning of the library can no more be questioned than the Chicago Fire. And yet the great Prescott relied on evidence that should have aroused his suspicions. It would be a dull business to review the heated controversy that raged over the issue many years ago, especially since it should have been laid for all time by Joaquín García Icazbalceta's masterly *Don Fray Juan de Zumárraga*, first published in Mexico in 1881. But Prescott is read and Icazbalceta is not, and so one still comes across bitter denunciations of the fanatical priest who destroyed a nation's literature. The great burning has been further fixed in tradition by the fine fresco painting by Diego Rivera which adorns the National Palace in Mexico City.

The difficulty is, however, that there is no contemporary record of such a burning, or even of the existence of such a library. There was plenty of destruction of temples and images for the purpose of breaking the power of the Indian priests. It was an object lesson in the superiority of the Christian God. If Zumárraga had in fact burned the library he would have been the first to take credit for it. But there is no mention of the burning of manuscripts (or, rather, of Indian picture records) until Father Diego Durán's *Historia de las Indias de Nueva España,* which was written sixty years after the conquest, and Durán says nothing about Zumárraga's part in it. After Durán's time the story accumulated details in a kind of snowballing process, until in 1776 the Scottish historian William Robertson, in his *History of America,* was able to denounce Zumárraga as an ignorant zealot, at whose order "as many records of the ancient Mexican story as could be collected were committed to the flames."

But it remained for Prescott to pronounce the bishop's doom. "The first archbishop of Mexico," he wrote, in his *Conquest of Mexico,* "Don Juan de Zumárraga,—a name that should be as immortal as that of Omar [the Caliph who in the seventh century is supposed to have ordered the destruction of the Alexandrian library]—collected these paintings from every quarter, especially from Texcoco, the most cultivated capital in Anahuac, and the great repository of the national archives. He then caused them to be piled up in a 'mountain heap'—as it is called by the Spanish writers themselves,—in the marketplace of Tlatelolco and reduced them all to ashes!"

The "mountain heap" detail, by the way, seems to have been added by the Jesuit historian, Francisco Clavigero, in 1780. It has also occurred to me that it was quite unnecessary for Zumárraga to have the mountainous records brought around or across Lake Texcoco in order to burn them in the marketplace of Tlatelolco (Mexico City). And in all the stories of the great burning it never seems to have occurred to the authors that Juan de Zumárraga was a medieval bishop with a very trying job on his hands, and not a modern archaeologist or antiquarian. This was the opinion (which I have borrowed) of Joaquín García Icazbalceta, in his *Zumárraga* (Mexico, 1881). Robert Ricard, in his *Spiritual Conquest of Mexico,* chapter 1, shows that the archives of Texcoco were destroyed in 1520, when the Tlaxcalan allies of Cortés burned the principal palaces of that city. Ricard also explores the compelling motives of the missionaries in obliterating all reminders of the natives' ancient religion, mostly idols and temples.

# 5

## THE UPRIGHT JUDGES

The sensational revelations of Bishop Zumárraga and the effective lobbying of Cortés convinced the Council of the Indies that something ought to be done about New Spain, and done at once. The Royal and Supreme Council of the Indies had been created in 1524, under the presidency of Fray García de Loaisa, general of the Dominican order, and was pretty well dominated by Dominican thinking. Since 1510 the Dominicans had been outspoken critics of the administration of the Indies, and especially of the barbarous treatment of the native races. Spurred on by the tireless Fray Bartolomé de las Casas and supported by the solid arguments of Francisco de Vitoria, a professor of philosophy at the University of Salamanca and one of the greatest legal minds of the age, the Dominicans were envisaging their ideal City of God in the New World, a City in which the children of nature would be ruled by their natural teachers and protectors, that is, the friars.[1] With the disastrous failure of Nuño de Guzmán and the first Audiencia, they seized the opportunity to inaugurate their long-delayed reform. It was to be expected that these stern legalists would select for the new Audiencia men of their own way of thinking.

The five men whom they sent to New Spain fully justified their expectations. The president, Bishop Sebastián Ramírez de Fuenleal, had been president of the Audiencia of Santo Domingo, then the seat of the overseas government of the Indies. The four associate justices (*oidores*) were all extraordinary men in their own right.

---

[1] For a more extended treatment of this important theme, see chapters 8 and 9, below.

Indeed, it would have been difficult to find men more able than the Licenciados Juan de Salmerón, Alonso de Maldonado (who earned the nickname of "the good"), Francisco Ceynos, and Vasco de Quiroga, the most extraordinary of them all, who was later famous as the bishop of Michoacán. Quiroga did much to erase the memory of the hated Nuño de Guzmán by setting up his own miniature City of God in the lake country, teaching the Indians, by his example, Christian charity and humility, along with a variety of useful trades, while at the same time he protected them with some success against the rapacity of encroaching settlers. He is still venerated as a saint by the people of Michoacán.

These men were the legal brains of the Spanish Empire, and they were the sort most feared by the feudal-minded conquistadores, for there was no place in the City of God for divided loyalties. Cortés, in one of his celebrated letters to Charles V, begged the Emperor to keep lawyers out of the Indies. The experience of New Spain with those of the first Audiencia certainly justified his strictures on the legal profession, but now Law in all her majesty was to be enthroned, and the conquistadores had to learn to behave themselves.

When the second Audiencia took over in 1530, acting as a caretaker for the forthcoming viceregal government, affairs in New Spain could hardly have been worse. The shysters and crooked bureaucrats put into office by Nuño de Guzmán had been making a profitable racket out of prosecuting people on the most frivolous charges and collecting outrageous fees. The tyranny of the first Audiencia had created a permanent rift between it and the city council of Mexico, which was made up largely of the old conquistadores, who naturally carried their resentments over to the new Audiencia. Their chief, Hernán Cortés, recently back from Spain, was still understandably sore from his treatment at the hands of Guzmán and, for all the second Audiencia knew, he was waiting for a chance to set up an independent government, as he might have conceivably done. Nuño de Guzmán, whose audacity and bad temper made him hard to control, was off in the west carving out a new kingdom for himself, while the capital was undergoing an orgy of unchecked corruption, and luxury and dissipation generally gave it the atmosphere of a mining camp during a boom. Crowds of idle

46

Spaniards, with no ties of any kind, were likely to pack up and leave at the slightest rumor in search of new bonanzas, and otherwise amused themselves by swarming over the country seizing loot and women. In addition to this formidable state of things, the Audiencia was faced with the grave danger of an Indian uprising, because, more than any other element, the native population had suffered heavily from the vicious government of Guzmán. The danger was soon realized.

That Bishop Fuenleal and the second Audiencia were able in five years to impose a régime of law and order upon such a chaos seems under the circumstances one of the most astonishing feats in the history of government. At the outset their work was complicated by the discovery of an active conspiracy among certain groups of Indians. In order to meet the threatened rebellion, the Audiencia regretfully had to turn the military power over to Cortés, who clanked through the capital in an unnecessary display of strength, in order to impress the new government and the populace with the fact that in a pinch he was still indispensable. To the dismay of the pious judges of the Audiencia, he smashed the uprising with characteristic vigor. They were new to the ways of conquistadores, and, when Vasco Porcallo, Cortés' lieutenant, brought in some two thousand Indian slaves "taken in rebellion," the shocked Quiroga promptly released them.

There was one task, however, in which the second Audiencia had the enthusiastic support of Cortés and all his old comrades, and that was the trial of Guzmán, Matienzo, and Delgadillo. The Audiencia long debated the question whether Guzmán should be brought back from New Galicia to answer charges in person. Unfortunately, although the stories of his atrocities were too notorious to be doubted, they decided that the work of completing the conquest of the province was too important to be interrupted, and Guzmán was allowed to stay until he had "pacified" his unlucky territory. The records of his residencia and those of his two stooges make dismal reading, being an unrelieved catalog of tyranny and extortion. But the hour of the two underlings had struck, and Matienzo and Delgadillo were arrested and sent back to Spain, where they died in prison. Guzmán, although a proved criminal, was not touched until

47

seven years later, when he too was shipped off to Spain and out of our narrative.

Except for their one colossal mistake in the Guzmán affair, the work of the second Audiencia was consistently good. President Fuenleal was tireless in his protection of the Indians. He called together a conference of the most experienced men in the country to study the problem: Bishop Zumárraga, the guardians of the Franciscan and Dominican orders, Hernán Cortés, the four justices of the Audiencia, and several of the more prominent among the old conquistadores. Their recommendations, which were adopted by the Audiencia, included: (1) the revision downward of the tribute; (2) abolition of the use of native carriers, whose ill-treatment in the transport of supplies had become a major scandal; and (3) (of great importance for the subsequent history of New Spain) *the granting to Indian communities the right of self-government and the administration of justice, under their own elected officers.* In other words, they were to be allowed to continue their old form of government, so long as it did not conflict with Spanish law, under the supervision of Spanish clergymen and Crown officers.

Indian towns were thus, at least theoretically, put on a basis similar to that of the Spanish-Roman municipalities, and their internal structure underwent little modification. By that wise measure Indian caciques were made over into officers of the Crown. They were given certain rights and privileges (not always observed, to be sure), such as exemption from personal services, tributes, and degrading punishments. They were allowed salaries which ranged from a few pesos a year to two hundred, depending upon the importance of their posts, and as a badge of authority they were allowed to carry the coveted royal wand of justice. They were, in short, elevated into a native nobility, and their responsibility was to keep the Indians quiet and enforce the king's law among them. They knew nothing, of course, about the king's law, but the priest and the *corregidor* were there to instruct them. This solution of the native political situation bears the stamp of genius, and the marked lack of further Indian trouble in the more civilized parts of New Spain is evidence of its wisdom.

One of the most exasperating problems facing the new government was caused by the attitude of Bishop Zumárraga and his unruly friars. The bishop had been instrumental in bringing about the new order, and he was reluctant to give up his authority as "protector of the Indians." Indeed, he kept his private court going in competition with the Audiencia. His Franciscans had the pride of old-timers and did not relish the ascendancy of the Dominicans, whom they did not like anyway. They continued to encourage the Indians to look to them for redress of their grievances and to ignore the officers of the Crown. The row has a somewhat comical look at this distance, but Spanish pride and touchiness made it a genuine crisis. The feudal tradition died hard, even among the religious. Zumárraga was a stubborn and opinionated old zealot, and it must have cost him something to see himself supplanted in what he considered his rightful prerogative. It was all the more to his credit, therefore, that, when he saw the justice of the Audiencia's stand, a timely rebuke brought him down off his high horse, and from that time onward he cooperated fully with the Audiencia. He was a welcome and powerful ally, for his ascendancy over the Indians and the respect he enjoyed among the old conquistadores were second only to those of Cortés.

I have mentioned the tendency of the unemployed to rush off on any new adventure that promised excitement or profit, or, preferably, both. A number of them followed Nuño de Guzmán to New Galicia in 1530. Others joined the Adelantado Francisco de Montejo in the conquest of Yucatan in 1528. Still others were attracted to Guatemala, where Pedro de Alvarado was collecting a force to take to Peru. He landed on the coast of Quito in 1534, but found his way blocked by the army of Diego de Almagro, Pizarro's lieutenant. At Riobamba, faced with the unpleasant alternatives of fighting Almagro or abandoning the enterprise, he realistically sold his army of five hundred men and all his supplies for the respectable sum of 100,000 gold pesos in bars. The comical sequel to the transaction was that when Alvarado got home he discovered that the bars were of lead concealed under a veneer of gold plate. At least, so he claimed in a long suit he filed against Pizarro—without success, it should be added.

The men who stayed in New Spain wandered about the country

lording it over the Indians and committing assorted crimes and extortions. Not the least prolific source of trouble was their promiscuous mating with Indian women, whom few of them intended to marry. This class of haughty vagabonds gave the worst possible example of the Christian life to the newly converted Indians, besides keeping the country in a turmoil with their lawlessness. The problem persisted for many years, as the supply of vagabonds seemed to be inexhaustible. The Audiencia attempted to abate the nuisance by obliging married Spaniards to send home for their wives, and by encouraging others to marry Indian women. Some were induced to settle down by being given town lots in the new city of Puebla de los Angeles (founded for the purpose), with Indians to do their work and the considerable privilege of membership in a municipal corporation.

The second Audiencia continued the Crown's policy of reducing the power of the feudal-minded encomenderos. This it did by removing all the encomiendas that had imperfect titles—all those, for example, granted by Nuño de Guzmán and the first Audiencia—and incorporating them in the Crown as *pueblos de realengo,* under salaried magistrates called *corregidores.* By way of appeasement the bereaved encomenderos were given preferment in the new posts, at a salary, generally, of two hundred pesos a year. The Audiencia was opposed, of course, by all those who looked upon New Spain merely as a source of quick wealth; but more and more of the older settlers, who had everything to gain from a stable government, were brought around to the support of the Audiencia.

The five years' rule of Fuenleal and his hard-working justices lacks the romance of the waving plumes and shining armor of military conquest, but it marked a conquest of far greater significance. The Mexican historian, Vicente Riva Palacio, sums up their work in a fine tribute: "[Under Fuenleal and the second Audiencia] the organization of the colony and the good government of the Indians began to be a fact. In the formless mass of the indigenous races and peoples, in the group of haughty and undisciplined adventurers, and among the enslaved and despised Indians, the severe profile of an orderly society began to be discernible, and the imperfect but visible forms of a government subject to law."

The second Audiencia had completed the first stage of its work by 1535, when the Kingdom of New Spain became a viceroyalty. By its courageous and intelligent rule it had set a high standard for succeeding governments to follow. If the great viceroys who took over their work made a conspicuous success of ruling New Spain, the credit belongs in very large part to these upright judges.

# 6

## DON ANTONIO DE MENDOZA

Assigning numbers to the viceroys of New Spain is done, I suppose, in the interest of efficiency, but the unfortunate result is that we are presented with a long line of indistinguishable abstractions, or fleshless automatons, inflexibly carrying out the orders of a narrow-minded despotism. If exceptions are allowed, they are as likely as not pictured to be vicious and corrupt men, prostituting their high office to amass a fortune, and even those admittedly superior are lost in the anonymity of an Arabic symbol.

But the fact is that the viceroys of New Spain, with singularly few exceptions, even in the slovenly period of the seventeenth-century Hapsburgs, were admirable public servants, trained for their profession, and possessing a high degree of personal integrity. They were necessarily given wide discretionary powers, for they were months away from Spain and had to be able to act when emergencies arose, or to modify laws to fit realities. They were usually chosen with the greatest care, for they were legally the king's person and had to uphold the majesty of the throne. Their office was one of the few, even when the Crown was reduced to beggary under Charles II (1665–1700), never sold to the highest bidder. Men of distinguished ability succeeded one another in a long and rarely broken line. This was especially true in the all-important sixteenth century, when the political structure of New Spain was taking shape. That now and then a crook appeared among them, or a stupid and small-minded tyrant, merely proves that New Spain could not hope entirely to escape the general fate of humanity. But it seems to me that the average stature of the viceroys of New Spain was so great that no country to my knowledge was ever more fortunate in its rulers. New

Spain had plenty of things the matter with it, as we shall discover, but it enjoyed a long life (three hundred years!) of relative peace, stability, and prosperity, in marked contrast to the squabbling nations of Europe. Some of the men who made this possible are worth our knowing.

Don Antonio de Mendoza was a member of one of the greatest families of Castile. The history of Spain during her most flourishing period is filled with Mendozas. They gave Spain such men as Iñigo López de Mendoza, the Marqués de Santillana, Queen Isabella's commander in the conquest of Granada, warrior and outstanding poet of the fifteenth century; Pedro González de Mendoza, Cardinal Archbishop of Seville, patron of letters, humanist, friend and supporter of Isabella the Catholic, and one of the greatest churchmen of Spain; and finally Diego Hurtado de Mendoza, one of the best writers of the Golden Age and brother of Don Antonio. Don Antonio himself had been trained as a diplomat and entrusted with delicate and important missions by the Emperor Charles V. I have included all this genealogy to indicate that by 1535 the Spanish Crown was convinced of the significance of the new dominions and was determined to keep them in the hands of loyal and able men who were tied to the throne by the closest bonds of tradition.

The arrival of the viceroy was hailed with joy by all elements of New Spain, with the probable exception of Cortés, who thus saw himself cheated of the high place which he might justifiably have looked upon as his by right, and who could have sensed the approaching demise of his feudal autonomy. But the rest of the citizenry were well pleased to see an end of the instability and factionalism which had cursed the country since the conquest. Mendoza reached Mexico City in November, 1535, and the whole place exploded in a grand fiesta, with games, jousting, music, parades, and free food for the people. No pains were spared to invest Mendoza with all the trappings of royalty. It was thought, moreover, to put him above temptation by giving him the substantial salary of 6,000 ducats a year, with 2,000 more for household expenses. His official titles were Viceroy, Governor-General, and President of the Audiencia of New Spain.

The Crown's colonial policy had two general aims at the time: the destruction of the quasi-feudalism of the conquistador–encomendero class and the erection of a centralized political structure, with all authority resting in the Crown. Practically, it meant the reconquest of the Indies from the conquistadores. The viceroyalty was no sinecure. Mendoza had to hem Cortés about with every restriction he could think of, without driving him into actual rebellion, and he had to do the same with the rest of the old conquerors, who were now a privileged aristocracy. He had to organize the administration of the Indians and protect them from irresponsible exploitation. He had to look after the Crown revenues, police the country, build towns and roads, establish public services, and insure mining, trade, agriculture, and commerce generally against interruption. Luckily, by the time Mendoza arrived in New Spain a great deal of spade work had already been done by the able men of the second Audiencia, who stayed on as his advisory council and supreme court.

The old conquerors looked with justifiable suspicion upon the viceregal government. Viewing with alarm had become a habit with them since their experience with Nuño de Guzmán. Cortés was sulky and still might make trouble. Nuño de Guzmán was unchecked and had been so for five years, making himself a little king in New Galicia. To ease these violent and ambitious men out of their hard-won privileges required tact, strength, and a devious cunning. Mendoza had these qualities, and he had with him besides the great prestige of the Crown and the full support of the highest tribunal in the land.

It would be pointless to retell in detail the everlasting feud between Nuño de Guzmán and Cortés, both of whom laid claim to all the territory their imaginations could encompass. They were bound to get in each other's way, and their enmity played into the hands of the viceroy. They had served their purpose, they had conquered an empire, and now the Crown's chief concern was to get rid of them with as little fuss as possible. Guzmán was by far the more vulnerable of the two, and Mendoza managed to have him sent back to Spain in 1537 to answer the old charges of his residencia. Two years later, Cortés, disgusted with Mendoza's effective checkmating of him at every move, also returned to Spain, where he remained until his death in 1547.

With the elimination of these two chieftains, Mendoza had little difficulty with the rest. The only one who offered a threat to the new order was Pedro de Alvarado, the toughest of Cortés' lieutenants and master of Guatemala. Alvarado was another Cortés, without the redeeming statesmanship of his chief. He was itching to undertake some spectacular new conquest of his own. He took over Cortés' plan to explore a route to the Spice Islands, which continued to be one of the never-never lands of Spanish ambitions. With this in mind he made a contract with the Council of the Indies; he borrowed a great sum of money; he collected a force of six hundred men and built a fleet of twelve vessels. His fleet arrived off the coast of Colima in 1540, but it was far from ready for the voyage. Moreover, Alvarado, by the terms of his contract, was obliged to admit Mendoza as a partner in his adventure. The money and supplies which he had to have could be procured only in New Spain. In short, Alvarado was thoroughly tied by the Council of the Indies.

Meanwhile, New Spain was in a fever over the report of another never-never land, the Seven Cities of Cíbola. The fabulous cities had first been reported by Alvar Núñez Cabeza de Vaca, who had heard of them during his remarkable eight years' wandering over what is now the southern United States and northern Mexico. Mendoza shrewdly saw in the new discovery a pretext for sending an expedition into the northwest, encircling the territory claimed by both Guzmán and Cortés. Before spending any money on it, however, he sent an agent, Fray Marcos de Niza, to verify Cabeza de Vaca's story. Fray Marcos set out in 1537 with a Negro slave named Estebanico, who had been with Cabeza de Vaca. But somewhere in northern Sonora Estebanico disappeared. (Fray Marcos said he was killed, although a persistent legend of the Southwest has it that he ran away and became an Indian chief.) So Fray Marcos returned with a lively account of a great city that he had seen from a distance, "larger than the city of Mexico." But, patriotic New Mexicans to the contrary, and in spite of a rock upon which his name is carved near Santa Fe, Fray Marcos could not have come within several hundred miles of the "seven cities," that is, the pueblos of New Mexico.

Mendoza had not waited for Fray Marcos to return, but had organized a vast expedition under Francisco Vázquez de Coronado, which was ready to go when the Cíbola story was confirmed. We have no clue to Fray Marcos' motive for spinning his preposterous yarn. There may have been an understanding between him and Mendoza to find the cities, whether or not they existed, because Mendoza was extremely anxious to get the expedition off before Cortés could do anything but protest, and before Alvarado should appear and demand a share in it. Fray Marcos, of course, could have been credulous enough to believe in their existence, for it was a credulous age, and greater marvels had been swallowed whole, the legend of El Dorado, for example. However it was, the yarn proved to be one of the most expensive ever told. The loss of money and lives in the Coronado expedition was so heavy that it brought a peremptory order from the Crown that no more money was to be spent on such nonsense. It should be noted, in passing, that with few exceptions the conquest of the New World was carried through by private initiative, the Crown contributing nothing, save, perhaps, the jewels that Queen Isabella is supposed to have pawned to help finance the first voyage of Columbus. The Coronado expedition got started in February, 1540, just six months before Alvarado anchored off Colima.

Mendoza's problem with Alvarado was to keep him out of the Coronado expedition and to bind him so tightly to the Crown that he could not hope to set up another of the semi-independent feudal states that were anathema to the Hapsburgs. The great importance he attached to Alvarado is attested by his making the long journey to the west coast to interview him in person. A mutually satisfactory agreement was patched up, and for the next few months Alvarado was kept busy getting his fleet into shape. Even so, he might have proved unmanageable if it had not been for the outbreak of the Mixtón War, early in 1541.

Coronado had drawn off from New Galicia a great many men, and the country was left without adequate defense. The semibarbarous tribes to the north of the barranca of the Santiago River (called Chichimecas by the Mexicans, which is to say, "wild men") had suffered grievously from the savagery of Nuño de Guzmán and were waiting for just such a chance to turn the tables. Their medicine men preached a war of extermination against the Spaniards, and soon the heights were swarming with excited and determined warriors. Unluckily for them, they were feared and hated by the people of the south; their propaganda campaign fell flat and they had to go it alone. The Indians followed their ancient custom of fortifying themselves on mountain tops (*peñoles*), while carrying on planless and uncoordinated raids against the Spanish settlements. Even so, the Spaniards were so vastly outnumbered, and their Indian allies were so terrified, that they were in grave danger of extinction. The governor of New Galicia, Juan de Oñate, a brave and able man, led a force of Spaniards against the Chichimecas and was badly beaten. He sent a frantic call for help to Mendoza, who in turn asked Alvarado to go to the defense of Guadalajara. Alvarado brought a body of a hundred men from Colima and, late in June, 1541, led an attack on the peñol of Nochistlán, Jalisco. For the first time in his life the great Alvarado was defeated by the despised Indians, and he died in the retreat when a horse rolled on him.

Mendoza was now free from the last threat to his authority, but he found himself with a first-class war on his hands. He had to take the field in person, and in a campaign of great ferocity put an end to the most dangerous uprising the Spaniards had to face in three hundred years. No one knows how many Indians were killed, but all who were captured, men, women, and children, were branded as slaves and distributed among the soldiery as booty.

Not only did Mendoza get rid of Alvarado, but he fell heir to his forces and his fleet of twelve vessels, with which he sent out two famous expeditions, that of Ruy López de Villalobos to the East Indies, and that of Juan Rodríguez Cabrillo to the coast of California. The immense amount of literature devoted to Columbus and his crossing of the Atlantic has quite obscured the more hazardous feats of Magellan, Cabrillo, Villalobos, and other early voyagers of the Pacific. Magellan, at least, had reasonably safe vessels, but Villalobos and Cabrillo set out on their voyages in Alvarado's home-made tubs, over uncharted seas, with inadequate provisions, and most of their men faced certain death from thirst, starvation, and scurvy. It may be argued, of course, that they did not know they were going to die, but my conviction is that they were indifferent to danger.

The Mixtón rebellion had hardly been crushed by Mendoza's army of old veterans of the Conquest when New Spain and the whole Spanish colonial empire were thrown into a panic by the news that a drastic code of laws had been passed by the Council of the Indies. Their nature was well known. For many years the Dominicans, the most vocal of whom was Fray Bartolomé de las Casas, had been agitating for more adequate protection of the native peoples of the New World. They had already been responsible for the adoption of a good many laws, some practicable, some utopian, such as their curious plan to put the government of the Indies into the hands of three Jeronymite friars (actually tried out by the regent, Cardinal Ximénez de Cisneros, in 1516). That most of their attempted reforms were abortive, or were successfully circumvented by the Spanish settlers, merely had the effect of making the Dominicans redouble their efforts. Meanwhile, their power in the Council of the Indies grew mightily until, after thirty years of labor, they were able, in 1542, to induce the Council to promulgate the famous code known as *The New Laws of the Indies for the Good Treatment and Preservation of the Indians*. That the Crown would jeopardize the very existence of the Spanish Empire by submitting to such meddling was the effect of long centuries of clerical domination, which made Spain a quasi-theocracy.

This remarkable code was based on premises established by Francisco de Vitoria (in two lectures delivered at the University of Salamanca in 1532, under the title *De Indis et de Jure Belli Relectiones*). He argued that the Spaniards had no right whatever to the land or labor of the Indians, and that their intrusion into Indian lands was justifiable solely on the ground that it was necessary for the propagation of the Christian faith. The Indians were defined as "free vassals of the Crown," but it was recognized that they were in an inferior state of development and that it was the Crown's duty, therefore, to exercise a protective tutelage over them until they should come of age, in this accurately anticipating the thinking of our own lawmakers. *This concept was behind all the Indian legislation of the Spanish Empire.* Now, since the Indians had been entrusted by God to the care of the Spaniards, it was manifestly wrong to enslave them or to use their labor for private ends. Hence the granting of Indians in encomienda was wrong, as were all forms of coerced services. Implementing this philosophy were two articles of the New Laws: one abolished the encomiendas, which were to revert to the Crown upon the death of the holders, while the other abolished Indian chattel slavery.

Such was the bombshell that exploded in New Spain in 1542. It should be borne in mind that the greater part of the wealth of the old conquistadores consisted of tributes paid by the Indians whom they held in encomienda, together with the more or less legal privilege of using their labor. The conquerors, with some justification, it must be admitted, looked upon themselves as a vested aristocracy, but for whom there would have been no New World for the Spanish Crown to rule. With the enforcement of the New Laws they saw themselves and their families dispossessed and reduced to beggary. The Council of the Indies was deluged with tear-compelling plaints and denunciations of Las Casas, of which the following, written by the city council of Guatemala to Charles V, is a fair sample:

"Your Majesty's most loyal vassals, the citizens of Guatemala, kiss Your Majesty's feet and hands. In reply to certain reports that have come to this province . . . we say that . . . we cannot believe them, and that we are as shocked as if you had ordered our heads to be cut off. If the reports are true it is as much as to say clearly that all of us here are bad Christians and traitors to God and Your Majesty, whom we have served with our lives and estates.

"According to this report, Catholic Caesar, we must abandon the hope that our children will enjoy the rewards which we their fathers enjoy and possess in the name of Your Majesty. We are stunned and out of our senses, because we do not see how our sins could have been grave enough to deserve such a rigorous and merciless punishment. . . . It is affirmed that the source of this cruel sentence is one Fray Bartolomé de las Casas. We are greatly astonished, unconquered Prince, that a matter of such antiquity, initiated by your grandparents, weighed by so many hands, considered by such good and clear minds so well versed in law and so abundant in good will, should be reversed by a friar unread in law, unholy, envious, vainglorious, unquiet, not free from cupidity (for all of which clear proof can be supplied), and, above all else, a troublemaker. . . . We say this not to speak evil of him; we say it because he is not competent to give testimony about the Indies. . . .

"What was Your Majesty's purpose in commanding us expressly to marry? And now that we are married and burdened with children, what recourse have we but to die in despair if [the New Laws] are enforced? . . . Let Your Majesty hear all sides . . . for we only desire and demand justice, that we be measured with the same stick with which your ancestors measured the vassals who won for them their kingdoms and seigneuries. . . ."

So ran the pleas of the desperate settlers. It was as if some English king of the seventeenth century had suddenly gone mad and ordered all the freeholds of the North American colonies incorporated in the Crown lands. It is a safe guess that we should have had a War of Independence just so much the sooner.

The roar of protest that arose from New Spain was deafening. The excitement was so intense that if Mendoza had attempted to enforce the new code New Spain would have probably rebelled. Fortunately, it was not the policy of the Crown to embarrass local governments with the job of enforcing unpopular laws. In this case a special officer was sent over in 1544, the royal visitor Francisco Tello de Sandoval. He was received with tight-lipped resentment. It was touch-and-go in New Spain. Mendoza knew it and Archbishop Zumárraga knew it, but Sandoval was determined to publish the New Laws at once. Mendoza and Zumárraga had the most ticklish problem on their hands. They had somehow to persuade the growling encomenderos to lie quiet while they patched things up, and they had the no less difficult task of arguing Sandoval into putting off the publication of the New Laws until they could get a lobby going in the Council of the Indies. If they had failed in either of these efforts New Spain would almost certainly have been devastated by the same civil war that broke out in Peru and Panama at that time. In those unfortunate provinces the tactless handling of the situation by inflexible officers caused hundreds of Spaniards to lose their lives, while the disastrous effect on native life can only be imagined. Mendoza has been blamed for blocking the humanitarian laws of 1542, but there can be no doubt that he chose the wiser course. The New Laws were later subjected to a critical revision and their harsher features were sufficiently modified so that the encomenderos accepted them. They still grumbled loudly, but did not rebel.

It should be pointed out that humanitarianism was not the only, or, possibly, the most important motive of the Council of the Indies in promulgating the New Laws. They were designed to be an effective weapon in the reconquest of the New World from the conquistadores. They were part of the vast centralizing movement that was going on all over western Europe. They were meant to remove the feudal privileges of the Spanish settlers and reduce them to the status of pensioners of the Crown. The Crown, in a word, intended to be the only encomendero.

The storm provoked by the New Laws passed for a time, and Mendoza was able to serve out the last five years of his reign in comparative quiet. No small part of his success was owing to his wisdom in handling the native population. It was imperative that he should supplant Cortés in the role of the Great White Father, and he did so by adopting the same policy of conciliation that Cortés had used so successfully. He set aside one day each week to hear Indian grievances. Crowds of Indians took advantage of the privilege of seeing the viceroy in person, and he listened patiently to their harangues. There is no record of his having done anything spectacular about their troubles, but the wisdom of the custom was manifest, and he advised his successor to continue it, "even though," he added wryly, "the heat and stench may be oppressive." This form of redress became so well established, and the press of Indian affairs so great, that in 1591 a separate tribunal was set up for handling them, the General Indian Court, which for two hundred and thirty years acted as a shock absorber between the races of New Spain.

Don Antonio de Mendoza ruled New Spain for more than fifteen years. When, in 1551, he reluctantly left to head the newly created viceroyalty of Peru, peace, order, and law were so firmly established, and the prestige of the Crown had attained such a height, that New Spain was to weather civil conflict until the whole Spanish machine collapsed, in 1808.

# 7

## DON LUIS DE VELASCO

The viceroys of New Spain were likely to reflect the character of their sovereigns. Thus Antonio de Mendoza was a magnífico in the grand tradition of the Renaissance. He represented the pomp and splendor, as well as the realistic imperialism, of the Emperor Charles V. In 1546 the management of the affairs of the Indies was put into the hands of the twenty-year-old Prince Philip, who was later to become famous as Philip II. Philip was very different from his father, who had always been regarded as a foreigner in Spain. Philip, on the other hand, was the most Spanish of Spaniards. He was a prince in the classical sense, a kind of Oriental god-king, with a strong mystic streak and an abiding conviction that he had been chosen by the Almighty to lead his country and the rest of the world into the paths of righteousness, which ran strangely parallel to those of Spanish aggrandizement. Under Philip, Spain enjoyed a rule of puritanical virtue comparable to that of England under Cromwell. The public service became for a time more or less free from the corruption that tended to creep in at the slightest opportunity. In this respect his rule resembled that of the great-grandmother, Isabella the Catholic, who swept grafting officials and venal judges out of office until Castile was the best-governed country in Europe.

Don Luis de Velasco, Mendoza's successor, was the kind of viceroy we should expect Philip to choose. He combined sagacity and humanity with a rigid sense of duty and dignity, and a capacity for hard work. He possessed precisely the qualities needed to continue the consolidation of New Spain. The New Laws of 1542, which had brought the colonies to the verge of disintegration, had undergone careful revision, but their fundamental principles had not been materially altered. That is, the Crown was still determined to set up in New Spain and the rest of the Spanish Indies a centralized, pyramidal form of government, in which all elements would be subordinate to the supreme power of the throne. The New Laws were not abrogated, nor were they a failure, as has so often been charged. They had to be revised in the direction of realism and workability, and they became incorporated into the great fabric of the Laws of the Indies. A gesture was made to ease the pain of the encomenderos, who were allowed to enjoy their encomiendas for "two lives," that is, for the life of the original holder and that of his heir. Their tenure was repeatedly extended, in fact, and the encomienda was not definitely abolished until the eighteenth century, when it no longer had any significance. The encomenderos, under the New Laws, still lived on Indian tributes, but their most valuable privilege was removed, that of using the labor of the Indians without pay. The law was not always enforced, and I suspect that local officials were usually lenient with the encomenderos, but it is noteworthy that in the voluminous records of the General Indian Court there are very few complaints against them. On the contrary, to protect their own interests they were obliged to protect their Indians. It is amusing to see our old friend Bernal Díaz del Castillo, at the age of eighty-odd, going to court to defend the Indians of his encomienda from a couple of land-grabbers, and winning his suit. In another important respect the New Laws remained unaltered: Indian chattel slavery stayed abolished, on the books, at least, for enslavement of "rebels" throughout the colonial régime continued to be employed as a punitive measure.

Indian slavery requires a word of explanation. From the time of Columbus it had been the practice of a good many Spaniards to enslave, on one pretext or another, as many Indians as they could capture, and sell them in the mines. Columbus himself had planned to go into the slaving business, but was stopped by Queen Isabella after he had shipped one batch of slaves to Spain. The usual pretext for taking slaves was "rebellion." Once the Indians had submitted to

Spanish rule and had taken the uncomprehended oath of allegiance to the Crown,[1] any act of rebellion could legally be punished by enslavement. It was common practice among certain Spaniards to provoke the Indians to armed resistance and then seize them as slaves. The Crown had placed many restrictions on slaving, but at the time of Velasco's appointment (1550) there was still a large body of these unfortunates scattered about the settlements and mining camps, estimated at between two and three hundred thousand in all the Indies—possibly 65,000 in New Spain alone. Their principal employment was washing gravel in the placer gold mines, grinding ore in the silver mines, and pearl diving. Others were used as domestic servants and field hands. The revised New Laws decreed the immediate release of all Indian slaves whose owners could not show proper titles of possession. Now, since records were rarely kept of the manner in which slaves had been acquired, it was fairly obvious that all slaves would be set free.

There was the expected bitter cry of protest. Slave owners rushed the usual lobbies back to the Council of the Indies, one of which was conducted by the indispensable Bernal Díaz del Castillo, of Guatemala. They were instructed to explain to the Council the disastrous consequences that the enforcement of this unjust law would have: Freeing the slaves would stop all the profitable activities of the country; the gold mines would cease operation; the Crown revenues would shrink to nothing; uncounted citizens would be ruined who had bought their slaves in good faith; in general, the colonies would go to the dogs. To the credit of the Council of the Indies, these arguments did not prevail and the Indian slaves were freed. What happened to the freedmen of New Spain is unknown. Elsewhere, as in Panama and Cuba, they were settled in colonies and given land and tools to give them a start. In New Spain, it is my guess that they drifted back to their native villages. The protests of the owners were

[1] Indians against whom the Spaniards might be leading an expedition (*entrada*) had to listen to a long manifesto (*requerimiento*), which explained to them the mysteries of the Christian religion, the nature of the Church, and the obligation of all men to acknowledge the sovereignty of the Spanish monarchs, etc., etc. Their bewilderment was no greater than that of the Spaniards who read it to them. Although the requerimiento was a dead letter by Velasco's time, some such rigamarole had to be gone through before any slaving party was legal.

correct in one respect, in that placer gold mining suffered a decline from which it never recovered, and the viceroy was embarrassed by a decline in the "king's fifth," the standard tax on the precious metals.[2]

It must be emphasized again that no act of the Council of the Indies was purely humanitarian, nor could it be. Its job was to govern the Indies. Its members were high-minded men, but they were also practical administrators, and it would not have been good administration (Philip II was always hard-pressed for money) to subject the Crown to a loss of revenue. Velasco's famous statement, that "the liberty of the Indians is worth more than all the mines in the world, and the revenue that the Crown receives from them is not of such consequence that the Crown would on that account crush under foot human and divine law," is not altogether accurate. For example, one of the arguments that made the emancipation of the Indian slaves palatable to the Crown was that the freedmen would become tribute-paying subjects, which they were not so long as they remained slaves. Since free Indians paid an annual tax of a gold peso a head, the argument had weight.

The profit accruing to the Crown from Indian tributes was, however, always disappointing. In the first place, at least up to the end of the sixteenth century, half the tributes, more or less, went to the encomenderos, who paid nothing to the Crown except the tithe, and that went to the Church. Besides, the collection of the tribute from the Crown towns proved to be a complicated business, especially in the early years, when it was assessed in kind. Tribute in gold dust could be collected only along the gold-bearing streams of the south coast, while in the rest of the country it was paid in textiles (*mantas*), fowl, maize, or in any produce used in commerce. It was brought to the corregidor and had to be stored and disposed of by sale. Moreover, it was brought in at fixed times, usually at the end of the harvest, and the resultant glut brought prices down. Corregidores complained that they had to spend all their salaries in the disposal of the tribute. Velasco remedied the situation to some extent by providing that tributes should be paid in cash, at the rate of one gold

[2] The placers were probably exhausted anyway. They have always been a superficial and temporary industry, doomed to early abandonment, as we have seen in California.

peso a year for each tributary, plus half a fanega of maize or its equivalent. In 1592 the tribute was increased by half a peso for New Spain and Guatemala, the so-called *real servicio,* to meet part of the immense cost of the Invincible Armada. Like most special taxes, it was never repealed, and was still being collected at the end of the old régime. Even so, the Crown made so little out of the tribute, and its collection was such a nuisance, that later viceroys recommended its abolition; but it was not done away with until the nineteenth century, when it was made a political issue to attract the Indians to the cause of Independence. Also, since the encomenderos were supported by it (at the rate of half a million pesos a year in Velasco's time), it may be that the Crown was reluctant to transfer this charge to the royal treasury, for veterans, even in those days, expected and demanded a bonus.

Long before Velasco's reign the tribute had been the subject of much discussion and dissension. In the good old days of free enterprise the encomenderos had let their conscience be their guide and had tended to collect all the tribute the traffic would bear. Attempts by men like Bishop Zumárraga to bring the tribute down to the Indians' capacity to pay had met with scant success, so one of the many duties assigned to Velasco was that of "moderating" the tribute. He was also charged with the inspection of encomienda titles and, in general, with continuing Mendoza's policy of putting the encomenderos in their place. In this thankless, indeed dangerous, task he chose assistants who were as stern and incorruptible as himself. The judges (or, rather, inspectors—*jueces visitadores*) whom he sent to all parts of New Spain were armed only with their commission and the inevitable notary. The treatment they might expect at the hands of the irritated encomenderos is illustrated by the experience of Diego Ramírez, who was sent into the northern and eastern provinces. In Metztitlán (modern Hidalgo) he was seized by agents of the encomenderos, thrown into jail, and sent back to the capital to answer a lot of trumped-up charges. The charges were eventually quashed by the Audiencia, and Ramírez continued to worry the encomenderos until his death, after which they managed to recover their losses.

Not all of Velasco's abundant energy went into internal administration. Ever since Hernando de Soto had explored "La Florida" in 1542, stories of its wealth kept circulating, probably fed by the survivors of the expedition, who had made their way from the delta of the Mississippi to Tampico in makeshift boats. Other motives also, such as the necessity of securing the eastern coast of Florida against the encroaching French Huguenots, induced Philip II to undertake its settlement, and Luis de Velasco was given the job. Velasco got together a large force of some 2,600 Spaniards and Indians and several vessels, and put Tristán de Luna in command. (Luna was a wealthy encomendero of Mexico City, and had been one of the organizers of the Coronado expedition, in which he had lost heavily.) Luna's expedition got away in 1559, but from the beginning was dogged by misfortune, and probably by mismanagement. He attempted a settlement on Pensacola Bay, but starvation, disease, storms, and hostile Indians took the heart out of the settlers in two terrible years, and Luna was relieved of his command. His successor had no better luck, and the broken remnants of the colony returned to New Spain in 1561.

Notwithstanding the expensive failure of the Florida adventure, Philip II had another project, which he also put into Velasco's hands. Ruy López de Villalobos, whom we last saw in one of Alvarado's tubs on his way to the Spice Islands, had actually reached them in 1542, by way of the Philippines, but could not make his way back across the Pacific. For twenty years the Crown had cherished the notion of making the Philippines an entrepôt for the lucrative China trade, which up to that time had been monopolized by the Portuguese. But first an eastward passage across the Pacific had to be found, because the Portuguese had closed the Cape of Good Hope route to all but themselves. The westward passage from Acapulco to the East Indies offered no difficulty. All one had to do was to steer into the belt of the northeast trade winds and stay there. The return was a very different matter. Tacking back and forth in the teeth of the trade winds would have taken an eternity, and no ship of the time could have carried enough provisions to make it. Spain, however, had never abandoned the quest of Columbus. After Magellan discovered the westward passage to Asia, several expeditions followed in an attempt to break into the Portuguese monopoly. One of these early expeditions was that of Jofre de Loaisa, in 1525. In his crew was an obscure Basque sailor named Andrés de Urdaneta.

Urdaneta was born late in the fifteenth century. In his youth he had been a soldier in Italy and had fought with the invincible legions of Gonsalvo de Córdoba, *el Gran Capitán*. When he reached the East Indies with Loaisa and found that he could not return, he spent eleven years sailing and trading in those waters, in defiance of the Portuguese. He finally completed the circuit of the globe in a Portuguese ship, landing at Lisbon in 1536. He was in New Spain in 1542 and refused Viceroy Mendoza's offer of a command in the Villalobos expedition. Ten years later he withdrew from the world and took the habit of St. Augustine. Twelve years after *that,* when Luis de Velasco was getting together a new expedition to explore the Philippines and look for an eastward passage, the only man in New Spain who knew anything about Asiatic waters was Fray Andrés de Urdaneta. Velasco vainly tried to induce the old friar to take command of the expedition, but he did get his consent to go along as observer and technical adviser.

The fleet sailed from Acapulco in November, 1564, under the command of Miguel López de Legazpi. Legazpi negotiated the westward passage without difficulty. He founded the city of Manila and decided to remain there and complete the conquest of the islands. The discovery of the eastward passage he entrusted to his nephew, Felipe de Salcedo, who sailed from Manila in a single short-handed vessel, a poor affair, or, as the old chronicle has it, a "gift ship." (It should be explained that in the frugal Spanish tradition one gives away only things of no value.) Urdaneta had a notion that the westerly winds which were known to prevail in the North Atlantic might also be encountered in the Pacific, so he instructed Salcedo to sail northward. A few days out from Manila the pilot and the sailing master died, and Fray Andrés had to take the helm. Scurvy began eating into the crew and soon there were not enough hands to work the vessel. But Fray Andrés beat his way northward, through calms and storms and contrary winds, for two thousand miles, and finally ran into the prevailing westerlies in about latitude 36°. At that point he turned east and sailed before the wind to the

Coast of California, and then rode the northwest gale down to Acapulco, arriving there on October 3, 1565.

Urdaneta had completed the first voyage on the Great Circle route across the Pacific, ten thousand miles, in four months and two days. Fourteen of the crew had died of scurvy, and at Acapulco no one had the strength even to drop the anchor. Only two men, in fact, were able to stand at all. One was the captain, Felipe de Salcedo, and at the helm, in his tattered friar's habit, stood the gaunt figure of old Fray Andrés.

The Eastward Passage had been solved. From that day forward heavy galleons were to bring to New Spain the silks, spices, and ivory of the East, and on their return trip were to flood Asia with good Spanish dollars from the mints of Mexico.

It is a pity that Luis de Velasco did not live to see the end of one of the most remarkable voyages in maritime history. I suggest that when another of our poets is casting about for a heroic theme on the order of Archibald MacLeish's *Conquistador,* he tell us the story of the Iron Friar.

It would be an injustice to Don Luis de Velasco to leave the impression that he was a monster of sternness and purity. Off duty he was an affable and kindly gentleman, fond of good living and exceedingly proud of his superb horsemanship. He loved to lead the hunt, and on holidays he joined in the colorful *juego de cañas,* a kind of jousting in which opposing squadrons of horsemen dashed at each other armed with light canes. The canes were thrown like javelins and caught on shields, while the horsemen galloped and cavorted about in a cloud of dust and with a highly satisfactory lot of noise. Don Luis was also addicted to bullfighting, which in those days of amateur sports was performed by men on horseback and which tried to the utmost the skill of the riders. In short, Don Luis was a very popular viceroy, and I suspect that he owed no small part of his popularity with the pleasure-loving Mexicans to his sportsmanship.

Don Luis deserved his popularity. What, possibly, he did not deserve was his mother-in-law. Doña María de Mendoza was a great lady from a famous family and the half-sister (illegitimate, but no matter) of Don Antonio de Mendoza. At the same time she was a stiff-necked and domineering old harridan, who soured the viceroy's domestic life. For Don Luis was a bit on the domineering side himself and liked, as the Spaniards say, to wear the pants in his own house. Everyone else, though—the servants, the palace guard, the vicereine herself—jumped when Doña María spoke, and she spoke often. The cast was well chosen for a farce in high place, and the rows between Don Luis and Doña María became the talk of the palace. Their feud soon took on the dignity of an affair of state, for Doña María's complaints were addressed to the Council of the Indies, no less. She had a long bill of grievances, the bitterest of which was that Don Luis hated her so ferociously that he would not allow her to see her own daughter. It is related that one day Don Luis went to Doña María's apartment and found her writing another letter to the Council of the Indies. He snatched it out of her hands and began to read. She snatched it back. High words were exchanged, and possibly other things. In the midst of the row it was announced that Archbishop Montúfar was in the antechamber. Don Luis emerged quite calmly, kissed the ring of His Grace, and excused himself. The archbishop entered and found Doña María sitting on the floor, disheveled and weeping. Blood was streaming from a gash in her forehead and beside her lay a silver candlestick. No one ever learned precisely what happened, but thenceforward peace reigned in the viceroy's household.

Peace had descended also on New Spain during the thirteen years of Velasco's reign. His unflagging zeal in enforcing the New Laws had earned him the honorable title of "Father of the Indians." He died in office on July 31, 1564, and in the universal grief of all classes was given the finest tribute a man can receive. The cathedral chapter of Mexico wrote to Philip II: "His death is mourned by all of us here in New Spain, for he governed with such prudence and rectitude, doing wrong to no one, that all looked up to him as a father. He died on the last day of July, very poor and in debt. He always held that his principal duty was to do justice, without fraud and without reward, serving Your Majesty and maintaining the realm in peace and quietness."

70

# 8

## THE FRIARS

For well over a century the *cuestión palpitante* in Mexico has been: What about the Church? In the fundamental conflict between traditional Catholic elements and the republican movements deriving originally from the Jacobin radicals of the French Revolution, the Catholic hierarchy has always upheld the autonomy of the Church in all matters which it considers its special province, namely, elementary education; the right (nay, the necessity) of preserving its ancient place as the single religious institution of the country; the right (again, the necessity) of being the sole judge of the qualifications of the clergy; the privilege of trying all criminal actions brought against its members; and the right to hold property. Its unyielding defense of these rights and privileges has brought on the bitterest and bloodiest conflicts in Mexican history. Divine Sanction *vs.* Popular Sovereignty! Historically, it is the struggle of the colonial régime, which lives on in the Church, with its authoritarian, clerical, and caste implications, to survive in the hostile modern world of middle-class liberalism and, lately, in the atheistic tenets which the present government carries on its back like an Old Man of the Mountains. All other political questions are, as the Spaniards say, "tarts and painted bread," compared with it. There is nothing peculiarly Mexican about it. Precisely the same struggle has been going on in Spain since 1812. There is not a phase of Mexican life that is not profoundly affected by it. The most incendiary invective is employed by both sides. The emotional content of the struggle is so high, in fact, that compromise or final solution is exceedingly unlikely, if not altogether impossible.

The dispute, punctuated with gunshots and spattered with blood, has been going on since Independence, with no end in sight. On the Church's side are the conservative elements: the clergy, of course; the landowners, large and small, especially in those sections of the country settled by Spaniards long ago (e.g., the Bajío district of Guanajuato, Michoacán, and Jalisco; Puebla, and Oaxaca); most shopkeepers and businessmen (but especially their womenfolk); a good part of the Indian and mestizo peasantry, and the unorganized pious generally. The strength of the Church is greatest in the country and the provincial capitals. On the other side is the Institutional Revolutionary Party, the PRI, which changes its name now and then, but not its nature. Its strength lies in the captive labor movement, the equally captive agrarian movement, the huge federal and state bureaucracies, and the army. This is an oversimplification, because all these elements are checked and split by a multitude of conflicting interests; but, by and large, the Revolutionary Party (i.e., the federal government) controls them all through patronage and the vast power of the national treasury. I do not know where the solution lies, or even that a solution exists. Meanwhile, it may do some good to understand the nature of the hold that Mother Church has on the people of Mexico, and how it came about.

The fight for survival is being carried on today by the secular clergy, whose history will be the subject of a later chapter. Back in the sixteenth century, however, the seculars were not the most numerous or the most powerful religious element. The mendicant orders of St. Francis and St. Dominic had held in Spain, since the thirteenth century, a special and privileged place. Organized as semiautonomous corporations, they lived under their own rules and owed direct obedience (at least until the time of Isabella the Catholic) only to their generals in Rome. They became something of an anomaly in the later centralized despotism of Spain, but, as the secular clergy fell under the control of the Crown, the value of the independent regular orders became apparent. Their comparative freedom from censorship made them a refuge for the finest intellects of the country: men who felt free, and considered it their Christian duty, to criticize everything of which they disapproved, including the acts of the monarchs themselves. They were the only ones who

72

enjoyed that privilege. By its exercise they had an influence on the history of Spain and America out of all proportion to their numbers. Mendicants had filled, and continued to fill, the highest offices of the state. Isabella's most trusted adviser was a Franciscan, Cardinal Francisco Ximénez de Cisneros, one of the greatest statesmen Spain ever produced. The man she put in charge of the important task of badgering the Moors and Jews into a Christian heaven (while destroying their will to resist) was Tomás de Torquemada, a Dominican and a rigid Pharisee, whose Inquisition captured the shuddering imagination of the world. The sweeping reform of the political structure of the Indies known as the New Laws (discussed above) was the work of the Dominicans of the Council of the Indies. The first bishops sent to New Spain were Fray Julián Garcés, bishop of Tlaxcala, a Dominican, and Fray Juan de Zumárraga, bishop of Mexico, a Franciscan, both great men by any standard.

The founders of the two orders were men of entirely opposite characters. St. Dominic was the embodiment of legalism. His God was the God of Law—Law supreme and inflexible—and woe to the wretch who transgressed it! It was St. Dominic who marched at the side of the ferocious crusader, Simon de Monfort, against the Albigensian heretics of Languedoc, and founded for their redemption the terrible Papal Inquisition. The God of St. Francis was the God of charity and humanity. Man to St. Francis was a weak and fumbling creature, to be led or coerced into righteousness, whose endless shortcomings were readily forgiven by his pitying Creator. The members of the two orders generally reflected the difference between the founders. The Dominicans bent their extraordinary legal talents to the erection of a City of God in the New World. The blueprints of their City were frequently drawn up in ignorance of the problems to be solved and in defiance of human nature (as we have seen in the New Laws of 1542), but the humanitarian legislation of the Council of the Indies was their accomplishment, based upon the noble assumption that the Indians were God's innocents, to be protected from abuse in this life and saved from damnation in the next.

The Franciscans, on the other hand, although they were convinced that God had chosen their order to establish His Millennial Kingdom in the New World,[1] were eclectic in method. They were practical men, a bit contemptuous, possibly, of legal formalities, and given to direct action. (Bishop Zumárraga's battle with Nuño de Guzmán was a bare-knuckle affair and no nonsense!) For that reason it was a fortunate thing that they were the pioneers in the conversion of New Spain. Their comfortable humanity, their readiness to make use of any device that came to hand, their tireless personal intervention for the protection of their charges, their mild rule and inexhaustible good will—these factors did more to win the affection and veneration of the Indians than any amount of orthodox theology could have done, although they were in such a hurry that they were accused of baptizing Indians wholesale without proper indoctrination. It is difficult to imagine how any other approach could have succeeded so well.

The original plan of the Council of the Indies was to send simultaneously to New Spain missions from the two great mendicant orders. The Franciscans were the first to get under way—I do not know why, unless it was that the Dominicans had virtually monopolized the Antilles and the Franciscans were thirsting to even the score. However it was, Fray Juan de Glapión, Franciscan confessor of Charles V, and Fray Francisco de los Angeles, general of the order, obtained a bull from Pope Leo X on April 25, 1521, granting them permission to preach to the people of New Spain. In addition, they were given certain extraordinary powers usually reserved to bishops: the power to administer all the sacraments; to absolve from all excommunications; to confer and confirm, in the absence of a bishop, minor orders in the hierarchy; to consecrate

---

[1] In John L. Phelan's *The Millennial Kingdom of the Franciscans in the New World*, he makes it quite clear that the Spiritual Franciscans (as opposed to the Conventuals) saw the discovery of the New World as the fulfillment of the Apocalyptic vision of St. John the Divine, heralding the Second Coming, when all mankind would be brought into the bosom of Jesus Christ. They worked against time, in the belief that the Day was close at hand. The prodigious energy generated by this belief was still functioning until late in the colonial period, as witness the evangelization of the northern frontier of New Spain in the eighteenth century. Father Junípero Serra's California missions are a prime example.

churches and provide them with ministers; and *no cleric or secular priest might interfere with them, on pain of excommunication.* This bull was the charter of the regular orders in New Spain. In effect, it set them up as semiautonomous feudal corporations, virtually independent of the civil authorities. The stout defiance of Nuño de Guzmán by the Franciscans was possible because they were beyond his reach. They also annoyed subsequent, and better, officers.[2]

The first small vanguard of the Franciscan mission arrived at Tlaxcala in 1522. Of the three friars who composed it, the most famous was Fray Pedro de Gante, a lay brother, reputed to be the

[2] The feudal nature of the missions is accurately described by the eminent Mexican historian, Manuel Orozco y Berra (*Apuntes para la historia de la geografía en México* [Mexico, 1881], pp. 173–174). It is worth quoting at length:

"It is curious to observe that the most ancient monuments of this class [the mission churches] had the double function of houses of prayer and fortresses. The ones I am acquainted with are built in the form of a parallelogram. The walls, thick and massive, rise to a height of many feet, reinforced by heavy buttresses. Around the top runs a crenelated parapet connecting the niches that rest upon the buttresses, with loopholes at the front and sides, capable of sheltering in complete safety one or two arquebusiers. . . . The doors and corridors cut in the thick walls were narrow, allowing the passage of only one man at a time. The churchyard . . . was the outer works of the fortress. It was also built in the form of a parallelogram, enclosed by a parapet topped with battlements; at intervals it had chapels, or rather redoubts, which could be used for crossfire. . . .

"The true conqueror, who really won and pacified the land, was the missionary. The church . . . was a castle. As soon as the church was erected, the villages roundabout considered themselves vanquished. The people came eagerly to learn doctrine and religious practices. They became the fief of which the missionary was the feudal lord. . . . In the absence of the vanished authority of the native lords, the missionaries, who had made themselves the indisputable conquerors of the land by their preaching and many virtues, established their authority in a land that always submitted to them gladly. . . . Nothing was more natural than that the missionary should take the place of that [authority] which no longer existed, and in so doing render a great service to society. His authority was based upon the unquestioned rights that his office of catechist gave him over his neophytes; those which his office of teacher gave him over his pupils. . . ; his rights over the conquered, as their ardent defender; his rights over the community, as its recognized temporal lord, because the missionary organized the police, suppressed lawlessness, administered justice, and imposed punishments upon those who rebelled against his discipline."

illegimate half-brother of the Emperor. They immediately perceived that their first task was to overcome the obstacle of language. They set up their first primary school (*doctrina*) in Texcoco, where they tried to teach the Gospel, reading, writing, singing, and the playing of musical instruments, to the sons of the Indian nobility, and themselves studied harder than any of their pupils. No formal organization, however, was attempted until two years later, when the first large company of Franciscans landed at Vera Cruz, the "Twelve Apostles," under the leadership of Fray Martín de Valencia. Obeying a pious impulse, with an astonishing intuition, the friars did precisely the thing best calculated to arouse wonder and veneration among the Indians. *Barefoot, in their coarse robes, they walked the three hundred miles over the mountains from Vera Cruz to Mexico City.* The men of Cortés would hardly have been human if they had not been as deeply moved as the Indians. When the friars reached the capital the conquistadores pressed around them to kiss the hems of their robes and beg their blessing, Cortés first. Bernal Díaz was among them. Fifty years later the scene was still fresh in his mind:

"When Cuauhtémoc and the other caciques saw Cortés fall to his knees and kiss the friars' hands, their astonishment was very great. And when they saw that the friars were barefoot and thin, and that their habits were ragged, and that they did not ride horseback, but walked, and were very pale; and when they saw Cortés, whom they considered an idol or something like their gods, thus kneeling, all the Indians followed his example, so that now, when the friars come, the Indians receive them with the same reverence and respect."

This admirable band of men, armed with nothing but goodwill and faith, set about their conquest of New Spain with an energy, daring, and intelligence equal to those of Cortés himself. *And their conquest endured.* Beginning with the three centers of instruction, at Tlaxcala, Huejotzingo, and Texcoco, within a few years they had set up their doctrinas in every Indian town of importance in the vast Provincia del Santo Evangelio, which covered the present states of Tlaxcala, Mexico, Puebla, Hidalgo, Michoacán, Jalisco, Morelos, Guerrero, and Vera Cruz. From their convents in the head towns (*cabeceras*) of the Indians they kept their friars continually on the move in the surrounding territory, baptizing, confirming, marrying, saying Masses, and teaching the elements of Christian religion and government. In addition to religious instruction, they taught European techniques of weaving, dyeing, ceramics, masonry, carpentry, silk culture, and agriculture generally. They acted as arbiters in the frequent disputes among their neophytes; they interceded for them with Spanish settlers and magistrates; they healed the sick,[3] punished the erring,[4] comforted the dying, and buried the dead. In short, in an amazingly brief period, the friars had completely replaced the native priests as the natural leaders of Indian society.

The "convent town" became the typical Indian town of the better sort. It was ruled by native officers under the direction of the friars, who intervened in village affairs whenever they thought it necessary; sometimes it may have been pure meddling, as was charged. The Indians complained now and then of the arbitrary interference of the friars, and the Spanish settlers complained a great deal, because, they said, the friars employed multitudes of Indians for building convents and chapels, and thus kept a considerable amount of labor out of circulation, labor which the settlers thought could be more profitably used in field or mine. But the friars took care of their own.

[3] Not only Indians. The Atlantic passage was so fatiguing that a great many passengers were landed sick at Vera Cruz. The Franciscans set up convalescent hospitals for them, at Jalapa, Perote, Oaxtepec, and Mexico City, as reported by the Commissary Fray Alonso Ponce, in 1588.

[4] The whipping post was considered an indispensable aid in implanting and maintaining the Christians virtues, as well as for the punishment of ordinary offenses. It need not shock us that it was part of the equipment of a mission. Our New England forebears took the scriptural injunction about sparing the rod quite as seriously. Fray Jerónimo de Mendieta in a letter to Philip II in 1587 explained the need of the lash:

"And hence one may perceive the error of those who think it is a cruel thing for a friar or priest to have the Indians flogged who are in his charge, whereas it is necessary for their well-being and profit. This error comes from ignorance of the character of the Indians, for the whip is as necessary to them as the bread for their mouths, and so natural that they cannot live without it among themselves. Indeed, they themselves say as much. When the whip is absent, like children they are spoiled, for if an Indian gets drunk, or takes a mistress, or beats his wife; or if she runs away from her husband; or if they refuse to go to Mass or the doctrina when they have not studied their lesson, then with a dozen lashes the matter is settled and they learn their lesson. But if the whip is withheld, not only is their correction impossible, but they become bolder and commit greater sins."

DURANGO(F)
Topia(F)
Peñol Blanco(F)
Nombre de Dios(F)
Sombrerete(F)

ZACATECAS(F)

Sentispac (F)

M        E        X        I

Juchipila (F)

Jalisco(F)

Ahuacatlán(F)

San Miguel el Grande(F)

Etzatlán(F)
GUADALAJARA (F)
Tonalá(F)
Tlajomulco(F)
Poncitlán(F)
Querétaro(F
Cocula(F)
Chapala(F)
Ocotlán(F)
Apaseo(
Axixic(F)
Zacoalco(F)
Yuriria(A)
Amacueca(F)
Cuitzeo(A)
Acámbaro
Huango(A)
Ucare
Atoyac (F)
Jacona(A)
Zacapú(F)
Zinapécuaro(F)
Jerécua
Autlán(F)
Zapotlán(F)
Tarécuato(F)
Cucupao(F) Charo(A)
Santa Fe(F)
Tajimaroa(F)
Zapotitlán(F)
Erongarícuaro(F)
VALLADOLID(F,A)
Tuxpan (F)
Tiripitío(A)
Pátzcuaro(F)
Tzintzuntzan (F)
Uruapan(F)

Colima(F)

Tacámbaro (A)

Cupándaro(A)

(A).  Augustinian
(F)  Franciscan
(D)  Dominican

*from R. Ricard "Spiritual Conquest of Mexico", 1966*

# MENDICANT ESTABLISHMENTS
## about 1570

O

TAMPICO (F)

Xilitla(A)

Tantoyuca (A)

Chapulhuacán(A)

Huejutla(A)
Pahuatlán(A)

Molango(A)

Culhuacán(A)

Metztitlán(A)

hapantongo(A)

Ixmiquilpan(A)

Tututepec(A)

Actopan(A)

Atotonilco(A)

Huauchinango (A)

Tula (F)

Acatlán(A)

Tulancingo(F)

ilotepec(F)

Tezontepec(A)

Epazoyuca(A)

Zempoala(F)

Otumba(F)

Tepeapulco (F)

Acolman(A)

Apan (F)

Cuautitlán(F)

Teotihuacán (F)

Atzcapotzalco(D)

Tetzcoco(F)

Tepetlaoztoc(D)

Huexotla(F)

yoacán(D) MEXICO

Chalco(D)

Chimalhuacán(D)

TLAXCALA(F)

uca(F)

Coatepec Chalco(D)

Xochimilco (F)

Tlalmanalco (F)

Huejotzingo(F)

Ocuila(A)

Mixquic(A)

Amecameca(F,D)

PUEBLA(F,D)

Quecholac(F)

Malinalco(A)

Tenango(D)

Cholula(F)

Ahuaca(F)

Tepoztlán(D)

Totolapan(A)

Tetela(D)

Ahuaca(F)

Acatzingo(F)

Cuernavaca(F)

Cuautinchán(F)

Tepeaca(F)

Tlayacapan(A)

Hueyapan(D)

Tecamachalco(F)

Yautepec(D)

Jantetelco(A)

Tecali(F)

Yecapixtla(A)

Oaxtepec(D)

Atlatlahuca(F)

Ocuituco(A)

Izúcar(Iztucan)(D)

Tehuacán(F)

Zacualpan(A)

Chietla(A)

Tepeji(D)

Chiautla(A)

Zapotitlán(F)

Teutila (D)

Tonalá(D)

Coixtlahuaca(D)

Tamazulapan(D)

Tanetze (D)

Tlapa (A)

Teposcolula(D)

Yanhuitlán (D)

Villa Alta (D)

Tecomaxtlahuaca(D)

Achiutla(D)

Ixtepexi(D)

Totontepec(D)

Tlaxiaco (D)

Etla(D)

Cuilapan (D)

OAXACA (D)

Ocotlán(D)

Nejapa (D)

Jalapa(D)

Coatlán (D)

Tehuantepec(D)

Huaxolotitlán

Huamelula(D)

They defended the complicated Indian hierarchy of the village, which included such officers as cantor, truant officer, and the like, as well as the alcaldes and a long list of minor officials.

The friars organized the Indians of their parishes into brotherhoods (*cofradías*), after the fashion of the church guilds of Spain, and each cofradía was made responsible for the celebration of some feast of the Christian calendar. These cofradías were among the most effective devices hit upon by the friars for the consolidation of the new society. Membership, and especially the privilege of playing a part in the village fiesta, were prized above all earthly honors, just as the loss of a part for drunkenness or some other naughtiness was a disgrace and a calamity. The power thus given into the hands of the friars was very great. The cofradías took their responsibilities with the utmost seriousness, and the plays were put on with considerable skill and originality. So thoroughly did the village play become an integral part of community life that even today, when there is not a friar in all Mexico, every self-respecting village has its special fiesta, managed and staged by its cofradía, playing such venerable mysteries as the Battle of the Moors and Christians, in which angels, devils, Moors, Christian knights, St. James, Hernán Cortés, Alexander the Great, Pharoah, and Julius Caesar appear, in fine disregard of the unities.

When Fray Alonso Ponce visited the convent town of Tlajomulco (Jalisco) on January 6, 1587, its cofradía was playing The Coming of the Magi. Even at that early date it was already the traditional fiesta of Tlajomulco, and Indians and Spaniards came from many miles around to see it. It was, and is, so typical of the Indians' beloved fiestas that I am including the description of it recorded by Father Ponce's secretary:

"For a long time past the Indians of Tlajomulco have had the custom of acting out the Coming of the Magi, just as our Holy Mother Church teaches us that it happened. . . . Against the tower of the church, near the door, they had built the gate of Bethlehem, and in it they had placed the Child and the Mother and St. Joseph. The gate was a poor affair made of sticks, woven together with twigs and covered with a kind of moss that grows in that country. . . . At one side of the courtyard, somewhat removed from the gate, was a shelter made of green branches, in which Herod was seated, together with a large company, in great majesty and dignity.

"The Magi descended on horseback from the summit of a high hill near the town, riding very slowly, not only to preserve their dignity, but also because the hill was very high and the way very rough. It took them almost two hours to come down to the church. Before them walked an Indian carrying a banner, and behind him another, an old man of over eighty, with a basket on his back full of offerings for the Child. And, while they were descending, a band of angels came out and danced before the gate, singing verses in the Mexican language and making many reverences and genuflections to the Child. Then appeared a band of shepherds, each with his pouch and a pumpkin and other things, and his crook and other implements of his trade, all very poor. While they were in the courtyard an angel emerged from a little wooden tower and sang *Gloria in Excelsis Deo,* at the sound of which the shepherds fell to the ground as if stricken senseless. But the angel comforted them and told them the tidings of the birth of the Child, at which they all got up and ran to the gate with great rejoicing and merriment, and offered the Child what they had: one, a kid; another, a lamb; a third, bread; a fourth, a mantle; and others, other things, and all this they did with such reverence that they inspired great piety among the onlookers.

"And then they began to dance and sing, telling each other what they had heard and seen, and repeating the words of the angel over and over again, saying *'Goria! Goria! Goria!'* jumping up and down the while and waving their crooks with great contentment and pleasure. And then they set to wrestling, and when two of them were thrown to the ground they rolled over and over tightly embraced, so quickly that everyone was astonished and pleased. . . . After this had been going for a long time two shepherds came out with their crooks and stopped them, and the director ordered them to be gone. Finally, when the shepherds saw the Magi approaching, they joined hands and made a circle, leaving some loose inside it, who with their crooks chased the others and knocked

81

down whomever they caught and rolled them from one side of the court to the other. And with this [that part of] the play came to an end, and truly it was worthy to be seen.

"The Magi were guided to the entrance of the courtyard by a tinsel star, which ran on two ropes from the top of the hill to the church tower. At intervals high wooden towers had been erected, from which the Indians pushed the star along on the ropes. When the Magi reached the entrance the star disappeared into one of the towers. Then they sent a messenger to Herod, begging permission to enter, and they dismounted and came before him. They asked him where the Child was, and Herod called his soothsayers, who at his command brought a great book and searched in it for a prophecy. But when they found it and read it to the king he became very angry and seized the book and threw it to the ground, and then ordered another of his wise men to pick it up and read the prophecy again. The poor wretch got down on his knees, confused and trembling, and turned the leaves until he found the prophecy, and he showed it to Herod. [This business is repeated many times, until Herod gives up in a tantrum.]

"The Magi left the presence of Herod and, guided by the star, which emerged from the tower, came to the gate of Bethlehem. There they prostrated themselves before the Child and offered Him their gifts, which were several silver vases, and each one knelt down and recited a short prayer in the Mexican language. The old Indian who carried the gifts and who, as the Father Commissary was told, had been playing that part for more than thirty years, put down his basket and made Him a speech, saying that he had nothing to offer save his labor and suffering. Thereupon the angel again appeared from the little tower and told the Magi to return to their own country; and so they left and the play came to an end. Ten or twelve friars attended this fiesta, and many Spanish laymen, and more than five thousand Indians, who came from that parish and other towns, because everyone in that province comes to it."

From a careful reading of Father Ponce's journal, it is evident that by his time (1584–1588) a very large part of the social and religious life of New Spain was directed by the Franciscans. The veneration in which the friars were held was manifested in every village through which Father Ponce passed. On September 13, 1584, he was approaching the town of Jalapa (Vera Cruz).

"For two leagues before [we arrived]," recorded his secretary, "the way was covered with arches made of branches and leaves, after the fashion of the triumphal arches of Spain, and at each arch there were many kinds of music—trumpets, flutes, *chirimías,* and other instruments—until we reached the town, where for half a league it was a sight to make one praise the Lord to see all the people, men and women, great and small, come forth in a procession and kneel down to beg the blessing of the Father Commissary."

Every day of the two weeks' journey from Vera Cruz to Mexico City there was a new celebration, with music, dancing, and feasting. The same thing happened in each of the convent towns in every part of New Spain visited by Father Ponce. His secretary was in a state of continual amazement at the piety of the Indians, the excellence of the music and dancing, and the lavishness of the entertainment. He never tired of cataloguing the abundance of native and introduced fruits and other produce. He noticed such Castilian fruits as oranges, lemons, walnuts, apples, quinces, several varieties of peaches, plums, apricots, pears, figs, and cherries, in addition to a "great abundance of vegetables," black grapes, olives, and bananas—all of which were offered to the friars. Thomas Gage, who forty years later followed the same route with a party of Dominicans, has left us a charming picture of their reception by the Indians:

"The first Indians we met was at Old Vera Cruz, a town seated by the seaside. Here we began to discover the power of the priests and friars over the poor Indians, and their subjection and obedience unto them. For two miles before we came to the town there met us on horseback some twenty of the chief men of the town, presenting unto every one of us a nosegay of flowers, who rid before us a bowshot, till we were met with another company on foot, to wit, the trumpeters, the waits (who sounded pleasantly all the way before us), the officers of the church . . . , though more in numbers on account of the many sodalities or confraternities of saints whom they serve; these likewise presented unto each of us a nosegay; next met us the singing men and boys, all the quiristers, who sang softly and leisurely walked before us singing *Te Deum Laudamus,* till we came to the midst of the town, where there were two great elm trees, the chief market place. There was set up one long arbour with green bows [arches] and a table ready furnished with boxes of conserves and other sweetmeats, and diet-bread to prepare our stomachs for a cup of chocolate, which while it was seasoning with hot water and sugar, the chief Indian officers of the town made a speech unto us, having first kneeled down to kiss our hands one by one. They welcomed us into their country, calling us Apostles of Jesus Christ, and thanked us for that we had left our country, our friends, our fathers and mothers, to save their souls. They told us they honored us as gods upon earth, and many such compliments they used until our chocolate was brought. . . .

"And thus we took our leave, giving unto the chief of them: some, beads; some, medals; some, crosses of brass; some, *Agnus Dei*; some, reliques brought from Spain, and to every one of the town an indulgence for forty years. . . . Wherewith we began to blind that simple people with ignorant, erroneous, and Popish principles. As we went out of the arbour to take our mules, behold the marketplace was full of Indians, men and women, who as they saw us ready to depart, kneeled upon the ground, as adoring us, for a blessing, which we as we rid along bestowed upon them with lifted up hands on high, making over them the sign of the cross." [5]

The first company of Dominicans sent to New Spain, in the charge of Fray Tomás Ortiz, did not get started until the beginning of 1526, and then ran into a great deal of hard luck. In the first place, Ortiz was not the kind of leader to inspire in his men that spirit of happy sacrifice essential to a successful mission. He shared with the heads of his order their gloomy forebodings of disaster in New Spain. He was convinced that Cortés was a scoundrel, and he managed to impose his conviction upon the Licenciado Luis Ponce

[5] Thomas Gage turned Anglican after abandoning his mission in Guatemala, in 1637. During the Cromwellian persecution of the Catholics Gage bought immunity for himself by denouncing Jesuits to the civil authorities. His book, *The English American, or A New Survey of the West-Indies* (London, 1648), was written as propaganda for Cromwell's "Western Design." Nevertheless, if we allow for the malice of the author, it is a unique description of life in New Spain and Guatemala, as well as one of the most entertaining travel books ever written.

de León, the royal visitor, who was on his ship. When they reached Santo Domingo a fresh crop of rumors from New Spain confirmed Ortiz's forebodings, and he decided to stay there a while. When the company arrived at Vera Cruz in May, 1526, most of the men were ill from the long voyage and bad food, and four of them died soon after reaching the capital. After a few weeks, Ortiz himself, on the pretext of having to return to Spain to recruit his company, shook the dust of New Spain off his sandals and embarked with four of the remaining friars, three of whom died on the way back.[6] Thus the first Dominican mission was left with only one friar and one lay brother. But that friar, Domingo de Betanzos, was a whole mission in himself. He had joined the mission in Santo Domingo, where he had already made a name by persuading Bartolomé de las Casas to take the habit of St. Dominic. In Betanzos, piety, austerity, and humanity were so great and so nicely proportioned that he became a mighty peacemaker in the evil days in New Spain while Cortés was off in Honduras.

Pedro de Alvarado had known Betanzos in Santo Domingo before the conquest of Mexico. He now persuaded him to undertake a mission to Guatemala. Betanzos accepted, but refused to go in Alvarado's company, because his conscience would not permit him the luxury of riding a horse. Instead, he walked the thousand miles with one companion. The year following, 1530, he walked all the way back again. Summoned to Spain for consultation about the organization of the Dominican province in New Spain, he walked to Vera Cruz, and from Spain he walked to Rome and back. In 1535 he brought a new company of Dominicans to New Spain and spent the rest of his useful life there, doing good to all men. Such a life would not be complete without a miracle. On his way across the Atlantic in 1535, it was related, his ship was caught in a violent storm, in the course of which it was driven directly at a great rock. When the ship was about to strike and all hands had given themselves up for lost, the rock opened and let it through.

Meanwhile, in 1528, the Dominican mission to New Spain was

---

[6] Ortiz never returned to New Spain, but was made bishop of Santa Marta, Venezuela, in 1529, where he died two years later.

begun in earnest, when Fray Vicente de Santa María brought over a company of twenty-four friars. The ground had already been broken and methods devised by the Franciscans. The Dominicans followed the same general lines, occupying territory not yet served by the Franciscans, the vast area of Oaxaca, Chiapas, and Guatemala, and sharing the tremendous task of converting the Indians. The third and last of the great Mendicant Orders to participate in the evangelization of New Spain was the Augustinians, whose first mission arrived in 1533. Some notion of the magnitude of that task may be had from the statement of Fray Toribio de Motolinía, who estimated that in the first fifteen years *no fewer than nine million Indians were baptized*—a statement that has usually been intrepreted to mean merely a very large number, although lately it has been given more credence.

This prodigious effort, which was to change the whole history of Mexico, was largely accomplished in fifty years (1523–1572). Such an expenditure of energy was bound to be followed by a period of relaxation, of emotional fatigue. Besides, the missionaries had done their work so thoroughly that they soon found themselves with time on their hands. A spirit of emulation and even of rivalry developed between the orders, a spirit that was not always evidenced in the saving of souls. It was not long before they were competing in erecting convents and churches on a scale beyond reasonable necessity. The smaller orders that came later were not to be outdone, with the result that, before many years had passed, New Spain was crowded with ecclesiastical edifices, the splendor of which caused a good deal of acid comment about the hard life of the friars. As early as 1531 the convent being erected by the Dominicans in Mexico City created such a scandal by its sumptuousness that the friars were reprimanded by the queen herself. The enormous mass of the Augustinian convent at Acolman, the rich and beautiful convent church of the Jesuits at Tepozotlán, the Byzantine luxury of the Mercedarian convent in Mexico City, the ruined but magnificent Franciscan church at Tlamanalco, the imposing Dominican convent at Yanhuitlán, and the jewel-like Dominican chapel in Oaxaca—all testify to motives other than a humble dedication to the conversion of the heathen. By 1596, according to Father Mendieta, there were churches in the four hundred convent towns of New Spain, and an equal number in the secular parishes, and he did not include the thousands of chapels in the smaller villages, the so-called *pueblos de visita*, served by circuit-riding priests and friars.

This immense amount of construction, however, should not be ascribed merely to perverse extravagance. The churchmen brought to the New World the Renaissance tradition of magnificence: the more beautiful the church the greater glory to God, and the greater credit to themselves. But in some cases their love of ostentation got out of hand rather badly. In 1556 Archbishop Alonso de Montúfar of Mexico, himself a Dominican, censured the friars in a letter to the Council of the Indies:

"The excessive costs and expenditures and personal services, and the sumptuous and superfluous works being erected by the religious in the Indian villages at the Indians' expense, should be remedied. With respect to the monasteries, in some places they are so grandiose that, although they are designed to accommodate no more than two or three friars, they would more than suffice for Valladolid. When a house is completed and another friar moves in and takes a notion to demolish it and remove it elsewhere, he does so. It is nothing for a religious to begin a new work costing ten or twelve thousand ducats . . . and bring Indians to work on it in gangs of five hundred, six hundred, or a thousand, from a distance of four, six, or twelve leagues, without paying them any wages, or even giving them a crust of bread. . . .

"The personal service of the Indians in the monasteries is very excessive: gardeners, doorkeepers, cleaners, cooks, sacristans, messengers, all without a penny of wages. There is a very large number of cantors in the service of the Church. In one monastery we found a hundred and twenty Indians serving as cantors, without counting the sacristans and acolytes and players [of musical instruments]. . . , and, since all the cost of such works and the rich and superfluous ornaments is met by assessing these poor people, the caciques and head men, who are supposed to take a hundred ducats from the community strongbox, take a thousand for themselves. No one knows this better than the friars, who have told me that the caciques and head men want the friars to ask them for money, so that with this pretext they can make an assessment for themselves."

One would think that the Indians would have been the first to resent such exploitation. There are, to be sure, occasional suits among the records of the General Indian Court which indicate that the Indians were not always the uncomplaining givers of their time and money, but by and large they seem to have served willingly enough. They were intensely loyal to the order under whose rule they happened to be, and they participated wholeheartedly in the rows and rivalries that disturbed the City of God. Father Ponce's secretary gleefully described the case of the Indians of Teotihuacán, "all the people of which are devoted to our Order. . . . The Royal Audiencia of Mexico wished to assign the doctrina of this town to the religious of another order, although the Indians did not like them and resisted for a long time. . . . At length the Audiencia sent a magistrate to put the said religious in possession of the doctrina, and, when he arrived and saw the resistance of the Indians, he had a gallows set up. And they believed that they were truly to be hanged, and they knelt down and began to recite that antiphony of St. Francis, which begins *Sancte Francisce prospera*, etc. And when the magistrate and the religious saw this they were confounded and gave up the attempt."

In 1559, at the very beginning of the Crown's long struggle to secularize the convent towns, Archbishop Montúfar got a taste of the Franciscans' power over the Indians. The friars, he complained to the Council of the Indies, were inciting the Indians to riot against the secular priests and drive them out of the villages.

On another occasion, ten years later, the feud between the Franciscans and the seculars threatened to end in a genuine rebellion. The friars of the convent of San José in Mexico City had been in the habit of going in a procession, with a large following of Indians, to celebrate the yearly feast of the Virgin in the church of Santa María la Redonda. This time they were met by a party of seculars, who ordered them back to their convent. The friars stood their ground and argued the point. Words led to blows, and the Indian partisans took the matter into their own hands and showered their adversaries with stones. The riot brought out the citizenry, but the Indians put them to flight likewise. Viceroy Don Martín

Enríquez finally had to send troops and arrest the Indian leaders, whereupon all the Indians, encouraged by the friars, it was charged, flocked to the jail and demanded to be imprisoned with the others, saying they were all equally guilty. The viceroy prudently released the leaders, and the friars won out.

The most serious impediment in the way of exercising any effective control over the orders lay in their quasi-feudal nature, and in the extraordinary powers granted them originally by the papacy. The Crown was fully aware of the anomaly and attempted to curb them by limiting their tenure to ten years. At the end of that time the Indians were presumed to be sufficiently indoctrinated to get along with the services of secular priests, and the native parishes would then become part of the Spanish church–state structure. Needless to say, the friars fought tooth and nail whenever secularization was mentioned. They argued, with plenty of reason, that ten years was too short a period of preparation and that their neophytes, if placed in the hands of "hirelings," would promptly revert to paganism. One would be inclined to give their argument more weight if they had not kept repeating it for a hundred years.

It was not until 1640 that the Crown found a man equipped to beat the friars at their own game. Don Juan de Palafox y Mendoza, Bishop of Puebla, was sent to New Spain as visitor general, with instructions to clean up the secularization business once and for all. Palafox was an extraordinary man, combining immense energy and learning with an unyielding character and devotion to the interests of the Crown. He wasted no time in argument, but turned the friars out of their jobs overnight. They retaliated by sending the expected lobby back to Spain with a portfolio of charges against the high-handed bishop. But their magic no longer worked, and Palafox was sustained by the Council of the Indies.

Palafox is most famous for the war of words that raged for ten years between him and the Jesuits of New Spain, a war brought on by Palafox's impious attempt to assess the Jesuits for tithes on their produce, a war in which both sides displayed a crushing erudition. Palafox was finally recalled to Spain, but in his fight he had achieved such popularity that his journey to Vera Cruz was a triumphal procession. His path was literally blocked by the great crowds that gathered to cheer him. In Spain he was speedily vindicated. He spent the remaining years of his life publishing his works, which fill twelve huge tomes, and after his death missed canonization only through the weakness of Charles II and the opposition of the Jesuits.

The fierce resistance of the friars to the secularization of their parishes provokes a few speculations about their motives: (1) They were genuinely convinced that the secular priests would undo their work among the Indians; (2) they never considered the Indians capable of education and expected to keep them in perpetual tutelage, out of contact with Europeans; (3) they had got fat with ease, wealth, and idleness, and worldly considerations may have had more to do with the case than was ever admitted. However it was, life in the convents of the metropolitan area did become scandalously free and easy. The Franciscan convent at Xochimilco on the lake was a delightful place where Viceroy the Marqués de Villamanrique and his court loved to frolic. The Franciscan Commissary, Fray Alonso Ponce (1585), was shocked at such looseness, but, when he threatened to do something about it, the viceroy banished him from the capital.

It would be the height of injustice to suggest that piety and decency had vanished from among the friars. When the fight against Satan had been won in the central provinces and the more serious friars found themselves with time on their hands, they engaged in various useful enterprises. Fray Francisco Tembleque, a Franciscan, drew up the plans and supervised the construction of the great aqueduct of Zempoala (Hidalgo), known as Los Arcos de Tembleque, which he finished in 1571, after seventeen years of work.[7]

It is also pleasantly ironical that the men whose pious frenzy had caused them to destroy everything that suggested heathenish beliefs

[7] A charming bit of folklore, of uncertain date and doubtful authenticity, grew up around the figure of Father Tembleque. His only companion, it seems, was a cat, whose duty it was to keep his master's larder filled, which he did by bringing in every morning a rabbit and a quail. Such a prodigy could not fail to cause head-waggings, for cats in those days were notoriously instruments of the devil, so a reverend commission was sent out from the capital to investigate. But the cat was more than equal to the test, and brought in additional rabbits and quail to feed the examiners, who naturally absolved Father Tembleque of any wrongdoing.

90

were the very ones who in later years did their utmost to preserve the art, history, literature, and folklore of the pre-conquest civilizations. Without the painstaking work of Toribio de Benavente (Motolinía), Bernardino de Sahagún, Jerónimo de Mendieta, Antonio Tello, Diego de Landa, and Francisco de Burgoa, to mention only the more eminent ones, our knowledge of ancient Mexico would be pretty much a blank.

From time to time the opening of new fields for missionary work stirred the old fire. The Franciscan, Jesuit, and Dominican missions of Texas, New Mexico, Arizona, Sonora, and the two Californias were as heroic as any undertaken in the early days. But in the great central plateau, after secularization, convent life drifted into a comfortable routine, always excepting the mission colleges, which meant that the friars' work there was done. It loses none of its significance, however, on that account. If it is true today that, for better or for worse, that great majority of the Mexican people are loyal to the Catholic Church and show little disposition to give it up in favor of modern state worship, the credit or blame goes to the stout friars of four hundred years ago who so thoroughly captured their love and imagination.[8]

[8] This slight sketch of one of the great adventures of all time is admittedly only a sketch. For a complete and authoritative account of it the reader is urged to turn to Robert Ricard's *The Spiritual Conquest of Mexico*, already mentioned.

# 9

## TOWNS, SPANISH AND INDIAN

There is little need to dwell upon the obvious fact that the various emigrating peoples of Europe brought their patterns of life with them to the New World. New England became a piece of Old England, New France a piece of Old France, and New Spain became, as nearly as the early settlers could make it, a replica of Old Spain. So it is pertinent to our quest to discover what notions of town planning the Spaniards had and what kind of society they had in mind to set up in New Spain.

To do so we must go back to Spain for a bit. The Spanish village or town, or municipal corporation (*comunidad*), is so ancient that its origin is lost in antiquity. The Phoenicians, Greeks, Carthaginians, and Romans found the Spaniards (Iberians, rather) living in organized communities. A community included the village proper and all the land used for its support. The comunidad may be thought of as a kind of social insurance society, whose fundamental reason for being was defense and the assurance of an adequate food supply. In a great part of Spain living has always been precarious. The scanty and variable rainfall, the thin soil with its poor crops, and the hard winters on the central plateau (which comprises two-thirds of the total area of the Peninsula) force the people to lead very frugal lives and to save their meager surpluses against the time of need. This necessity brought about community enterprise, because only by pooling its resources could the safety of the group be assured. The public granaries (*alhóndigas*) of Spain are the visible symbols of collective life.

The necessity of providing against scarcity required a working political organization. In the Spanish community a government was devised which is still fundamentally unchanged from pre-Roman times. The legislative and judicial body of the village was a council (*cabildo*) of elders called *regidores*. The regidores appointed or elected the mayor or mayors (*alcaldes*), the constables (*alguaciles*), and themselves served as a court of justice. The citizens (*vecinos*) were not mere residents, but privileged and responsible members of the corporation. They tilled their plots individually, but the harvesting and threshing were generally the work of the whole village. Each village had a threshing floor (*área*) where the wheat was threshed (as it still is in many places) by driving cattle over it, or by flailing. The comunidad had a common pasture (*ejido*) and a common wood (*monte*).

The comunidad was welded into a unit, not only by the practical necessity of defense and assuring the food supply, but by an intensely local religion and a patriotism that bordered on the fanatical. The most powerful figure in the village was the priest, long before Christianity had been thought of. He was the medicine man, in charge of propitiating the fickle deities of rain and generation, and he was the sage who was consulted in all affairs of state. Not the least of his duties was to lead his people in war, not as a military commander, perhaps, but as a spiritual tub-thumper. The fierce Spanish priests were the centers of resistance in the early invasions of Spain, and they spurred their followers on to unheard-of sacrifices. In the siege of Numantia by Scipio Africanus, in 133 B.C., the last of the defenders are said to have thrown themselves into the flames of their burning town rather than yield to the Romans. The early Spanish priest seems to have been a close kin to the North African *marabout*, that wild ascetic who from time to time has led the Moslem world in its religious wars.

The six hundred years of Roman rule altered somewhat the primitive structure of the Spanish comunidad by removing its political functions. It was expanded into the Roman *municipium* and became one of the cells that made up the Empire. The acceptance of Christianity was slow in Spain, and when it was finally adopted it resembled the ancient local religion. The Christian priest was still the priest of the comunidad, and the Christian Church in Spain was first of all a Spanish Church. The intense

93

vitality of the Spanish comunidad made it survive the many centuries of Moorish–Arabic domination. A great part of the population remained to live under Moslem rule. In manners, dress, and speech they became Moslems, but their religion continued to be a primitive Christianity, and their comunidad did not change.

In the long process of reabsorption into Christian Spain known as the Reconquest, the Spanish communities were so powerful that they were courted and respected by the Spanish monarchs and were admitted by treaty into the emerging Spanish nation. They frequently, in fact, assumed independence and, in strong federations known as *hermandades* (brotherhoods), imposed their will upon feudal lord and monarch alike.

The Spaniard, then, was by tradition a town dweller. His first loyalty was to his comunidad, the members of which were bound together by ties stronger than blood. He was proud, but his greatest pride was in being a vecino, a member of his comunidad. His town, or at most his province, was his *patria chica,* which he loved (and loves) with an astonishing strength.

And so it was that when the Spaniards came to the New World their first political act was to organize themselves into their familiar comunidades. The municipal corporation was recognized as a proper source of authority, next to the Crown. When Hernán Cortés illegally undertook the conquest of Mexico and badly needed some color of legality, he organized the municipality of the Villa Rica de la Vera Cruz, which thereupon elected him Governor and Captain-General and gave him enough legality to justify his irregular conduct at court (aided by a thumping gift to the Emperor). The Spanish comunidad revolutionized the political structure of the New World, and an understanding of its working is necessary to our understanding of Mexico.

One of the lieutenants of Cortés, Luis Marín, was given the assignment of "pacifying" the province of Chiapa in 1523. When it was completed, he returned to Espíritu Santo (Vera Cruz) to resume his duties as regidor. But the Indians of Chiapa did not stay pacified, so the job had to be done all over again. It was undertaken by Diego de Mazariegos, who assembled a company in 1527 and, with arms supplied by Cortés, led a new expedition south. This time it was decided to occupy the country permanently, and Mazariegos brought along for the purpose a number of Spanish settlers and Aztec "friends." The Indians of Chiapa put up a game resistance, fortifying themselves, as was their suicidal habit, on the heights, from which many jumped to their death rather than surrender. The survivors were magnanimously treated by Mazariegos. Instead of branding them as slaves (the common fate of Indian "rebels"), he settled them in a village, Chiapa de los Indios (now Chiapa de Corzo), on the Grijalva River. As soon as the shooting was over, Mazariegos set about establishing his new town.

According to Antonio de Remesal, the early (1619) historian of Chiapa and Guatemala, quoting the lost minutes of the cabildo, on March 1, 1528, "Captain Mazariegos brought together in his house all the chiefs of his army and spoke to them. He told them that his aim in founding a town there was to conserve what they had won with such hardship. He said that he had not chosen that as a permanent site, but that it would have to serve until a better one could be found. But [he said], whether they remained there or removed elsewhere . . . he was naming it Villareal, so that he might be reminded of his *patria*, Ciudad Real, in Spain.

"Then he named as his first alcaldes Luis de Luna and Pedro de Orozco, and he delivered to them their staves of justice, under a solemn oath that they would perform their duties well and faithfully, always bearing in mind the service of God Our Lord and that of His Majesty, and that of the common good."

Mazariegos also named six councilmen (regidores), a treasurer (*mayordomo*) of the new villa, and an attorney (*procurador*). "And on the sixth day of March [1528] . . . all the aforesaid alcaldes, regidores, and other officers met in the house of Captain Diego Mazariegos to take possession of their offices. Then they made a schedule of the salaries of the chief constable (*alguacil mayor*) and his assistant, and those of the jailor and town crier, and they delivered to the alguacil mayor five pairs of handcuffs and some leg irons. . . . They also ordered the said alguacil to erect in the square a wooden stock and to place on the hill at the entrance of the town . . . a wooden gallows for the execution of justice."

The cabildo further enacted that all persons who desired to remain there and become vecinos of the new villa should enter their names in the book of the cabildo, "and they would be received, and they would enjoy the privileges and the liberties enjoyed by the citizens of other villas and cities of this New Spain, and those who did not desire to become vecinos would not enjoy them."

About eighty men entered their names in the book of the cabildo. "After this important act had been completed, without which the community and republic would have no existence," Mazariegos brought the officers and vecinos of the new "republic" to a site he had discovered, some two and a half leagues east of the Indian town of Zinacatlán. And there, "in the presence of me, the said secretary, and of the council of the said Villareal, they said that although the villa had been founded and first situated in the province of Chiapa, because at that time the territory had not been explored, the captain and the regidores had decided to change, because the first site was in the hot country, where there were many marshes and mosquitoes. The present site had been chosen because it had all the necessary qualities: It was in the cold country; there was an abundance of good water, pasture, and dry land, and land for cattle, woods, etc."

One reason given for the selection of the new site was that the villa could be placed there without harm to the Indians. The removal was duly authorized by a vote of the cabildo, and the villa was marked out, with a square, places reserved for a church, a town hall, and the houses of the governor and principal vecinos. The Indian "friends" were put to work clearing the ground and erecting houses; the indispensable stocks and gallows were reinstalled, and Villareal was a fact. "All of which, as described above, they commanded me, the said secretary, to enter in this book of the cabildo, and they signed it with their names."

For the next month the vecinos busied themselves with laying out streets and assigning building lots. Which done, on April 24, 1528, they met with the cabildo and were officially given possession of their lots. The matter of allocating agricultural lands had still to be done, but the founding of Villareal had first to be confirmed by the Audiencia in Mexico City. Then, "on August 22 they began to mark out the land in caballerías and peonerías. A caballería was the estate given to him who had supplied a horse during the war; it was

600 feet long and 300 feet wide. A peonería was that given to a foot soldier; it was 300 feet long and 50 feet wide." [1]

In this wise was founded the charming old town now known as San Cristóbal de las Casas, in the state of Chiapas, which for three centuries was the center of Spanish culture for the region between Oaxaca and Guatemala. Most of the graceful colonial towns that are now the pride of Mexico had a similar origin.

In one important respect they were different from their Spanish prototypes: Each town had a native quarter (*barrio*), from which mechanical and domestic services could be drawn. In Villareal the Aztec and Tlaxcalan "friends" were settled in such a quarter. But so many of them had fallen in the campaign, or had succumbed to the hardship of carrying supplies, that the population of the native quarter was not large enough to meet the needs of the town. So in 1537 the cabildo petitioned the Audiencia of Mexico "to beg His Majesty to command that up to two hundred Indians, with their wives, come to this country and settle near this villa, provided that they come from the land of Mexico, and we will give them very good lots on which to live and pursue their trades and commerce, because it will be of great assistance in peopling and maintaining this villa and in the pacification of this country. This is what has been done in Guatemala and in other Christian [Spanish] towns of this New Spain, and it will be a good thing here."

It should be mentioned again that wherever the Spaniards went, in military expeditions or for the purpose of founding towns, they were invariably accompanied by considerable numbers of Indians from the Plateau, who were as useful to the Spaniards as they were destructive of the country to which they were brought. Mexican "friends" were settled in barrios and were given preferment over the surrounding natives. They became completely urbanized. It is still interesting to see the contempt that their descendants have for

[1] About 4 acres and ⅓ acre, respectively. These plots are so tiny that I think Remesal must have misread the minutes, putting down *pies* (feet) for *pasos* (two yards). The latter measurement would have made the plots about 108 and 9 acres respectively, which would conform more closely to general practice. In 1536 Viceroy Mendoza fixed the official size of the caballería at 1,104 by 552 *varas de Castilla,* which comes to about 105.4 acres.

*inditos* of the country. It might even be argued that, with the help of the Spaniards, the Aztecs continued their interrupted conquest of Mexico and Central America. From Sonora to Nicaragua the map is studded with Aztec place names, many of them reminders of the Mexican "friends" who passed that way. Some of the Aztec barrios, such as Escuintla in Guatemala and San Esteban de Tlaxcala in Saltillo, Coahuila, preserved their language and identity until very recent times.

After what has been said of the town-dwelling habits of the Spaniards, it should be apparent that they considered their kind of community life the normal and proper pattern of society, not only for themselves but for the Indians as well. In New Spain they found well-organized, advanced Indian communities not unlike their familiar Spanish towns and worthy of the privilege of self-government. The second Audiencia of Mexico (1531–1535) did in fact give them essentially the same status as Spanish towns. Let me hasten to add, lest the reader jump to the conclusion that the millennium had been reached, that Indian rule turned out to be no whit less corrupt than Spanish rule. The records of the General Indian Court are crowded with suits brought against Indian officers for the usual charges of graft, extortion, nepotism, and general cussedness. Bishop Manuel Abad y Queipo of Michoacán (who to be sure was a tremendous *gachupín* and, as such, contemptuous of Creoles and Indians alike), describing native rule after two centuries of it, wrote to the Council of the Indies: "The Indians govern themselves, and all the [local] magistrates are of the copper-colored race. In each village there are eight or ten old Indians, who live at the expense of the rest in absolute idleness, basing their authority either upon their claim of illustrious birth, or upon political trickery which has become hereditary. These chiefs have a great interest in keeping their fellow citizens in profound ignorance, and thus they contribute more than anyone to the perpetuation of the prejudices, ignorance, and barbarism of ancient habits."

Nevertheless, it was political wisdom on the part of the Spanish overlords to interfere as little as possible with native hierarchies and customs, and it made for successful government. Custom (*cos-*

*tumbre*), indeed, was recognized as the common law of the country, and a plea of "costumbre" was always allowed if it did not conflict with Spanish law. There were other and more potent factors in that success, of course, such as the vast influence of the religious orders. The wisdom of the policy is indicated by one startling fact, namely, *that by the end of the sixteenth century there was no regular military establishment in all New Spain south of the Chichimec frontier.* By way of contrast, the government today maintains garrisons in every part of the Republic.

In that first century—to get back to our story—a considerable part of the native population lived in scattered hamlets and isolated clumps of houses called *rancherías,* in every nook and cranny where a few square yards of earth offered a roothold for maize. These odd corners had the additional advantage for the Indians in that they allowed them to evade the tax collector and the *mandón* in charge of rounding up labor gangs.

The problem of administering these inaccessible communities had been recognized from earliest times. The Laws of Burgos of 1512 attempted a solution by ordering the concentration (*congregación*) of Indians in towns where, by observing the habits of the Spaniards, they might be induced to live in an orderly manner and adopt a Christian way of life. No humor was intended. When the Spanish conquerors accepted encomiendas in New Spain, one of the obligations they assumed was the settlement of Indians in towns. But the indifference of the encomenderos and the cost of building, as well as the natural resistance of the Indians, made the process slow. The Council of the Indies, however, had no intention of relinquishing the project of making town-dwelling and tax-paying citizens out of the Indians. Between 1546 and 1574, after the civil administration of New Spain had become firmly established (i.e., after most of the old conquerors were dead or past active resistance, and a large part of the encomiendas had escheated to the Crown), the Council decided to complete the concentration of the scattered population.

In 1584, Viceroy (and also Archbishop and Inquisitor) Pedro Moya de Contreras was so instructed by the Council. But he was a wise and humane man, and knew the cost in suffering that the concentration was bound to inflict on the Indians, so, using the ancient prerogative of Spanish officials, he "obeyed but did not fulfill" his instructions.

In 1590, Luis de Velasco II (son of the great viceroy of the same name) was sent over with the same instructions regarding the congregation of the Indians. Velasco (who otherwise was an intelligent and able ruler) in this instance failed to visualize the magnitude of the task or the vast organization necessary for its success. The result was that the men he commissioned to congregate the Indians acted without preparation and with great severity, uprooting populations and moving them about with little regard for their welfare. Confusion and suffering followed them like a plague. Many Indians were said to have died from starvation and exposure. One critic, the Franciscan Fray Juan de Torquemada, even charged that Velasco had undertaken the congregation in the rainy season for that very purpose. Velasco was no such monster, but the effect was the same. Many of his congregations had to be abandoned for lack of subsistence.

Philip II and the Council of the Indies were getting impatient over the interminable delay, and Viceroy the Conde de Monterrey was instructed in 1598 to complete the congregation forthwith. He gave the difficult project his full attention. The congregation was, in effect, a political and economic revolution for some hundreds of thousands of people. Since it clearly reveals the whole Spanish scheme of government and explains to some extent the present structure of the Mexican community, it will be of interest to go into it in some detail.

The preamble of the first law of Title III of the Laws of the Indies summarizes the matter: "We have always given our greatest care and attention to . . . the most convenient means of instructing the Indians in the Holy Catholic Faith and the evangelical law, in order to cause them to lay aside their ancient erroneous rites and ceremonies, and to live in concert and order. To bring this about, our Council of the Indies has met several times with other religious persons, and the prelates of New Spain were called together in the year 1546 by order of the Emperor Charles V (of glorious memory); and they, with the desire of promoting the service of God, and ours,

100

resolved that the Indians should be congregated in villages and not allowed to live scattered in mountains and wildernesses, where they are deprived of all spiritual comforts, the aid of our ministers, and those other things that human necessities oblige men to give one to another. Therefore . . . the viceroys, presidents [of Audiencias], and governors were charged and ordered to execute the congregation, settlement, and indoctrination of the Indians, using in this such kindness and gentleness that . . . it will encourage [others] . . . to come and offer themselves of their own free will. . . . And, because the above has already been put into effect in the greater part of our Indies, we order and command that it be carried out in all the rest. . . ."

The ideal village is then described: It was to be placed where there was good land for cultivation, with a sufficiency of wood and water; it was to have at least a square league (about six and a half square miles) of land, *which might not be alienated*; it was to have a public grazing ground (ejido); where practicable it was to be established near the mines, so that the Indians working there might have the same benefits as their fellows—and, the law should have added, where their labor would be available to the miners, as in the Code of Burgos of 1512. It is apparent that the ideal Indian village was to be a replica of the ancient Spanish comunidad.

The political structure of the village was defined in great detail: The church was to be the center of society; attendance at Mass was compulsory; the priest was to have an assistant, a kind of truant officer, with the duty of seeing that the Indians did not absent themselves from Mass. Two or three cantors and a sexton were provided for each village, exempted from tributes and personal services. Each village was to have one or more alcaldes and two or more regidores, to be elected yearly in the presence of the priest, "as is the custom in Spanish and other Indian villages." The Indian alcaldes were given the power of arrest and investigation; they might inflict punishment to the extent of one day's imprisonment and six to eight lashes, for drunkenness and absence from Mass; graver offenses were to be turned over to the nearest Spanish authority. Indian alcaldes had the power to arrest and detain in jail Negroes and mestizos, whose punishment, however, was reserved to the Spanish

101

magistrates. In order to assure the permanence of the congregation, its members might not remove to another village.

Cattle farms (*estancias de ganado mayor*) might not be located within a league of any Indian village; sheep farms (*estancias de ganado menor*), half a league. The Indians might kill any cattle invading their lands.

Spaniards, Negroes, mestizos, and mulattoes were forbidden to dwell in Indian villages. Travelers might remain overnight, and merchants three days; but none of these might lodge with the Indians unless no inn was available. All supplies must be paid for in cash and must not be taken by force. Even the overseers of encomiendas might not remain in the villages without the special permission of the Audiencia or of the Spanish governor of the province.

Unlike a good part of the Spanish legislation, this organization of the Indian village was based on reality. It was comprehensible to the Spaniards, because it was modeled on their familiar comunidad; also to the Indians, because it altered very slightly their traditional pattern of village life. *It is still the political structure of the Mexican village today,* with some modifications resulting from changes in the superior government.

To return to the congregations: the Conde de Monterrey appointed a large number of teams, each composed of a judge, an alguacil, and, of course, a notary. These teams were sent to all parts of New Spain to gather information about native settlements and to make a survey of established villages, with respect to their productive land, water supply, communications, and the like. The larger villages were to be expanded to the point where they might support a priest and the regular Crown officers.

The investigators worked a full year and brought back to the special Court of the Congregation a large body of information. For the next five years officers (*jueces de congregación*) busied themselves marking out new barrios and transferring people to them. They worked against the opposition of the encomenderos, of the regular clergy, and, above all, of the Indians themselves. Denunciations, obstructive tactics, the flight of Indians to the hills, lawsuits, and appeals to the Audiencia made the work slow and stopped it in many cases. Nevertheless, a large but unknown number of congregations were completed.

The hardships resulting from the dislocation of native life, and the inevitable mistakes and ineptitude of some of the officers, gave critics of the congregation the opportunity of denouncing it as the heaviest affliction the Indians had ever suffered. But it is not safe to take such criticisms at their face value, even when they came from the pens of churchmen, for everybody was grinding an ax of some kind. The severest critic of the congregation was Fray Juan de Torquemada, already mentioned, and the ax he was grinding was the prevention of the secularization of the Indian parishes. I have examined all the fragmentary records of the great congregation of 1598–1605, and it seems to me from this distance that the officers in charge of it were as moderate as the circumstances would allow. It is true that a great many Indians were removed from their beloved milpas in odd corners and were forced into better quarters in the new congregations, while they saw their old houses go up in smoke, and they naturally did not like it. But the milpas were not destroyed. Even the expense of building the new houses was credited to the tribute account of the village. If there was not enough land available for the congregation, it was taken from the Spanish holdings in the vicinity.

Pedro de Cervantes was the juez de congregación of the province of Tlanchinol (northern Hidalgo). He was commissioned to transfer the populations of eleven scattered rancherías to the four villages of Tenango, Tlalol, Lontla, and Coacuilco. In the eleven rancherías were 392 families (roughly, 2,000 people). Cervantes had to lay out eleven new barrios, complete with streets, squares, and building lots. Three hundred and ninety-two houses had to be erected, together with eleven *casas de comunidad* and eleven chapels (for each barrio remained a self-governing entity), and the work had to be done without interfering with planting and harvesting. He organized the men of the eleven rancherías into squads of ten, each of which was given a particular task: clearing streets, staking out lots, carrying lumber and building materials, and the like, while squads of women took care of the commissary. By keeping everlastingly at it, with no force but his own authority, and by traveling on horseback from village to village, urging on the laggards and threatening the unwilling, this admirable administrator completed the job in eight months. On February 4, 1605, Cervantes was able to report to the Court of the Congregation in Mexico City that the new communities were in their houses and were operating under their own officers. No lives had been lost and no active opposition experienced.

The congregation of Tlanchinol was, possibly, the happy exception in a pretty grim affair; but, whatever we may think of the wisdom or humanity of uprooting populations and moving them about according to some planner's dream, the congregation was designed to complete the monolithic organization of New Spain which was then thought necessary. The vast modern collective farms of Mexico are not dissimilar in purpose, although they are probably better managed. In any case, the indelible Spanish stamp on thousands of Indian villages testifies to the magnitude of the revolution wrought by the Spanish town builders.[2]

[2] It should be emphasized that the civil congregation here described was the outgrowth of the Christian communities that the missionaries organized everywhere among the Indians.

# 10

## WORK IN UTOPIA

*The two Republics, of Spaniards and Indians of which this Kingdom consists, are so repugnant to each other . . . that it seems that the conservation of the former always means the oppression and destruction of the latter. The estates, buildings, plantations, mines and herds, the monasteries and religious orders—I do not know whether it would be possible to maintain them or improve them without the service and aid of the Indians.*—Viceroy Luis de Velasco II to his successor, the Count of Monterrey, 1595

The story of work in New Spain impinges upon all other questions, because *every part of its economic structure depended in the end upon the labor of the Indians.* The Indians were not the only ones who worked, but they formed the great reservoir of labor without which society could not exist. The Conquest of Mexico was in a real sense the capture of native labor. The various shifts to which the Spaniards were put to get necessary work done is relevant to the whole history of Mexico from that day to this.

Few aspects of the Spanish colonial régime have been the object of more furious denunciation than its treatment of the Indians. Abuse of the Indians was, with few exceptions, tied up with the matter of getting work done. The scowling conquistador lashing the naked and cringing Indian is the traditional picture and one that shows no sign of dying out. On the contrary, the excellent mural decorations which since 1920 have covered the public buildings of Mexico rarely omit it. The lesson to the spectator is that, no matter how bad things may be at present, they are infinitely to be preferred to the slavery of olden times. Like all such facile theses, however, deliberately propounded for indoctrination, this one contains a deal of bad thinking and misinformation. What has been done is to take the desperate plight of the Indian as it was within the memory of many still living and project it back into colonial times. Not that the Indian's life was a continual fiesta under Spanish rule, for it is evident that the elaborate system of protection set up by the Laws of the Indies was evaded as often as not, and that the colonial authorities were in a tacit conspiracy with hacendados, mineowners, and operators of textile mills to keep men securely tied to their jobs. At the same time the necessity of preserving the Indians from extinction made the Audiencia more vigilant in enforcing the laws than is commonly believed. In any case, no part of our survey of Mexico is more important or more necessary to understand than the story of work.

Necessary work always has to be done. In conquered countries, if the population is capable of exploitation, necessary work is always done by the conquered. That may not be sound ethics, but it is history. Our New England ancestors tried to enslave the Pequot Indians of Connecticut and failed only because the Pequots would rather have died than become slaves, and did. The problem of procuring labor had to be faced from the moment Columbus founded his unlucky settlement of Isabella on the island of Española.

The great discoverer, upon his return to Spain in 1493, wrote the Catholic Monarchs a famous letter, which may be considered the first real estate prospectus of the New World. "There are in that island," he wrote, "mountains and valleys and fields, and beautiful fat lands for planting and sowing, for raising cattle of all kinds, for cities and villages. The ports are such as you would not believe unless you saw them, as are the many broad rivers of sweet waters, most of which are gold-bearing. . . . The people all go naked as their mothers bore them, save only that some of the women cover a single part with a green leaf, or with a cotton cloth made for the purpose. They have no iron or steel or arms, nor are they apt for such things, not because they are not well set up and beautiful, but because they are wonderfully timorous. . . . They are so guileless and so generous with what they possess that you would not believe it without seeing it."

Free rich land and a docile population waiting to be put to work! The appeal to the poverty-stricken and land-hungry soldiers of Spain was irresistible—the same soldiery who had lived on loot in the conquests of Granada and Naples, and had always found the loot too little. There were many thousands of these unemployed warriors in Spain at the close of the fifteenth century. Each was a nobleman in his own mind, for the bearing of arms was a patent of nobility. For many centuries a whole class of society had had no trade but arms and no income but the spoils of the enemy. The Spanish crusader, who became the conquistador of the New World, was a hardy, brave, ruthless, and usually illiterate barbarian. The noble state, however, postulated land and retainers, and he had only his arms. Work? Everyone knows that in the great tradition of nobility useful work is degrading. Cortés himself said that if he had wanted to plow he would have stayed home in Spain.

Small wonder, then, that Columbus had no difficulty in enlisting a considerable army of these adventurers, some fifteen hundred of them, for his second expedition to the Garden of Eden. But one important item had been overlooked, namely, the food supply. In those days armies lived on the country, and Columbus evidently anticipated no difficulty in feeding his men in Española. Native economy, however, was not equal to the added burden. The Indians had got along well enough on a diet of manioc bread, sweet potatoes, and fish, but they produced only what they consumed. The Spaniards ate all the food they could seize, and invaders and Indians alike were soon reduced to a state of permanent starvation. The problem of procuring food was immediate and the situation was heavy with disaster. "Nothing in those days," wrote Las Casas, "gladdened the people here more than to learn that ships were coming with provisions from Castile, for all their sufferings were from hunger." Conditions became so hideous that in the next few years Española was all but abandoned and could be kept up only by sending over shiploads of convicts, *whose sentences of death had been commuted to two years' service in the Indies.* "Indeed," wrote the historian Oviedo, "I saw many of those who at that time returned to Castile with such faces that, if the king had given me his Indies, were I to become as they, I should not have gone thither." The necessity of procuring food, as I shall have occasion to repeat, was the greatest and most continuing modifying factor in the settlement of the Spanish Indies.

Now, the cultivation of manioc (or *yuca*, from which we get tapioca) is extremely laborious, although the yield is generous. The brush must be grubbed up, hillocks built, and the encroaching jungle must be fought back unceasingly. Then the tuberous roots are dug up, grated, and the poisonous juice squeezed out, after which the fibers are made into heavy flat cakes, which have the virtue of lasting indefinitely if kept dry. In that first generation manioc bread was the staple food of the colonists. It was such an important item in the Conquest that it is hardly too much to say that the New World was conquered on manioc. At least, it is hard to see how it could have been conquered without it.

The aversion of the Spanish conquistadores (and others) to manual labor in the tropics is notorious, and the new parasite class insisted on being fed and made rich. What were the heathen for if not to work for their betters? So the Indians of the Antilles were forced to plant manioc and wash gold, and were kept at it so unremittingly, with so little regard for their strength and habits, that the greater part of the population died off in the first twenty years of the Spanish occupation. It was that frightful catastrophe which inspired Las Casas' *Brief Relation of the Destruction of the Indies*. Conditions were so incredibly bad that it may be said that not even Las Casas could exaggerate them.

The Spaniards, however, had not been sent to the Indies merely to drive the Indians to the gold pits. Back in the queen's council were those who remembered that, by the terms of the bull *Inter caetera* of Alexander VI, which gave Spain and Portugal the Indies, she had undertaken to make Christians of the natives. The paradox involved in saving the souls of the aborigines, while using their bodies for profit, agitated the legal minds of Spain for many years, and was solved only after the New Laws of 1542 had come perilously close to destroying the Spanish Empire.

In Española in the time of Columbus the matter was settled summarily by recourse to a proposition which may be somewhat

108

baldly stated as follows: "Is it not just to make the heathen work for us in exchange for the ineffable gifts of Christianity and the profit system?" Lest this proposition shock the reader, it should be added that one of the most persistent criticisms directed for centuries against the Indians was that they had no sense of values. They would not work for wages like Christians, and they exchanged things of great price for things of little price. Their inferiority was manifest. All of which, of course, strikes us as the flimsiest sort of rationalization, but it served. Work had to be done in any case, and Columbus and his successors ground the helpless islanders in a deadly round of unceasing toil. When the despairing Indians resisted (as they did under Queen Anacoana), well, then they were heathen rebels and could legally be enslaved. Columbus's project for establishing a trade in Indian slaves, as I have mentioned elsewhere, was stopped by Isabella herself. The fearful stories of Spanish barbarity which came back from the Indies finally aroused the queen to the necessity of redeeming her pledge to the pope.

So out of starvation, slavery, and death came the first New Deal to the Western Hemisphere. It was entrusted to Don Frey Nicolás de Ovando, Lord Commander of the military order of Calatrava, one of those extraordinary warrior monks who had governed conquered Granada. In 1502 he was made governor of Española, with the mission of repairing the damage done during the misrule of the Columbus brothers, suppressing Indian and Spanish rebels, and restoring order. The old *comendador* was equal to the task. Within the year the Indians who were left alive had been thoroughly subdued, as well as those turbulent spirits among the Spaniards whom Columbus had so signally failed to control.

But Ovando, like every other administrator sent to the Indies, still had to face the problem of feeding the population, getting useful work done, and making Christians and Spanish subjects out of the Indians. It was he who introduced the much discussed and lamented encomienda system (a trusteeship or guardianship) by which the conquered Moorish provinces in Spain had been governed. He divided the Indians into lots of varying size, depending upon the category of the recipient, and put them under the tutelage of presumably God-fearing and high-minded Spanish laymen. Some of the largest encomiendas were given to King Ferdinand and the men of his court. It is well to remember that this was before the establishment of religious missions. The encomendero, in fact, was supposed to assume the obligations of a lay missionary and at the same time to act as collector of the tribute and general overload of the Indians. It was a quasi-feudal arrangement: the encomendero accepted the responsibility of looking after the Indian's soul, while the Indian discharged his end of it by raising foodstuffs and washing gold. *This legal fiction, by one name or another, was behind all measures by which the Indian was coerced into doing work.*

To the conquistador of 1500 it was a reasonable and logical solution of the labor problem. He evidently looked upon the encomienda merely as a contrivance for avoiding the ugly name of slavery. The matter becomes clear in the light of his action after the population had become too scanty to support him. Slaving expeditions to the Bahamas and other "useless" islands (i.e., islands where no gold was to be found) grew to be a profitable traffic. One such expedition, under Francisco Hernández de Córdoba, led to the discovery of New Spain in 1517. The ill-defined status of the encomienda Indians made their lot worse, if possible, than that of the out-and-out slaves. Fray Bernardino de Manzanedo, one of the three Jeronymite governors of the Indies, wrote to Charles V in 1518: "Since no one has the assurance that he will be able to keep the Indians given him in encomienda, he uses them like borrowed goods, and thus many have perished and are perishing."

The blind and fumbling policy of the Spanish Crown during the tragic first thirty years of its government of the Indies makes it easy to drift into a denunciation of the whole Spanish effort. When the policy was not one of squeezing the last *maravedí* out of the natives, as under Ferdinand the Catholic, it was such quixotic nonsense as attempting to restore them to a state of independence under clerical government (the Dominican thesis). The irreconcilable conflict between priest and layman, piety and practicality, was further confused by the fact that Spain had gone into the empire business with no adequate machinery of administration and, naturally, no knowledge of the New World. Moreover, the center of government was so distant that months and even years had to elapse between the recognition of a problem and any remedial measure. The wonder is that anything constructive was ever done.

With all its faults and manifest hypocrisy, the encomienda was a halting but intelligent step toward setting up a stable economy in the colonies. It need not astonish us that it had no immediate beneficial effect on native life, or that the encomendero took his missionary duties lightly. He was too intent upon procuring the necessities of life and the scanty grains of gold that his Indians washed out of the earth, to allow the new legal fiction to alter his murderous course. By 1510, conditions among the miserable remnants of the population were so ghastly that the first Dominican missionaries to arrive there were horrified and at once embarked upon their long and heroic campaign to remedy them.

The year 1510 marked the beginning of the curious politico-humanitarian pact between the Spanish Crown and the Dominican order, by which the two were joined in a common effort to suppress the New World feudalism (the encomienda) of the conquistadores and to preserve the Indians from extinction. The first target selected by the Dominicans for attack was the encomienda, to which they ascribed most of the evils of the Indies. Their violent denunciations of the encomenderos (in which they were opposed by the Franciscans) brought about a tardy and, in some respects, ludicrous attempt to save the situation by setting up an ecclesiastical régime over the Indians. It was embodied in the Code of Burgos of 1512.

This famous Code, the first written for the New World, is an excellent example of the idealism, irrationality, and ignorance of the early Spanish clergymen who legislated for the relief of the Indians. The proper government of the innocent aborigines, according to the reverend lawmakers, included such measures as teaching them to say their prayers in Latin and restricting their heathenish custom of taking baths. The Code of Burgos was stillborn in any case, because the natives of the Antilles were past saving. It did lay down several principles, nevertheless, which were never abandoned. The first of them, of course, was that the most imperative duty of the Crown was to convert the Indians to Christianity and bring them to a "reasonable" (Spanish) way of life. In spite of Dominican protests,

111

the encomienda was retained as an instrument toward that end. It may not be coincidental that King Ferdinand held 1,400 Indians in encomienda. A further reason for its retention was, I suspect, that the Crown had always rewarded its soldiers with loot taken from the enemy; indeed, it did not pretend to pay them otherwise. Of great significance to the subsequent history of the Indies, the Code of Burgos also postulated the necessity of gathering the Indians in regular European-style communities, in which they should live under Spanish tutelage, and in which their services would be more readily available for useful work. It was this typical mismating of economic necessity with humanitarianism which was to confuse Indian legislation for a century, but which was to result in that not altogether useless code known as the *Recopilación de las Leyes de los Reynos de las Indias.*

Cortés and most of his men had lived for years in the Antilles before undertaking the Conquest of New Spain. They had grown up with the encomienda, so to speak, and were fully aware that their true wealth was the labor of the Indians. Cortés had some doubts about the wisdom of allowing the encomienda to be transferred to New Spain, or, at least, he so expressed himself to the Emperor. When, however, the Conquest was accomplished and his men clamored for their reward, there was nothing to give them but Indians in encomienda, and so they all became little feudal lords— Cortés really a big one—all this in direct disobedience to the command of the Emperor, but his edict had come too late. The Crown accepted the *fait accompli,* but from that time on pursued the policy of seizing for itself all the encomiendas whose holders died or otherwise forfeited title. In the Hapsburg system there could be only one logical encomendero, the king himself.

Fortunately for New Spain, the encomienda there turned out to be a very different thing from the disguised slavery it had been in the islands. This was partly owing to the character of Cortés and partly to the character of the mainland Indians. In New Spain the conquistadores found a hardy agrarian people, long inured to the exacting labors of the field, living under the primitive feudalism of their native overlords. They accepted a change of masters with some indifference. The status of the pre-Conquest peasant (*macehual*)

112

made the transition easy. There is a curious document in the National Archives of Mexico, a petition sent by the chief men of Huejotzingo (Puebla) to Viceroy Velasco in 1554, begging him to allow them to donate certain of their lands to the peasants.

"We principales," they wrote, "have held our lands from time immemorial, ever since our forefathers left them to us, whereas the macehuales had none; and they cultivated our lands and brought us wood and water, and built all the buildings we had need of, and gave us chickens [turkeys] and chili and everything for our maintenance, and their wives and children served us in everything we commanded. They did all this so that we might allow them to sow their crops on our lands." The macehuales receiving the donation were to bind themselves to cultivate the land of their chiefs.

The reader is not to infer that the Indians of New Spain were better off under the encomenderos than under their native lords, but at least the change was not one from heaven to hell, as we read in the storybooks. And then, as routine and familiarity rubbed some of the sharp edges off mutual intercourse, and especially when the New Laws of 1542 removed the right of the encomenderos to use the labor of the Indians at pleasure, there developed between them and their charges some sort of tolerable relationship, with a healthy basis in common interest, the Indians supporting the encomenderos with tributes, the encomenderos protecting the Indians from the rapacity of other Spaniards.

Bernal Díaz del Castillo was such an encomendero. His encomienda embraced a number of villages in Guatemala. In 1579 a certain Martín Ximénez obtained from the Audiencia of Guatemala a grant of some lands lying within the encomienda of Bernal Díaz, and his Indians appealed to him to stand by. The old conquistador, then eighty-six, took the case to court, and won.

"To this [petition for the grant]," he argued, "I reply and swear that if the said lands could be granted without harm to the Indians, I myself should have asked former governors to grant them to my six legitimate sons. But, as I have said, these lands are the ones on which the Indians have their crops of maize, peppers, and cacao, and from which they pay their tributes, and it is their ancient holding, and

113

that is why I have not asked for them, because it would mean the destruction of the Indians."

Melchor de Pedraza, encomendero of Atotonilco and Zacamal (Hidalgo) in 1580 appealed to the Audiencia to protect his Indians from their own governor and caciques, who were forcing the Indians to work on their lands and in their commerce the greater part of the year, with the result that the Indians had no time for cultivating fields for their maintenance *and for the payment of their tribute.* The frequency of such cases in the fragmentary records leads me to believe that this attitude was fairly universal among encomenderos.

It would be hazardous to assume that the conquistador of New Spain, after the middle of the sixteenth century, turned into a gentle patriarch, intent upon the well-being of his charges. I merely wish to suggest that he did not necessarily continue to be the monster which he had assuredly been in the macabre days of Española. He learned in time that he needed Indians, lots of Indians, live Indians. He had to accept his feudal obligation toward them, and the Indians themselves recognized this community of interest. Bernal Díaz, who was typical of his class, seems to have settled comfortably into the unexciting life of a country squire, living on his tributes and playing the part of the great white father to the Indians of his encomienda. The encomenderos, it should be added, did not for long continue to be the most numerous or the most representative of the Spanish settlers. In the early days they were a privileged aristocracy, but they were constantly being diminished by death, and their encomiendas were gradually taken over by the Crown. By the end of the sixteenth century the Crown held about three-fifths of all the Indian towns of New Spain. The encomenderos had, in effect, long since been reduced to the status of pensioners by the law of 1571, which says: "The encomienda is a right granted by Royal Grace to the deserving of the Indies, to receive and collect for themselves the tributes of the Indians given them in trust for their life and the life of one heir . . . with the obligation of looking after the spiritual and material welfare of the Indians and of dwelling in and defending the provinces of their trust, and of doing homage and taking personal oath to fulfill all this."

After the Conquest New Spain rapidly filled up with men from every stratum of Spanish society, and the more there were of them the more acute was the problem of feeding them and getting necessary work done. The conquistador–encomendero class did not disappear—far from it. As a rule they had large families (Bernal Díaz mentions his six legitimate sons on all occasions, leaving the number of his natural children to our imagination), and their offspring continued to enjoy preference in land grants and government jobs. Generally, I suspect, they were spoiled brats, as will appear later on. Out of the needs of this rapidly growing white society of Mexico grew the extraordinary institution of the *repartimiento,* that is, a work allotment, or corvée, in Peru called the *mita.*

It was based on the sound principle that the state might force its citizens to do such work as was necessary for the existence of the commonwealth. It was the eminent-domain principle applied to labor. Necessary work was defined as the production of foodstuffs, the operation of mines, the erection of public buildings, churches, and convents, the opening and maintenance of roads, harbors, and irrigation ditches, the laying out of new towns and congregations, and the care of travelers. It is apparent that few mechanical services were *not* considered necessary for the good of the commonwealth. The important thing about the repartimiento, however, as far as the Indians were concerned, was that (at least in theory) *no one could be forced to work for private gain and that all services must be paid for in cash.* The authors of the repartimiento were convinced that coercion was an evil, but that at times it was a necessary evil. Anyway, they hopefully believed that it would serve as a stopgap in the transition to a more desirable state of things; that is, it would be an educational interlude during which the Indians would learn to work for wages like civilized human beings. But the repartimiento lasted, at least in agriculture, its field of widest application, for two and a half centuries, and even after Independence coercion was continued for another hundred years under the cheaper and much worse regulated system of debt peonage.

From about 1550 to the repartimiento's codification in 1609, it led to appalling abuses, which excited the condemnation of the Franciscans, especially that of their chief spokesman, Jerónimo de

Mendieta. There may be some clerical bias here, but there is none in the most trustworthy of contemporary critics, Don Gonzalo Gómez de Cervantes, who in 1599 addressed a bitter memorial to Don Eugenio de Salazar, Oidor of the Council of the Indies.[1]

Cervantes was corregidor of Tlaxcala and quite likely a member of the powerful Cervantes clan founded by the Comendador Leonel de Cervantes, who achieved fame by bringing his seven daughters to New Spain in 1524 at Cortés' expense and marrying them off to the more prosperous of the conquistadores. Don Gonzalo's indictment of the system clearly reflects the views of the Creole aristocracy and does not pretend to be fair to his opponents. It is, nevertheless, so circumstantial and agrees so closely with Mendieta's account that it commands respect.

In Mexico City, he wrote, there were large numbers of Indian workmen skilled in the mechanical trades: tailors, embroiderers, painters, silk spinners, blacksmiths, cobblers, masons, and carpenters, whose regular wages were four reales (½ peso) to one peso a day; but the juez repartidor made no distinction between them and the unskilled workmen, and pressed them all into work gangs, in which they earned only one real a day. This naturally led to bribery and corruption, for the skilled workmen either hired substitutes or greased the palm of the juez repartidor to let them off, the bribery rate being as high as three or four pesos a week.

The immense amount of labor, he continued, required for the erection of the four great cathedrals (Mexico City, Puebla, Guadalajara, and Valladolid), and the large number of churches, chapels, convents, schools, and ecclesiastical edifices of all kinds, kept a veritable army of workmen occupied and aggravated the labor shortage, which was already acute because of the diminishing population. The shortage was especially felt in the haciendas, where the lot of the Indians was grim. "They send a Negro or servant along with the Indians who speeds them up and forces them to work faster than their weak constitutions can support. On top of this, they beat,

[1] This unique document eventually found its way to the British Museum and was published by Alberto María Carreño under the title, *La Vida Económica y Social de la Nueva España al finalizar el Siglo XVI* (Mexico, 1944).

116

whip, and mistreat them, and even take away their food and blankets to keep them from deserting. . . . Some farmers, after having kept them for two or three weeks, give them back their bundles of clothing and remove their guards . . . and the miserable Indians, seeing themselves at liberty, leave without collecting their wages, thinking themselves well paid just to get away. . . . These Indians, it should be noted, are assigned to the repartimiento for only one week, but the farmers, faced with the loss of their crops . . . keep them, as I have said, two or three weeks and more. Since the wretched Indian has left his house for [only] a week, his food gives out, and when he returns he finds his wife or his children dead, and his fields ruined for lack of cultivation, or destroyed by cattle.

"The Indians are assigned to the mines in the same fashion, and, since the miners have been short of hands since the epidemics of 1575–1576 [*matlazahuatl* or *cocoliste*, probably spotted fever or typhus, the most deadly of the scourges, which was endemic until well into the eighteenth century], they hold for two or three weeks the Indians who have been assigned to them for one. I am a witness of the abuse that the Indians receive in some of the mining haciendas, especially in those where they are forced to carry the ore to the mouth of the mine, from there to the mill, from the mill to the mortars, from the mortars to the sieves, and thence to the mixing troughs, using their blankets for the purpose, blankets worth at least five or six reales. The rough ore tears the blankets, so the Indian, after serving his week, is paid four reales and left with a ruined blanket that cost him five or six. Thus he works for nothing and even spends his own money."

All officialdom, he wrote, all troops, and all Spaniards who could afford them kept horses in the city, which meant that a large supply of fodder had to be brought in by the Indians pressed into this service. "But only the viceroy and the officers of the Audiencia enjoy this repartimiento, and no citizen or hidalgo does; hence it is of little value to the militia. . . . Every day a great many canoes come in loaded with grass, which is cast into the lake two, four, or six leagues from the city. . . . Many Spaniards make a business [monopoly] of bringing it in canoes, with Negroes in charge of them. . . . The result is that this repartimiento benefits only the [Crown] officers,

117

who thus get their fodder more cheaply than the rest of the citizens. . . . This is a matter that demands correction, because the strength of this kingdom lies in its horses."

It may be a coincidence that Cervantes' *Memorial* was written just after the last petition of the encomenderos to have their encomiendas made perpetual (1597); but they are of a piece, and both repeat the arguments of the Franciscans, that is, that the Indians were better off under the encomienda. However it was, the mounting criticism stirred the Council of the Indies to undertake a complete codification of Indian employment, free or forced.

The Ordinances of 1609 show a great advance in the science of lawmaking, in their frank recognition of the problem, and in their practical and realistic approach to it. They also afford a glimpse into the working of the paternalistic mind. (It is well to remember that this was in 1609 and the Rights of Man were a long way in the future.) Some of their more important provisions were: (1) Indians might not be brought from excessive distances, more than one day's journey, or from different climates; (2) their wages were to be adequate and proportioned to their work; (3) they must be paid for time spent in traveling to and from their work; (4) they must be paid in cash, in person, and in the presence of a magistrate; (5) their hours of labor were to be fixed by the viceroy; (6) they were to be allowed to go home at night whenever practicable; (7) to prevent their being considered as serfs or bound to the land, they might not be mentioned in any deed as belonging to such and such an estate or mine, for they were by nature "as free as the Spaniards themselves"; (8) they might not be employed, even voluntarily, in sugar mills or pearl fishing, for their weak constitutions unfitted them for such labor; (9) their tributes might not be commuted to personal services (an old practice among encomenderos).

Thomas Gage, that somewhat disreputable but indispensable reporter, has left us a lively and accurate account of the new repartimiento at work: "The Spaniards that live in that country [Guatemala] . . . allege that all their trading and farming is for the good of the commonwealth, and therefore whereas there are not Spaniards enough for so ample and large a country to do all their

118

work, and all are not able to buy slaves and blackamoors, they stand in need of the Indians' help to serve them for their pay and hire; whereupon it hath been considered that a partition of Indian laborers be made every Monday, or Sunday in the afternoon, to the Spaniards, according to the farms they occupy, or according to their several employments, calling, and trading with mules, or any other way. So that for such and such a district there is named an officer, who is called *juez repartidor,* who according to a list made of every farm, house, and person, is to give so many Indians by the week. . . . They name the town and place of their meeting upon Sunday or Monday, to the which themselves and the Spaniards of that district do resort. The Indians of the several towns are to have in a readiness so many laborers as the Court of Guatemala hath appointed to be weekly taken out of such a town, who are conducted by an Indian officer [*mandón*] to the town of general meeting; and when they are come thither with their tools, their spades, shovels, bills, or axes, with their provision of victuals for a week (which are commonly some dry cakes of maize, puddings of *frijoles,* or French beans, and a little chilli or biting long pepper, or a bit of cold meat for the first day or two), and with beds on their backs (which is only a coarse woolen mantle to wrap about them when they lie on the bare ground), then are they shut up in the town house, some with blows, some with spurnings, some with boxes on the ear, if presently they go not in.

"Now being all gathered together, and the house filled with them, the *juez repartidor,* or officer, calls by order of the list such and such a Spaniard, and also calls out of the house so many Indians as by the Court are commanded to be given him . . . and delivereth unto the Spaniard his Indians, and so to all the rest, till they be all served; who when they receive their Indians, take from them a tool, or their mantles, to secure them that they run not away; and for every Indian delivered unto them, they give to the *juez repartidor,* or officer, half a real, which is threepence an Indian, for his fees, which yearly mounteth to him a great deal of money. . . . If the complaint be made by any Spaniard that such and such an Indian did run away from him, and served him not the week past, the Indian must be

119

brought, and surely tied by his hands in the marketplace, and there be whipped upon his bare back. But if the poor Indian complain that the Spaniard cozened and cheated him of his shovel, ax, bill, mantle, or wages, no justice shall be executed against the cheating Spaniard, neither shall the Indian be righted, though it is true that the order runs equally in favor of both Indian and Spaniard. Thus are the poor Indians sold for threepence a week for a whole week's slavery, not permitted to go home at night unto their wives, though their work lie not above a mile from the town where they live; nay, some are carried ten or twelve miles from their home, who must not return till Saturday night late, and must that week do whatsoever their master pleaseth to command them. The wages appointed will scarce find them meat and drink, for they are not allowed a real a day, which is but sixpence, and with that they are to find themselves, but for six days' work and diet they are to have five reals, which is half a crown."

All forms of coerced labor were subject to grave abuses, but even so Gage's indignation is not to be taken at its face value. Gage and his kind, for one thing, lived by virtue of the system. Then, the Indians serving as much as a fourth of their time in the fields for hire were probably no worse off than the peasants of Europe, as Humboldt remarked. They were certainly not slaves. The pittance they received was insufficient to support life at any level; but the Indians did not depend upon their wages for a living. Their wages went toward paying their tribute (a peso a head of family yearly, plus the half-peso of the *real servicio* after 1592) and incidental expenses, mostly connected with their religious life: fees for baptism, marriage, burial, and the like. For the rest, they had their milpas and a good part of their time for cultivating them.

The common criticism of Spanish colonial legislation for the amelioration of the lot of the Indians is that it was evaded as often as not. The labor code of 1609, however, did not aim at the destruction of a system, like the New Laws of 1542, but at a reasonable regulation of long-established practice. It did not, therefore, arouse much opposition. On the contrary, the severity with which the Audiencia came down upon offenders is sufficient proof that it had the support of a substantial majority of its beneficiaries. Labor was getting critically short by 1609 and wastage of manpower could no longer be tolerated, as Gómez de Cervantes had made clear ten years before.

Several factors contributed to make the repartimiento bearable. The first is that it did little violence to native customs. All the evidence we have indicates that before the Conquest the Indian peasant was obliged to contribute part of his time and labor to the cultivation of the common land set aside for the support of priests and officials. He worked the land on a kind of sharecropping basis. He was also accustomed to contributing personal services and tribute in kind. Alonso de Zorita, writing in 1575 in support of the Franciscan thesis against the repartimiento, said of the personal services of the peasants under the Aztecs: "The ordinary daily personal service of wood and water was assessed by the day, by villages, and by districts (*barrios*) in such wise that at most each Indian had to serve only twice a year, and, as has been said, it was assessed among those living close by, and for that reason they were exempted to some extent from the tribute paid by the others."

The pre-Conquest macehual, then, was accustomed to paying tribute and rendering personal services for the support of his rulers. The good-of-the-commonwealth principle must have struck him as right and proper, or, at least, as something to be expected and put up with. In the large number of cases of abuse of the repartimiento heard by the General Indian Court, no objection was ever made to the principle of the thing, but only that such and such a person had violated law or custom. *Costumbre*, let me repeat, was Indian law and was always respected by the Spanish courts so long as it did not run counter to Spanish law.

A second factor in the control of the repartimiento was the endemic shortage of labor. During the century following the Conquest the native population died off at a staggering rate. Smallpox, measles, typhus, and other epidemics wiped out vast numbers of people, while the dislocation of the economy and the normal scourges of famine, flood, and drought made recovery very slow. At the time of the Conquest central Mexico (the settled part of the Plateau) had an estimated population of at least eleven million, of which by 1600 no more than a million and a half remained

(Gómez de Cervantes puts the decline at ninety per cent). As a result, competition for labor in the mines raised wages to such a point, even before the Ordinances of 1609, that the miners begged for relief. The same phenomenon occurred in the Spanish towns, where Indian mechanics could earn several times the wage paid in the repartimientos (as we have seen in the memorial of Gómez de Cervantes), and the surrounding agricultural lands were, as a consequence, drained of needed labor. The cry of the hacendados was that the Indians were being spoiled by high wages, a complaint that was repeated for centuries.

A third and very interesting factor in the modification of the repartimiento arose from the nature of New Spain's most vital industry, silver mining. In 1540 a survey of Indian communities was made which showed that a considerable part of the population was being employed in the mines, which at that time were mostly gold placers, in which forced gangs could be used effectively. The huge silver deposits discovered a few years later could not be worked by any such pick-and-shovel technique, but required a specially trained group of men. *By the end of the eighteenth century the silver mines of New Spain were generally operated with free Indian labor,* according to Humboldt. Such an astonishing development demands our attention.

Silver mining was a complicated business of sinking shafts and running drifts, ventilating and draining the mines, and preparing the quicksilver amalgam and roasting it. All these tasks require special skills and cannot be performed by occasional gangs brought in from the fields. Also, the mineral deposits were usually in remote, arid, sparsely settled, nonagricultural regions, to which the repartimientos had to be brought from great distances—a costly procedure and one provocative of much discontent. Moreover, the weekly or fortnightly changing of the labor gangs was destructive of the continuity necessary to efficient operation and prevented the building up of a body of skilled workers, which became progressively more essential as the processes of mining became more complex.

The repartimiento disappeared from mining, then, because it was a clumsy and inefficient device for procuring skilled and specialized labor. A potent cause of discontent with it was the disparity in wages between the free *peóns* (who earned as much as a peso a day) and the men of the repartimiento (who earned an eighth as much). This discontent led to dangerous riots (strikes) in the eighteenth century. But the most powerful factor of all, perhaps, in the elimination of the repartimiento from mining was the unceasing demand for the precious metals (mostly silver) in Europe and Asia, which made it profitable for mine operators, especially in the eighteenth century, to work their properties to capacity and to offer relatively high wages and bonuses to their workmen. Thus it came about that in the course of time the mines gathered about them communities of skilled mechanics, who in turn depended for their subsistence upon the outlying haciendas which had been established to meet this need. The rich farming and stock-raising country in the present states of Guanajuato, Querétaro, San Luis Potosí, Aguascalientes, Jalisco, and Zacatecas was supported by, and supported, the new mining communities.

Baron von Humboldt was struck by the prosperous condition of the mine workers. "In the Kingdom of New Spain," he wrote, in 1803, "at least within the last thirty or forty years, the labour of the mines is free, and there remains no trace of the mita [repartimiento]. . . . Nowhere does the lower people enjoy in greater security the fruit of their labours than in the mines of Mexico; no law forces the Indian to choose this species of labour, or to prefer one mine to another; and when he is displeased with the proprietor of one mine he may offer his services to another master who may perhaps pay more regularly. . . . The labour of a miner is entirely free throughout the whole Kingdom of New Spain. . . . The Mexican miner is the best paid of all miners; he gains at least from 25 to 30 francs (£1 to £1 4s) per week of six days. . . . The miners, *tenateros* and *faeneros* [ore carriers and piece workers] occupied in transporting the minerals to the place of assemblage (*despachos*) frequently gain more than 6 francs per day of 6 hours (4s 10d)."

The miners earned their high wages. In a deep mine, such as La Valenciana at Guanajuato, lack of ventilation was a continual hazard. There was no hoisting machinery available before the late eighteenth century, and the ore had to be carried to the surface,

1,500 feet, on men's backs. This was one of the most expensive operations, for the tenateros could make only five or six trips a day up the long chicken ladders with their 100-pound sacks of ore. By 1790 the hoisting was being done by horse-powered winches (*malacates*).

The determination of real wages in colonial times is a very difficult problem. Average prices do us little good. Maize might be worth two reales a fanega (hundredweight) one season and four times as much the next. It might sell for two reales in an agricultural community, while in a mining community in the mountains it might sell for a peso, that is, four times as much. Prices fluctuated violently from the irregularity of the crops, because there were no adequate storage facilities. The wages of the repartimiento Indian were hardly more than a token wage in any case. In 1550 he earned two and a half reales a week. By 1600 he was earning generally a real a day, and the rate tended to stick at that point. John Stephens found the debt-peonage system working in Yucatan in 1840 on the same weekly quota basis as the old repartimiento, and the men, called *luneros,* that is to say, "Monday men," were still receiving a real a day, which was credited against their "debt." In the repartimientos destined for service in a Spanish town or mine, where expenses were higher and where the men competed with free labor, the pay was substantially better, averaging about two reales a day, although it rarely exceeded half the rate paid for free labor.

One of the arguments by which the repartimiento was rationalized was that it would serve to educate the Indians and elevate them to the status of free workers. Obviously, it did no such thing. A class of free workers did develop on the cities and mines, but it was not through any desire on the part of the employers, who did everything they could to prevent it. The motive, of course, was cheap labor, and the standard excuse was that the Indian would not work without coercion. That assumption was dignified by being made law as early as 1512, when the Code of Burgos postulated: "It has been seen by long experience that the natives are by nature inclined to a life of idleness and vice." The thesis is weakened by the experience of the mining industry, which found it possible to attract workers by paying them adequate wages.

Although in principle the repartimiento was restricted to tasks performed for the benefit of the state, local magistrates took a very broad view of the matter and were prone to define a great many activities within the good-of-the-commonwealth framework. At the same time the law was specific about sugar manufacturing, pearl fishing, and the processing of indigo (the fumes from which were supposed to be injurious). It was argued that the Indians were not strong enough for these occupations, so the operators were obliged to employ Negro slaves. The high cost of slaves, however, and the Negroes' tendency to run away and form colonies of dangerous outlaws (*cimarrones*) in the mountains made the employment of Indians more desirable, so Indians were bootlegged into these industries and paid enough to keep them quiet. By the end of the eighteenth century the silver mines were running on free Indian labor, and Humboldt noted that the sugar mills were also.

In the plantations it was necessary to have a dependable labor force, preferably cheap. The problem was serious because, without continuity, it was impossible to operate. Take the case of Don Manuel Garrote Bueno. Don Manuel had a cacao plantation in Guatemala and operated it with Indian workmen under the repartimiento. On March 5, 1798, he addressed a complaint to the Audiencia of Guatemala which illustrates the situation. The Indians, he stated, refused to serve in his repartimiento, alleging that it left them no time to work their own lands. This, he averred, was nonsense, because they were willing to serve for higher pay. In other words, they were striking. "The hope that the superior government," he continued, "would be able to enforce its provisions [for the repartimiento] had stimulated me to undertake the planting of cacao . . . , but now I am completely discouraged . . . During the past year I planted 8,000 trees, and at present I have in the nursery more than 9,000. If the repartimiento is going to be enforced I shall be glad to continue planting, but if the stubbornness of these natives and their habit of disobeying the orders of the superior government bring about its suspension, it will expose me to disaster and I shall have to abandon my undertaking . . ."

As resistance to the repartimiento grew, the device of tying men to their jobs by contract and debt came into general use. The practice

125

had been forbidden long ago during the reign of Charles V, but it was too obvious a solution of the labor problem not to be used surreptitiously, and it became so widespread that it was finally accepted as legal.

The working of debt peonage was simplicity itself. What Indian could resist accepting an advance of a few pesos against his wages at the price of putting his cross on a piece of paper which he could not read? Once having done so, he was caught, and the local alguacil could haul him off to work whenever he was needed. Debt peonage became so general that the complete transition to it after Independence was entirely logical. In the nineteenth century, up to the Revolution of 1910, the pulque plantations of the Plateau, the grain and cattle haciendas, the sugar, coffee, banana, cacao, tobacco, henequen, indigo plantations, and the mines all depended upon debt peonage to secure a cheap and constant supply of labor. Meanwhile, after Independence, the Indian little by little lost the land that the Spanish government had wisely set aside for his subsistence and sank to the level of a landless serf, living at the mercy of his employer.

To supply labor for the many textile mills of New Spain, the operators had recourse to other methods which kept the General Indian Court full of complaints. Long before the Conquest the Indians had developed high skill in the manufacture of cotton goods, and after it they continued to supply the country with fabrics, which became one of the most profitable items of tribute collected by the encomenderos and the Crown. Weaving was the most important industry of New Spain, outside of mining, and has continued to be so down to the present day.

Wool began to rival cotton very early. By 1580 the annual commercial clip had attained the imposing figure of 300,000 pounds, and large numbers of people were employed in its manufacture. The ancient problem of ensuring cheap and continuous operation led to the establishment of one of the ugliest of colonial institutions, the *obraje*, which was the worst kind of sweat shop, usually a small affair of a few spindles, dyeing vats, and looms. The commonest means of procuring labor were the press gang, the purchase of convicts from the local jails, contracts, and debt. The men were kept on the job by the simple expedient of locking them in. The textile industry was either too profitable, or the workers were too far beyond the fringe of respectability, to make control effective. Cheap Mexican textiles invaded markets as far away as Peru, but no improvement in the lot of the workers accompanied the growth of the industry.

Father Agustín Morfi, visiting the obrajes of Querétaro in 1777, says of them (in his invaluable *Viaje de Indios*): "There were once many factories here, where serge, flannel, blankets, and ponchos were made, but they have decayed through the tyranny of the management. Since the majority of the operatives are convicts and are cruelly treated, they do not work with the care which they might otherwise exercise, and the free workers who might make a living in them, will not work because of the horror with which these workshops are regarded."

Humboldt was profoundly shocked by the obrajes. "On visiting these workshops," he wrote, "the traveler is disagreeably struck, not only by the great imperfection of the technical process in the preparation for dyeing, but in a particular manner by the unhealthiness of the situation, and the bad treatment to which the workmen are exposed. All appear half naked, covered with rags, meagre, and deformed. The doors, which are double, remain constantly shut, and the workmen are not permitted to quit the house. Those who are married are only allowed to see their families on Sundays. All are unmercifully flogged if they commit the smallest trespass on the order established in the manufactory."

In other trades, such as carpentry, masonry, ropemaking, tanning, saddlemaking, and the like, Indian workmen were extensively used, but they were kept in the lower ranks of the medieval guild system brought over by the Spanish workmen. In the hierarchy of apprentice, journeyman, and master, the Spaniards took care to save the better paid jobs for themselves by making it impossible for an Indian to advance beyond the rank of journeyman. It was difficult, in fact, for an Indian to get himself accepted as apprentice, and he was usually employed only in the unskilled operations. There was nothing to be done about it, because the guilds were powerful and their privileges were sanctioned by laws and customs that reached far back into the Middle Ages.

There was still a wide field for Indian craftsmen in the manufacture of articles for native consumption. Most native crafts survived because they were despised by the white workers, and there was no money in them anyway. So the Indians continued to make and use their own domestic wares without much interruption, and the humble markets of remote villages today are full of handsome pottery, textiles, and leather goods. Native crafts have been discovered in late years by tourists in search of the picturesque, with the unfortunate result that many "Mexican Curious," as one enterprising dealer used to advertise, are now turned out by factories in the capital. The virus has infected crafts along the more frequented tourist routes. Some years ago I visited the old textile village of Teotitlán de Valle, Oaxaca, looking for some honest handicrafts, and found the Zapotec workmen weaving hideous imitations of Aztec designs in shrieking aniline colors. "Why," I protested to the *maestro*, "do you make these ugly things instead of your own beautiful blankets?" "That's the way they order them," he answered. "But doesn't anyone make the old blankets?" "No, señor. One maestro refused to change and made the good blankets with cochineal and indigo, but he died. It is all gone now." I found the most dreadful example of this vandalism in the town of Santa Ana, Tlaxcala, one of the oldest textile centers of Mexico, where one shop advertised "Genuine Imitations of Saltillo Blankets!"

This chapter has a happy ending. Twenty-five years later, I am delighted to add, Mexican cotton and woolen textiles, silver and lapidary work, leather and pottery, in beauty of design and excellence of workmanship, have taken their place among the best in the world. These flourishing new industries were begun by certain enterprising foreigners (for example, in Taxco, Guerrero, and San Pedro Tlaquepaque, Jalisco) and have been intelligently encouraged by the government's Ministerio de Fomento, whose Museo de Artes Populares in Mexico City is a treat to the eyes.

# 11

## THE SECOND GENERATION

The sons of the conquerors, with few exceptions, did not go in for a career of conquering. They dug in and held on. Their fathers' prowess had made them a privileged aristocracy, and their ambition tended to be satisfied with defending their property and position. Content with being a parasite class, they argued that the Crown owed them a living, and they kept up a ceaseless bombardment of the Council of the Indies for more Indians, more land, more money. They exploited to the utmost their prestige as "sons of first conquerors," or relatives, and as such were legally given preference in the distribution of land and offices. Diego de Ordaz, nephew of the old conqueror of the same name, presented himself before the Council of the Indies in 1538 and persuaded the Council to grant him about twenty square miles of the rich volcanic soil on the eastern slope of Ixtaccíhuatl, in his uncle's encomienda of Calpan (Puebla). The Council sent the royal order (*cédula*) to Viceroy Mendoza, who duly "obeyed" it, but kept young Ordaz cooling his heels for four years while his claim was investigated. The Audiencia finally assigned him a piece of land elsewhere and less than a tenth the size of his claim. His bitterness at such injustice was shared by all his kind, who looked upon the viceregal government as their natural enemy, as it was.

Their fathers had set the pattern for their conduct. As one by one the old conquerors fell on evil days, or felt that they could do with a little more land, or what not, their first act was to file a petition (*probanza*) with the Council of the Indies, setting forth at length the services they had performed in the conquest, and how in their old age they were facing beggary, and their precious offspring the same, unless they were properly rewarded.[1] Not many years after the Conquest, some of its stalwart heroes, to judge by their petitions, were a sniveling and shameless lot of beggars—which in no wise deflated their pride and presumption. Their sons carried on.

It was an unfortunate thing for New Spain that Don Luis de Velasco died when he did. The unheralded crisis that was about to threaten the existence of the kingdom was such that only a man of his caliber could have met successfully. As it was, deprived of his wisdom and strength (New Spain was governed by the Audiencia during the interregnum), the country came as near disintegration as at any time since the ugly days of Nuño de Guzmán and the first Audiencia, thirty-four years earlier.

In 1563, the year before Velasco's death, the son and heir of Hernán Cortés came to New Spain to take over his father's vast estate. Martín Cortés, second Marqués del Valle de Oaxaca, was a spoiled darling of privilege. He had been reared at the sumptuous court of Charles V, and had been sent with Prince Philip to England among the crowd of young magníficos who dazzled the eyes of the British at the unlucky wedding of Philip and Mary Tudor. In New Spain, the Marqués, full of arrogance and ostentation, was bent on persuading the country to accept him as the son of his father—a thing that the country, as it turned out, was very willing to do. In his train were his two bastard brothers, Don Luis and Don Martín, the latter the mestizo son of Cortés by his Indian mistress, Doña Marina. Both boys had been legitimized by Pope Clement VII, and both had received the coveted habit of Santiago from Charles V. (Since Cortés whimsically named two of his sons Martín, I shall refer to his legitimate heir as the Marqués and to the other as Don Martín.)

The Marqués set up his household in Mexico City in the regal style befitting his great name. Such was the magic of that name, and such the wealth, swank, and presumption of the Marqués, that he

[1] These petitions are legion. Most of them are of scant historical value. An extraordinary exception is Bernal Díaz del Castillo's *True History,* which, according to Ramón Iglesia, began as a simple probanza. The appearance of Francisco López de Gómara's *Historia de la Conquista* in 1552 infuriated Bernal Díaz and led him to expand his probanza into the delightful chronicle that we know (Ramón Iglesia, *El Hombre Colón y otros Ensayos.* Mexico, 1944).

soon gathered around him a regular court of the young bloods of New Spain. They looked upon him as their natural leader in their concern to protect their encomiendas, which it was the evident purpose of the Crown to take away from them. To make the power of the Marqués more formidable, the Indians transferred to him the blind adoration in which they had held his father. Not the least element of his strength was supplied by the Franciscans, who had always been hot partisans of Cortés, and who were now in a bitter fight with the Council of the Indies and Archbishop Montúfar to save their parishes from secularization.

This dangerous coalition of forces was bound to cause uneasiness in the mind of the jealous and aging Velasco. Friction between him and the Marqués was made inevitable by the latter's insufferable arrogance and childish vanity, which led him openly to show his contempt for the viceroy. A row between Velasco and the Audiencia had brought over a royal visitor to investigate, the Licenciado Jerónimo de Valderrama, who otherwise turned out to be an intriguing and unworthy officer, ready to bend a listening ear to gossip, and greatly flattered by the attention that the magnificent Marqués did not fail to show him.

Flanked by the favor of Valderrama, the Marqués and his satellites grew in boldness and soon had the capital split into two factions. It resembled the old conflict between the Crown and the feudal conquistadores which had come so close to bringing on civil war in 1544, when the New Laws were published by Tello de Sandoval. Rumors of the impending abolition of the encomiendas kept the fires of discontent well stoked, and the more hardy spirits among the followers of the Marqués began to toy with the idea of cutting loose from the old country. Several things seemed to favor the success of such a movement. The endless wars of Charles V and Philip II had weakened Spain so badly that it was unlikely that an effective force could soon be sent to put down a rebellion. The royal treasury was exhausted, and the Crown had sunk to the point of having to ask for outright gifts. The fatuity of Valderrama, the short-sighted timidity of the Audiencia, and the untimely death of Velasco were so many additional encouragements to conspiracy.

The active leaders of it were the two daring and popular sons of an old conqueror, Gil González de Avila,[2] Alonso and Gil González, who had inherited their father's rich encomienda of Cuautitlán in the Valley of Mexico, which was yielding at that time a yearly tribute of 7,430 gold pesos. These young men, aged twenty-five and twenty-six, met with their fellows in the palace of the Marqués, kept their grievances fresh and their courage up, and in time hatched out a plot. The plan agreed upon was intelligent and thorough. On a certain Friday, when the city council met, the conspirators were to divide themselves into squads of eight or ten. One squad was to bar the door of the council chamber; another was to seize the armory; a third was to penetrate into the quarters of the Audiencia and kill the oidores and Valderrama. After these necessary preliminaries, a man in the cathedral tower was to give two strokes on a bell, whereupon the conspirators were to kill the treasury officers and all others who should·oppose them. The populace was to be overawed by a show of strength. Don Luis Cortés was detailed to dash to Vera Cruz and hold the fleet in port, to prevent news of the rebellion from reaching Spain. Don Martín's job was to seize Zacatecas and its silver, while Puebla and other strong points would be taken by the squads assigned to them. Then the Marqués would be proclaimed king, and a parliament would be convoked to endow him with the proper cachet. The conspirators did not neglect to allow for a new nobility, including the Indian caciques;[3] the land would be redistributed among the deserving, and then let Philip of Spain stop them if he could!

[2] Gil González de Avila had earned Cortés' gratitude by joining Francisco de las Casas in Honduras and eliminating Cristóbal de Olid (see chap. 4, above).

[3] The establishment of an Indian nobility, with the titles and privileges of Spanish nobles, had been proposed to the Council of the Indies twenty-five years before by Viceroy Mendoza, as a means of tying the ruling class firmly to the Crown. His recommendation was not accepted, for it was considered too dangerous, but the policy of recognizing Indian hierarchies had much the same effect. The power of the caciques was legally very limited, but they had, and continued to have, a great ascendancy over their people, which led to innumerable abuses: extortion, corruption in the distribution of work stints, theft of community funds, forced services, and the like. They were kept in power because they would presumably aid in the conversion of the Indians. Sons of caciques were singled out from the beginning for instruction in the Christian doctrine.

The plot of the Avila brothers was not necessarily foredoomed to failure, as is usually held. On the contrary, if it had been carried through with daring and dispatch, it could very well have succeeded. Its first requisite, however, was effective leadership, another Cortés. The only possible head of it was the young Marqués, for success depended upon his wealth and name. But the Marqués blew hot and cold: at one moment he seemed to be leading the conspiracy, and at the next he was fearfully currying favor with Valderrama and the Audiencia. Inaction sapped the enthusiasm of the plotters. News of the affair reached the Audiencia, but that body was in a blue funk and could do nothing. Finally, Alonso de Avila, impatient, and suspicious of treachery, decided to carry on by himself, apparently counting on forcing the Marqués to take a stand. But at the moment when the plot was to be sprung, Don Alonso fell seriously ill, and nothing came of it. It seems to be certain, however, that if at any time in 1565 or 1566 the Marqués had said the word, nothing could have saved New Spain from civil war and possibly independence. But success required intelligence and audacity, qualities that the Marqués had not inherited along with his father's name and title.

It was not until July 16, 1566, when the leaderless conspiracy had died aborning, that the Audiencia plucked up enough nerve to face the issue. Even so, the oidores did not dare to come out in the open. By a ruse they got the Marqués to attend one of their sessions. When he was safely inside, the doors were locked, and he was put under arrest. At the same time the Avila brothers were seized by a squad of bailiffs and thrown into prison. The ensuing panic that immediately took possession of the other conspirators led to a general rush on their part to denounce one another before the Audiencia. Thus fortified, that body tried the Avila brothers for high treason, and they were beheaded with fitting solemnity in the public square of Mexico City on October 3, 1566.

The terrible fate of the two young men shook New Spain to the foundations. The Audiencia, frightened by its own boldness and by the general indignation of the public, took cover and delayed the prosecution of the rest of the conspirators. Meanwhile, the arrival of a new viceroy, Don Gastón de Peralta, put the Audiencia in an embarrassing position. While still at Vera Cruz, Peralta had heard the details of the abortive plot and had made up his mind that the danger had been greatly exaggerated. Upon reaching the capital he dismissed the heavy guard that the Audiencia had stationed at the palace, and in general was inclined to treat the whole affair as a boyish prank. The Audiencia was in a very bad light, and its predicament was further heightened by Peralta's insisting that the Marqués be sent back to Spain for trial, with the obvious implication that he would not receive a fair hearing before the Audiencia. Both the Audiencia and the viceroy hastened to patch their fences with the Council of the Indies by sending back separate reports of the business. That of the viceroy was intercepted at Vera Cruz by agents of the Audiencia, and the Council of the Indies received a highly colored account of the conspiracy, together with a thoroughly false lot of charges against Peralta—one of them being that he had raised an army of no fewer than 30,000 men, with the manifest intention of carrying out the plot on his own account.

It took little to arouse the suspicions of Philip II, and here was evidence of a full-fledged rebellion against his divine authority, and no denial of it from the viceroy. The situation called for the most violent measures. Philip picked out his toughest judge, the Licenciado Alonso de Muñoz, and sent him to New Spain armed with the terrible power of doing the king's justice with his own hand.

Muñoz arrived at Mexico City in October, 1567. He was the embodiment of everything sinister in the Oriental despotism of Philip II. His ferocious sadism thrived on blood. He was the Judge Jeffreys of New Spain. For six dreadful months his minions, operating in secrecy, entered the homes and seized the persons of all whom the breath of suspicion touched. The prisons of the capital were immediately crowded to suffocation with his victims, and more and more prisons had to be built, airless dungeons which for a century afterward bore the hated name of Muñoz. Scaffolds were erected and the headsman's ax dripped with the bluest blood of New Spain, until it began to seem that Muñoz intended to wipe out the whole class of encomenderos. The trials were a farce. To be accused was to be condemned. There was no appeal from the mad Muñoz. This was his hour, and woe to those who stood out above the crowd!

The most famous and pathetic episode of the reign of terror was

134

the trial of Don Martín Cortés, the scapegoat mestizo half-brother of the Marqués. Powerless to touch the latter, who was safely in Spain, Muñoz sated his ferocity on Don Martín. This brave and unfortunate man stood fast where so many of his companions had bought their safety by betraying their fellows. He was put to the torture of water and the cord,[4] but in his agony refused to testify. The record of his torture for January 7, 1568, after six pitchers of cold water had been forced down his throat, ends with an admirable bit of understatement: "And in this condition, the said Don Martín being ill . . . and since it was evident that he was fatigued by the torture, it was ordered suspended, to be repeated if it seemed best. . . . And the said torture was suspended this day at about nine o'clock of the morning."

Nothing definite was proved against Don Martín, but the suspicion against him was so strong that he was sentenced to perpetual banishment from the capital, on pain of death if he should return, and to a fine of a thousand pesos. There is no evidence, incidentally, that the sentence was ever executed. The only further record of the shadowy and tragic figure of the first mestizo, after his torture, shows him imprisoned in his own house a few months later, after which he disappears from view.

The disgusting conduct of Muñoz aroused fear and resentment to such a pitch that a full account of his atrocities was soon in the king's hands. To Philip's credit he immediately reversed himself and sent two royal commissioners to New Spain in a fast dispatch boat. These two men, the oidores Vasco de Puga and Luis de Villanueva Zapata, proceeding with the utmost secrecy, surprised Muñoz in his quarters in the Dominican convent and read him the king's order, which allowed him three hours in which to leave the city. Thereupon the terrible visitor and his assistant, in imminent danger of their lives from the outraged citizenry, slipped out of the city on foot like a couple of criminals. Poetic justice was further served by their having to return to Spain in the same ship with the deposed viceroy (deposed by Muñoz). Philip II received Peralta with marked cordiality; but, when Muñoz presented himself, the king spoke one glacial sentence: "I sent you to New Spain to govern, not to

[4] See below, chap. 17.

destroy!" Muñoz was found dead in his chambers the next morning.

The Marqués del Valle spent several years under house arrest, but there was not enough evidence against him to convict him of treason. His estate, which had been sequestered by Muñoz, was restored to him in 1569, and he was let off with a fine of 50,000 pesos. A personal loan to the king of 100,000 more may have helped to erase the suspicion of disloyalty. The Marqués never returned to New Spain.

The conspiracy of the Avila brothers was the dying flicker of military feudalism in New Spain for long years to come. From that time onward, the descendants of the conquerors offered no threat to the Crown, but chose wealth and comfort, and became a superfluous and idle anachronism. What ailed the second generation? With their wealth, numbers, and influence they had a fair chance of success. They seem to have been infected by a kind of slow poison. They were unable to make up their minds, and they frittered away precious time until they could not avoid the awful vengeance of the king. Their fathers, in circumstances certainly as unpromising, had brought off the most audacious conquest in the history of the New World. Something had been lost in those forty years: spirit or vision; or it may be that men fighting merely to preserve inherited wealth and privilege lack a conviction of rightness, or that a life of well-fed ease destroys the military virtues. It may also be that the prestige of the throne had grown so mightily by their time that it unhinged the knees of those amateur warriors and they fainted at their own daring. However it was, the sons of the old conquerors were soon replaced by vigorous and hard handed men, who wrested fortunes from mines and commerce, and who in their turn left great wealth to sap the vitality of their sons.

An epoch ended in 1568. Back in Spain the crisis had the good effect of making Philip II see the danger of turning loose upon his dominions visitors with unlimited powers. He chose the next viceroy with care, and the prudent and intelligent Don Martín Enríquez de Almanza was allowed to enjoy a long and undisturbed reign of peace and construction, a work in which all classes joined with thanksgiving. The Silver Age was at hand.

# 12

## THE SILVER AGE

How shall we measure the weight of time? How make clear the deep mark of its pressure on the habits of mankind? How, to be specific, shall we gauge the effect of the two hundred and fifty years of what I have termed the Silver Age of New Spain? Even within the narrow and arbitrary limits I have set, say, from 1570 to 1820, it spanned a mighty period. At its beginning soldiers were still debating the merits of the crossbow against the clumsy and new-fangled arquebus. At its end steamboats were plying the Hudson.

During that long age the Invincible Armada of Philip of Spain was destroyed by the English Channel and the heavy guns of Elizabeth's sea dogs; Shakespeare and Milton wrote; the Pilgrims landed on Plymouth Rock; Newton and Descartes blew to bits a comfortable world built upon established authority; Cromwell led the middle class of England against an outworn despotism; the Glorious Revolution enthroned common sense; Voltaire laughed the Old Régime to death; Jean-Jacques Rousseau poured out the heady liquor of the Rights of Man; the tinsel court of Louis the Unlucky ended on the guillotine; Napoleon collected crowns and set the pattern for a new breed of earthshakers. Across the sea the young American republic chanted somewhat noisily the glories of Liberty, while Whitney's cotton gin double-riveted the fetters of black men, and land-hungry pioneers drove West over the ruins of once-free Indian nations. And all this long while the people of New Spain were born and died, lived and mated, built and delved, and began to forge a new race behind the bulwark of Spain's might and the Atlantic Ocean. Two hundred and fifty years!

The Silver Age of New Spain was literally the age of silver. The little metal disks, which some thousands of years ago were invented

137

to facilitate trade, in time took on a magic virtue of their own, and mankind became obsessed with the notion that they were wealth in themselves—which is still the case, as the Shrine of Fort Knox should prove to the skeptical. The fortunate possessors of gold and silver could enjoy power and material comforts denied to most mortals. The pawnbroker and banker could command kings and armies. To discover new sources of the magic metals became the consuming desire of noble and commoner. Their quest fired men to make unheard-of efforts in exploring the ends of the earth. Every discoverer and explorer of the New World (not just the greedy Spaniards) reflected the thirst for the precious metals which was devouring Europe. Europe had become a trading society; trade depended upon the precious metals, and there was not enough currency to meet the growing need.

As it turned out, New Spain contained an inexhaustible reservior of silver. A mint was established in Mexico City in 1535, and a thin trickle of silver coins began to flow to Europe. In 1557 the invention of the quicksilver amalgam process greatly reduced the cost of separation, and the flow of coins grew to a torrent which in time inundated the world. "Pieces-of-eight! Pieces-of-eight! Pieces-of-eight!" The chant of John Silver's parrot echoed the chant of mankind. The clumsy wooden machinery of the Casa de Moneda in Mexico City stamped out bright Spanish dollars year in and year out. The mints of New Spain, in the course of time, coined some *two billion* dollars, in a world which still counted in pennies. Two billions more were exported in ingots, and another billion or so was contributed by Peru. Two-thirds of the entire silver supply of the world was eventually shipped from the port of Vera Cruz. The single *real de minas* of Zacatecas is credited with having yielded a fifth of the world's silver before the nineteenth century.

The treasure of the Spanish Indies was the vortex in which the economy of Europe whirled for three hundred years. It did not occur to anyone, apparently, that the stream of metallic treasure and the increasing poverty of Spain had anything to do with each other. As early as 1520 gold dust from the placers of Española was upsetting the price structure, and the people of Seville were rioting against the rising cost of bread. By the end of that century a mechanic's wages or a farmer's income would no longer support life. Spanish economy

138

was all but destroyed, the cities filled up with hungry beggars, and thousands upon thousands of men and women who had no place in the world sought refuge in religious orders. It was the first modern inflation.

The "King's fifth" of the treasure of the Indies was never enough to finance the costly wars of the Hapsburg monarchs. The gold placers were soon exhausted, and with the heavy decline of the population they could not have been worked anyway. Toward the end of the sixteenth century the shallow and more easily exploited silver deposits began to fail also, and New Spain went into its "Century of Depression," as Woodrow Borah calls it. The Crown taxed Spain to suffocation, and was driven to the desperate expedient of mortgaging its income for generations to come, in a vain attempt to finance the huge military establishment in the Low Countries. The Crown could not pay its troops, and in 1575 they mutinied and subjected the city of Antwerp to one of the most terrible sacks in history, the so-called "Spanish Fury." The bankruptcy of the Crown became manifest to all the world when Philip II arbitrarily lowered the murderous rate of interest (12 to 18 per cent) on his debts and brought down the banking houses of Germany and Italy in the sixteenth-century equivalent of the Great Crash of 1929. The dismal practice of auctioning public offices corrupted the civil service, but the income from it proving inadequate, the Crown took to inventing and selling titles of nobility, virtually at wholesale, thereby creating an upstart aristocracy of money, upon which the legitimate nobles could look with scorn not unmixed with envy. Disillusionment and cynicism in high office replaced the crusading spirit of Isabella the Catholic. Don Quixote awoke from his dream.

"At length he wak'd, and with a loud Voice, Blessed be the Almighty, cry'd he, for this great Benefit He has vouchsafed to do me! Infinite are his Mercies; they are greater and more in number than the Sins of Men. The niece hearkening very attentively to these Words of her Uncle, and finding more Sense in them than there was in his usual Talk, at least since he had fallen ill; What do you say, Sir, said she, has anything extraordinary happen'd? What Mercies are these you mention? Mercies, answer'd he, that Heaven has this Moment vouchsafed to shew me, in spite of all my iniquities. My Judgment is return'd clear and undisturbed, and that

139

Cloud of Ignorance is now remov'd which the continual reading of those damnable Books of Knight-Errantry had cast over my Understanding."

Society and the public service became so corrupt that thoughtful men saw nothing ahead but final dissolution, and the great Quevedo dipped his pen in bile and wrote:

> Sir Money is a doughty knight!
> Mother, I bow to Milord Money;
> He is my lover and my honey.
> His passion is indeed so burning
> That he is pale from constant yearning;
> And since, although he wants in size,
> Milord my every wish complies,
> Sir Money is a doughty knight!
>
> Well born of Indies' noblest blood,
> While all the world in homage stood,
> He cometh home to Spain to die,
> But leaves his bones in Italy. . . .
>
> He is a gallant, shining fellow,
> Although his color runs to yellow;
> His valor is beyond all doubt
> In Christian or in Moorish bout;
> And since the noble and the lout
> Are equal in his lordly sight,
> Sir Money is a doughty knight!

Spain's admiring and envious rivals, never suspecting her disease, hung on her flanks like a pack of wolves, greedy for their share of the spoils. Anti-Spanish propaganda, embittered by the religious conflict, had the very practical purpose of rationalizing the seizure of Spanish treasure. Las Casas' masterpiece of horror, *A Brief Relation of the Destruction of the Indies,* was the most widely translated book of the time, while Thomas Gage's *New Guide to the West-Indies* was written to justify Cromwell's "Western Design," that is, the capture of the Spanish colonies. An undeclared war was waged against Spain from the beginning of the Conquest. A long line of famous pirates became the heroes of their respective countries, and

Queen Elizabeth herself was a joint partner in some of the more lucrative raids on Spanish commerce. Hawkins, Frobisher, Raleigh, and a host of others kept the Spanish authorities in a continual state of nerves for two hundred years. Drake's raids on Nombre de Dios, Panama, and the Pacific ports made his name such a legend that at the dread cry of "Draque!" the people of the coast towns took to the hills. Thomas Cavendish sailed round the Horn and picked up the rich Manila galleon *Santa Ana* off the coast of Lower California, with a cargo of gold and Chinese silks. In 1628, the Dutch pirate, Piet Heyn, seized the whole Spanish treasure fleet in Matanzas Bay, Cuba, and carried off twelve million pieces of eight, an exploit which his grateful government rewarded with knighthood. Legalized piracy did not go out of fashion until the eighteenth century, when the merchants of England discovered that it was more profitable to smuggle goods to the Indies in exchange for silver, while the British navy discouraged freebooting among her rivals. And so it was that the treasure of the Indies played a large part in the birth of the commerical age, and great segments of the population of Europe, fleeing the unbearable depression, emigrated to the New World and began the slow building of what was to become the United States of America. Pieces of eight!

In New Spain silver was king. To increase its production was the first responsibility of every viceroy. About the mines stately cities sprang up, with large and industrious populations. The people of the new cities had to be fed, and agriculture flourished in the provinces near by. Long trains of mules laden with silver bars unloaded at the Casa de Moneda in Mexico City, which became the silver metropolis of the Spanish Empire. Where the treasure was, there the power gathered also. The capital was the goal of the ambitious and the refuge of the disinherited, who flocked in to live like rats on the alms and refuse of the rich.

A silver nobility appeared in New Spain, complete with purchased titles and shaky coats of arms. Antonio Obregón spent a few thousand of the two hundred million pesos he had taken from La Valenciana mine of Guanajuato and became Conde de Valenciana. Jesús Salado went him one better and became Conde de Matehuala and Marqués de Guadiana. The Marqués de Aguayo, the Marqués de Mal Paso, the Conde de Regla, the Marqués de Apartado, the

141

Marqués de Vivanco, the Marqués de Jaral, and the Conde de Santiago were among the glittering dignities bought by the miners from the bankrupt Crown, together with the privilege of painting a crest on their carriages and having their ears titillated by a murmured "Señor Marqués" or "Señor Conde." [1]

The grateful and pious miners lavished their riches on the Church in propitiatory offerings, until the churches and cathedrals of New Spain were incrusted with the precious metals. The new aristocracy had to be housed and clothed befittingly. Their palaces studded the capital, and their taste for luxuries brought galleons from China laden with silks, jewels, brocades, ivory, and spices. Their ready alms supported an army of professional beggars of all classes. The magnificence of their habits and the splendor of their households transcended vulgarity. They struck the very English Thomas Gage in the same way in which the riches of Rome must have affected the barbarians.

"In my time [1625]," he wrote, "Mexico City was thought to be of between thirty and forty thousand inhabitants, Spaniards, who are so proud and rich that half the city was judged to keep coaches, for it was a most credible report that in Mexico in my time there were above fifteen thousand coaches. It is a byword that at Mexico there are four things fair, that is to say, the women, the apparel, the horses, and the streets. But to this I may add the beauty of some of the coaches of the gentry, which do excel in cost the best of the Court of Madrid and other parts of Christendom; for there they spare no silver, nor gold, nor precious stones, nor cloth of gold, nor the best silks of China to enrich them. And to the gallantry of the horses the pride of some doth add the cost of bridles and shoes of silver. . . .

"Both men and women are excessive in their apparel, using more silks than stuffs and cloth. Precious stones and pearls further this their vain ostentation; a hat-band and rose made of diamonds in a gentleman's hat is common, and a hat-band of pearls is common in a tradesman; nay, a blackamoor or tawny young maid and slave will

[1] This unquenchable thirst for titles was remarked by Humboldt. "The largest piece of gold found in El Choco," he wrote, "weighed twenty-five pounds. The Negro who discovered it fifteen years ago did not even gain his liberty. His master offered the nugget to the King's cabinet [museum] in the hope that the court would reward him with a title, which is the object of the most ardent desires of the Spanish Creoles."

make hard shift but she will be in fashion with her neck-chain and bracelets of pearls, and her earbobs of some considerable jewels. . . .

"There are not above fifty churches and chapels, cloisters and nunneries and parish churches in that city; but those that are there are among the fairest that ever my eyes beheld, the roofs and beams being in many of them all daubed with gold, and many altars with sundry marble pillars, and others with brazil-wood stays standing one above the other, with tabernacles of several saints richly wrought with golden colours, so that twenty thousand ducats is a common price for many of them. . . ."

Gage's description of this New World Babylon, evidently written to impress Cromwell with its wealth, to be had for the taking, does not inspire confidence, but there are few contemporary accounts against which to correct it. An exception is the precious *Diario de Sucesos Notables* (1648–1664) of Don Gregorio Martín de Guijo, who seems to have been a useful but undistinguished citizen. The minutes of the Venerable Chapter of the cathedral record that "he exercised his pen with singular talent." This talent is not conspicuous in his diary, in which he amused himself by jotting down street-corner chitchat: autos de fe (for which see chapter 17), deaths, marriages, births, the arrivals and departures of viceroys, bishops, *flotas* and dispatch boats from Spain, floods, famines, epidemics, miracles, piracies, crimes, hangings, and the frequent feuds with which the young bloods of the city banished boredom. Indeed, the Diary is the forerunner of the modern tabloid and allows us to see life in the capital during the Silver Age through the eyes of the man-in-the-street. A selection of his entries (condensed) follows:

April 26, 1648. A frigate sailing from Campeche, with a cargo valued at 100,000 pesos, is driven ashore by pirates and looted.

December 9, 1648. The Manila galleon has been sighted off the south coast, the first one to arrive in two years. Great rejoicing and ringing of bells.

March 7, 1649. A Portuguese, in jail charged with murder, commits suicide, for which his body is mounted on a mule, paraded to the scaffold, and there hanged.

March 21, 1649. The office of Accountant General is repossessed by the Crown because the buyer paid only 20,000 pesos for it, instead of the former price of 40,000.

July 8, 1649. Juan de Alcocer, administrator of the sale of papal bulls, has a corn removed. Gangrene sets in, his leg is cut off, and he dies eleven days later.

July 29, 1649. A free mulatto is hanged for stealing a lamp from the Augustinian convent.

November 19, 1649. Five large ships, believed to be hostile, are sighted off Acapulco. Troops are dispatched to reinforce the garrison.

July 3, 1650. The new viceroy, the Conde de Alva de Liste, enters the city riding under a pallium carried by members of the city council. He and the gentlemen of his entourage are dressed in costly brocades; his pages and servants are in livery, green velvet capes embroidered in gold. He is seated upon a throne of crimson velvet on a stage before the palace of the Marqués del Valle [now the Monte de Piedad]. The archbishop in full canonicals, and the canons in white capes bearing crosses and candlesticks, emerge from the cathedral. The viceroy has to listen to the story of Hercules, composed in verse by a certain Father Matías de Bocanegra, S.J., after which he repairs to the cathedral to receive the archbishop's blessing.

December 26, 1650. Don Guillén de Lombardo has escaped from the prison of the Inquisition (see chapter 17). No ships have arrived from China, and the resultant scarcity of cinnamon has raised its price to a peso a pound. [Cinnamon was, and is, considered indispensable in the manufacture of chocolate.]

January 18, 1651. The viceroy witnesses the blasting of a hill on the route of the Huehuetoca Canal.

May 7, 1651. The butchers' guild stages a three-day celebration of the Feast of the Holy Cross, with a brilliant procession of maskers: Indians, Moctezuma, Hernán Cortés, Moors, and the Great Turk. It ends with a series of bullfights, over the protest of citizens who are shocked by this desecration of the Holy Cross.

September 23, 1651. The flota from Spain arrives at Vera Cruz. It had put in for water at the island of Virgita [?], where the landing party was attacked by Indians and thirty men were killed, among them two Jesuits and a Dominican. One vessel sank in Vera Cruz harbor.

April 17, 1652. The Indians of Parral are reported to be in rebellion. They have eaten a Jesuit.

May 27, 1652. A tavern keeper is hanged for coin-clipping.

January 19, 1654. The viceroy, who is in the habit of roaming the streets at night, surprises two Augustinian friars eating buns in a bun shop. Their superiors are warned to put a stop to such license.

March 24, 1654. "Doña María," the great bell of the cathedral, weighing 44,000 pounds [it actually weighed 15,000], is hoisted into place. The operation takes a week and is witnessed by the viceroy.

April 8, 1654. During the celebration of the king's birthday one of the viceroy's pages makes an insulting remark about the wife of Don Cristóbal de la Cerda, knight of Santiago, who stabs the page in a fury. The page's companions set upon Don Cristóbal and cut him up. He is given Supreme Unction, arrested, tried, and sentenced—to what, Guijo does not say.

May 18, 1654. The French and Dutch pirates of the island of Tortuga quarrel over division of their spoils. The Audiencia of Santo Domingo sends two vessels; the pirates are surprised, and a million pesos in treasure are recovered. The pirates are brought to Santo Domingo and, it is a safe guess, are hanged.

July 8, 1655. The English under Penn and Venables attack Santo Domingo with sixty vessels and 20,000 troops [actually, about 6,000]. They are beaten off with heavy loss by Negro cowhands and slaves.

August 15, 1655. A fifty-gun ship from Spain arrives at Santo Domingo and forces the enemy to lift the siege. The enemy loses 3,000 men. Great rejoicing in Mexico City, with bell-ringing and thanksgiving services at the cathedral.

September 8, 1655. The English take Jamaica. Prayers are ordered in all the churches.

October 21, 1655. Two Augustinian lay brothers are arrested for the murder of their superior. They are sentenced to 250 lashes and life imprisonment, on a vegetable diet three days a week.

November 13, 1655. Twenty-two English "Calvinists" are captured at Tampico by mulatto cowhands and brought to the capital.

145

November 26, 1655. The *alcalde de corte,* Don Juan Manuel, attempts to arrest a mulatto, who attacks him with a dagger and takes sanctuary in a church. Don Juan has him arrested anyway, gives him two hours in which to defend himself, and then has him garroted. Don Juan is excommunicated for violating sanctuary, but the Audiencia orders him absolved.

January 30, 1656. The greatest event of the diary, the completion of the cathedral, to which Guijo devotes twelve pages.

June 6, 1656. The flagship of the treasure fleet sinks off Havana, with a loss of 5,000,000 pesos and 400 passengers.

June 17, 1653 [flashback]. Miraculous intervention of the Virgin to relieve a drought. Her image is paraded through the streets for two weeks, at the end of which a violent storm interrupts the procession.

March and April, 1657. The Manila galleon, *Nuestra Señora de la Victoria,* having lost a good part of her crew in a slow crossing, is reported to be beating up and down the coast between Acapulco and Guatemala.

June 4, 1657. An 85-year-old Spaniard, after being tortured until his arms are broken, is hanged for robbery. His accomplices, an Indian woman pulque vendor and an old Chinese, are given 200 lashes and sold to the obrajes for six years.

September 8, 1658. The loss of Jamaica is confirmed. Of the 400 men sent [from Santo Domingo] to its relief, 300 have been hanged from balconies, or have had their throats cut.

November 6, 1658. Fourteen men are burned at the stake for sodomy.

November 16, 1658. Fire breaks out among the wooden stalls of the Zócalo. The cathedral bells are rung; the archbishop brings out the Host; all the religious orders surround the fire. While they cast holy relics into the flames, the stalls are torn down and the populace loots the shops.

July 13, 1659. Cromwell is dead! Thanksgiving services at the cathedral.

March 12, 1660. The viceroy is attacked in the cathedral by a demented soldier, who is tortured, found guilty, dragged through the streets, and hanged.

146

June 14, 1661. One of the worst droughts ever recorded causes heavy losses of cattle. The image of Nuestra Señora de la Asunción is paraded through the city, followed by an immense crowd. A few drops of rain fall. The procession is repeated on the eighteenth, with the Sacred Host added as a further inducement, whereupon it rains for twenty-eight days without stopping.

February 7 and March 28, 1663. The office of treasurer of the mint is sold to Juan Vázquez de Medina for 300,000 pesos. He is jailed for failure to deliver 200,000 pesos of the price.

June 22, 1663. Violent outbreak of smallpox. Dreadful heat by day and frost by night, which kills the crops. Religious processions bring a little rain. They are repeated, and it rains steadily until July 8, when the epidemic ceases.

April 3, 1664. Bad blood between Viceroy the Conde de Baños and his appointed successor, Archbishop Diego Osorio. The viceroy and his sons try to murder the archibishop's secretary.

June 28, 1664. The feud continues. The viceroy banishes the archbishop from the city. Fearing a popular tumulto, the Audiencia tries to persuade Osorio to return. He refuses. A letter from Spain confirms his appointment. General rejoicing. Baños and his sons take refuge in the palace.[2]

September 9, 1664. A Negro girl is accused of assaulting her mistress with a machete. While she is being led to the gallows, her owners withdraw their complaint and she takes refuge in a church. The viceroy sends a halberdier to fetch her out. Two Mercedarian friars and a secular priest protest this violation of sanctuary. A mob of Negroes, Indians, and mulattoes rescue the girl and bring her to the cathedral. She is given in custody to the convent of La Concepción. She is not otherwise punished.[3]

[2] This row was a sequel to that between Bishop Palafox and the Jesuits of twenty years before. The Jesuit historians Vetancourt and Alegre defend Baños, whom Alegre calls "one of the most just and exemplary of viceroys." However it was, Baños died in the odor of sancity as a barefoot Carmelite.

[3] Guijo was not entirely unnoticed by his contemporaries. Antonio de Robles, whose dry-as-dust *Diario* (1665–1703) purports to be a record of "notable events," has this entry for August 10, 1676: "Monday the 10th: today was buried the Licenciado Gregorio del Guijo, a man noted for his pen and good sense. . . . He was interred in the presbytery of the Regina. The whole chapter [of the cathedral], whose secretary he had been, attended."

The capital was a city of violent contrasts, as, indeed, it still is. The silver-incrusted coaches of the rich plowed their way through crowds of drunken and debased Indians, Negroes, mulattoes, and mestizos, who lived by begging in the daytime and by thieving at night. They were the army of the disinherited, expressively called *léperos,* whose control was an all but insoluble problem for the police. Two hundred years after Gage's and Guijo's time, the plague of léperos was still unabated. Fanny Calderón described them in 1840 with her sharp pen: "Whilst I am writing this a horrible lépero, with great leering eyes, is looking at me through the window, and performing the most extraordinary series of groans, displaying at the same time a hand with two long fingers, probably the other two tied in. 'Señorita! Señorita! For the love of the most Holy Virgin! For the sake of the most pure blood of Christ! By the miraculous Conception!—' The wretch! I dare not look up, but I feel his eyes are fixed upon a gold watch and seals lying on the table. . . . There come more of them! A paralytic woman mounted on the back of a man with a long beard. A sturdy-looking individual, who looks as if, were it not for the iron bars, he would resort to more effective measures, is holding up a *deformed foot,* which I verily believe is merely fastened back in some extraordinary way. What groans! What rags! What a chorus of whining!" Fanny Calderón, it should be added, had a Scottish and New England background.

According to the most accepted theory of the time, léperos were the result of pulque. The evidence was certainly strong enough, save that cause and effect were reversed. Drink was the only escape of the lépero, and the pennies he could beg or steal speedily found their way into the pockets of the *pulqueros.* Fortunes were made, and are still made, out of this utter misery. Early in the seventeenth century it was estimated that there were fifteen hundred *pulquerías* in the capital alone. The intolerable nuisance and the danger from unrestricted drinking led to a series of edicts that recall the abortive attempts to enforce prohibition in the United States. One such edict aimed to reduce the number of pulquerías in Mexico City to a hundred and fifty, each of which was to be operated by an old woman of proved virtue. She might sell pure pulque (*pulque blanco*), but no spirits or Spanish wine. Pulque was commonly adulterated with a root which turned it yellow and increased its intoxicating power. A white man who adulterated pulque, or who otherwise violated the edict, was subject to a heavy fine and a term in the galleys, while the luckless Negro, mestizo, or mulatto who was caught at it might suffer mutilation or death. Indian violators were let off with a sound beating, the universal remedy for all their shortcomings. But there was too much money invested in the traffic, the government's income from it was too great, and the populace was too addicted to pulque, for the ordinances to have any appreciable effect. Their constant repetition is sufficient proof of their sterility. Mobs of drunken léperos continued to be a menace to public safety, for they could always be counted on to loot and riot whenever the authorities weakened or some feud split the city. Two such riots, or *tumultos,* were grave enough to threaten the existence of the state in the seventeenth century. They are worth describing in some detail, for they were symptomatic of the disease that was eating at the heart of New Spain.

# 13

## TUMULT AND SHOUTING

Mexico City was the center of the wealth and political power of New Spain. It was also the battleground for the factions that were always ready to fly at each other's throats. It may be that the many rows that shook the capital from time to time arose from boredom, love of excitement, and Creole frivolousness (as the Spaniards were inclined to charge), but they all had one constant: the deep and bitter hatred that the Creole felt for the Spaniard. That hatred was the motive power behind the ill-fated conspiracy of the Avila brothers. It split all classes. It set the cabildo of the city (Creole) against the Audiencia (Spanish). It divided the religious orders more sharply than any other group. In his journey from Mexico City to Guatemala in 1625, Thomas Gage found all the convents along the way in a perpetual feud, which was so violent that the friars were kept apart, *criollos* in one convent, *gachupines* in another. He was much taken with the beauty of Oaxaca and would have liked to settle there, but the Dominican convent was occupied by Creoles, who would have none of him. Juan de Solórzano y Pereyra, a wise and gifted jurist, and member of the Council of the Indies, laid the blame for the feud mostly on the regular orders, which discriminated against Creoles on the doubtful ground that the climate of the Indies had a softening effect on their character and that the Creoles, therefore, were too fickle to be trusted with responsible posts. Whether the orders believed this nonsense or not, they acted in accordance with it, and lacerated Creole pride did the rest.

The weakness of the Crown in the seventeenth century under the last three Hapsburgs and their venal favorites was reflected inevitably in the weakness of the viceregal government of New Spain.

The Hapsburg machine was creaking with internal stresses. The weaker it got, the more restless, impatient, and furious the Creoles became. The heavy lesson of 1566 was forgotten in time, and in the first part of the next century the Creoles were again caressing the notion of freedom and whispering defiance of the Crown. An opportunity soon arose to bring the struggle into the open.

The lack of definition between the civil and ecclesiastical jurisdiction had always been a prolific source of trouble, and it took a wise head to keep the peace between them. A row was almost inevitable when two such hotheads as Archbishop Don Juan Pérez de la Serna and Viceroy the Marqués de Gelves ruled at the same time. Serna was a heavy-handed despot who had ruled New Spain pretty much as he pleased, with no interference from the easygoing Marqués de Guadalcazar, viceroy from 1612 to 1621. In the latter year Gelves took over. Gelves was an able and vigorous administrator, but otherwise was afflicted with the same harsh and uncompromising temper as the archbishop.

From the moment Gelves landed at Vera Cruz he set about cleaning-up the appalling mess left by his predecessor. One of the most urgent needs was to rid the country of the swarms of bandits who infested every road, exacting tribute from unescorted travelers. Gelves organized small companies of troops to run them down, and, thanks to his energy, within three years most of the robbers had turned to more peaceful occupations, while the bodies of the others swung by the hundred from crossroads gibbets.

A notorious abuse that had been allowed to go unchecked was the practice of certain alcaldes mayores and corregidores of buying up the grain supply and holding it for famine prices, while the public granaries (alhóndigas), which had been established to prevent just such a situation, were allowed to fall into disuse. The viceroy attacked the problem in his usual hobnailed fashion, arresting on the charge of malfeasance one of the most prominent offenders, Don Melchor Pérez de Varáez, knight of Santiago and corregidor of the province of Metepec (Mexico). At the same time Gelves undertook to break the grain monopoly by purchasing 10,000 fanegas of maize and dumping it on the market.

These measures threatened the privileges of a whole class (mostly

151

wealthy Creoles) and raised up against the viceroy a host of enemies, for no one knew where his foolish rage for reform was going to stop. Even so Gelves might have ridden out the storm if he had not made the mistake of including in his reforms certain irregularities of Archbishop Serna, the most notorious of which was the operation of a private slaughterhouse in the archepiscopal palace. The slaughterhouse may not have been doing any harm, but it violated a strict law which put the meat supply of every community under royal license. Gelves wrote the archbishop a sharp note begging him to desist from the practice. Serna, of course, took the viceroy's action as a direct invasion of his rights, and he straightway put himself at the head of the growing faction whose privileges were threatened. Gelves, for his part, displayed a positive genius for making enemies. One day at a function in the cathedral he seated the members of the city council (wealthy Creoles all) below certain of the Crown officers and so wounded their pride that they walked out in a body. Instead of overlooking this bit of peevishness, Gelves took it as an insult to the throne and had the offenders jailed.

The city was split wide open: Creoles against Spaniards, secular priests against friars, friars against friars, most of the populace against the viceroy, and the léperos happy to join any movement that promised excitement, free drinks, and booty. Every lawsuit and petty dispute became a political issue, and nothing was decided on its merits. The focus of the row was the trial of the grafting corregidor of Metepec. After three months of hearing accusations and counter-accusations, and possibly evidence, the Audiencia found him guilty and sentenced him to pay a fine of 70,000 pesos. Dismay and fury cemented the archbishop's party, which resolved to break Gelves.

To insure payment of his fine, Varáez was confined in the Dominican convent under military guard. The convent was an immense building, and the hospitable friars allowed the guard to take up quarters inside. Here was the opening for which the archbishop was waiting, for was not the guard violating sanctuary? He ordered the provisor of the convent to expel the guard. The point was argued up and down, and the upshot of it was that the guard stayed, on the viceroy's order. Serna then went into action and blasted the viceroy, the Audiencia, and even the soldiers of the guard with an excommunication. An *escándalo!* A dog of an excommunicate was in the palace! The archbishop's notary led a mob of priests in an attack on a constable. The viceroy retaliated by confining the notary in the fortress prison of San Juan de Ulúa at Vera Cruz. More excommunications. The viceroy appealed to the apostolic judge. The judge ordered Serna to withdraw the excommunications. Serna refused. He not only refused, but he locked up every church in the capital and laid the whole city under an interdict.

Now, an interdict was the most awful weapon in the arsenal of the Church. All services, all sacraments, were suspended. The bells tolled night and day as for the dead, and the terrible ceremony of anathema was read from the pulpit of the cathedral. The dying could not receive the final comfort of Extreme Unction and must go before their Maker with their sins fresh upon them. The interdict was a command to the faithful to rise and smite down the enemies of God. Funeral processions bearing lighted candles wended their lugubrious way through the city streets, and the dread edict was posted on the door of every church for all to see.

The apostolic judge ordered the rebellious archbishop to lift the interdict, and himself suspended the excommunications. Finding himself blocked by the apostolic judge and the viceroy, the archbishop retaliated by stopping the tolling of the bells, and the sudden silence was even more terrifying than the noise had been. Then it was that Serna decided to play his last trump. Without his customary ceremonial robes he went before the Audiencia in the guise of a humble suppliant for justice. His act had been well advertised, and a large crowd of partisans and léperos gathered before the palace. The Audiencia, badly scared by the demonstration, ordered him to leave. The archbishop refused. The Audiencia had been forced into a position that Serna must have foreseen: He was put under arrest, sentenced to pay a fine of 4,000 ducats, and banished from New Spain. The news was greeted with a roar of defiance from the crowd outside. Nevertheless, the archbishop was escorted to San Juan Teotihuacán under guard. Once there, he fired an excommunication at the entire government and sat down to await developments.

The government, however, had no intention of allowing the

archbishop to remain within striking distance of the capital, and ordered him to continue to Vera Cruz. His escort prepared his carriage. Several officers entered the church to notify his Grace that it was time to go, and were met by their prisoner with the Host in his hands. No priest could be touched while performing his sacred office, and the guard had to retire. The comedy was repeated until the guard gave up in disgust.

Back in the capital the archbishop's party had not been idle. Rumors were circulated to the effect that the high price of grain was the viceroy's doing. Priests tacked up more excommunications on church doors, and the partisans of Varáez held daily councils of war. The square was never free of angry crowds. The Audiencia weakened under the attack and lifted the decree of banishment against the archbishop. Gelves, however, was not to be intimidated, and his evil genius made him commit the last folly of imprisoning the whole Audiencia for exceeding their powers. This new scandal brought a boiling mob to the palace. It was ordered to disperse; it refused, and two léperos were seized and flogged as an example for the rest.

On top of it all, the archbishop, from his sanctuary at Teotihuacán, blasted the city with a new interdict. The churches were again closed and the bells resumed their tolling. The mob churned. A secretary of the Audiencia tried to push his way through and was roundly cursed. His escort undertook to punish the offenders. Rocks flew, and the great tumulto of 1624 was on.

Led by a priest on horseback, the rioters pulled up the paving stones of the square and showered them at the windows of the palace, shouting "Long live Christ! Long live the King! Death to the heretic! Death to the excommunicate!" The call to arms was blown by the trumpeter of the palace guard, but the militia did not respond. The mob yelled for the release of the Audiencia, and the viceroy made one gesture of appeasement by liberating the oidores and allowing them to show themselves at the windows. It was too late, and the gesture was futile in any case, for the leaders of the riot were out to destroy him. These leaders were the priests, the Creole citizenry, and the city council itself, which was still smarting from the viceroy's insult. One of its members was so carried away by his enthusiasm that he got out the city banner and led the mob in person.

The doors of the Dominican convent were battered down and Varáez was carried out in triumph. The hated gachupines were too frightened to show themselves. The only friends the viceroy had left were the Franciscans, who paraded through the square and persuaded some of the mob to follow them off. But the rioters were back the same day armed with heavy beams with which to break down the doors of the palace. Which done, they roared through the courtyards, opened the jail, and set fires, while a priest mounted on a table offered absolution to all who would fight the heretic. The Audiencia by this time had escaped and joined the archbishop's party. They demanded the viceroy's surrender and announced his deposition. To give their demand more weight, armed men were posted on the surrounding roofs and sniped at the palace guard. With the palace burning over his head and his men dying, Gelves saw that further resistance was useless and escaped in disguise to the Franciscan convent.

By January 16, 1625, the disgraceful affair was over. Victory (for the time being, anyway) lay with the archbishop, the Creoles, the crooked bureaucrats and their friends. The glad tidings were sped to Teotihuacán, and the archbishop was escorted to the capital by an admiring crowd. All the bells of the city were set to ringing in a deafening welcome. Satan had been vanquished. The interdict was lifted, as well as the excommunications—all save that of the viceroy. The grafting corregidor of Metepec was whitewashed by the same oidores who had convicted him and was allowed to return to Metepec, there presumably to carry on his profitable speculations in grain. Gelves was confined in the Franciscan convent under a heavy guard, which oddly enough did not violate sanctuary, and, after long and unavailing negotiations, was allowed to go back to Spain—not, however, before the Audiencia had sent the Council of the Indies an account of the tumulto. The archbishop could not have felt altogether easy about his part in it, because a month later he accepted a handsome donation made by his flock and went to Spain himself, there to be coldly received by the king. He was never sent back to Mexico.

155

The Council of the Indies was not taken in by the representations of the Audiencia, and in November of that same year of 1626 a new viceroy, the Marqués de Cerralvo, landed at Vera Cruz, accompanied by the inevitable and dreaded royal visitor, Don Martín Carrillo, Inquisitor of Valladolid. For two years Carrillo conducted a quiet and thorough investigation of the riot, but his mildness was so pronounced that I am tempted to speculate about what would have happened if Philip II had been alive. Only four leaders of the mob were executed. Five of the priests implicated in the tumulto fled to Spain, but were caught and sentenced to the galleys. Two of the oidores lost their jobs. The Marqués de Gelves, on the other hand, was exonerated and restored to an honorable career in the king's service.

The lesson of the great riot of 1624 is best given in the words of the visitor Carrillo: "[The tumulto shows] three facts of great importance to the Spanish government: first, the conspiracy was organized, directed, and led by the clergy, that is to say, by the class believed at court to be the principal and most firm support of the government of the mother country; second, if the matter were followed through, it would be found that all, or almost all, the populace were accomplices; third, the hatred of the mother country's domination is deeply rooted in all classes of society, especially among the Spaniards [Creoles] who come to establish themselves in Mexico City, and was one of the principal means used to excite the populace to action."

*Carrillo anticipated by two centuries the motives of the wars of independence.*

Sixty-eight years later Mexico City was again threatened with destruction. The tumulto of 1692 had varied and confusing causes, as usual. No matter what happened, it immediately assumed political implications. In this case the prime cause of the riot was meteorological. In the first two chapters I gave a good deal of emphasis to the unpredictable weather of the Plateau. The year 1691–1692 was an extreme example of the fickleness of the Mexican climate. The winter was exceptionally severe. Heavy snowfall and frost destroyed crops and interrupted commerce. Later on, unseasonal and excessive humidity brought on a blight of mildew (*chahuixtle*) and killed the whole wheat crop. The price of wheat reached the famine level of twenty-six pesos a *carga de mula* (200 pounds). Heavy and continuous rains flooded the Valley of Mexico and destroyed about half the maize crop. Maize sold for six pesos a carga (about six times its usual price). The viceroy, the Conde de Galve, obliged the provincial towns, as far away as Celaya (Guanajuato), to send their grain to Mexico City, until they too were threatened with famine and refused to send any more.

The public granary of the capital was besieged by the hungry, and a popular rumor was circulated, to the effect that the shortage was owing to manipulation on the part of royal officials. The general discontent was further aggravated by the faulty system of distribution at the granary, where women were allowed to crowd in to suffocation and fight for places. The officer in charge could think of no better way to handle the situation than to use the whip.

Popular irritation was brought to a head on a Sunday, June 8, 1692, when an Indian woman got beaten and trampled at the granary. She was picked up by the angry crowd and brought to the palace of the archbishop, Don Francisco de Aguiar y Seijas, a generous and charitable man, several cuts above Archbishop Serna of the earlier tumulto. His Grace kept out of sight, so the Indians carried the woman to the government palace and demanded to see the viceroy. Unable to penetrate the quarters where they believed, correctly, that he was hiding, the Indians grew more and more excited and began to throw stones. The guard drove them away from the palace, but the rioters gathered reinforcements and returned to the attack, killing two soldiers and obliging the rest to take refuge inside.

"Long live the King! Death to the cuckold gachupines! Death to the viceroy! Death to the corregidor!" The shrieks of the mob were punctuated by the thud of paving stones against the palace gates. The rioters soon got the idea that it would be a fine thing to sack the mint. The myriad stalls of the marketplace supplied fuel for the fires set against the doors. The ranks of the mob were constantly swelled by more Indians, léperos, half-castes, and riffraff, until the square was choked with ten thousand yelling men and women. Some

157

attempted to scale the balconies of the palace and were shot down by the soldiers. According to Don Carlos de Sigüenza y Góngora, a professor at the university and himself a horrified witness of the riot: "There were so many people, not only Indians, but of all castes, the shouting and roaring were so loud, and the rain of stones upon the palace was so heavy, that the noise they made at the doors and windows exceeded that of a hundred drums beaten at once. The few who were not in the square waved their blankets like banners and threw their hats into the air; others mocked, and the Indians supplied stones with unwonted diligence."

His Grace the archbishop thought to quiet the mob by showing himself in the square. On the box of his carriage sat a lackey holding the archiepiscopal cross, but lackey and cross were both knocked down by a well-aimed paving stone, and His Grace retired. Friars, Jesuits, and secular priests were for once united. They paraded and exhorted, but met with the same reception.

The first targets of the mob's fury were the gibbet and the stocks, which went up in flames, along with the carriage of the corregidor. Fire ate through the thick palace doors, and soon the inner compartments, the chambers of the Audiencia, and the jail were burning. The town hall was also fired. The shops surrounding the square, particularly the wineshops and pulquerías, were looted, and the mob, now gloriously drunk, danced and howled in a frenzy. The respectable citizens, thoroughly frightened, barricaded their houses. Toward evening groups of militia recovered somewhat from the general panic and began to fire on the crowd. At the same time the alcohol began to wear off, and, at ten o'clock, when a party was sent out by the viceroy to reconnoiter, it found the square deserted, save for the dead lying among the embers. The great tumulto of 1692 had burned out like a grass fire. It was the most expensive of all such riots, the property loss being estimated at two million pesos. If the rioters had had a purpose and a leader nothing could have saved the city from destruction. As it was, the government was to stand until the respectable elements themselves should lead tumultos.

The gibbet and the stocks were soon rebuilt. A few ringleaders were hanged, one was burned alive, while the whipping post and stocks took care of the rank and file. There was much learned discussion about the cause of the tumulto. Don Carlos de Sigüenza was inclined to blame it on pulque and the natural perversity of the Indians. To prevent a recurrence, the grain supply from the provinces was increased and maize was distributed free to the poor. The sale of pulque was prohibited, for a while. The Indians were restricted to their barrio of Santiago Taltelolco, also for a while. The police force was strengthened. In short, everything was done except to inquire into the reason for the huge slum population of Mexico City, and the léperos continued to lend picturesqueness, squalor, and disease to urban life, as they still do.

# 14

## TRANSPORT AND COMMUNICATION

Before the Conquest and the introduction of pack animals, most goods were transported on the backs of men. Among the Indians there existed a class of professional carriers, called *tamemes*, while every peasant toted his own provisions, tributes, and household goods. The Aztecs had, moreover, developed a highly efficient relay postal service, the speed of which astonished the Spaniards. Cortés, for example, sending a message to Moctezuma from Vera Cruz to Mexico City, a hundred leagues away, could expect a reply within six days. Indian merchants with their trains of carriers roamed from Sinaloa to Nicaragua, respected everywhere even by warring nations. The Spaniards employed vast numbers of tamemes to carry their provisions, guns, and baggage. The brigantines with which Cortés destroyed Aztec naval power on Lake Texcoco were brought there in pieces by eight thousand Tlaxcalan tamemes, who made a gay fiesta of the occasion. The first ships that Cortés launched in the Pacific after the Conquest were carried in the same fashion across the Isthmus of Tehuantepec.

The Spanish missionaries, who were prone to be shocked by everything that differed from European customs, were loud in their denunciations of the use of God's creatures as beasts of burden, although they were obliged to employ them themselves. They had plenty of reason to protest. In the early days the conquistadores and miners drove the tamemes beyond endurance. In 1530 Nuño de Guzmán forced them to carry all his supplies for the conquest of New Galicia. Many thousands were pressed into service for the mines, and their bones lay whitening in heaps along the roads. In his famous letter of August 27, 1529, Bishop Zumárraga railed against this abuse.

"The Indians," he wrote, "are very badly treated by Spanish travelers, who take them, loaded like pack animals, without even feeding them, wherever they wish to go, and for this reason the Indians suffer great harm and even die along the road. It is worst among the gold miners, who load the Indians of their encomiendas and send them thus burdened thirty, forty, or fifty leagues, more or less, and many die on the way. I have in mind one province called Tepeaca [Puebla] from which it is said that more than three thousand free men, by the account of the cacique of that place, have died on the road from carrying supplies to the mines."

Remedial legislation, as usual, was principally noteworthy for its lack of realism. The early prohibition of the use of carriers brought an understandable complaint from Spanish merchants, who had to meet the competition of Indian merchants, to whom the prohibition did not apply. The use of tamemes by Spaniards was by turns prohibited, allowed, regulated, and the question was finally abandoned, as the introduction of pack animals solved the worst abuses. There were many regions, however, which were either too poor to support pack animals or too inaccessible to allow their use. San Ildefonso (Villa Alta, Oaxaca) for many years could be approached only by foot trails and continued to be served by tamemes until fairly modern times.

A century after Bishop Zumárraga's outburst, Thomas Gage found the carrier system working apparently undiminished in Guatemala. "So likewise," he wrote, "are they [the Indians] in a slavish bondage and readiness for all passengers and travelers, who in any town may demand unto the next town as many Indians to go with his mules, or to carry on their backs a heavy burden, as he shall need. . . . A *petaca*, or leathern trunk, and chest of above a hundredweight, they will make those wretches to carry on their backs a whole day, nay, two and three days together, which they do by tying the chest on each side with ropes, having a broad leather in the middle, which they cross over the fore part of their heads, or over their forehead, hanging thus the weight upon their heads and brows, which at their journey's end hath made the blood stick in the foreheads of some,

161

galling and pulling off the skin, and marking them in the foretop of their heads, who as they are called *tamemes,* so are easily known by their baldness, that leather girt having worn off all their hair."

In its attempted regulation of the use of Indian carriers the Council of the Indies was up against geography, economics, and, the toughest problem of all, Indian *costumbre.* Although the Indians readily accepted pack animals when they could get them, tamemes continued to be used everywhere. In 1794, Don Agustín de las Quentas Zayas, Governor-Intendant of the Province of Chiapas, undertook the ambitious project of opening a road from Salto de Agua on the Tulijá River to Comitán, where it would connect with the *camino real* to Guatemala and afford an outlet for Guatemalan commerce on the Laguna de Términos. He built a new town at Salto de Agua, but when it came to moving supplies he found himself stopped by the lack of pack animals. The remedy was at hand. "In the pueblos of Tila, Tumbalá, and Palenque," he wrote to the Audiencia of Guatemala, "all of them a little more than a day's journey distant, there are twelve hundred Indian bearers, who will carry burdens of seven *arrobas* [175 pounds], *sillas de cabeza,* etc." *Sillas de cabeza* were chairs for carrying passengers.

These tamemes were professionals. In 1840 John Lloyd Stephens used such human pack trains to traverse that same back country of Chiapas, and on one occasion was properly shocked at being carried in a *silla de cabeza* over the very rough stretch between San Pedro (Sabana) and Palenque. "Though toiling excessively," he wrote, "we felt a sense of degradation at being carried on men's shoulders. . . . We had brought a silla with us merely as a measure of precaution, with[out] much expectation of being obliged to use it; but at a very steep pitch, which made my head almost burst to think of climbing, I resorted to it for the first time. It was a large, clumsy armchair, put together with wooden pins and bark strings. The Indian who was to carry me, like all the others, was small, not more than five feet seven, very thin, but symmetrically formed. A bark strip was tied to the arms of the chair, and, sitting down, he placed his back against the back of the chair, adjusted the length of the strings, and smoothed the bark across his forehead with a little cushion to relieve the pressure. An Indian on each side lifted it up, and the carrier rose to his feet, stood still a moment, threw me up once or twice to adjust me on his shoulders, and set off with a man on each side. It was a great relief, but I could feel every movement, even to the heaving of his chest. The ascent was one of the steepest on the whole road. In a few minutes he stopped and sent forth a sound, usual with Indian carriers, between a whistle and a blow. . . . My face was turned backward; I could not see where he was going, . . . but in a few minutes, looking over my shoulder, I saw that we were approaching the edge of a precipice more than a thousand feet deep. . . . My carrier moved along carefully, with his left foot first, feeling the stone upon which he put it down, . . . and by degrees, after a particularly careful movement, brought up both feet within half a step of the edge of the precipice, stopped, and gave a fearful whistle and blow. I rose and fell with every breath, felt his body trembling under me, and his knees giving way. . . . The poor fellow was wet with perspiration, and trembled in every limb. Another stood ready to take me up, but I had had enough."

Every traveler in Mexico and Central America today sees Indian carriers (no longer called tamemes, but *cargadores*) competing with pack animals and motor trucks, even in the cities. In Guatemala it is considered a mark of virility to be able to carry a heavier pack than one's neighbor, and competition among boys is so strenuous that it frequently leads to hernia.

A very important part of Aztec commerce—virtually everything, in fact, brought to the markets of Mexico–Tenochtitlán—was waterborne, as it continued to be for a long time after the Conquest. The heavily populated lacustrine towns of the Valley of Mexico were all connected with the capital, and with each other, by an immense fleet of canoes, estimated by Gómara to number 200,000. "And I am understating rather than exaggerating the number of these *acalli*," he adds, "for some affirm that in Mexico [City] alone there are commonly 50,000 of them, used for bringing in provisions and transporting people. The canals are covered with them to a great distance beyond the city, especially on market days." Gómara's statement is supported by all contemporary accounts. The people of the valley were amphibious. At the back of every house built upon

163

the shores of the lakes and canals, as most of them were, was a landing where the family canoe was moored. During the siege of Mexico in 1521, a major problem faced by Cortés was to protect his flanks from attack by water, which he solved by building his famous fleet of brigantines and driving the canoes off the lakes. "Wooden canoes," writes George Vaillant, "were essential for life on the lakes. Some were dugouts hollowed out by fire, but others . . . were flat-bottomed punts constructed of planks which were probably tied together in Aztec times, rather than pegged, as they are today." Most of them were probably the one- and two-man craft that are still to be seen on Lake Xochimilco, but others were fairly large transports propelled by as many as twenty men, like the one in which Cuauhtémoc was captured.

Canoes served another essential purpose. Sanitation in a water-bound city like Mexico was of the first importance. The Aztecs kept their city sweet by collecting offal in canoes and removing it daily to the maize fields to be used as fertilizer. Urine was carefully saved in earthenware pots and sold to the dyers as a mordant in fixing colors.

When the city was pulled down during the siege in 1521, the canals were filled with the debris and the sanitation system was seriously impaired, but many canals continued in service. Gonzalo Gómez de Obregón wrote (1599): "This city is served by canals drawing water from the lakes. A large number of canoes come in daily loaded with fodder, maize, wheat, stone and sand for building, merchandise, flour, barley, and lumber, . . . but there is such negligence in the city government that garbage and offal are thrown into the canals from all the houses that give upon them, in such quantities that the poor Indians can hardly force their canoes through." With the gradual silting up of the lakes and the consequent flooding, the city was frequently inundated in its own filth and became a pesthole. Epidemics were a scourge for centuries and were not brought under control until the opening of the Tequixquiac drainage tunnel in 1900. The last canal, La Viga, which brought flowers and greenstuffs from Xochimilco, was filled in only a few years ago.

Transport in New Spain, as it is in present-day Mexico, was one of the most vital and difficult problems of government and economy. From the opening chapter of this volume the reader might get the impression that it was all but insoluble, but necessity and ingenuity partly overcame the formidable obstacles offered by the terrain. The transport of silver, quicksilver, lead, and other supplies for the mines, and the heavy demands of commerce and the military, forced the government to open many roads. In most cases its work was simplified by the existence of ancient Indian trails, which spread out like a spider web in all directions from the capital. A great many of the *caminos reales* were not roads in any sense that we should recognize, being merely mule and donkey tracks. The only carriage and wagon roads were the necessary artery over the eastern escarpment from Vera Cruz and those over the easy gradients of the Plateau connecting the capital with the principal mining centers of the west and north. The rest of the terrain was too difficult for wheels to negotiate, and all the trails and roads were such that only sheer necessity forced the traveler to use them.

The hardship and expense involved in supplying and maintaining the missions and garrisons of the northern frontier were fairly staggering. In 1616, for example, Viceroy the Marqués de Guadalcazar ordered the treasury officials of Zacatecas to defray the cost of fitting out a caravan to convey seven Franciscan missionaries and their military escort from Zacatecas to New Mexico, a thousand miles over the arid and trackless waste that lay between. The train was to be composed of eight vans or *carros*, huge, two-wheeled, iron-shod affairs, each drawn by eight pairs of mules. They were expressively called *chirriones* (from *chirriar*, to squeak). To equip such an expedition was so formidable an undertaking that only one could be dispatched every two years. Provisions and spare parts had to be taken along, as on an ocean voyage. Progress was slow, say, ten miles a day, to allow for the pace of the sheep and calves of the commissary. Forage and water had to be found, game and fish when available, camp pitched every night, repairs attended to, and a guard mounted against possible Indian attack. The expedition of 1631 had thirty-two carros and 512 mules. The total cost of the year-and-a-half journey from Zacatecas to New Mexico and return was 19,475 pesos. In 1680, when the news of the revolt of the Pueblo Indians of New

165

Mexico reached the capital, a train of twenty-eight carros was dispatched for the relief of the province. It caused enough excitement, according to Juan Antonio Rivera (*Diario Curioso de Mexico: 1676–1696*), for the archbishop and the viceroy to go in person to Guadalupe to watch its departure.

For two hundred years a freight and passenger service was operated between Lake Izabal and the interior of Guatemala by the Indians of San Luis Jilotepeque, partly on mules, partly on their own backs. The frightful difficulties of transport in that stretch were typical of much of the communication in the remoter parts of New Spain. They inspired one of John Stephens' best descriptions: "The ascent [of Mt. Mico] began precipitously, and by an extraordinary passage. It was a narrow gulley, worn by the tracks of mules and the washing of mountain torrents so deep that the sides were higher than our heads, and so narrow that we could barely pass through without touching. Our whole caravan moved singly through these muddy defiles; the muleteers scattered among them and on the bank above extricating the mules as they stuck fast, raising them as they fell, arranging their cargoes, cursing, shouting, and lashing them on. If one stopped, all behind were blocked up, unable to turn. Any sudden start pressed us against the sides of the gulley, and there was no small danger of getting a leg crushed. . . . The woods were of impenetrable thickness, and there was no view but that of the detestable path before us. For five hours we were dragged through mudholes, squeezed in gulleys, knocked against trees, and tumbled over roots; every step required care and great physical exertion; and, withal, I felt that our inglorious epitaph might be, 'tossed over the head of a mule, brained by the trunk of a mahogany tree, and buried in the mud of Mico Mountain.' . . . The descent was as bad as the ascent; and, instead of stopping to let the mules breathe, as they had done in ascending, the muleteers seemed anxious to determine in how short a time they could tumble them down the mountain. . . . This is the great high road to the city of Guatemala, which has always been a place of distinction in Spanish America. Almost all the travel and merchandise from Europe passes over it."

Freighting was a huge and profitable enterprise. Rates were so high that European goods sold for three to four times their original cost. To supply animals for transport was another large industry. Mules were bred everywhere, but particularly in southern Oaxaca and northern Vera Cruz (the Huasteca). Certain Indian communities (Thomas Gage particularly mentions the rich Indian mule raisers of Chiapas) became expert breeders and trainers, while every town of any size had a barrio where the mule trains stopped. These barrios were carefully avoided by peaceful and respectable citizens.

The free life of the road attracted vagabond spirits of every color and degree of mixture, skillful, tough, fond of drink and women, dangerous in a brawl, and profane beyond description. Indians and mestizos took to the life as a duck takes to water, and their morals were such that scandalized pastors along the roads kept up a continual lament. The most famous muleteer (*arriero*) of all time, however, was a woman, Doña Catalina de Erazu, better known in folklore as the Nun Ensign.

Rebelling against the discipline of her convent, where a pious family had mistakenly made her take the veil, Catalina fled in stolen male attire and swashbuckled her way from Spain to Peru and Chile. She became famous as a swordsman. Serving now as arriero, now as soldier, her dueling and killing kept her continually in hot water with the authorities, and on one occasion she escaped execution only by revealing that she was a woman, a nun, and a virgin. Her case baffled the legal minds of Peru, and she was sent back to Spain for disposal. The Spanish authorities also gave up, and she was turned over to the pope, who was so intrigued by her story that he gave her dispensation to wear male clothing for the rest of her life. Philip IV of Spain granted her a pension of five hundred pesos a year from his bankrupt treasury. Doña Catalina landed in (and on) New Spain about 1640, took up her old trade of arriero, and became the terror of the Vera Cruz road. Her career reached a fitting climax when she fell madly in love with the wife of a young hidalgo. When shown the door by the outraged husband, she challenged him to mortal combat. The duel was prevented, and Doña Catalina sulked back to her mules, dying in harness in 1650.

167

Her escapades were so famous that three years after her death she was made the heroine of the first American novel, *La Monja Alférez*, printed in Mexico in 1653.

Long transport trains had to be fed and their attendants housed. In the early days the arrival of a train of mules and their drivers caused something like a famine in the Indian communities through which they passed. A system of *posadas*, or stopping places, was set up along the more frequented routes. The villages nearby had to supply them with food and forage, while the town house (*casa de comunidad*) was utilized as a shelter by the arrieros. The Indians were supposed to be paid for supplies and services, and in compensation were exempted from working in the repartimientos. Regular inns (*ventas*) for travelers were evidently a profitable investment, to judge by the large number of licenses issued for their operation, even in the sixteenth century. It is refreshing to come across the names of famous conquistadores, such as Diego de Ordaz and Francisco Vázquez de Coronado, among the first innkeepers.

The system of posadas continued in use until fairly late times. Humboldt wrote of them (1803): "The metizos and Indians engaged in freighting (preferring this life to sedentary occupations) spend their nights in the open or in the *casas de comunidad* built for the accommodation of travelers." John Stephens, stopping at the casa de comunidad of Chimalapa, Guatemala, in 1840, described it as it must have been for centuries: "This, besides being a town house, is a sort of caravansary or stopping place for travelers, being a remnant of Oriental usages still existing in Spain, and introduced into her former American possessions. It was a large building, situated on the plaza, plastered and whitewashed. At one end the alcalde was holding a sort of court, and at the other were the gratings of a prison. Between them was a room about thirty feet by twenty, with naked walls, and destitute of chair, bench, or table. The luggage was brought in, the hammocks hung up, and the alcalde sent me in my supper." Ordinarily Stephens stopped with the village priests, whose hospitality and good cheer he never tired of praising.

One of the charges regularly made against the Spanish administration of the Indies is that it neglected to build adequate roads. So it did, and so did every other government in the modern world up to the eighteenth century, when post roads and diligences came into general use in Europe. Even in the English colonies of North America traveling was such an ordeal that few would willingly undergo it. Although everyone complained of the discomfort of traveling in New Spain, the cost of opening roads anywhere but in the flat places was so prohibitive that a general system covering the country was out of the question. Even now, with dynamite and modern machinery, road building is such a difficult and costly business that many parts of Mexico are still cut off from the world.[1]

[1] The engineers of the Pan-American Highway will testify to the enormous difficulties of road building through southern Mexico. The stretch between Oaxaca and Tuxtla Gutiérrez, Chiapas, bedeviled by steep gradients, cloudbursts, and landslides, took ten years to complete. The first trip over it was made by an inspection car in June, 1945. The great highway was formally opened by President Alemán in May, 1950. It extends from Ciudad Juárez (opposite El Paso, Texas) to Ciudad Cuauhtémoc, on the border of Guatemala, a distance of 2,135 miles. It cost 267,083,000 pesos and twenty-four years of hard and skillful work.

# 15

## THE SECULAR CHURCH

The Silver Age in New Spain was preeminently the age of the secular Church. The friars had been the shock troops of the spiritual conquest; the secular priests were the army of occupation. Their function was to strengthen the hand of the government in the difficult task of holding the loosely joined empire together. The first and most important thing about the Spanish Church which must always be borne in mind is that *the Church was a State-Church, just as the State was a Church-State.* So intricately were the two interwoven that it is quite impossible to discover the fine line that divided one from the other. Their overlapping jurisdictions sometimes led to violent conflict, such as that between Archbishop Serna and Viceroy the Marqués de Gelves, described in chapter 13. To understand the completeness of the fusion we must go back to the Middle Ages, or even back to the Emperor Constantine, when that sagacious ruler saw the need of replacing the anemic state religion of Rome by something more robust, and made Christianity the official religion of the Empire. By his act the Christian priesthood became an essential part of the civil hierarchy.

The political function of the Church was reaffirmed in Spain when the semibarbarous Visigoths, who had overrun the country in the fifth century, finally realized that they had not the faintest notion of how to govern it and had to accept, at a price, the help of the Spanish-Roman bishops. The bishops had, in fact, been the real rulers of Spain since the withdrawal of the Romans. The price they exacted of their barbarian masters was the acceptance of Roman Catholicism (the Visigoths had been converted to the Arian heresy) as the state religion and the surrender of all real power into the

170

hands of the Church. Thenceforth the Visigothic kings were hardly more than puppets: they had to accept consecration by the bishops before they could legally rule, and their legislative and administrative functions were exercised by a council of churchmen. The pact between King Reccared and the bishops was made at Toledo in 587 and marked the beginning of the quasi-theocracy that made Spain unique among the early Christian states.

In the nine centuries between the surrender of King Reccared and the discovery of the New World the relationship between Church and state was not always well understood, and the monarchs often fell out with their priestly advisers, but in the fifteenth century it grew very close indeed. Isabella the Catholic envisaged a new holy state, and she brought it into being with the help of such able churchmen as Tomás de Torquemada and Francisco Ximénez de Cisneros, who, to be sure, were not seculars. In the ranks the secular priests played a part no less important. Through their work the long centuries of sporadic warfare between Christian and Moslem became a holy crusade to drive the infidel from the sacred soil of Spain. Bishops and priests fought side by side with Castilian warriors, more fanatical and, not infrequently, equally ferocious. Spain achieved nationhood through a *religious* war that embraced all classes.

The religious nature of the crusade was not always apparent, for Christian knights had no compunctions about hiring themselves out to Moslem chieftains when they needed the money—which was chronically—but in the conquest of Granada, personally directed by the astonishing Isabella, the religious aims were always in the foreground. The importance of that conquest for Christendom was so great that, in recognition of it, Isabella was granted the right by the papacy to nominate men for all offices in the Spanish Church. That right was called the *real patronazgo*, and it was extended to the Indies in 1508 by Pope Julius II. By his act, every secular priest, from village curate to archbishop, became a salaried servant of the Crown, bound by honor and interest to support it, particularly against the jealous and powerful feudal lords, who viewed with alarm the growing threat of Isabella's despotism.

The discovery of the New World occurred at the very moment that the energy and enthusiasm of Castile had been channeled under the direction of Isabella and her clerical army. Spain had become a kind of theocracy somewhat like that of the Hebrews under King David. To the queen, state and Church were merely different aspects of the same thing, having one common and fundamental purpose, to establish on earth a Spanish City of God, with one monarch, one creed, and one way of life, as St. Augustine and St. Isidore of Seville had long since preached. Thus treason became heresy, and heresy treason. Isabella established the terrible Spanish Inquisition to impose her ideals upon dissident minorities. "Spaniard" and "Christian" had to be synonymous. The Spaniards were the new Chosen People and Isabella was their prophetess. Church and state were welded into one intricate machine; to touch either was to touch both.

The political function of the Church was perfectly understood by all Spanish monarchs from Isabella onward. The Church's political task was to uphold the sanctity of the Crown, to preach obedience to it and chastise disobedience (disobedience was heresy), and to act as an intelligence service by which the Crown might keep an eye on the volatile loyalty of its subjects. Thus, the seculars were the very backbone of conservatism. The Crown favored them in every way. Service in the Church was made an attractive career for men of all classes. It became the ambition of every family, peasant or noble, to have a son in the priesthood, for honor and security, because the priest was frequently the supporter of a large number of indigent relatives. The son of a peasant could usually aspire to be a parish priest, although there are instances of able peasants who attained the highest ranks. The upper strata of the clergy were generally occupied by the sons of nobles. The Church of Spain resembled in its political aspects the later Established Church of England.

It should be clear, then, why the visitor Carrillo was so scandalized by the participation of secular priests in the riot of 1624. They were betraying their age-long trust. As he put it: "The conspiracy was organized, directed, and led by the clergy, that is to say, by the class believed at court to be the principal and most firm support of the government." It should also be clear why the viceroys, from the time of Don Luis de Velasco (1551–1564), supported the seculars against the friars in the secularization of the missions, for the quasi-feudal regular orders were becoming more and more an anachronism in the Hapsburg state, although they still had valuable work to do. The dangerous missions of the northern frontier, from Texas to California, remained in their hands until the eighteenth and nineteenth centuries, and their large establishments and colleges in every part of New Spain continued to be a feature typical of colonial life. Generally speaking, however, the Silver Age was the age of the secular Church. The secular priest was the Crown's insurance against the endemic tendency of Spaniards to cut loose from authority. In fact, the authority of the Crown was not to be seriously threatened again until the seculars themselves joined the rebels, in 1821.

Every Indian village of any size supported a priest, who was the highest civil authority next to the usually distant corregidor or alcalde mayor. His immediate authority was almost absolute. Every self-respecting hacienda had a priest. Every *real de minas* had a priest, the larger ones many. Like all bureaucracies, the secular clergy tended to proliferate. Large parishes were split into smaller ones, small parishes into still smaller ones, until, by the end of the Silver Age, there were more than 8,000 secular priests in New Spain.

These men were supported by a special tax, the tithe (ten per cent of the income of the Spaniards, and ten per cent of such crops of the Indians as had been introduced from Europe, usually limited to cattle, wheat, and silk), by salaries paid them by encomenderos and hacendados, by gifts and bequests, by fees collected for marriages, burials, and the like, and by the income from mortgages and other investments. *All the property of the Church, as well as that of individual clergymen, was exempted from taxation,* on the ground that it was employed for religious purposes. In the inevitable accumulation of three centuries a very large part of the real wealth of New Spain found its way into clerical hands. Lucas Alamán, the Mexican statesman and historian, himself a conservative Catholic, estimated that fully half the wealth of the country belonged to the clergy and pious foundations by the end of the Spanish régime.

The wealth of the clergy of New Spain has been a bitterly disputed subject for more than a century, both the liberals and the devout making such conflicting and extravagant claims that they cannot be taken seriously. All the evidence at my disposal, however, points to its having been very great. There was no rule forbidding the secular priest to engage in commerce or to hold property, and that he had ample opportunities for doing so if he felt inclined, can hardly be doubted. The records of the General Indian Court, of which I append a few samples, are replete with evidence of clerical enterprise.

In 1629 the parish priest of Suchitepec (Oaxaca) was investigated by the Court for collecting two reales (a fourth of a peso) from all the married men in his parish, to pay for Masses on certain feast days, in default of which they were whipped or exposed in the stocks.

In 1631 the priest of Cuescomatepec (Vera Cruz) was investigated for a long list of extortions: He obliged the Indians of his parish to furnish him daily with: two cocks, two hens, two wax candles, two *almudes* (about half a bushel) of maize, one real of butter and chili, two reales of firewood, twenty loads of hay (worth ten reales), two Indian women to make tortillas, a boy to take care of his fifteen horses, and an Indian to work in his kitchen. He assessed each married man one real (a week?) for masses; bachelors, widows, widowers, and spinsters, half a real. He assessed the village five pesos (a week?) for wine. He obliged the Indians to work in his fields without pay. If they complained, they were punished by heavy beatings, exposure in the stocks, and imprisonment. He borrowed money from the Indian cofradía and never paid it back.

In 1654 the priest of Santa María Ocelotepec (Vera Cruz) was forcing each of the villages of his parish to give him a pound of cochineal (worth twenty reales) during Lent. He collected two reales a head from adults for confession; from children, one real. Each adult was obliged to bring him, besides, two almudes of maize, and during his absence from his home church he collected thirteen reales a day in "salary." All these sums were extorted, with the whipping post or the stocks as persuaders.

In that same year of 1654 the priest of Calpan (Puebla) was forcing each of his parishioners to bring a load of hay to Mass, or lose his blanket, and each was obliged to confess during Lent at two

174

reales a head. One Indian who failed to turn over to the priest the alms of his cofradía was hung up in church and whipped. Another died from the beating he received for disobedience, and it cost the village ten pesos for his burial service (the legal tariff being four pesos).

These incidents are selected from a multitude of cases. It is not to be inferred that all priests were rascals, or that the seculars were the only sinners, for the friars sinned with about the same frequency. There were always quiet and godly men who did their duty with no thought of gain and who gave their goods to the needy. But there was no adequate control over the priest who abused his power. Clerical immunity (the *fuero*) put him beyond reach of the civil courts, except in certain criminal cases, and the worst thing that could happen to him for the kind of peccadillo I have described was to be transferred to a leaner parish. There was a great difference, of course, between the incomes of those at the bottom of the ladder and those at the top; but the humblest priest enjoyed economic advantages well above those of his Indian parishioners.

In the vast estate known as the Marquesado de Aguayo, which covered about 30,000 square miles in what is now the state of Coahuila, there were many haciendas, each with its priest. The priest at the Hacienda de los Patos (near Parras) received a salary of 300 pesos a year in 1787, in addition to which he was given a farm to cultivate for his own profit, all his food, a servant, and all the fees for marriages, burials, and the like. The priest at San Esteban de Tlaxcala (near Saltillo) earned 600 pesos a year above expenses. Father Agustín Morfi, who supplies these details, says of the priest at Monclova: "The fertility of the soil is proved by the fact that, although the curacy is worth only 2,000 pesos a year (which does not pay the expenses of the priest's household), he has made a fortune of 80,000 pesos, and this in spite of the loss he has suffered at the hands of the Indians." This same priest, according to the historian Vito Alessio Robles, lived to see Mexico independent, and when he died left an estate valued at 240,189 pesos.

It goes without saying that the priest shared the psychology of the landed class that employed him. Not infrequently he was a landlord himself, enjoying decided advantages (mostly tax exemptions) over his lay competitors, and using their same methods of exploiting land and labor. "Behind the chapel [of the Sanctuary of Guadalupe, Durango]," wrote Father Morfi, "is a spring of very good water, which used to be brought across the plain to irrigate a grove of poplars and to supply part of the city; but a priest bought a small farm in its vicinity and on his own authority cut the pipe in order to bring the water to his own land, thus depriving the city and the poplar grove of its benefits."

Aside from his religious duties on the hacienda, the priest's responsibility was to induce obedience among the workers. So powerful was his voice that labor troubles were unusual, although it must be said to the priest's credit that at times he was a moderating influence with his employer. This traditional duty of the priest in the native village was still a political force in the nineteenth century. The superintendent of a large American mining company told me that in the good old days of Don Porfirio his first recourse in the event of labor difficulties was to call in the priest to straighten things out, at a trifling cost in alms. The strong anticlerical bias of the Revolution of 1910 is understandable against this background.

# 16

## EDUCATION AND LETTERS

If the Church entered into every phase of the political and economic life of New Spain, in the field of education, from parish school to the university, the priest was master—as was true, to be sure, throughout the western world. There were no fewer than forty colleges and seminaries in New Spain by the end of the Spanish régime. All of them were ecclesiastical, serving as training schools for the priesthood, but they also had a large enrollment of lay students preparing to enter the university. Before their expulsion in 1767, the Jesuits were supreme in the preparatory field, operating some twenty-three institutions of learning, one of which, the College of St. Peter and St. Paul in Mexico City, competed with the university in influence, and was almost certainly superior to it in accomplishment. The granting of higher degrees was, however, a jealously guarded monopoly of the Royal and Pontifical University of Mexico.

Founded in 1553 (some eighty years before Harvard, as is always pointed out, for some reason), the University of Mexico was a faithful copy of the medieval University of Salamanca. Education, like political philosophy and, indeed, like all learning, was based upon an authoritarian concept of the universe. All knowledge was either revealed in the Scriptures, established by the Doctors of the Church, or handed down from the more respectable ancients, such as Aristotle and Galen. The seven pillars of learning were Theology, Scripture, Canon and Civil Law, the Decretals, Rhetoric, and the Arts (that is, Logic, Metaphysics, and Physics), all of which were taught in Latin, presumably to keep the sacred precincts unpolluted by the vulgar. The highest chair, and the best paid, was that of Theology, the Mother of Science, which was established "to impugn, to destroy, to vanquish, and to extirpate that which does not conform to the Faith." The place of the university as the guardian of the accepted order of things is best illustrated by the Laws of the Indies, which are quite specific in the matter: "In conformity with what has been disposed by the Holy Council of Trent . . . those who in the universities of our Indies receive the degrees of Licenciado, Doctor, and Master shall be obliged to profess our Holy Catholic Faith . . . and they shall also swear obedience [to us] and to our viceroys and audiencias in our name, and to the rectors of the university." No one might receive the degree of Bachelor of Theology, or that of Master or Doctor in any faculty, without first swearing "that he will always hold, believe, and teach by word and writing that the Virgin Mother of God, Our Lady, was conceived without original sin in the first moment of her natural being, as she was."

Scholastic education at the university consisted mainly of memorizing answers—which was the only logical course to follow, since all knowledge was revealed and set down in books. The bright scholar proved his brightness by showing that the book was right. "In ordinary circumstances," writes John Tate Lanning in his excellent study of colonial universities, "the regimen produced men of stupendous rote memory, along with imposing but inappropriate and artificial allusions to the ancients and the myths. These had long been symbols of the 'compleat' intellectual, the proudest result of education and the surest mark of the colonial scholar. Prodigies at thirteen or fourteen held degrees in law, practiced before the royal audiencia, and competed against their professors for their posts."

It was originally intended to restrict the higher learning to persons without "blood taint," that is, to those without Negro, Jewish, or Moorish ancestry, but, as Lanning points out, "there was little effective prejudice against the Negro and mulatto [in the universities] before the eighteenth century. . . . The rule against blood taint had not been enforced, and some persons of color found their way into the professions, especially medicine, which was not held in high repute much before the eighteenth century." Blood taint also included those whose parents or grandparents had been punished by the Inquisition.

The Royal and Pontifical University of Mexico was a very busy place. In the 268 years of its existence, up to Independence, it ground out 37,732 bachelors, and 1,655 licenciados and doctors. This industry did not necessarily represent a thirst for knowledge. The university offered an opportunity for the ambitious or the talented to join the ranks of the privileged, in the clergy or in the professions. A very considerable number of the students were poor, and the university administration was continually pestered by petitions for exemption from fees. Some of these indigent students were taken care of by scholarships donated by wealthy patrons.

The moment a student was admitted to the university he fell within the ecclesiastical fuero, which meant that he could be tried by the civil courts only for certain grave and specified crimes: murder, treason, and the like. Otherwise he was protected by his cap and gown. From freshman to rector all members of the university hierarchy were heavily swathed in dignity, which went to the length of permitting the rector to go through the streets preceded by two armed Negro lackeys in livery, a privilege much resented by certain of the viceroys, who were not allowed that distinction.

The teaching and practice of medicine came within clerical jurisdiction. Authority and mysticism were the essential equipment of a physician. Medicine, in fact, was not quite respectable, and the best people did not go in for it. It was the stepchild of the university. During the Middle Ages Spanish physicians, because of their association with Arabic and Jewish practitioners, had an advantage over their European competitors; but running against this salutary current was a prejudice against accepting anything from the infidel. So Spanish medicine fell into the hands of the Schoolmen, and the art of healing was learned by consulting Latin translations of Galen and Hippocrates.

Medicine was held in such poor esteem at the university that students of doubtful antecedents were occasionally granted degrees. Instruction was, of course, in Latin, and the ability to patter diagnoses and write prescriptions in that mysterious tongue was an essential part of the witchcraft that passed for medicine. The difficulty and expense of getting a medical degree, however, and the high fees collected by licensed practitioners, brought into being, or rather perpetuated, a class of popular physicians, male and female, known as *curanderos,* who knew no Latin and had to practice their art in Spanish. There was so much agitation on the part of the Latin-speaking medicos against their Spanish-speaking rivals that we get the impression that the principal efforts of the profession in the public welfare were directed toward keeping the curanderos out of circulation. Curanderos, incidentally, still pursue their craft in Mexico and still annoy the professionals.

Among the nostrums prescribed by the learned physicians we can recognize the standard remedies of the medieval authorities. There was a bewildering assortment of troches, suppositories, electuaries, clysters, ointments, powders, purges, and plasters, whose complicated ingredients included calomel, opium, verdigris, white lead, mercury, gums, turpentine, vinegar, herbs, oils, and other things not so nice by half. One bill of medicines prescribed for Doña Catalina Xuárez, the first wife of Cortés, came to 172 gold pesos, which he characteristically refused to pay, and, anyway, his wife was dead when the apothecary sued him. The excessive cost of medical services limited the physician's activity to the more prosperous. The rest of society got along with curanderos and Indian herb doctors— which, perhaps, was just as well. It is understandable why a person stricken by disease first called a priest.

Medicine remained generally at this paleolithic level throughout the Silver Age, although toward the end there were some stirrings toward modern methods of treatment and investigation. Particularly worthy of note was the Protomedicato, a kind of state medical board, founded in the sixteenth century, which had charge of the examination and certification of physicians. It did a great deal toward controlling quackery and malpractice, although it might be argued that popular quacks could do no more harm than certified ones. Still, the Protomedicato had a good deal of power, and, when vaccination against smallpox was accepted by the profession, the Protomedicato was of great value in obliging physicians, and persuading the people, to accept it. This last was not easy. Viceroy José de Iturrigaray had himself publicly vaccinated as part of the propaganda campaign in the anti-smallpox expedition of 1803, by Francisco Xavier Balmis, which was the beginning of modern medicine in the Spanish Empire, but it occurred at the very end of the old régime.

Meanwhile, the ignorance of the nature of disease and the unspeakable sanitary conditions of cities and villages brought a monotonous repetition of devastating epidemics: smallpox, measles, whooping cough, influenza, typhoid, typhus, cholera, and the rest, while malaria, enteritis, syphilis, tuberculosis, yellow fever, and a number of obscure native maladies were endemic. The first century after the Conquest witnessed the disappearance of many millions of Indians, who had no protection against the introduced diseases of Europe and Asia. Some of these plagues depopulated whole provinces, and large stretches of vacated land were made available for exploitation. Epidemics, therefore, may be considered a prime cause of the early spread of cattle raising and the growth of the hacienda system.

If the theologian and the bachelor-at-law could look down upon the physician, the latter could heal his ego by looking down upon the apothecary and the curandero, and they could all unite in scoffing at the lowly surgeon. Surgery was practiced by barbers, who were duly licensed by the Protomedicato, and was restricted to bleeding, to the opening of abcesses, dressing wounds, and the like. But interest in surgery was growing in Europe and was reflected in New Spain by the opening of a school of surgery in Mexico City in 1770, although it was opposed by the Protomedicato on the ground that the surgeons could not speak Latin.

I should not like to leave the impression that medicine in New Spain was more than relatively backward, for, up to the defeat of scholasticism in medicine in the eighteenth century, the ignorance, superstition, and conservatism of the medical profession in Europe and the English colonies were hardly less notorious.

The literary and intellectual life of New Spain during the Silver Age was completely dominated by clerical pedantry. The sixteenth century had produced a robust literature, mostly historical, inspired by the Conquest. Bernal Díaz del Castillo's *True History* is one of the greatest chronicles of all time, but it was written by a soldier in a soldier's language. His crudities could not be tolerated by the learned of later centuries, who imitated only too successfully the wearisome obscurities then considered good taste in Spain. Letters were chiefly concerned with endless elaboration of the commonplace; they were the embroidery and fancywork of an idle class. Cervantes was not unknown in New Spain, but it is a dismal commentary on the times that there is little evidence of the impact of that prince of laughter on his Mexican contemporaries. One great exception to the rule was the playwright, Juan Ruiz de Alarcón, who went to Spain early in the seventeenth century and, in spite of the savage ridicule directed at his deformity (he was a double hunchback), wrote plays of such insight and invention that they are still read with pleasure. Another exception was Sor Juana Inés de la Cruz.

The last viceroy appointed by Spain's playboy king, Philip IV, arrived in 1664. The Marqués de Mancera was a vigorous and effective administrator. He was also young and a good fellow, and he soon gathered about him a company of the pleasantest and most hell-roaring blades of the capital. By great good fortune the Marqués had married a beautiful and talented woman, Doña Leonor Carreto, who formed a court or literary salon of her own and attracted to it the most ornamental young women of the aristocracy. Her favorite lady in waiting was a girl named Juana Inés de Asbaje, who had been brought to the city at the age of eight and who even then was beginning to draw attention by her precociousness. At fifteen she was writing graceful and witty verses, full of conceits after the fashion of the day, bookish and infinitely remote from the strong colors of Mexico, but somehow beautiful.

This extraordinary girl became the constant companion of Doña Leonor. Some of her best poems were dedicated to her "Laura," as she called her patroness (the members of the vicereine's circle had such-like fanciful names for each other). She spent a year or so in this intoxicating atmosphere. Juana Inés particularly delighted the viceroy by defeating the stuffy professors of the university at their own game of citing authorities. She seemed clearly destined for a great place in the world and was courted and sought after above all others. And then, with a fine sense of the dramatic, or possibly because the viceroy was paying her too much attention, as it was whispered, she retired with her books and her learning to the convent of St. Jerome, where she provoked the disapproval of her superiors by continuing her studies and writing.

For the next twenty-five years Sor Juana Inés de la Cruz (as she was to be known thenceforth) devoted herself to letters. Then one day in 1693, in an access of piety, she gave away her rich library and renounced her writing. Two years later her convent was invaded by one of the epidemics that were the scourge of the capital, and Sor Juana gave herself to nursing her sisters. Within a few days she had caught the infection and died, on April 17, 1695.

Sor Juana is deservedly considered the first and best of Mexico's poets, although she was Mexican only by an accident of geography, for she was Spanish in sympathy and inspiration. "The entire work of Sor Juana," writes the distinguished poet and critic, Arturo Torres-Rioseco, "conforms with the best tradition of the Golden Age [of Spain]. It would be useless to try to discern in her work traces of Mexicanism, for they are nonexistent, whether in her sensibility or in her subject matter. Her occasional references to local events and her use of native words are not sufficient reason for characterizing her as a Mexican poetess; they serve merely to lend the grace of popular inspiration to her poetry.

"In her-role as a Spanish poetess Sor Juana fulfills a historic mission, that of linking two continents by means of her poetry and her insatiable curiosity. Not only did she perpetuate Spanish lyric verse in Mexico; she also maintained a close epistolary friendship with the great figures of the court. And even in her cell the nun held a kind of literary cenacle, which was attended by all the cultured men of the time, including the viceroy, all eager to foster in the New World a renascence of the cultural atmosphere of the Iberian peninsula. In her work, and in the example she set for others, the genius of Sor Juana shone forth against the dull background of an era of general artistic decline."

The poetry of Sor Juana necessarily reflects much of the artificiality then in vogue. She wrote with grace, charm, and good sense, and somehow her careful attention to the niceties of versification did not interfere with her music and her thought. At the risk of doing Sor Juana an injustice, I have translated below one of her best-known sonnets. It is certainly not representative of her great poetry, and my rendition misses the curious light music of her lines, but it will serve to give some notion of her erudite playfulness and intelligence.

183

## Sonnet to Her Portrait

The painted counterfeit that you perceive,
With syllogisms false of colors made,
Where niceties of art make brave parade
And cunning craft the senses doth deceive;
Where lying flattery hath dared conceive
To hide the years by ravages betrayed,
Obliterate the scars where Time hath stayed,
And triumph o'er oblivion—believe
Me, is a frail device yet more forlorn
Than silly flowers tossed upon the wind,
Against a certain fate a broken door;
A foolish enterprise, of Folly born,
A sorry, senile thing, which to my mind
Is dust, a corpse, a shadow, nothing more.

Sor Juana stood out above her contemporaries; indeed, she stood alone in the long expanse of three centuries. It would be a dull and profitless business to review the others, who were mere tinkers in belles-lettres.

In the scholarly field, however, Don Carlos de Sigüenza y Góngora, whom we have already met wringing his hands at the tumulto of 1692, was a figure of some stature. Educated by the Jesuits, those excellent schoolmasters, Sigüenza showed an extraordinary proficiency in mathematics and the physical sciences. At the age of twenty-seven he won in open competition the chair of mathematics and astrology at the university. His interests were broad and his activity was prodigious. Physics, astronomy, cosmography, history, archaeology, and Indian languages absorbed most of his energy, while the rest of it was unhappily devoted to versifying. In the physical world Sigüenza was an apostle of common sense. His argument for the natural origin of comets (as opposed to the official doctrine that they were divine portents of disaster) led him into a bitter controversy with the Jesuit scholar and missionary, Father Eusebio Kino, but won him respectful consideration abroad.

At the university Sigüenza advocated the adoption of the Cartesian method and the abandonment of the slavish acceptance of classical authority. Although he was a student of the ancient culture of Mexico, he failed to see any connection between it and the Indians about him, for whom he expressed the greatest contempt, reflecting the prejudices of his class, according to which Indians were inferior beings to be controlled by force and kept in perpetual tutelage.

Sigüenza wrote voluminously in his many fields; in his prose he was the Sandman in person, while in his verse, of which he was extremely proud, he touched the highest point that obscurity ever attained. Since the more involved and incomprehensible a poem was, the greater its merit, it is significant that he carried off prizes in the poetic contests of the capital.

Sigüenza is credited with being the first modern scientist of Mexico. It may be that in him we have a hint of the revolt against the suffocating scholasticism of the university, a revolt that in the following century led to an awakening interest in the world of thought. Toward the end of the old régime timid theses in bad Latin began to appear, which discussed the revolutionary ideas that were to destroy the university and all it stood for. But it would be hazardous to assume that these feeble stirrings of the mind went much beyond the closed circle of the elect. The great mass of colonial society— Spaniard, Creole, Indian, and mestizo—remained untouched by foreign heresies, under the sheltering wings of Mother Church and the Inquisition.

# 17

## THE HOLY OFFICE

No institution in the Spanish Empire has been more publicized than the Holy Office, and no institution has brought more opprobrium upon the Spanish Church. Its prototype of the thirteenth century, the Papal Inquisition, was invented by a Spaniard, Domingo de Guzmán (St. Dominic), and was used by Pope Innocent III to crush the Albigensian heretics of Languedoc and to unify the papal dominions. It was received with particular hostility in Spain, where it was looked upon, not without reason, as another attempt to bring Spain under papal suzerainty, which had been going on since the time of Pope Gregory VII (1073–1085). It was not until Isabella the Catholic was confronted with the similar task of unifying Castile, and the Castilians saw the opportunity of getting rid of Moorish and Jewish competition, that the usefulness of the Inquisition was recognized there, but it was established as a *Spanish* corporation, over the strong opposition, incidentally, of the papacy, and with a good deal of growling by the Aragonese, who liked Castilian domination as little as they did the papal.

The Holy Office of Isabella was a politico-religious engine. Forcibly converted Jews and Moslems of dubious loyalty, known as New Christians, existed in Granada in such numbers that they were considered an anomaly and a menace in the ideal Christian state that Isabella and her great minister, Cardinal Ximénez de Cisneros, were creating. Moreover, ancient ties with the Berbers across the Strait of Gibraltar could make the New Christians a dangerous fifth column should the Moslems attempt the reconquest of Granada, a project that was cherished for many years in Barbary. The Inquisition was set up to control or annihilate these dissident elements. It was backed by the new might of Castile. The liberty-loving Spaniards were obliged to accept it, and in time even came to approve of it. It turned out to be an extremely effective engine. It did its work so thoroughly that within a few generations Spain had achieved religious unity, save for odd groups of poor Jews called *marranos* and the indigestible gypsies, and had been forced into the Procrustean bed of orthodoxy.

Although Bishop Zumárraga (1527) had been given the additional duty of acting as inquisitor, as had the visitor Tello de Sandoval (1544) and Archbishop Montúfar (1551), the Holy Office did not have a regular establishment in New Spain until 1571, when rumors of large numbers of Portuguese Jews in New Spain persuaded Philip II that the danger warranted its introduction. Dr. Pedro Moya de Contreras, a distinguished jurist and a high-minded and zealous churchman, was the first to enjoy the honor of heading it. His inauguration was a solemn ceremony designed to impress upon the people of the capital his awful responsibility in the extirpation of heresy and other abominations. On November 4, 1571, Contreras was escorted to the cathedral by Viceroy Martín Enríquez and the senior oidor of the Audiencia. Contreras' secretary read from the pulpit the King's instructions to all Crown officers, commanding them, under heavy penalties, to aid the Inquisition in its work and to execute faithfully the sentences that it should impose. The citizenry were commanded to denounce all suspects, *even in their own families,* and run them down like mad dogs.

It is difficult to discuss the Holy Office objectively, so easy is it to bemoan its dreadful methods. We must bear in mind that its inventors considered it a justifiable and necessary police force to protect Isabella's new Christian state. Most civilized peoples have rejected its procedures, although, not long since, the Gestapo and kindred organizations have found them useful. The comparison is not altogether just, for the Holy Office was governed by a strict code, however mistaken its principles, and even attempted to protect the falsely accused. Its higher judges, moreover, like Moya de Contreras, were usually men of great integrity. The trouble with the Inquisition as part of the machinery of government was that it enjoyed almost absolute power and the civil authorities had little control over it, for

187

its highest court, the *Suprema* in Madrid, was answerable only to the king. The Inquisitor and all his staff, down to the humblest *familiar*, were subject only to the court of the Inquisition—a system that inflated its officers with a sense of importance and allowed them to indulge in petty tyranny without hindrance. The familiars were the nastiest element, unpaid volunteers who, clad in the protective livery of the Inquisition with its green cross, infested every community, irresponsible, hated, and feared, for at their word any citizen could be haled before the court and jailed, with the most calamitous consequences to his reputation and estate, even if nothing worse befell him.

That the administrative chaos implicit in the Mexican Inquisition did not do irreparable damage to the state may be attributed to: (1) the comparatively small scale of its operations; (2) the high character of most inquisitors; and (3) the general approval, indeed, enthusiastic acceptance, of the citizenry. After all, the Inquisition was a menace chiefly to Portuguese Jews and foreign heretics, whom no one liked anyway, and then the *autos de fe* were the most thrilling public spectacles in a city where life tended to be dull.

For two years Contreras and his staff worked hard at rounding up and trying suspects, which done, scaffolding was erected and the whole population was invited to witness the truly blood-chilling performance. On February 28, 1574, the long line of seventy-four convicts, clad in the yellow *sambenito*, were paraded before their judges and listened to their sentences. Their wickedness covered a wide range, from holding that fornication was no sin, to solicitation in the confessional, bigamy, blasphemy, witchcraft, Lutheranism, Judaizing, and so on. Thirty-six foreigners, mostly from the rich bag of Englishmen taken when John Hawkins was surprised at San Juan de Ulúa by Viceroy Martín Enríquez in 1568, were quite justly found guilty of being Protestant schismatics and received varying sentences. Two of them were garroted and burned at the stake. Most of the others were ferociously beaten as they were led through "the customary streets" at the tail of a horse and suffered the jeers and curses of the populace, while some of the youngsters were condemned to menial service in the women's convents. After serving their sentences several of them recanted and lived to become good Mexican Catholics.

The immense popularity of the *auto de fe* is attested by the windy Don Gregorio de Guijo, whose gossipy *Diario* has already been extensively quoted in chapter 12. He reports the autos, particularly the stupendous one of 1649, with the delight of an aficionado:

April 10–12, 1649 (condensed). The first act is a procession directed by the Inquisition, whose standard is carried by three eminent citizens and escorted by the Knights of Calatrava and all the nobility of the capital, followed by the familiars, the Dominican friars singing responses, their prior dressed in black wearing the green cross of the Holy Office, and by the members of that tribunal in full regalia. The procession comes to a halt before the scaffold, where the Dominicans spend the night, praying and guarding the Cross.

All night long the people crowd into the square. They sleep on the scaffold, or in rented rooms overlooking it. At six in the morning the convicts are paraded, escorted by five companies of troops, who have to fire their pieces in the air to keep back the curious. Effigies of sixty-nine men and women who have died "in the sect of Moses" are carried by Indians at the head of the procession. Next come eight men and five women condemned to be burned; after them, twenty-seven others and the effigies of a man and a woman who died repentant. The great crosses of the principal churches bring up the rear, followed by all the clergy, the familiars, and the civil servants with their black wands of office, who lead a horse, saddled and bridled, bearing a small box covered with scarlet taffeta, in which the records of the condemned are contained.

The convicts are led up a stairway constructed for the occasion, facing the university, and are seated in an amphitheater. The judge, the city councilmen, the mayor, the corregidor, the inquisitors, and the archbishop, with their retinues, parade through the square and take their seats in a convent looking out upon the scaffold. By three in the afternoon the ceremony is over and the convicts are delivered to the secular arm for execution. They are marched to the court of the corregidor, who orders those condemned to die by fire to be led to the stake, the living as well as the effigies of the dead; but all save one are mercifully garroted before burning. The exception, a certain Tomás Temiño, for being rebellious and contumacious, unconfessed and insulting, is burned alive. Those convicted of lesser crimes are

189

remanded to prison, some to await transport to Spain, where they will expiate their sins rowing in the king's galleys.

The burning place (*quemadero*) is surrounded on three sides by wooden stands rented to the spectators. To the very end the convicts are exhorted to repent and die in the Faith. One by one they are garroted and burned. Temiño is saved for the last. Even the Indians, to the embarrassment of the Spaniards, beg him to believe in God, failing which, they and the street urchins set fire to the fagots. Seven of the convicts repent at the last moment. They are whipped through the streets and consigned to the penitentiary for life. Guijo notes that the scaffolding cost 6,000 pesos.

Reporting the auto de fe of November 19, 1659, Guijo describes with more than his usual gusto the execution of the famous impostor, Don Guillén Lombardo (William Lampart), an Irishman of prodigious learning who had served the Spanish Crown in its plotting with the Catholic rebels of Ireland. Thinking, perhaps, to profit by the weakness of the home government, and by the confusion in New Spain caused by the row between Bishop Palafox and the Jesuits, Lampart came to Mexico in 1640 and busied himself in a plot to set up an independent government. With the help of an Indian forger, he prepared a complete set of documents, royal seals and all, which identified him as viceroy. In a bid for popular support, he let it be known that he was the bastard son of Philip III. But his timing was bad. He had no more than put his fantastic plot in motion when the real viceroy, the Conde de Salvatierra, arrived. Don Guillén was arrested on October 25, 1642, and spent the next eight years in the dungeons of the Inquisition, whence he bombarded the judges with petitions. In 1650, with the help of an accomplice, he broke jail, but, instead of fleeing the city, he spent the night of his escape posting denunciations of the inquisitors on the doors of the palace and the cathedral. He was soon back in his cell, where for nine more years he wrote furiously. Although manifestly insane, he was finally tried and found guilty of heresy, treason, and a long list of other crimes, for which he was sentenced to be paraded on the back of an ass, followed by the public crier announcing his misdeeds, after which he was to be burned alive. On the day of his execution the streets were blocked by the multitudes who swarmed in to see the show. Nor were they defrauded. The prisoner was suspended by his right arm, a gag in his mouth, while his sentence was read to him, after which he was chained to the stake with an iron ring about his neck. But the mad Irishman cheated his tormentors by hurling himself against the ring and dying of strangulation. The auto de fe was unquestionably a popular diversion.[1]

A good deal of nonsense has been written about the tortures of the Inquisition, as if the Holy Office were unique in that respect. Most of our popular notions come from such doubtful sources as Edgar Allan Poe and Charles Kingsley, who discovered that spine-chilling horrors sell books. But the Inquisition was a tribunal and, following the universal procedure of contemporary law courts, it employed judicial torture to establish the guilt of the guilty and the innocence of the innocent. It did not inflict torture as a punishment, although that was probably a purely academic distinction from the victim's point of view. Its sentences were executed by the "secular arm," to which the convicts were "relaxed," as the cant of the time had it. Kind and degree of torture were carefully prescribed, to avoid maiming and death. The witness to be "questioned" was duly warned that in case of obduracy he alone was responsible for any injury he might sustain. Methods of torture varied from one Holy Office to another, but the most common ones employed in New Spain were water and the cord.

The cord was a cheap and effective device. Knotted ropes were tied around the witness's arms and legs and twisted with a stick until the knots bit into the flesh. Five turns of the stick were ordinarily sufficient to loosen his tongue, but if he proved stubborn his discomfort was increased by drenching the ropes with water, which caused them to shrink. Sometimes the cord was applied to the head, but the practice was not recommended because the subject's eyes were likely to pop out. Care was also advised in the use of the cord on women, whose fragile bones broke more easily than men's.

The cord, or the threat of it, was usually enough to make the

[1] Lampart occupies a firm niche in Mexican folklore. In 1872 he was made the hero of a romantic novel by Vicente Riva Palacio, *Don Guillén de Lampart, Rey de México*. More seriously, the historian Luis González Obregón made him a precursor of Mexican independence, in *Don Guillén de Lampart: La Inquisición y la Independencia en el Siglo XVII* (Mexico, 1908).

witness "sing," but in cases of extreme obduracy he was secured to the rack and a leather funnel was thrust down his throat, after which a prescribed number of pitchers of cold water were poured in. The water treatment was so painful that few were able to support it. Those who lasted out the course were declared "to have vanquished the torment" and were pronounced innocent, that is, unless the suspicion against them was substantiated by other witnesses, as frequently happened. Judicial torture was a vestigail survival of the primitive trial by ordeal. It is interesting to note, in passing, that it lasted in New England, at least on the statute books, until early in the nineteenth century. The curious reader might look up the grisly institution of "pressing," by which our ancestors extracted information from the unwilling.

In the event that the accused or a witness incriminated himself, as he usually did, he was sentenced to a punishment designed to fit the crime, ranging from scourging and wearing the *sambenito,* to long prison terms, service in the galleys, or the ultimate penalty of the stake. Conviction was always accompanied by fines, or the confiscation of the estate of the accused. The most inhuman part of the sentences was guilt by association, for the convict's family and the second and third generations of his descendants were barred from all honorable posts in state or Church and became, in fact, social outcasts. Guijo reports a pathetic case of the kind, with a happy and unexpected ending.

A certain Captain Luis de Olivera, of the Vera Cruz garrison, had been dismissed from the army because his father had been executed as a Judaizer in the auto de fe of 1649. Olivera protested the sentence and proved, to the satisfaction of the court, that his father had been an Old Christian, with no taint of Portuguese or Jewish blood. The judges handsomely reversed their decision, Olivera was restored to his commission and, seated among the city councilmen, had the honor of hearing the sermon of exoneration. The novel event was celebrated with the inevitable procession, in which the captain was paraded through the streets of the capital in a richly appointed carriage, "for all the world to see."

Although the practice of torture by the Holy Office was the feature that has always excited the most morbid imaginings, its most

192

effective device for making its power felt was a complete and terrifying secrecy. Nothing that took place within its walls could be known outside. The first intimation a man had that he was being investigated was the appearance of uniformed familiars of the Holy Office at his door, usually at night. From that moment until his release or his condemnation in the auto de fe it was as if he had vanished from the earth. The effect of his arrest on the minds of his family and friends can readily be imagined. Terror seized them and they were avoided like the plague, for who knew what the accused might say in his agony? The accused could never learn the precise nature of the charges made against him. He was never confronted with his accusers, and his only part in the examination was to answer a series of questions so ambiguously worded that it was a clever man who did not incriminate himself. If his preliminary examination proved inconclusive, or if the evidence against him was strong enough, he was put to the torture to clarify the matter, or to expose his accomplices. The procedure might take months, or even years. Some trials were never finished, presumably because the accused died under torture, or otherwise. The cumbrous machinery of the Holy Office was so slow-moving, indeed, that at the height of its activity it completed an average of only thirty-four cases a year.

It would be unprofitable to review many of them beyond the samples already submitted, so monotonously alike are they in their outrageous flouting of the rights of the accused (twentieth-century rights, that is) and in the idiocies solemnly recorded by the notaries as the accused vainly sought to satisfy his questioners. Perhaps the most famous and pathetic case was that of the luckless Carvajal family. Don Luis de Carvajal was a New Christian from Portugal. He was also one of the more enlightened and humane conquistadors. His conquest of Nuevo León was the most successful ever undertaken in New Spain, and in a few years he had transformed that remote corner of the kingdom into an orderly and prosperous community. Carvajal's piety was unquestioned, but, unfortunately for him, Philip II had given him permission to bring a hundred families from Portugal to Nuevo León, and most of them turned out to be unrepentant Jews. Carvajal was denounced to the Holy Office for failing to report their presence, and in 1590 was sentenced to six years' exile. The net was spread, and within a short time had gathered in a hundred and twenty victims, including the whole Carvajal family. The most harrowing part of the affair was the torture and trial of his niece and nephew, who, with a number of his relatives, were strangled and burned in the quemadero of the capital.

Even so, the Holy Office of Mexico was a poor thing as compared with the frightful engine of Isabella the Catholic. Not many heretics and Jews found their way to New Spain and, by a humane decree of Charles V, the Indians were exempted from its ministrations as early as 1538. The occasion for it was that in 1536 Bishop Zumárraga had condemned the cacique of Texcoco, Don Carlos, to be burned at the stake for relapsing and practicing human sacrifice. In exempting the Indians, it was argued that in view of the heavy penalty for becoming Christians they would be reluctant converts. Also, and more humanely, it was held that they were in an imperfect state of conversion and could not be regarded as having the same responsibility as Europeans for knowledge of the Faith. It has further been suggested that the Indians, like the gypsies, were too poor to bother with, since the Holy Office derived its income from fines and confiscations.

One of the principal functions of the Holy Office was the censorship of books and the exclusion of all literature listed in the *Index Librorum Prohibitorum*. Indeed, it made up its own *Index* and jealously scrutinized every piece of writing before granting its necessary *imprimatur*. Colonial literature was feeble enough in any case (with the miraculous exception, of course, of the works of Sor Juana Inés de la Cruz), and it is tempting to lay the responsibility for its poverty at the door of the Inquisition; but in Spain the glorious flowering of letters known as the Golden Age occurred during the ascendancy of the Holy Office.

In the seventeenth and eighteenth centuries the Holy Office was gradually undermined by modern rationalism, and it went into a rapid decline under the anticlerical Bourbons, until, in the words of Thomas Buckle, "it was reduced to such pitiful straits that between 1746 and 1759 it was able to burn only ten persons; and between 1759 and 1788, only four." Actually, the last burning recorded in

Spain was that of a witch, in 1781. Judicial torture was falling into disuse at the same time everywhere in the western world.

In New Spain the modern spirit was even more manifest. The Holy Office was openly defied by Viceroy the Marqués de Croix, himself an emancipated son of the Age of Reason. Summoned before that tribunal for certain insults that he was accused of having offered to one of its dignitaries (and very likely did), he appeared, but took the precaution of posting several pieces of artillery in the square outside. The judges took the hint and the viceroy was dismissed with apologies. The last flickers of its old fire burned faintly in 1811 and 1815, when the two insurgent priests, Miguel Hidalgo and José María Morelos, were tried for treason, blasphemy, heresy, and other crimes. The solemn trial of Hidalgo lasted until a year after his death, for the inconsiderate army officers had shot him without waiting for the decision of the Holy Office. Perhaps on that account it was unwontedly expeditious in the trial of Morelos and had the satisfaction of unfrocking him and reading over him the once-dreaded ceremony of anathema before the firing squad could interrupt the proceedings.[2]

Apart from these belated stirrings, the terrible tribunal spent its declining years censoring books and excluding dangerous foreign publications—all to no purpose, it may be added, for British and American smugglers were by this time doing a fine business selling forbidden literature to the famished intellectuals of New Spain.[3]

[2] It is a commentary on the waning prestige of the Holy Office that Father Hidalgo had long since been denounced for reading forbidden books and teaching foreign heresies, but he was not condemned and unfrocked until he was taken in open rebellion.

[3] In 1812, for example, Lucas Alamán, who was to become Mexico's great statesman and historian, then a student of twenty, ran afoul of the Holy Office for having in his possession such notoriously subversive works as William Robertson's *History of America* and Oliver Goldsmith's *The Vicar of Wakefield,* both in English! His books were confiscated, but he was not otherwise punished. A more striking instance of the decline of the Holy Office is afforded by José Joaquín Fernández de Lizardi (1776–1827), founder of *El Pensador Mexicano* (1812), whose acidulous criticism of the old régime and open propaganda for independence would have brought him to the stake in the days of the Hapsburgs.

# 18

## THE BENEVOLENT DESPOTS

The Silver Age in New Spain was an era of consolidation. The fire of conquest had long since burned out, and the Spanish government had to undertake the less spectacular but no less difficult task of making its conquests stick, in the face of hungry and aggressive rivals. In the wild north country, from Louisiana to the Pacific, missions and garrisons were strung out in a thin line. The Jesuits in Sinaloa, Sonora, and Lower California; the Franciscans in Texas and New Mexico, and, toward the end of the old régime, in California; and the Dominicans, in the province of Fronteras of Lower California, braved death and often faced it, to spread the Word of God among the heathen, while soldiers stood by to suppress uprisings, and the settlers got a firmer hold on the Indians' land.

The rich trade with the Orient, by way of Manila, obliged the government to undertake its protection against pirates and scurvy. The seizure of the Manila galleon *Santa Ana* by Thomas Cavendish in 1587, following the terrifying raids of Francis Drake and Drake's invasion of "new Albion" in 1578, led to the exploration of the west coast by Sebastián Vizcaíno in 1602. Seeking a convenient port for the revictualing and protecting of the galleons, Vizcaíno sailed north beyond Cape Mendocino. He missed San Francisco Bay, as they all did, but discovered the port that he named Monterrey, in honor of the viceroy. Upper California, however, was many months away, for the voyage up the coast against the northwest gale was a desperately slow business of endless tacking, during which the crews were decimated by scurvy. So a hundred and sixty-odd years were to elapse before the expansion of Russia induced the Spanish government to establish from San Diego northward the typical line of missions and presidios, the "outposts of empire," as the late professor H. E. Bolton aptly named them.

In the sixteenth century New Spain had been organized into administrative districts known as *corregimientos* and *alcaldías mayores,* under their corresponding officers. These magistrates were courts as well as executives, and their power for good or evil (particularly for evil) was very great. The execrable system of selling public offices had its most vicious effect among them. Suppose, for instance, that an alcalde mayor had paid 500 pesos for his job, as Father Morfi reports. The sale naturally carried with it the implication that he would not be interfered with when he reimbursed himself. He was allowed to defraud the people of his district in various ways. A favorite device of the corregidor or alcalde mayor (there was no essential difference between the two offices, as far as I can determine) was to impose a sort of gabelle called a *repartimiento* (not to be confused with the forced labor repartimiento). He would stock up with seeds, tools, salt, textiles, and other commodities, and apportion a yearly purchase of them among the towns of his district. Since he could drive competitors out of business (he was the Law), he could put prices up as high as he liked.

Local government jobs in New Spain came to be regarded as private monopolies with vested interests, and they could be, and were, sold, traded, or bequeathed like any other commodity. Thus, the corregidores and alcaldes mayores degenerated into regional bosses known as caciques, who tended to interpret the Laws of the Indies to their own and their friends' advantage (as did the corregidor of Metepec cited in the description of the tumulto of 1624, in chapter 13). As they became rich and formed connections with the landed gentry and the higher Crown officers, it became increasingly difficult to control their rapacity. Even the powerful Bourbon viceroys of the late eighteenth century were unable to break their hold, and *caciquismo* (personal and irresponsible government) came to be the pattern of provincial administration. This great evil was one of the principal obstacles in the way of setting up a working government under the Republic and is today still one of the unsolved political problems of Mexico.

All things considered, it is remarkable that the viceroys of New

Spain during the century of the last three Hapsburgs were not altogether bad. Although they did not measure up to the standard set by the excellent civil servants of Philip II, most of them were far from being the conscienceless grafters we read about. In any case, the Spanish Crown was in such a state of prostration that they would have been helpless to cope with the intricate hierarchy of linked privilege that bound together the magistracy, the clergy, and the mining and landed interests of New Spain. The result was that New Spain, for all practical purposes, was virtually independent at the end of the seventeenth century.

The Spanish Hapsburgs luckily died out with the imbecile Charles II, "the bewitched," who had been the helpless tool of intriguing foreign agents, the clergy, and his own mother, Mariana de Austria, regent during his minority. The Bourbons brought a different kind of despotism to Spain in 1701. For some centuries they had been emancipated from clerical domination; they meant to rule in fact, not by sufferance of the clergy. They were "benevolent despots," model Louis XIV.

The Augean stable of Spanish government and economy left by Charles II would have dismayed Hercules himself; but the Bourbons, although "they never learned anything and never forgot anything," did have the virtue of pertinacity. Slowly, with the help of able ministers, such as Orry, Alberoni, and Grimaldi, Philip V and his successors dug Spain out of the muck and began the long job of remodeling her after the French system of Richelieu and Colbert. Those two statesmen had successfully broken feudal and local independence in France by redividing the country into large administrative districts (intendancies), under powerful officers (intendants) responsible only to the Crown. The intendant system was introduced into Spain by Philip V in 1718.

A vast program of reform was undertaken at the same time. The collection of state revenues was taken out of the hands of tax farmers. Handouts to the clergy were cut down, clerical meddling in the government was eliminated, and the sale of public offices was curtailed. Commerce and manufacturing were relieved of some of the suffocating taxes and restrictions that had ruined Spanish economy, and foreign competition was reduced by high tariffs and outright prohibitions. The army and the navy were reorganized along modern lines, and promotion was made the reward of merit. The new royal academies of language and history, the new University of Barcelona, and the technical and medical schools of Madrid and Seville began to gnaw at the foundations of medieval scholasticism. It was revolution from above in the best authoritarian tradition, and very few Spaniards liked it. Ancient prejudice against foreigners, and pride, custom, and privilege, died hard. Those honest men who saw in the revolution the birth of a new and better Spain were dubbed *afrancesados* and were more bitterly hated than the foreigners themselves.

The first half-century of Bourbon rule had no great impact on New Spain. The new viceroys administered the old system somewhat better than their predecessors, but it was not until Spain herself had become strong again that the Bourbon reform was brought to the Indies. The greatest of the Bourbon monarchs, Charles III (1759–1788), needed money, and under the Bourbon system colonies existed solely for the purpose of supplying it. To increase the revenues of the Crown Charles III had to reform the administraton of the Indies. Overseas commerce had long been a monopoly of the single port of Cadiz. Cadiz was a very narrow bottleneck, and the resultant scarcity of goods and their high prices made the colonists trade openly with British smugglers, who during the first half of the eighteenth century handled over half the commerce of the Indies. The monopoly of Cadiz was gradually broken by opening more Spanish ports to colonial commerce, until in 1778 all trade within the empire was made free. Internal trade and protection from foreign competition brought life to Spanish industry and shipping. Traffic between Spain and the Indies doubled and tripled, and the Crown revenues soared to five or six times their level in 1700.

The reform of New Spain was put into the hands of one of the most remarkable men ever sent to the Indies, Don José de Gálvez, visitor-general from 1765 to 1772 (later Charles III's Minister of the Indies and Marqués de Sonora). Gálvez was expected to carry through the revolution in New Spain that had been only partly completed in the mother country in half a century. His formidable commission was made possible by his having as partner a strong viceroy who shared his views and responsibilities, the Marqués de

Croix, whom we have already seen in action defying the Inquisition. At the outset the two were given their most delicate assignment, the expulsion of the Jesuits.

The motives of the expulsion have been debated ever since, and one guess is as good as another. Mine is that Charles III, in his desire to emancipate the Crown from clerical influence, chose the most vulnerable point to attack it. The Jesuits had grown too powerful for their own good. From their humble beginning as the spiritual militia of the Church, they had become in time a kind of praetorian guard of the throne of St. Peter. Their institutions in the Spanish Empire were jealously defended autonomies, which popular imagination (even official imagination) endowed with great wealth. In the totalitarian state of Charles III the Society of Jesus was an anomaly. The order was expelled from Spain in March, 1767, and was suppressed by the pope four years later.

In New Spain the expulsion was planned and executed with amazing efficiency. Not a word of it leaked out. Indeed, the necessity for the utmost secrecy was apparent. The Jesuits, by their domination of the schools, by the reverence in which they were held by all classes, and by their admirable system of missions in the northwest, had made themselves the most influential body in New Spain. However peaceful and law-abiding they might be, their friends were bound to raise a storm of protest which could (and did, in some cases) develop into armed rebellion. Fully aware of the danger, Gálvez and Croix sent military parties with sealed orders to every Jesuit establishment in the kingdom, and simultaneously, in the small hours of the morning of June 24, 1767, officers entered the convents, schools, and missions, and arrested the 678 members of the order and started them off on their sad journey.[1]

[1] In the haste of the expulsion no proper accommodations had been prepared, and the unfortunate men were herded into miserable quarters in various ports, while the government got together a convoy at Vera Cruz. They were not embarked until October 24, and arrived at Cadiz March 30, 1768. Now reduced by disease to 528, they were sent off to the Roman states, where they were not permitted to land. Confined to their ships, they wandered about the Mediterranean suffering from hunger and harsh treatment, and finally found refuge in the Papal States. The total number affected by the expulsion was about 6,000.

The public was thunderstruck. In certain communities, always on the verge of trouble anyway, the expulsion supplied the excuse for such an outburst of rioting and stone-throwing as had not been seen since the famous tumultos of the century before. In San Luis de la Paz, Guanajuato, and San Luis Potosí the jails were stormed, public officials were insulted, and the old cry of "death to the gachupines!" was heard again. In Valladolid (now Morelia) and Pátzcuaro mobs got out of hand and terrorized the town authorities.

But things were very different from the mild days of the late Hapsburgs. In the Bourbon system the single duty of the citizen was to obey, failing which, he had to be taught. Gálvez took charge of the situation in person. With a small army of 600 men he descended upon the disaffected parts, set up criminal courts, and dealt out summary justice in a way that would have shocked Philip II himself. Eighty-five men were hanged, 73 were lashed into bloody ribbons, 674 were condemned to prison, and 117 were banished. All the convicts were Indians and mestizos. It may not be a coincidence that the jacquerie of Miguel Hidalgo broke out in those same places forty-three years later.

Whatever reason of state Charles III may have had for expelling the Jesuits, for New Spain the expulsion was a calamity. Their missions among the virile tribes of Sonora had kept that troublesome region quiet for over a century. The resentment of the Indians was so great that military expeditions had to take over the "pacification" of Sonora, and some of the tribes were never reconciled. Another great loss was the closing of the Jesuit schools, which were by long odds the best in the country. Without the Jesuits to uphold the shaky standards of colonial education, ignorance and superstition became too frequently typical of the clergy and the public generally, and afforded an excellent culture for breeding the germs of unrest that were blowing in from Europe. A substantial material loss resulted from the seizure of the Jesuit plantations, which were models of efficiency and formed an appreciable part of the agricultural wealth of New Spain. The wealth of the Jesuits lay, in fact, not in the hoards of gold and silver that they were supposed to have hidden, but in their ability to make things grow.

The riots of 1767, Gálvez believed, were chargeable to the weak and corrupt government of the alcaldes mayores, and he determined to replace them by intendants as soon as possible; but the intendancies were not established in New Spain until 1786, when Gálvez was Minister of the Indies, just a year before his death.

The weak external defenses of New Spain were a source of uneasiness to the Crown. Bound up with France by the Bourbon "family compact," Spain was dragged into the interminable wars between France and England for world domination, which made the eighteenth century literally "the century of conflict." Gálvez speeded up the organization of a large body of militia, composed of Indian and mestizo conscripts under Spanish and Creole officers. It was the forcible recruiting of this militia which caused the outbreaks of 1767, along with the resentment over the expulsion of the Jesuits. In 1769 Gálvez undertook the settlement and protection of the vast and exposed northwestern section of the country. While on this expedition he got word of the threatened occupation of Upper California by the Russians. To meet this new menace the tireless Gálvez organized and sent off the famous religious and military expeditions of Fray Junípero Serra, Gaspar de Portolá, and Juan Bautista de Anza, which brought the limits of New Spain to San Francisco Bay.

It would require a sizable book like Herbert I. Priestley's *José de Gálvez, Visitor-General of New Spain*, to give an adequate notion of the scope of the Bourbon revolution in New Spain. It touched every phase of colonial life. In spite of themselves the people of New Spain profited by the irritating efficiency of the new régime. It again became safe to travel over the roads. The new trade regulations cut out a good deal of illegitimate gain from the smuggling business, but goods were cheaper and more plentiful for the rest of the population. New Spain not only defended herself, but expended large sums for the fortification of Cuba, Santo Domingo, Puerto Rico, and the Philippines. Ocean commerce (in the short intervals between wars) was safer than ever before. The government went into business, to the great distress of private monopolists, and the tobacco *estanco* established by Gálvez produced a net revenue for the Crown of three to four million pesos a year for forty-five years. The state-operated gunpowder monopoly (gunpowder was used mostly for blasting in the mines) brought in another three million, and minor projects (e.g., the playing card monopoly) prospered in proportion. Outside the government monopolies, private enterprise was encouraged and flourished as never before.

The new prosperity made the eighteenth century in New Spain a century of building. Cities competed with one another in erecting public monuments in the severe neoclassic style. Great aqueducts brought water to the cities and haciendas. Interest in the natural sciences was awakened, and expeditions were sent to explore the geography and resources of New Spain. Juan Pérez in the *Santiago* sailed from San Blas to Monterey and as far north as Nootka Sound, partly to spy on the Russians and British, partly to map the coast and verify the existence or nonexistence of the fabled Northwest Passage. Alejandro Malaspina and José Bustamante, in the *Descubierta* and the *Atrevida,* sailed around the world, stopping at Monterey for a quick look at California. An elaborate botanical expedition under Dr. Martín Sessé spent twelve years exploring the plant life of New Spain, carrying forward the great work of Dr. Francisco Hernández begun in the sixteenth century. The new School of Mines in Mexico City was one of the best equipped and probably one of the costliest in the world. After a hundred years of the Bourbon revolution New Spain was on her way toward taking her place among modern nations. She was certainly the most solvent. She not only paid her own way and had no debt, but increased the Crown revenues to the imposing sum of twenty million pesos a year, of which, to be sure, ten million were earmarked for military and other expenses. Baron von Humboldt, although not blind to the shortcomings of the colonial régime, was nevertheless so enthusiastic that his *Political Essay on the Kingdom of New Spain* reads like a panegyric.

The prosperity of the country was more or less confined to the upper crust. The agricultural workers on the haciendas continued in their status of virtual serfdom, at one real a day, although, as Humboldt remarked, they were no worse off than their contemporaries in Europe. The textile industry, as we have seen, was nothing but a lot of sweatshops—but so were the factories of England. The point here is that we must not expect the people of one age to anticipate the ideas of a later one. An exception, already mentioned, was mining, in which the skilled worker was relatively well paid at a dollar a day.

New Spain and Old Spain both, however, were being driven

beyond their natural gait. The Bourbon threat to established custom and privilege aroused a sullen resentment. And then it was an intolerable affront to Creole pride to have to play second fiddle to gachupín busybodies and meddlers and to see the best jobs go to middle-class nonentities from Spain. As the visitor Carrillo had remarked back in 1626, the feud between Creoles and Spaniards was deeply rooted. It spread among all professions and classes. It split families, churches, colleges, religious orders, and government bureaus into Montagues and Capulets. It was a highly dangerous and irrational phenomenon, and the Bourbon system exacerbated the matter beyond endurance. Let the government weaken again and the country would blow up like an overheated boiler.

When the great Charles III died in 1788 and left the complicated mechanism of the Bourbon state to his fatuous son, Charles IV, stresses began to appear in all directions. The humiliating spectacle of seeing the proud empire ruled by the adulterous queen, María Luisa of Parma, and her guardsman lover, Manuel Godoy, did much to destroy the wholesome respect for the Crown which had silenced open criticism for nearly a century.

The effects of the change were not immediately apparent in New Spain. On the contrary, the last viceroy appointed by Charles III, the second Conde de Revillagigedo, ranks among the greatest. Revillagigedo was the ideal servant of a benevolent despot. His wisdom, vigor, and integrity were matched by his loyalty. His curiosity penetrated every branch of government. He innovated little, but strove to make effective the reforms of José de Gálvez. It was he who finally attacked the problem of rescuing New Spain from corrupt local officials and inaugurated the badly needed intendant system. He so purified the civil service that during his reign the Crown revenues reached their highest point in history. He even mollified the outraged Creoles somewhat by beautifying and cleaning up Mexico City.[2] If benevolent despotism can ever be justified, the fate of New Spain under Revillagigedo would be an excellent argument for it. His stature is evident in the analysis of

[2] Revillagigedo saw the possibilities of the great Zócalo, which he turned into a circular park surrounded by a stone balustrade, in signal contrast to the screaming ugliness of the present paved desert.

colonial government which he wrote for the guidance of his successor upon leaving office in 1795, his famous *Instrucción Reservada,* or Confidential Advice—advice which the next viceroy entirely lacked the ability to follow.

Revillagigedo's reign was the triumph and final flowering of benevolent despotism. From the time of his departure until the end of the old régime New Spain suffered under a series of mediocrities. The first was the Marqués de Branciforte, who was a creature of the queen's lover, Godoy, and who reflected only too faithfully the character of his patron. At his touch the new civic spirit began to wilt. Justice and favors were again put up for sale, and ancient privilege could once more breathe freely.

In Europe the French Revolution had released the storm that was to destroy the very foundations of a system that could produce a New Spain. The frivolous Godoy led Spain down the disastrous course to her eventual extinction as a great power. His first folly was to enter the alliance against revolutionary France in 1793 to avenge the death of Louis XVI. The result was a series of crushing defeats administered by the enthusiastic republicans, and the dishonorable treaty that Godoy made with Napoleon in 1795 earned him the ridiculous title of "Prince of the Peace," conferred by his cuckold master. Godoy became the tool of Napoleon in the absorption of Spain. He brought his country into the dictator's "Continental System" and lost the fine navy of Charles III to Nelson at Trafalgar. The cup of folly was already full, but it spilled over in 1808, when Godoy did nothing to prevent Napoleon's kidnaping of Charles IV and Crown Prince Ferdinand at Bayonne, and all Spain flamed up in a wild rebellion and chased the favorite across the border into France, where he spent the rest of his long life writing his inevitable memoirs, and died in 1851.

The "principle of authority" was no more. New Spain followed the mother country into the abyss of anarchy. Passions and resentments that had lain for so long just under the surface could now be released without the fear of a royal visitor, and New Spain could indulge in an orgy of bloodletting that was not to cease until exhaustion, or until some new tyrant should impose order at the point of a gun.

# 19

## THE GREAT MUTINY

The movement that I am calling The Great Mutiny, meaning the Wars of Independence, was as complicated as Chaos. It was really one of the long series of Creole mutinies that began back in 1566 and, in a way, are still going on. From mutiny to Revolution, we might call it. It did not begin among those who had every reason to rise, namely, the Indians. At first it was not even an armed rebellion.

It began in Spain. Three shocking bits of news exploded in Mexico City at the same time: Napoleon's kidnaping of Charles IV and Crown Prince Ferdinand at Bayonne in 1808, the king's abdication in favor of Ferdinand, and the elevation of Joseph Bonaparte, "Pepe Botellas," to the throne of Spain. The confusion in Mexico will easily be imagined, particularly since it supplied the excuse for each faction to claim the right to take over the government. The city council of Mexico, which was composed mainly of rich Creoles, said: "We shall not recognize the puppet of Napoleon. The king (whom God preserve!) is in the enemy's hands. The Audiencia and the viceroy have not, therefore, any source of authority, since their power derives from the king. Let us follow the example of the free cities of Spain and set up a provisional junta of municipalities to govern until the king is restored." Said the royalist Audiencia: "Nonsense! We were constituted the highest power in the land by our sovereign (whom God preserve!) and he still rules through us. We shall, therefore, continue to rule in his name until his restoration." Viceroy José de Iturrigaray, being one of Godoy's appointees, said nothing.

The Audiencia and the Spanish elements of the capital suspected, with some reason, that the Creoles' enthusiasm for municipal rule was a thinly disguised move toward independence, in spite of the Creoles' vociferous loyalty to Ferdinand VII. (Since 1776 independence had been a word to conjure with in the Western Hemisphere.) The question of who was to rule in New Spain was argued with great erudition on both sides. The merits of the case, of course, had nothing to do with the matter. The talking was a lawyer's game. The real issue was the ancient struggle for power between Creoles and Spaniards.

The equivocal attitude of the viceroy made it impossible to settle the question. Iturrigaray was apparently convinced that Spain could not stand against Napoleon, that New Spain would become independent, and that he stood a very good chance of heading the new nation. So he secretly encouraged the Creoles, who became more insistent in their demands for a provisional government. Finally, the viceroy submitted the question to a general election, in which the Creoles elected all the delegates, and a junta of municipalities was created in August, 1808. Viceroy Iturrigaray began to put on airs of royalty, while the alarm of the Spanish elements grew. When at last it became evident that the Creoles were bent on independence, the Spaniards decided to take things into their own hands.

Don Gabriel Yermo was a wealthy Spanish sugar grower. His Hacienda de San Gabriel, in what is now the state of Morelos, was a model of thrift and good management. His humanity and good sense had led him to set free all the Negro slaves of his plantation, several hundred of them, and they showed their loyalty and gratitude by serving him as militia in the stormy days to come. Yermo was, in short, a benevolent despot in miniature and the highest type of industrious and intelligent Spaniard. So when his countrymen in the capital looked about for a figurehead that would attract the best people to their cause, they chose Don Gabriel. By appealing to his patriotism and by proving to him the treason of Iturrigaray, they persuaded him to lead the conspiracy that was to have such far-reaching and fatal consequences.

In the night of September 15, 1808, a small band of armed men, very probably with the knowledge of the Audiencia, penetrated the palace, shot the only sentry who had not been suborned, and arrested the viceroy. Which done, they proclaimed old General Pedro de Garibay viceroy in his place, and their act was recognized by the Audiencia—illegally, because the Audiencia did not have the power to appoint viceroys in any circumstances. Just as Napoleon had knocked the keystone out of the arch of Spanish authority, Yermo and his fellow conspirators destroyed the principle of legality in New Spain. Their provocation was great, and their concern for their own interests probably greater. Yermo seems to have been a man of integrity, honestly convinced that only by force could New Spain be prevented from seceding. However it was, thenceforth the *coup d'état* was to be the thing, and legality merely a cloak to cover rule by force, as would become abundantly evident in the course of the next half-century.

The Creoles were apt pupils in power politics and soon bettered their instruction. Outplayed by the gachupines for the control of the government, they organized "literary" clubs and secret societies after the French models, particularly one called Los Caballeros Racionales, which is to say, "Gentlemen of Reason,"—"reason" here to be understood in the connotation of the French Revolution. Napoleon's agents were busily spreading in New Spain the new gospel according to the Jacobins, and the Gentlemen of Reason began to see themselves as the founders of the ideal republic. It was all very flattering to starved egos, and it was as contagious as the cholera.

The puppet viceroy, Garibay, put in by the "Europeos," turned out to be a doddering old man incapable of decision. The Audiencia got word of it back to the Junta Central of Seville, which had gained general recognition as the provisional government of insurgent Spain, and the Junta appointed Archbishop Francisco Xavier de Lizana to supersede him. But the archbishop also turned out to be a mediocrity and was, moreover, suspected of being under the influence of the Creoles. This chronic and incurable weakness of the government encouraged more and more people to join the underground movement for independence, until New Spain was honeycombed with secret societies. One of the most active groups was the Literary and Social Club of Querétaro, whose leader was a Creole officer in command of the local milita, Captain Ignacio Allende. The club grew and prospered, and in time came to count among its members influential citizens from the wide stretch of country between Querétaro and Guanajuato. Perhaps the most enthusiastic of them was the parish priest of the little town of Dolores. His name was Father Miguel Hidalgo y Costilla.

Miguel Hidalgo is a very delicate subject to discuss. Mexican patriotism has made him the Father of Independence and a symbol of the revolt against all the evils of the old régime. He has become the Scourge of Tyrants, the Friend of the Oppressed, the Man of Mexico.

All group movements must have symbols and myths. In the United States we have distorted the images of our country's great men until their own mothers would not recognize them. We have made Washington a prig and Lincoln a god. In Mexico the figure of Hidalgo has of late years been deified in school texts and mural paintings until he has little resemblance to the puzzled and sanguinary enthusiast who emerges in the documents of the time. The best thing we can do is to recognize two Hidalgos, the symbolic figure and the man. Of the two the man is infinitely the more interesting.

Hidalgo was not a great man before he was caught up in the insurrection and placed at the head of it. He had lived for fifty-seven years without achieving more than moderate distinction. He taught Latin, theology, and philosophy for some years at the ancient (1540) College of San Nicolás in Valladolid (Morelia, Michoacán), and rose to be rector of it. His unorthodox teaching and his reading of prohibited books was resented by the faculty, and in 1792 he resigned from the College and accepted the curacy of Colima. Ten years later he was posted to the parish of Dolores, Guanajuato, having meanwhile incurred the suspicions of the Holy Office, although the case against him was dismissed for lack of evidence.

Hidalgo loved words and had the power to move people. He certainly thought he had been relegated to the unimportant parish of Dolores because he was a Creole—in which he may have been right. Then, as he saw the better posts in the Church go to men who had no greater recommendation than to have been born in Spain, his sense of injury grew to a bitter hatred of all things Spanish. His personal grievances and the miseries of his country he laid to the diabolism of the gachupines. As his phobia matured, he practiced a number of innocent compensations. He read forbidden books; he raised forbidden grapes and pressed out forbidden wine; he planted forbidden mulberry trees and spun forbidden silk. He also busied himself by operating a small pottery in Dolores. His discontent might have spent itself in these activities, and he might have ended his days in harmless obscurity, if the Literary and Social Club of Querétaro had not offered him an outlet for his forbidden learning and eloquence. He acquired a taste and discovered a talent for conspiracy. The Rights of Man, the Social Contract, and the rest of the intoxicating doctrines of the French Revolution became woven in his mind into a beautiful fabric of the perfect republic, from which gachupines should be excluded.

But even Hidalgo could not forego a "principle of authority." Popular sovereignty had no place in his republic. Its head, he proposed, was to be none other than the incompetent son of Charles IV, although, to be sure, Hidalgo did not know that Ferdinand VII (the "Beloved") was incompetent. It is strange to see the sullen figure of Ferdinand held up in the manifestos of the time as the last hope of the Mexican people. Hidalgo may have been simple-minded enough to think that independence from the gachupines could be achieved by calling in a gachupín ruler, one who was, moreover, still a prisoner of Napoleon, but it is doubtful that the Creoles generally had any such illusion. In any case, Hidalgo could not conceive of a state without a semidivine sovereign, for, with all his oddities, he was a pious man.

The conspirators got beyond the talking stage. The Literary and Social Club of Querétaro hatched out a plot, a very simple plot, far too simple, as it turned out. According to it, at the annual fair in San Juan de los Lagos, on December 8, 1810, an armed force under Captain Allende was to "pronounce" for independence in the name of Ferdinand VII. The populace would join up, and the rest of the country would be invited to go along. To put the movement on a sound financial footing, the property of the Spaniards would be seized and incorporated into the national treasury.

The meetings of the Literary and Social Club were not very secret, and news of the impending revolt soon got around. The conspiracy was denounced to the Crown authorities of Querétaro and Guanajuato, and to the Audiencia itself. But such was the confusion in the government that a fatal lethargy paralyzed action. On September 13 a few arrests were made at Querétaro and the arms of the conspirators were taken. The whole affair, indeed, might have died there if Juan Aldama, one of its leaders, had not ridden the fifty miles to Dolores and brought the news to Hidalgo and Allende. Hidalgo had to decide, and he decided for war. With no military training or preparation, with apparently little concept of the terrible responsibility he was assuming, drunk with the idea of an independent and gachupín-less state, with himself at the head of it, Father Hidalgo gathered up a score of Indians from his pottery on the morning of September 16, 1810, and raised the celebrated *Grito de Dolores*: "Long live Our Lady of Guadalupe! Long live Independence!" But his more realistic followers answered with the old cry of the tumultos: "Death to the gachupines! Death!"

This was a real tumulto, with a real priest at the head of it, and there was no José de Gálvez to string up the participants. The original handful of men from the pottery was soon swelled by a multitude of shouting Indians and mestizos from the haciendas. They knew nothing about the Rights of Man, the Social Contract, or Ferdinand VII, but they did understand *death to the gachupines*: death and booty and a glorious fiesta of blood. They roared through the countryside, burning, looting, and attracting more followers, until at the end of a week Hidalgo and Allende found themselves leading a riotous mob of 50,000 men.

Ignacio Allende, an experienced soldier, had every right to expect that he would be chosen military leader of the insurrection, but he reckoned without Hidalgo, and without the Indians. This was a religious tumulto, and no leader would do but a priest. Allende was swept aside at San Miguel el Grande (now ironically called San Miguel de Allende), and Hidalgo was named *Generalísimo*, although he was totally ignorant of the elements of military science. His vanity was nowhere more evident than in his acceptance of the military leadership of the insurrection. The series of murderous disasters into which he led his mob of half-armed and untrained men had no other cause. Mobs do not win battles. His love of titles

211

became proverbial. He named himself "Captain-General of America" and had himself addressed as "Serene Highness," while he filled his staff with generals and field marshals, appointed without reference to ability or military experience.

From San Miguel el Grande the "Army of Independence" moved on Celaya. People fled before it as before a forest fire. Celaya was taken without resistance. Enthusiasm mounted. The liberators would take Guanajuato; they would take Guadalajara; they would take the capital itself. They were irresistible. Hidalgo decided to march on Guanajuato, a rich mining town then almost as large as Mexico City.

The intendant of the province, Don Juan Antonio Riaño, was one of the most enlightened officers put in by the Bourbons. Under his inspiration Guanajuato had become a center of arts, letters, and science. Among the many civic improvements he had introduced was a large granary, the Alhóndiga de Granaditas, to prevent a recurrence of the terrible famine of the "year of the hunger" of 1784–1785. The Alhóndiga was (and is) a heavy square structure in the heart of the city. Its great solidity induced Riaño mistakenly to choose it as a stronghold when he heard that Hidalgo's army was approaching. All the treasure of the city was brought there, the Spanish residents with their families took refuge in it, and the walls were manned by a battalion of militia.

Hidalgo's forces reached Guanajuato on September 28 and took up positions on the surrounding hills, from which they could command the Alhóndiga. Unfortunately for the defenders, Riaño was killed at the beginning of the attack, and a squabble over the appointment of his successor demoralized the garrison. In any case, it is doubtful that the defenders could have stood off the huge crowd of insurgents, now at the height of their excitement. What followed was one of the most shocking massacres of that fearful time. In Guanajuato there was a lad of eighteen named Lucas Alamán, who was later to play a prominent part in his country's destiny. The massacre at the Alhóndiga made an indelible impression on him and probably gave his mind the conservative bent which has so often been lamented by liberals. Forty years after the massacre Alamán described it in his *Historia de Mexico*.

212

"When the insurgents had taken the Alhóndiga they gave rein to their vengeance. In vain those who had surrendered begged on their knees for mercy. . . . Most of the soldiers of the battalion were killed; others escaped by taking off their uniforms and mixing with the crowd. Among the officers many young men of the most distinguished families perished. Some tried to hide in Bin Number 21 with the dead bodies of the Intendant and others, but they were discovered and mercilessly slaughtered. All were stripped of their clothing. Those who were left alive were tied together and brought naked to the public jail, which was empty because the prisoners had been turned loose.

"The populace gave itself up to pillaging everything that had been stored in the Alhóndiga, and it was all scattered in a few minutes. The building presented a most horrible spectacle. The food that had been stored there was strewn about everywhere; naked bodies lay half-buried in maize, or in money, and everything was spotted with blood. . . .

"The people who stayed on the hilltops to await the outcome of the action came down to share in the looting. . . . That afternoon and night and the following night they sacked all the shops and houses in the city belonging to Europeans. On that fatal night the scene was lighted by great numbers of torches, and nothing was heard but the noise of blows crashing against the doors and the ferocious howling of the rabble applauding their fall and rushing in in triumph to remove goods, furniture, and everything else." [1]

It had been a good tumulto. A satisfactory amount of blood had been spilled, and Hidalgo's war chest had been enriched by three million pesos in cash. The startling success of the insurrection emboldened the conspirators of other groups. Uprisings took place in cities and provincial capitals, and in a very short time all New Spain except Mexico City and a few of the larger towns was in the hands

[1] The horrible sequel to the September massacre occurred three months later. In the interim the Alhóndiga was used by the insurgents as a prison for captured Spaniards. When General Calleja marched west to put down the insurrection, hanging and shooting as he came, Hidalgo's men abandoned Guanajuato. As a last gesture of defiance and hatred, they entered the Alhóndiga and hacked all their prisoners to death with machetes.

of jubilant patriots. Their success was deceitfully easy. They had no organization worthy of the name. Their troops were untrained, undisciplined, and ill-armed. The numerous groups were jealous of one another. Then, little by little the stories of horror and pillage revealed to the Creoles the true nature of Hidalgo's uprising. It was a servile revolt, and in a war of classes they had to stand with the Spaniards or perish. Their private feud could wait. Defenses were organized. Two bodies of militia were put in the field: one under General Torcuato Trujillo, the other under General Félix María Calleja, a total perhaps of 13,000 men.

Hidalgo's forces had overrun the west in a single month and were now approaching Mexico City. Their only opposition was Trujillo's small army of about 7,000 men, which intercepted them at Las Cruces, between Toluca and Mexico City. Hidalgo's huge numerical superiority should have enabled him to smother his enemy. He almost did so, in fact, but the insurgents' fatal lack of leadership and their confusion saved the better disciplined militia from annihilation. Even so, it was a victory of sorts for the insurgents, and Allende tried to persuade Hidalgo to follow it up and march on the capital. Precious time was wasted in quarrels and indecision, until Hidalgo learned that Calleja was descending on him from Querétaro. By this time the original enthusiasm of the mob had given way to lethargy and indifference. The spirit that Hidalgo's insurgents had shown against Trujillo had vanished. An unaccountable panic, or boredom with the game, started them homeward, and nothing could stop them.

Hidalgo and Allende, with a fraction of their forces, retired to Guadalajara, where Allende belatedly undertook to hammer them into some kind of striking arm, while Hidalgo indulged his maniacal frenzy by murdering Spaniards in batches, an estimated six hundred of them. The more sober Allende cast cannon and manufactured hand grenades, to compensate somewhat for his lack of muskets. He recruited the army until it numbered some 80,000 men. But he was not given time to train them properly, and they were still hardly more than a mob when Calleja, who in energy and military ability, as well as ferocity, was the most formidable soldier in New Spain, marched on Guadalajara with a force of 6,000 disciplined troops.

Again faulty leadership condemned the insurgents to almost certain destruction. Generalísimo Hidalgo allowed his Indians to continue their suicidal habit of immobilizing themselves on hilltops, as they did at Puente de Calderón on the Lerma River. The two armies met on January 17, 1811. Calleja's skill, mobility, discipline, and superior arms more than made up for the disparity in numbers. He took the initiative and kept it. For several hours the insurgents defended themselves desperately, but finally, confused by a grass fire, it was said, they broke and ran. Those who were not cut down deserted in droves.

Now the folly of having their forces commanded by a religious enthusiast was sufficiently patent to all, and Hidalgo was deposed and Allende put in his place. It was far too late. Split by dissensions, the insurgent government fled from Guadalajara and set up headquarters in Zitácuaro, a mining town in the difficult terrain of eastern Michoacán.

Hidalgo and Allende, with a small force of about 1,000 men, set out northward in the hope of finding support among the erstwhile rebels of Coahuila and Texas; but no friends appeared, and the ragged little army was surprised and captured by ex-insurgent Colonel Ignacio Elizondo near Saltillo on February 21. The lesser officers were taken to Monclova, tried by drumhead courtmartial, and shot. Hidalgo and Allende, with their senior officers, were put in irons and driven on pack animals two hundred miles across the desert to Chihuahua, where they also were tried and shot through the back as traitors. Hidalgo's trial lasted four months, for he was a priest and had to be properly condemned and unfrocked by an ecclesiastical court before execution. He was shot on July 31, 1811.

Even if we allow for a certain mystical belief that Hidalgo evidently had in himself, and the ascendancy that it gave him over his followers, it is difficult to avoid the conclusion that his leadership of the insurrection was calamitous, not only in its immediate consequences, but in his legacy of bloody violence which all but destroyed the country. To judge by his proclamations, Hidalgo was one of the great spirits of the age. *"We are resolved to enter into no arrangement which does not have as its basis the liberty of the nation*

215

*and the enjoyment of those rights which the God of Nature has given to all men, inalienable rights which will be sustained by the letting of rivers of blood, if necessary."*

Jean-Jacques Rousseau and rivers of blood! Well, the rivers of blood, at any rate, were not a figure of speech. Hidalgo shot his prisoners, military and civilian, with religious conviction for the glory of liberty. We should not, of course, look for sweet reasonableness in a jacquerie, but I cannot help thinking that if the movement had been directed from the beginning by a soldier like Allende, or by the statesmanlike Morelos, the outcome would not have been such unrelieved tragedy. *Death to the gachupines* worked both ways.

Then, as a fitting climax to his brief day in the sun, the old man, after four months in chains at Chihuahua, four months of contemplation and prayer, came to himself and, in his words, "the sleep left my eyes." At the threshold of death his early beliefs returned to comfort him, and he poured out his soul in a *mea culpa* that for sheer poignancy has few equals.

"Who will give water for my brow and fountains of tears for my eyes? Would that I might shed from the pores of my body the blood that flows through my veins, to mourn night and day for those of my people who have perished and to bless the eternal mercies of the Lord! Would that my laments might exceed those of Jeremiah . . . so that in clarion tones I might tell the chosen people of their crimes, and in my deep grief call upon the world to see whether there is pain as great as mine!

"Ah, America! Ah, Americans, my compatriots! And ah, Europeans, my progenitors! Have pity, have pity upon me. I see the destruction of the soil that I have wrought, the ruins of the fortunes that have been lost, the infinity of orphans that I have made, and—this I cannot say without fainting—the multitude of souls that dwell in the abyss because they followed me!

"All ye who inhabit the earth be my witnesses! Be my witnesses all ye who have shared the excesses into which I have plunged, blind and ungrateful! I have offended the Almighty, the Sovereign, Europeans and Americans. . . . I desire and beg that my death make for the glory of God and His justice, and that it be a convincing plea for the instant cessation of the insurrection. And I conclude these last weak words with the protest that I have been, am, and shall be throughout eternity a Catholic Christian, and that as such I believe and profess everything that our Holy Mother Church believes and professes, and that I abjure, detest, and retract whatsoever I have said to the contrary; and, finally, that I hope that the prayers of the Faithful throughout the world, and especially those of these dominions, shall interpose for me, so that the Lord and Father of Mercies, who grants me death from love and pity for my sins, may vouchsafe me His Blessed Presence.

Royal Hospital, Chihuahua. May 18, 1811.

[signed] Miguel Hidalgo." [2]

Hidalgo abjured the insurrection, and the insurrection abjured Hidalgo—which brings us to the second figure of the movement, and by far the greatest. José María Morelos was also a parish priest. He was born in Valladolid in 1765. In spite of the family's poverty, he seems to have had some schooling. He spent his youth, to the age of twenty-five, working on his uncle's farm and driving mules on the "China Road" between Acapulco and Mexico City, although he was never actually in the capital before his capture. In 1790, probably influenced by his pious mother, Doña Juana María Pérez Pavón, he enrolled in the College of San Nicolás in Valladolid and began to study for the priesthood. He was ordained in 1797 and was eventually assigned to the obscure parish of Carácuaro in the hot country of southern Michoacán, where he eked out his minute living by raising livestock for the Valladolid market. In common with many of the Creole clergy, Morelos resented the preference given to Spaniards in the higher posts of the Church, which may explain his

[2] It was inevitable that some doubt should be raised about the authenticity of this famous and explosive document, but all the evidence is in favor of its being genuine. It is written in Hidalgo's hand and signed by him. It is in character, given his mystical and romantic bent, and it is borne out by the correspondence that he carried on with the Holy Office during his imprisonment, although we may allow that he was subjected to almost unbearable pressure by the Church authorities. The documents were thoroughly examined by the noted Chilean scholar, José Toribio Medina, in his *Historia del Tribunal del Santo Oficio de la Inquisición en México* (Santiago, Chile, 1905).

joining Hidalgo in October, 1810. Quite typically, Hidalgo appointed the inexperienced Morelos to his staff and sent him off to recruit an army in the south country. Morelos set out from Carácuaro on October 25, 1810. He had perhaps twenty men and no guns. He gathered up some 2,000 men and marched to Zacatula. From Zacatula he moved on Acapulco, where he arrived on November 12. Powerless to storm the fortress, he had to content himself with blockading the port and cutting communications with Mexico City, a doubtful gain in exchange for wasting six precious months.

Morelos finally realized the hopelessness of his task, lifted the blockade, and moved on Chilpancingo, Tixtla, and Chilapa (Guerrero), where he captured badly needed arms and supplies, and set about training his men. His army was to be the opposite of Hidalgo's. Seeing how the latter's untrained mob had been cut to pieces by the royalists, he wisely decided to build up a small, mobile force of *guerrilleros,* with which to surprise and cut off royalist garrisons and escape into the rough country that he knew so well from his days as a mule driver. He soon showed himself to be a born guerrillero, in a land where the word has meaning. He earned the respect of Calleja, who was given the thankless task of running him down, which kept Calleja busy for four bloody years. Morelos attracted a number of able leaders who achieved distinction in their own right: Hermenegildo Galeana; the Bravo brothers, and especially the son of one of them, Nicolás Bravo, of whom we shall hear more later on; two future presidents, General Manuel Félix Fernández (better known by his adopted name of Guadalupe Victoria), and General Vicente Guerrero; and the man who was to become Morelos' most brilliant field commander and his "right arm," Father Mariano Matamoros.

One might think that the formidable task of creating an effective army and equipping it would have occupied Morelos to the exclusion of everything else, but he was a legalist and a statesman, and had to have a government to make his revolution respectable in his own eyes and in those of the world. As early as November, 1810, he announced the principles upon which it was to be built. "The revolution was justified, Morelos, insisted, because the perfidious *gachupines* were the enemies of mankind, who for three centuries had enslaved and subjugated the native population, stifled the natural development of the kingdom, squandered its wealth and resources, and violated the sacred cult. Now [that] Spain was in the hands of the French, and the *gachupines* were conspiring with Bonaparte to perpetuate their power, all Americans must unite in defense of country and religion." [3]

Morelos' violent demagoguery about the "enemies of mankind" and his nonsense about the gachupines' conspiracy with Napoleon are manifestly echoes of Hidalgo. It is hard to believe that he took it seriously, but it had the dismal effect of convincing the royalists that he and his followers would have to be exterminated, so the war continued to be fought without quarter on both sides. In one respect Morelos deviated sharply from Hidalgo: He abandoned the fiction of bringing over Ferdinand VII to head his state and proclaimed the "manifest heresy" of popular sovereignty (so denounced by the Inquisition in 1808). In his message to the Congress of Chilpancingo in November, 1813, Morelos elaborated his principles in ten articles, as follows (condensed):

1. America is declared independent of Spain and of any other foreign power.
2. The Catholic religion is the only one tolerated, but the Church is to be supported by tithes only, all other subventions being abolished. The sole interpreters of Catholic dogma are the secular priests. [He apparently marked the regular order for dissolution; Morelos was a secular.]
3. Sovereignty resides in the people and is exercised by them through their elected representatives. Government is divided into three functions: legislative, executive, and judicial.
4. All government employees must be American.
5. The only foreigners to be tolerated are skilled mechanics, free of political ties and capable of giving instruction in their trades.
6. Slavery and all caste distinctions are abolished; all citizens are to be known simply as Americans.

[3] W. H. Timmons, *Morelos of Mexico*, p. 51.

7. Laws are to be applied to all alike, without exception or recognition of any privilege. "Since good law is superior to any man, the laws passed by our Congress should be such that they will encourage constancy and patriotism, and moderate both opulence and poverty; [they should] increase the wages of the poor in such wise as to improve their habits and banish ignorance, rapine, and theft."

8. The right to possess property is sacred; a man's house is inviolable.

9. Judicial torture is abolished.

10. Government monopolies are abolished, as are the sales tax (*alcabala*) and tributes; the government will be financed by an income tax of 5 per cent and an import duty of 10 per cent on all foreign goods.

Morelos' ideas about government (none of them original with him) show him to have been a political and economic liberal revolutionary—a very moderate one at that—but they also explain why he had no enthusiastic following among the clergy and the more affluent Creoles, who were certainly not attracted by a program that contemplated the destruction of the landed estates and higher wages for the workers, to say nothing of an income tax! Morelos had signed his own death warrant, although his program in its essentials has been the heart of every radical movement from that day to this.

To go back a bit—Morelos' strategy in the war was to occupy strong points, such as Izúcar, Cuautla, and Taxco, and slowly extend the ring around the capital and strangle the royalist forces. He took these three towns in November, 1811, and fortified himself strongly in Cuautla (present state of Morelos). Calleja, fully aware of the danger to the capital, advanced on Cuautla in March, 1812, but he was without siege guns, and his light artillery did little damage to the adobe walls of the town, so the operation was reduced to blockading and skirmishing. For seventy-two days the defenders stood off Calleja. Their food gave out, and they were obliged to eat all manner of vermin. The death rate from starvation was appalling. Finally, on May, at midnight, the insurgents evacuated Cuautla under cover of darkness and in complete silence. It was two hours before the royalists saw what was up, and then they charged; but in the confusion a large part of Morelos' forces escaped, although his losses, mostly among the civilians, were heavy.

It is the fashion among Mexican historians to consider the defense of Cuautla as Morelos' greatest military feat. Perhaps it was, but from this distance his strategy appears mistaken. He lacked the force to occupy the ring of towns around the capital. It immobilized his army, gave his enemy freedom of movement, and destroyed the effectiveness of the hit-and-run guerrilla tactics in which he excelled, although, to be sure, wars are not won by guerrillas.

After his retreat from Cuautla, it took Morelos six months to rehabilitate his badly mauled army, while he carried on desultory raids in the Valley of Puebla without accomplishing anything of importance. By November of 1812 he felt strong enough to move against Oaxaca, which his unruly troops sacked. Captured royalist officers were shot. Morelos was himself anathemized and excommunicated by Bishop Bergosa y Jordán of Oaxaca, much to Morelos' distress, for he, like Hidalgo, always held that he was a true son of the Church. By a coincidence, Bishop Bergosa later presided over Morelos' trial and distinguished himself by his violence.

With the capture of Oaxaca Morelos' prestige reached its highest point. He now had a base of operations and a rich province to supply his troops. He published a newspaper, *El Correo Americano del Sur*, and opened a mint, although he lacked gold and silver and was obliged to issue copper coins, which, of course, immediately drove out all the hard money and caused a great deal of resentment.

In the spring of 1813, he decided to make a new attempt on Acapulco, which he had failed to take in 1810. Having no siege guns, his army had to sit down to a long blockade. After seven months of it Morelos stormed and took the fortress. It was a spectacular feat, but the victory was an empty one, for the rich shipping of Acapulco had naturally been diverted to San Blas, while the tireless Calleja was given time to plan Morelos' destruction. With the twin victories of Oaxaca and Acapulco behind him, Morelos now undertook the more ambitious project of taking Valladolid. His army numbered about 5,000, and was reasonably well equipped and trained. Valladolid was defended by an able young officer named Agustín de Iturbide, who charged and put to flight the vastly superior insurgent army, capturing Morelos' most valued officer, Father Mariano Matamoros, who was at once unfrocked and shot.

The shocking disaster at Valladolid was the end of Morelos' career as generalísimo of the insurgents, who, split by quarrels and without effective leadership, never recovered from the blow, although they did manage to write a constitution, that of Apatzingán of 1814, which incorporated Morelos' principles, as given above. Apatzingán, in western Michoacán, was, however, too vulnerable to royalist attack, so the insurgent government determined upon the desperate step of marching across the wild mountain country of Michoacán and Guerrero, with the thought of making Tehuacán, Puebla, their headquarters. Morelos was given the task of protecting their rear; but they were surprised by a royalist force at Texmalaca, Guerrero, on November 5, 1815. Morelos stood off the enemy until his government had escaped, and then gave himself up. His men were shot, and he was hurried off to the capital, where the news of his capture was received with rejoicing, incredulity, and dismay.

Excitement in the city was intense, and throngs of the curious blocked the road to get a glimpse of the famous guerrillero. After a hasty trial, the Holy Office unfrocked him, convicted him of the usual crimes of blasphemy, heresy, treason, and the rest, and "relaxed" him to the secular arm. The authorities could not risk a public execution in the city, which was full of sympathizers, so Morelos was taken to San Cristóbal Ecatepec, where, proud and unrepentant, the most formidable leader of the insurrection met his death, on December 22, 1815.

About Morelos' prowess as a soldier one may have reservations, but he was truly noble in this: In spite of his power as head of the military establishment, he refused to accept the dictatorship, as he was repeatedly urged to do, and subordinated himself to the civil authorities, rejecting every title but that of "servant of his country." In this course, high-minded as it was, he was clearly mistaken, for circumstances did not allow time for the long deliberations of a confused government. His humility and selflessness made it possible for the small spirits of his party to sacrifice him for their own safety, and the great Morelos died serving his ideal to the end.

The death of Morelos meant the death of the insurgent movement, although scattered bands, now hardly distinguishable from bandits, continued to harass the remoter parts of the country. By offering amnesty to some and by shooting the others in batches, Calleja gradually imposed peace on the land—a badly needed peace, for the six years' war had brought commerce, agriculture, and mining almost to a full stop. The best lands lay idle; many rancheros and hacendados had been driven off or slaughtered; the country was hungry. A large professional army had been created, with Indian and mestizo troops and Creole officers, who had fought alongside the Spanish regulars and discovered that they were in no respect inferior to them. Most ominous fact of all, perhaps, was that in military service, with its immediate satisfactions in honors, brilliant uniforms, and loot, a great many young Creoles had found their true calling. *From then on, all governments were to stand or fall by their consent.*

Meanwhile, affairs in Spain had followed a dizzy course. The Spanish insurgents had been fighting Joseph Bonaparte and his tremendous brother for six years, with the effective help of the Duke of Wellington and the British army. The question of government during the Peninsular War was a very difficult one. Rival juntas sprang up like mushrooms all over the country, each claiming to represent Ferdinand VII and the Spanish people. In the course of time the strongest of them, the Junta Central of Seville, was recognized by most as the legitimate provisional government, but was itself split by all manner of notions, ranging from conservatism to extreme radicalism. The leaders of the Junta Central, although committed to the restoration of Ferdinand, were very far from favoring a return to the old autocracy. They had imbibed many of the concepts of the French Revolution and British liberalism, and planned a new and liberal Spain—all this, of course, without consulting Ferdinand in his prison at Valencay. The outcome of their debate was the calling of a convention at Cadiz, which gave birth to the famous Constitution of 1812. It proclaimed a constitutional monarchy, with guarantees of the rights of man, freedom of speech, freedom of the press, representative government, and our familiar parliamentary apparatus. It did away with the Inquisition, but appeased the alarmed clergy by establishing the Catholic Church and tolerating no other. The overseas dominions were given equal representation with the Peninsula, but the seat of government was to remain in Spain.

Representatives from the whole Spanish world met in Cadiz, and the congress was immediately split into the usual factions of Spaniards and Americans. The American delegates insisted on rights of local government which would have made the dominions virtually independent. The Spanish delegates would tolerate no such heresy. The congress was a lawyer's paradise. Its abiding faith in the efficacy of the written word led to endless argument and amendment, until the constitution attained vast dimensions. Meanwhile, the half-starved soldiers of Spain fought the French in the mountains of Castile, and in New Spain conspiracy and treason flourished, with the results that we have seen.

Napoleon's defeat in 1814 brought the longed-for Ferdinand back to Spain, where he was received with delirious joy. A delegation of doubting representatives from the Cadiz government made him swear to observe the new constitution, and the *liberalitos* sat back to enjoy the millennium. Ferdinand, however, had not the slightest desire to become a constitutional monarch. He speedily gathered about him the numerous reactionary elements of the country, scrapped the constitution, and inaugurated a reign of terror. The liberals were jailed or exiled, and the Inquisition was restored. In a word, Ferdinand VII, with the backing of the Holy Alliance, was out to obliterate even the memory of the French Revolution and its Spanish echoes. The monarchist party took heart everywhere. In New Spain the Creoles had their Ferdinand at last, and their argument had lost its punch. The gachupines were in the saddle and meant to stay there. They had learned nothing from the insurrection.

Ferdinand's stupidity led him to undertake the suppression of the liberties which even the reactionaries had begun to enjoy under the enlightened Bonapartes. The exiled liberals, operating principally from London, kept up a steady fire of criticism and propaganda. Ferdinand's complete bungling of the government of his prostrate country alienated his supporters. Masonic clubs and secret societies plotted his overthrow. The army was shot through with Masonic doctrines. For six long years Spain seethed and bubbled with plots and repressions, until one day in March, 1820, the troops of Colonel Rafael Riego, on their way for service in Buenos Aires, did a rightabout and marched on Madrid.

Spain was electrified. Liberals and Masons came out of their holes and flocked to Riego's banner. The reactionary government fell without striking a blow, and Ferdinand VII hastened for the second time to swear to uphold the Constitution of 1812. Liberal light-heartedness and wishful thinking could hardly go farther than to accept the word of that proved trickster. Two years later, in 1823, a French army (the "100,000 Sons of St. Louis") under the Duc d'Angoulême, crossed the Pyrenees to teach the liberals of Spain that royalty could not be thus lightly insulted, and within weeks the country was again groaning under the ferocious despotism of Ferdinand, which lasted until his death in 1833.

In New Spain the *coup d'état* of Riego was welcomed by liberal and separatist Creoles (not by any means by all Creoles), and unrepentant insurgents. The Spaniards, of course, heard the news with consternation. And then, when the Spanish Cortes showed itself to be radical and anticlerical, and when the restored freedom of the press made public all the ancient feuds and rivalries, the rift between Creoles and gachupines widened beyond hope of healing. The Constitution of 1812 was proclaimed for the second time in Mexico City on May 3, 1820, and the whole political deck of New Spain was reshuffled and dealt. The new alignments were astonishing: *For immediate independence from Spain, the conservative Creoles, the Spaniards, the upper clergy, and the Audiencia.* The erstwhile liberals and insurgents were in a state of confusion and did nothing.

What the new reactionary conspiracy needed was military force, and it was at hand in the person of Colonel Agustín de Iturbide, who had crushed Morelos at Valladolid, and who very likely already saw himself at the head of the new nation. In the south country the remnants of the insurgent army were still active under General Vicente Guerrero. Iturbide had no difficulty in persuading that honest and simple-minded patriot to join the new and glorious movement for independence. The two met at Iguala. The outcome of their meeting was the first of the endless series of "plans" that make the history of modern Mexico so confusing. A "plan" is the proclamation of the aims or principles of the leaders of a rebellion. It is their justification for the seizure of the government by force. Hence, the "plan" is the instrument by which a military leader tries to make his act palatable to the rest of the country. "Plans" sometimes mean something. More frequently they mean that someone wants power and what goes with it. *All governments of Mexico, from Iturbide's day to this, have been established by military force and justified by "plans." The "plan," then, may be considered the fundamental constitution of Mexico.*

Iturbide's "Plan of Iguala," published on February 24, 1821, had many things to recommend it to a war-weary country. It proclaimed immediate and complete independence from Spain, thus pleasing the Creoles and the insurgents; it proclaimed equal treatment for Spaniards and Creoles, thus easing the chronic alarm of the gachupines; and it proclaimed the supremacy of the Catholic religion and the intolerance of all others, thus appeasing the clergy and the pious. Most portentous and significant item of all, it placed the guarantees of these three principles in the hands of the army, which thereupon took the name of the Army of the Three Guarantees, shortened to *Trigarante*.

The skeptics, the Masons, the liberals, were outnumbered and outmaneuvered. The Army of the Three Guarantees had a walkaway. A new viceroy, Don Juan O'Donojú, although himself a Mason, speedily came to face-saving terms with Iturbide's overwhelming force. Royalist officers and troops were readily suborned and did little to oppose the Trigarantes, and so, after a spell of parading about the country to let it know who was master, Iturbide took the capital on September 27, 1821, and proclaimed the new Empire of Mexico. Mexico was free at last!

The tragedy of Mexico cannot be measured. Her spurious "freedom" was the logical outgrowth of the Spanish plot of 1808, which had brought about the destruction of orderly government. Iturbide's seizure of power was the triumph of lawless force and lawless privilege. Perhaps the alternative was anarchy, as Lucas Alamán and Iturbide's modern apologist, José Vasconcelos, suggest, but it is difficult to see in Iturbide anything more than a shallow adventurer bent on power. He did win independence from Spain, but at the price of delivering his country into the hands of the very forces that had made independence desirable, for it should be borne in mind that Iturbide's *coup d'état* was a reaction against the constitutional monarchy of Spain. If we compare Iturbide with the lofty Morelos, the "Liberator" shrinks to his true dimensions.

The new rulers of Mexico were the military of Iturbide's complexion. Their will was law; assassination and betrayal were their weapons; their price was the wealth of their country. Under their rule Mexico was to be the scene of bloody *opéra bouffe* for long years, until the whole inglorious farce was knocked into a cocked hat by Winfield Scott and a handful of Yankees.

Iturbide wasted no time in showing his colors. He used the ragged patriots of General Guerrero for parade purposes until he was safely seated in the capital, and then quietly scuttled the whole party of the insurgents. A hand-picked "Committee of Notables" proving to be more difficult to manipulate than he had reckoned with, Iturbide called a Constitutional Congress in February, 1822, to determine the form of government of the new Empire. The congress was split by the usual feud, but was not sufficiently docile to his will either. It not only attempted to finance the government by reducing the salaries of the military, but had the temerity to propose the reduction of the army to half its size! Mexico, however, could not hope to elude her fate by any such legalistic nonsense. In the night of May 18, 1822, troops rushed through the streets of the capital shouting "Long live the Emperor! Long live Agustín I!" Léperos and a hired claque joined in the uproar, and by dawn Mexico City was witnessing a classical tumulto. It also found Iturbide willing to sacrifice himself for the fatherland, and he accepted the imperial crown from his own hands.

There is no need to review in detail the ridiculous spectacle of Iturbide's "reign." The Emperor dressed himself up to look the part. Court etiquette and rules of protocol became the most pressing business of the palace. A brand-new flock of condes, marqueses, princes of the blood, and lords and ladies in waiting was created, and they strutted about with their "riband, star, and a' that," while a desperate Congress exhausted its ingenuity to finance the extravagant show.

Forced loans disgusted the rich; clerical reaction suppressed liberties; Masons and liberals renewed their secret meetings; and lampoons and pasquinades at the expense of the make-believe royalty were scrawled in public places. Finery filled no bellies. Worst of all, Iturbide treated his ancient comrades in arms with a more than regal condescension.

The commandant of the port of Vera Cruz was a dashing young Creole with the gift of gab and a boundless ambition, who had been one of the first to "pronounce" for the "Liberator and Emperor." On his way to Mexico City to receive his expected reward, he was met by the news that he had been removed from his command, and he furiously turned back to Vera Cruz nursing dark thoughts. His name was Antonio López de Santa Anna.

Iturbide had shown the way for his own undoing. His calamitous government, his ruinous fiscal makeshifts, his idiotic pretensions, his clericalism—all these things rapidly cemented a powerful opposition. The patriots, the Masons, the old republicans and insurgents, and disappointed army men had plenty of reason to destroy the emperor they had so recently acclaimed. Santa Anna, whose greatest gift was to smell out a popular cause and put himself at the head of it, "pronounced" against Iturbide in December, 1822. By February he had attracted enough adherents to formulate the indispensable "plan."

The "Plan of Casa Mata" had nothing extraordinary about it. It demanded the abolition of the "empire," the exile of Iturbide, and the establishment of a federal republic under a constitution. The nominal head of the "Plan of Casa Mata" was insurgent General Guadalupe Victoria, who thus became the first president of Mexico. News of the pronunciamiento spread with great rapidity, and, almost before he knew what was going on, Agustín I was on his way into exile, under penalty of death if he should return. Badly advised by optimistic friends, Iturbide returned to Mexico a few months later, armed with a printing press. He was arrested and, on July 19, 1824, the state legislature of Tamaulipas ordered him shot. Iturbide died well. Iturbide to his executioners: "Fellow Mexicans, in the moment of my death I recommend to you the love of our country and the observance of our holy religion. . . . I die for having returned to help you, and I die happy, for I die among you!"

Iturbide's fatal legacy to his country was a method which was to be perfected by the most mischievous figure in the history of the Republic, the actor Antonio López de Santa Anna.

# 20

## SANTA ANNA'S LEG

It is not easy to follow the thread of reason through the generation following the Independence of Mexico. The loosely cemented strata of colonial society had split apart in the cataclysm of 1810–1821, and their mending is still an uncertain and remote aspiration. The various strata, broadly speaking, may be labeled: conservative (the upper clergy, and the landed and moneyed elements generally); liberal (anticlerical, anti-Spanish, democratic, at least in theory); military (the growing officer caste, mostly Creole, usually running with the conservatives, but likely to favor the winner); and the forgotten Indians, who supplied most of the cannon fodder. It was the beginning of the age of *caudillos*. A caudillo is a military chieftain, like Iturbide, Santa Anna, or Juan Perón (or like a thousand others who will occur to the reader), ruling by force, whatever the pretext. All Spanish America fell into the hands of caudillos a hundred-odd years ago. Most of the "republics," in fact, are still in their hands.

When the old authoritarian system of Spain collapsed, it left no body of citizens, in the Peninsula or in America, trained to assume the responsibility of government. If a situation came up in the old régime it was the autocrat's business to meet it. Those outside the bureaucratic hierarchy were supposed to obey and ask no questions. Autocracy was irresponsible and it tended to foster irresponsibility. The so-called ruling class of New Spain was not a ruling class in the sense that it could take over the machinery of government and run it, say, as the upper and middle classes of England did. The wealthy and privileged of New Spain were as irresponsible as the Indians they despised, and, when their wealth and privileges were threatened, they acted like spoiled children and threw things around. It was this recklessness and frivolity that made it impossible to set up a working government after Independence, and that same element continued to overthrow every government that in any way menaced its privileges and comfort. It was a lawless society; it had destroyed law. So it fell an easy prey to the first uniformed brigand who had the power to enforce his will. There were, unfortunately, a great many uniformed and unemployed brigands left over from the late wars, and one had to make the doubtful choice of the least threatening of them.

The more respectable Creoles, as a rule, avoided politics. The type of self-made general with whom they would have to associate filled them with disgust, and they were content to live apart, paying blackmail and extortion, while the country was bled white by its military parasites. (I am referring, of course, to those like Iturbide and Santa Anna, for there were noble exceptions, like the magnanimous Nicolás Bravo, who achieved deserved fame *by refusing to kill his prisoners*.) There is no other explanation for the toleration of *santanismo* (Santa Anna-ism). With a modicum of civic spirit the numerous Creoles could have shaken off their incubus; but the comfortable habits of generations were more precious, and, anyway, a great many of them were in uniform themselves. Life in the capital continued to be as gay and reckless and frivolous as if the massacre at the Alhóndiga had never taken place: cockfights and bullfights and the eternal round of flirting and parading on the boulevards—the amusements of a class that had no useful thing to do.

There were honorable exceptions among them also: men who fought on the conservative or liberal side for a new and finer country, men like Lucas Alamán, Miguel Ramos Arispe, and Valentín Gómez Farías, but the exceptions were too few to alter the picture materially. While Santa Anna's unpaid army was fighting to keep Texas in the Republic, there was little indication in the capital that Mexico was facing the gravest crisis in her history. That was the generals' business, and what the better people thought of the generals may be gathered from the fact that no great opprobrium attached to Santa Anna for his disgraceful defeat at San Jacinto and his more than disgraceful explanation of it. Generals were expected to lie and steal and betray one another, and sell out to the highest bidder—in a word, santanismo. And santanismo existed because those who might have prevented it did not make the effort. Perhaps the deadliest heritage of Spanish autocracy was the psychology that kept the Creole class in a state of resentful aloofness.

Meanwhile, Mexico lay prostrate, and her body was fought over by uniformed bandits in and out of the government, and by the foreigners who thought to inherit the wealth of the Indies, now that Spain was out of the way. The misery of Mexico under her gay exterior can be imagined, but Creole society carried on. A new upper class appeared, the military, parvenu and jealous of its position, the men overdecorated, the women overdressed. Fanny Calderón was shocked by their vulgarity.

"18th [of January, 1840]," she wrote in her incomparable *Life in Mexico*, "for the last few days our rooms have been filled with visitors, and my eyes are scarcely yet accustomed to the display of diamonds, pearls, silks, satins, blondes, and velvets, in which the ladies have paid their first visits of etiquette. . . . The Señora B—a, the wife of a general, extremely rich, and who has the handsomest house in Mexico. Dress of purple velvet, embroidered all over with flowers of white silk; white satin shoes and *bas à jours*; a deep flounce of Mechlin appearing below the velvet dress, which was short. A mantilla of black blonde, fastened by three diamond aigrettes. Diamond earrings of extraordinary size. A diamond necklace of immense value, and beautifully set. A necklace of pear pearls, valued at twenty thousand dollars. A diamond sévigné. A gold chain going three times round the neck, and touching the knees. On every finger two diamond rings, like little watches. . . ."

The political life of the time has the elusive quality of a masque. We read the lines, and they seem to mean something, but they are confusingly remote from the action. The best actor and leading man of the masque was Antonio López de Santa Anna, the incredible Santa Anna, whose first public appearance of importance was at the overthrow of Iturbide. Santa Anna had an uncanny stage sense and could time his entrances and exits to a second. He also knew when to stay in the wings.

Iturbide's fall had left the national affairs in a terrible muddle, and Congress hastily patched up a provisional government, the *Poder Ejecutivo,* which was put into the hands of three tried insurgent generals, Guadalupe Victoria, Nicolás Bravo, and Pedro Negrete. Generals had inherited the "principle of authority." These three men had proved their worth on the battlefield, but civil government was a mystery to them, so they were given a cabinet to administer the various services. The man chosen for the key position, Minister of State, was the young man whom we first met at the Alhóndiga in 1810, Don Lucas Alamán.

Alamán was a Creole aristocrat who had somehow escaped the sloth that too frequently paralyzed the members of his class. He had been educated as a mining engineer, first at the School of Mines in Mexico City, later in France and Germany. He had visited England in the spring of 1815 and there saw the light, for in England's industry, her conservative and (relatively) responsible aristocracy, her opulence, and, above all, her orderliness, he discovered the qualities that his own country needed. There could be no Alhóndiga massacre in England. Alamán's admiration for England and English institutions was to guide him in all the plans he conceived for the rehabilitation of Mexico. Order became Alamán's god; to achieve order he allied himself with those who had destroyed order, and with the man who was to destroy Mexico, Antonio López de Santa Anna.

Alamán had served as Minister of State under Iturbide, and his youth (he was thirty), energy, knowledge, and integrity make him the one bright spot in that fantastic adventure. In his philosophy he was a benevolent despot of the eighteenth century, born out of his time. He despised and dreaded the half-baked Jacobinism of the liberals and did his utmost to create a strong centralized government. He had a clear vision of the growing might of the United States, and opposed Manifest Destiny at every turn. At that time we were looking at the Isthmus of Tehuantepec as a possible corridor to the Pacific, but Alamán blocked us with a plan to colonize it. To remedy Mexico's thin population and its lack of capital (most of which had gone with the Spaniards), Alamán proposed the admission of skilled foreign mechanics and foreign capital under strict supervision—one of Morelos' ten points. Above all he insisted on a strong government

233

for the protection of capital and industry. He was bitterly opposed by the radicals in Congress and by the men who wanted a weak government for purposes of their own. For a year he was attacked as a monarchist, priest-lover, autocrat, hispanophile, crypto-gachupín, and a number of less pleasant things. It all came to a head in a tumulto and pronunciamiento led by General José María Lobato in January, 1824, and Alamán was forced to resign.

At the opposite pole from Alamán stood the liberal leaders, Miguel Ramos Arispe and Valentín Gómez Farías, whose political creed was a rationalization of *death to the gachupines*. Under their inspiration the liberal Congress wrote the first Constitution of Mexico, that of 1824, a naïve document incorporating a good many features of the Constitution of the United States. Their prescription for the government of Mexico was complete decentralization, a federation of semiautonomous states. The federalists did everything they could to weaken the executive. They even made our early mistake of having the two highest offices go to the competing candidates for the presidency, a mistake that was to cause endless confusion and bloodshed in the years to come.

The federal system was probably the worst that could have been adopted in the circumstances. It was based on the fallacy that the old Spanish administrative districts were independent entities, each with a culture and destiny of its own. Throughout Spanish America, indeed, the endemic anarchy of the first half-century of independence in chargeable largely to that assumption. The liberal authors of the Constitution of 1824 took it for granted that everything in the Spanish system was bad and that the only thing to do was to throw it all out and make a fresh start. They ignored the immense weight of three centuries of habit, and they chose to ignore also the fact that the old system, with all its faults, was a tried and working system, while the new Constitution erected a weak and unfamiliar government in a country ravaged by civil war and overrun by bandits; riveted upon it the tyranny of provincial caciques; allowed for no effective check on the Church or the army, which by that time was a privileged caste, infinitely more rapacious than anything seen in colonial times; and it imposed an uncomprehended democratic ideology upon a people who had known nothing but rule from above for a very long time. In short, the federal system was an invitation to anarchy.

With all its pretensions of democracy, the Constitution of 1824 was another "plan," imposed by the radicals in Congress, with the backing of foreign agents and provincial satraps. But there it was, and nineteen more or less independent republics were created, each with the fatal power of accepting the Constitution or ignoring it—a tradition that still persists, making the state governments of Mexico something of a puzzle to outsiders, although of late years the strong Revolutionary Party (PRI) has successfully suppressed the tendency of local caciques to shake off control from Mexico City.

The first president chosen under the new Constitution was the amiable and patriotic insurgent general, Guadalupe Victoria, who had been Santa Anna's figurehead in the "Plan de Casa Mata." The vice president and choice of the minority was one of Morelos' former generals, the decent and civilized Nicolás Bravo. But always generals! The government was a hodgepodge selected from all factions. The hated but indispensable aristocrat, Lucas Alamán, was again called to head the Ministry of State, and, through innocence or patriotism, he worked for the crazy-quilt government as if he thought it stable or desirable. He negotiated with George Canning for the recognition of Mexican independence, and signed a commercial treaty with England at the same time. He continued to oppose Manifest Destiny and became the thorn in the flesh of our meddling minister, Joel Poinsett. He refused to open the Santa Fe Trail to American commerce until we should conclude a commerical treaty with Mexico, while at the same time he discreetly put obstacles in the way of that treaty. His "perfidy" (according to Poinsett) led him to oppose the admission of American settlers into Texas. The radicals and Poinsett's "York Rite" Masons labeled Alamán antiprogressive, Anglophile, undemocratic, despotic; they accused him of high crimes, misdemeanors, and treason; and they brought about his second fall in September, 1825. Alamán's defeat was a triumph for the centrifugal forces of Mexico and, as Poinsett wrote to Secretary of State Henry Clay, it was also a victory for the United States over England.

President Guadalupe Victoria lasted out his full term of four years

—a phenomenon that was not to be repeated for a long time. His administration was threatened only once, in December, 1827, by the vice president, General Bravo, now the hope of the conservatives, whose "plan" demanded the suppression of secret societies (the Masons) and the expulsion of Joel Poinsett, and, of course, the creation of a strong central government. Bravo was unsuccessful and had to flee the country. The exile traffic was to strain the scanty capacity of the Vera Cruz road for many years.

In the election of 1828 the radical "York Rite" party, supported by Poinsett, backed the old Indian insurgent, General Vicente Guerrero, against the "Scottish Rite" conservative candidate, General Manuel Gómez Pedraza, a former officer in the royal army. (The reader should not let himself be confused by the Masonic labels. The lodges only in the loosest sense represented opposing philosophies, but were hardly more than pressure groups supporting this or that candidate according to their interests.) Pedraza won the election by the close margin of ten to nine (each state having one vote), and Guerrero was persuaded to "pronounce."

For four years Santa Anna, like Br'er Fox, had lain low, but now his nose told him that the wind was blowing liberal, and so from his lair in Vera Cruz he "pronounced" Guerrero president. Santa Anna was arbiter of Mexico.

One of the incidents of the Victoria administration was the first of a series of expulsions of the Spaniards who had remained in Mexico under Iturbide's "Three Guarantees." The expulsion was a reprisal against Spain for refusing to recognize Mexican independence. At the same time it was a triumph for the patriots who were carrying on their ancient feud with the gachupines. It was also a triumph for Joel Poinsett and those foreigners who aimed to replace the Spaniards as the exploiters of the country's resources. But for Mexico it was a disaster, for the Spaniards were the middle class of Mexico. Many of them had Mexican wives, and their children were Mexican. They ran the shops and the small factories; they managed the haciendas; they owned a substantial part of the vanishing capital of the country, and they took it with them. A second expulsion in 1829 was a reprisal against the silly attempt of Ferdinand VII to

236

reconquer Mexico by landing a small expeditionary force at Tampico, under the command of General Isidro Barradas.

What! With Santa Anna in Vera Cruz! President Guerrero gave the leading man his cue, and Santa Anna led a division against the sick and starving Spanish troops, who had already been defeated by the heat and the mosquitoes. A short but violent action ensued, and the fatherland was saved by Santa Anna.

It was high time, because Guerrero, having been given dictatorial powers to meet the Spanish invasion, was suddenly discovered to be trampling under foot the most sacred heritage of the fatherland. He was accused of being a Jacobin, an atheist, a Mason, a destroyer of religion, and the rest—the usual outcry of the centralists. Vice President Anastasio Bustamante "pronounced," evidently without consulting Santa Anna, who countered with one of his famous Napoleonic proclamations: "I shall stubbornly oppose those who, on any pretext whatever, would temerariously hurl from the presidential chair the Illustrious General, Citizen Vicente Guerrero, and they will succeed in doing so only over my dead body, when I shall have perished defending the Chief Magistrate of the Nation!"

Santa Anna's nose had failed him. The conservatives were strong. More pronunciamientos. Soon the whole country, except for a few diehard liberals under General Juan Alvarez, had accepted Bustamante. Santa Anna made the best of it and retired to Manga de Clavo, his hacienda in Vera Cruz. Congress legitimized Bustamante, who occupied the uneasy seat of the presidency for the first time, on January 1, 1830. At his back "he had the good will of the clergy, the applause of the well to do, the effective support of the army, the clericalism of the Senate, and the indecision of the Chamber of Deputies."

The wheel had made a complete revolution back to despotism. For three years Bustamante's conservative party ruled Mexico through terror, imprisonment, and assassination, all in the name of law and order and the protection of property. Lucas Alamán was again Minister of State. The foulest blot of the Bustamante administration was the murder of Guerrero. That old insurgent had joined forces with Juan Alvarez in his ancient stamping ground in the south.

Defeated at Chilpancingo by General Bravo, he retired to Acapulco and took refuge on the Italian brigatine *Colombo,* commanded by his friend Francisco Picaluga, who sold him to the government for 50,000 pesos in gold.[1] That Alamán should allow himself to be a party to this sordid affair shows how even a man of his principles could be deluded by jesuitical reasoning. He must have order! And Vicente Guerrero, one of the finest old stalwarts of Independence, faced a firing squad in Cuilapa, Michoacán, February 14, 1831.

The country went wild with rage and grief; that is, the "mob" did. The *yorkinos* made capital of that and the natural reaction against Bustamante's despotism. The uproar was so loud that the sensitive nose of Santa Anna informed him (after three years) that the will of the people was being flouted, and he "pronounced" in favor of General Gómez Pedraza, a *moderado.* A chorus of pronunciamientos notified the conservatives that the game was up, and Pedraza was installed as provisional president on January 3, 1833. The new Congress showed its gratitude to Santa Anna by voting him the titles of "Liberator of the Republic" and "Conqueror of the Spaniards," and, on March 30, 1833, elected him president. The radical Valentín Gómez Farías was elected vice president. But Santa Anna, who detested the dull routine of government, pleaded ill health and left the Poder Ejecutivo to Gómez Farías.

The liberal leader was fifty-two years old at the time. He had studied medicine and political science, and was a tremendous anticlerical. Under his lash Congress indicted the ministers of the ousted Bustamante government and was especially ferocious against Lucas Alamán, who was obliged to go into hiding to avoid arrest and worse. Congress worked hard for forty-five days. Its program was a complete liberal house cleaning. It worked in the knowledge that its time was short. It meant to put in a whole liberal program, regardless. The liberals attacked the Spaniards who had escaped the expulsion; they secularized the missions of California; they encouraged emigration to California by exempting the colonists from tithes; they decreed the seizure of the Cortés estate; and they limited the

[1] The reader will be pleased to learn that Picaluga, the Judas of the tragedy, was executed as a bandit in Genoa, in 1836.

jurisdiction of the military and ecclesiastical tribunals to the army and the clergy, for those courts had long been a refuge of privileged laymen.

The conservatives were panic-stricken and sounded the alarm. The uproar grew. A certain Colonel Ignacio Escalada "pronounced" in Michoacán. His "plan": "The garrison protests that it will sustain with all its strength the Holy Religion of Jesus Christ and the immunities and privileges of the clergy and the army, which are threatened by the usurping authorities." It proclaimed "the Illustrious Conqueror of the Spaniards, General Don Antonio López de Santa Anna, Protector of the Cause and Supreme Chief of the Nation."

Santa Anna heard his country's call. His return from Manga de Clavo was the occasion for a popular demonstration. More pronunciamientos demanded that he be named dictator. Santa Anna was puzzled. After twenty days in power he left the stew to cook a while longer and went back to Manga de Clavo. The liberal Congress also made a bid for the support of the Illustrious Conqueror of the Spaniards by putting him in command of the government forces. But Santa Anna's actions were ambiguous. He allowed himself to be "taken prisoner" by the conservative General Mariano Arista, until he should consent to become "Supreme Dictator and Redeemer of Mexico." Gómez Farías managed by some miracle to put down the insurgents in the capital and generally showed more strength than Santa Anna had expected. So Santa Anna "escaped" from his captors and appeared before Congress, swearing "to defend the Constitution till death," and vowing that his hatred of tyranny was "eternal." Congress simply did not believe him. Meanwhile, the insurgents laid siege to Puebla, and Santa Anna met the challenge in his best style: "We march to bring aid to the brave sons of Puebla who . . . are defending their sacred walls with a valor worthy of being perpetuated in the annals of our history!"

While the two armies sparred harmlessly at Puebla, Santa Anna had one of his frequent strokes of luck. The capital was invaded by the cholera. The superstitious populace was told that the plague was a sign of divine wrath against the impiety of Gómez Farías and the liberals. On the very day that Congress proved its atheism by

239

abolishing tithes throughout the Republic and by secularizing the university, Santa Anna returned to Mexico City, announcing that he had suppressed the revolt. The government was delighted. It declared the clergy subject to civil action for using the pulpit for propaganda against the government and it exiled Bishop Labastida y Dávalos. Then it reached the height of madness: It cashiered all the officers who had taken part in the rebellion!

Pronunciamientos. Santa Anna was invited by the army chiefs to cut loose from the liberal rabble. Their slogan: *Religión y Fueros!*—meaning, the clergy and the army above the law. It was still too early for Santa Anna to decide, and he had to retire to Manga de Clavo because his health had been broken in the service of the fatherland.

Meanwhile, the liberal Congress went on destroying religion and the army. The country was in danger! And who do you suppose came forward to sacrifice himself for the fatherland? Right!

In April, 1834, the garrison of Cuernavaca "pronounced" for Santa Anna. Its "plan" called for the dissolution of the liberal Congress, the expulsion of Gómez Farías, the suppression of the militia (liberal), the protection of religion, and the rest. Provincial caciques "pronounced" in unison, all except the cacique of Zacatecas, which Santa Anna took and sacked. In the capital: Te Deums and solemn Masses of thanksgiving. Religion was saved. Santa Anna, paladin of the Cross. Gómez Farías in flight to New Orleans. From a newspaper of the day: "Yesterday the execrable Gómez Farías at last left this capital, crushed under the weight of the just imprecations of a whole city . . . and his terrible and lawless deeds. . . . Like a comet of ill omen, Gómez Farías brought cholera and misery, immorality and tyranny, espionage and treachery, ignorance and sacrilege, the exaltation of criminals and the abasement of honest men, the triumph of the filthy rabble and the crushing of the select, the terror and mourning of families, proscription, tears, and death in a thousand most horrible forms. . . ." A fair sample of the long litany of vituperation which has been leveled at every liberal leader from José María Morelos to Lázaro Cárdenas.

Santa Anna now felt strong enough to dispense with his mask. For eight months he reigned as absolute dictator, with soldiers and

240

martial law. He dissolved Congress; he discharged all government employees suspected of liberal leanings; he put his own men into all national and state offices. When he had the situation well in hand, and the liberal house cleaning of Gómez Farías had been completely undone, he called a new hand-picked Congress in December, 1834. But it turned out to be so incredibly reactionary that even Santa Anna was frightened at the thoroughness of his job. The conservative Congress meant to settle once and for all the nonsense of popular sovereignty. It ignored the Constitution of 1824 and set up a new "principle of authority" in the shape of a Poder Conservador, a supreme executive responsible to no one, not even to its creators. It was the *Fuehrer-Prinzip* in all its purity. And Br'er Fox, he lay low. He knew his people.

In spite of Alamán's warnings, Texas had been allowed to fill up with Yankee immigrants, rude men who despised the "greasers" and who had some reasonable complaints about Mexican notions of justice and administration. The inevitable happened, and Sam Houston and his Texans, supported, incidentally, by liberal Mexicans, "pronounced" for the restoration of the Constitution of 1824 and against the dictatorship of Santa Anna. The Liberator of the Republic and the Conqueror of the Spaniards was not one to let slip this opportunity of saving the fatherland in true Napoleonic style, and he unsheathed his unconquerable blade, which, as he put it in his inimitable prose, "was the first to descend upon the necks of the rash enemies of the fatherland!"

Santa Anna established his headquarters at San Luis Potosí, where he set about creating an army out of several thousand green recruits rounded up by his press gangs. He had energy, and he had a colossal nerve. There was not a cent in the war chest. His men had nothing to eat for days at a time. Using his authority as president, Santa Anna borrowed money from the *agiotistas* (a new class of bloodsuckers who financed the bankrupt government at three and four per cent a month); he manufactured munitions; he requisitioned horses, oxen, and carts; he drilled his men into the semblance of an army; and in the dead of winter he set out across the desert on the six-hundred mile march to San Antonio.

It was a frightful ordeal. Men and animals died from cold and

241

hunger, drowning, exposure, and disease. Santa Anna, however, was above all that. Human life meant little when the fatherland was in danger. And then he had to keep ahead of the revolution that was threatening to break out at home from one day to the next. Six weeks of marching brought him to San Antonio and the old Franciscan mission of the Alamo, where the Texans had imprudently fortified themselves.

On March 6, 1836, the Alamo was surrounded—Bill Travis and his hundred and fifty against Santa Anna's thousands of half-starved recruits. An hour's fierce fighting, brave men against brave men. Numbers and fire power won, and Santa Anna continued the savage tradition of the wars of independence by shooting his prisoners. And, just to prove to the Texans that he was serious, he ordered General José Urrea, over Urrea's protest, to shoot the garrison of Goliad. Santa Anna was to learn that *death to the gringos* also worked both ways.

At San Antonio the news of the expected revolution overtook him, and he had to decide between saving the fatherland by going back to Mexico, and saving it by completing the conquest of Texas. He chose the second alternative as offering the greater glory. He divided his army into three divisions, which overran the country, spreading terror and desolation. Santa Anna himself acted the great conqueror. He issued orders and counterorders in such profusion that his troops marched until they dropped from exhaustion. He resembled Stephen Leacock's general, who mounted his horse and rode off in all directions. He led his division on a forced march of *forty miles* in one day and descended upon Harrisburg, the capital, which he took without firing a shot. Santa Anna was invincible and the Texans were cowards.

And then came the climax, or tragic ending. Santa Anna met Sam Houston's Texans at San Jacinto and with unparalleled frivolity encamped on a rise a short distance from the enemy. The day was warmish and the Conqueror was tired. He did not even bother to post sentries. He was awakened from his siesta by a yell that was to haunt him for the rest of his life: *"Remember the Alamo!"* Sam Houston's revenge was complete. He lost three men killed and eighteen wounded. Santa Anna lost his whole army: 400 dead, 200 wounded, and 730 prisoners. In fifteen minutes!

Santa Anna escaped on horseback. He disguised himself in some cast-off clothing that he found in a hut, but was captured and betrayed by the salutes of his own men. The Texans were for shooting him on the spot, but Sam Houston was too humane or too canny to allow it, and Santa Anna, with the pistols of scowling Texans nervously twitching, dictated the orders that freed Texas of Mexican troops.

Sam Houston started his fallen enemy off for Mexico, according to agreement, but at Galveston a crowd of new men insisted on shooting "Santy Anny." They were argued out of the notion, and the Liberator again escaped death by a hair's breadth. The Texans then sent him to Washington to have a talk with Andrew Jackson, who got nothing out of him but a lot of meaningless protestations, and Santa Anna was back in Mexico in the spring of 1837, just a year after the Alamo and San Jacinto.

In some unexplained manner Santa Anna in that year had undergone a complete metamorphosis. The traitor who had lost San Jacinto and Texas was now, at least in the minds of his admirers, the hero who had saved the honor of the fatherland at the Alamo. They put on a great display of fireworks when he landed at Vera Cruz. Concerts, speeches, poems to the savior of the fatherland. And wouldn't he consider resuming the presidency? But Br'er Fox knew better than to rush things. He could afford to wait. He retired to Manga de Clavo and dictated his version of the war in Texas—a version in which he won all the victories and his subordinates suffered all the defeats.

During the past few years a number of claims had been filed by French citizens against the Mexican government, one by a M. Remontel, who had a pastry shop in Tacubaya. It seems that some army officers had invaded his shop one night, locked him in a back room, and devoured all his pastries. They knew how to insult a Frenchman. The indignant proprietor claimed 800 pesos in damages. It was the smallest item in the huge bill for 600,000 pesos presented by Louis Philippe's minister, but it gave its name to the famous

243

"Pastry War" that ensued. The Mexican government ignored the claims, and, on April 16, 1838, the port of Vera Cruz was blockaded by a French fleet.

Six months of tiresome haggling having come to nothing, Admiral Baudin opened fire on the decrepit old fortress of San Juan de Ulúa on November 27. From his retirement at Manga de Clavo Santa Anna heard the distant cannonading. What! A war going on and he had not been informed! He shouted for his famous white horse and galloped off toward Vera Cruz, arriving during the negotiations for surrender. Treason! He borrowed a skiff and had himself rowed out to the fortress, where he tried to persuade the commandant to blow the place up rather than surrender. But the capitulation had already been signed, and Santa Anna raged back to Manga de Clavo. He may have had a hand in President Bustamante's refusal to accept the terms, and orders came that Santa Anna was to take the field against the French. San Jacinto was forgotten.

Santa Anna against the King of France! A good match. But the bored Admiral Baudin refused to fight. Indeed, if it had not been for the Prince de Joinville, there would probably have been no war at all. The Prince, however, was cut out of the same Byronic cloth as Santa Anna, and thirsted for glory. France, *la douce France,* had been insulted, and only blood could wipe out the stain. *Revanche!* So Baudin prepared a landing party, and Santa Anna was awakened by shouting and firing in the streets. In his underclothing, with his unconquerable blade tucked under his arm, the hero escaped, leaving General Arista to hold the French. Once outside, Santa Anna was his old self. Orders flew, and soon a detachment of Mexican troops was exchanging shots with the Prince de Joinville's marines from behind a barricade. French honor was appeased after several hours, and the Prince withdrew to his ships. Victory! Santa Anna mounted his white horse. Charge! At that moment the god of luck took him by the hand and led him into the path of a French cannonball. His left leg was shattered below the knee. Never would the fatherland be allowed to forget Santa Anna's leg.

The death that the hero expected momentarily resembled that of a romantic opera star, who manages to sing lustily while his life blood flows in a red torrent. On his carefully arranged deathbed the wounded hero lay, while strong men wept unashamed, but his agony did not prevent his dictating a fifteen-page last message to his beloved fellow citizens, which ended: "I also beg the government of the fatherland to bury me in these same sand dunes, so that my companions in arms may know that this is the battle line I have marked out for them to hold."

The death scene was what is known in Hollywood as a "wow." Santa Anna might well have said: "Mexico is worth a leg!" The pitiful stump of Santa Anna's leg was to be paraded with such effect that revolutions and more revolutions would have to be fought, thousands upon thousands of Indian boys would have to die, and half the territory of the nation would have to be sacrificed, before the leg could be paid for. Santa Anna loved his wound with pathological intensity. He never tired of talking about it. He affected invalidism, and a romantic pallor ennobled his features. Fanny Calderón was impressed.

"In a little while entered General Santa Anna himself; a gentlemanly, good-looking, quietly-dressed, rather melancholy-looking person, with one leg, apparently somewhat of an invalid, and to us the most interesting person in the group. He has a sallow complexion, fine dark eyes, soft and penetrating, and an interesting expression of face. Knowing nothing of his past history, one would have said a philosopher, living in dignified retirement—one who had tried the world and found that all was vanity—one who had suffered ingratitude, and who, if he were ever persuaded to emerge from his retreat, would only do so, Cincinnatus-like, to benefit his country. . . . It was only now and then that the expression of his eyes was startling, especially when he spoke of his leg, which is cut off below the knee. He speaks of it frequently."

Santa Anna had two great loves: himself and his fighting cocks. Next came the gaming table, where his gambler's vanity made him coolly risk large sums on the flip of a card with the same unconcern with which he staked men's lives and his country's destiny. And now his leg, which became almost as dear to him as his fighting cocks.

By 1839 unhappy Mexico had become so inured to "plans" and pronunciamientos that they no longer caused a ripple of excitement. The capital fell a prey to its ancient plague of tumultos, with mobs yelling for this or that general, or against this or that action of the government, or just yelling. Banditry had become a semirespectable profession, and gallant highwaymen who apologized to their female victims were not unknown. In the north, Santa Anna's old companions, Generals Urrea and Mejía, upon whom he had laid the blame for the loss of Texas, "pronounced." The Poder Conservador was frightened. Would the mutilated Liberator accept the presidency?

The death scene at Vera Cruz had had the touch of genius, but it was only a rehearsal as compared with the Return of Cincinnatus. Slowly and painfully the carriage of the great man bumped over the stones of the neglected Verz Cruz road. At every stop: triumphal arches, bands, bunting, rockets, speeches, poems, and military parades, while the pallid hero lay limp and unsmiling, acknowledging the ovations with a wave of his languid hand, his empty trouser leg mutely reminding the fatherland of his sacrifice. Who so small now as to remember San Jacinto?

The grateful Poder Conservador voted him the new title of *Benemérito de la Patria* (Well-Deserving of the Fatherland) and made him president for the fifth time. Why he should wish to rule is a mystery for the psychologists to solve. The treasury was exhausted, as usual, and a rebel army was descending upon the capital. Never mind. He would rule with or without money, by terror, confiscation, and oppression. Mejía took Vera Cruz and marched on Puebla. Santa Anna's order to his generals: "The firing squad for all captured officers!" Mejía's last speech: "Santa Anna is doing to me what I should have done to him, only he is shooting me three hours after my capture, while I should have shot him in three minutes!"

The fatherland had been saved again, and Santa Anna began to put on unmistakable airs of royalty. But he was bored. The eternal financial crisis was a bore. The "plans" and pronunciamientos that continued to pop were a bore. He was homesick for his cockpit at Manga de Clavo. "Ill health" compelled his retirement, and General Nicolás Bravo was left to face the music.

Hell itself broke loose as soon as the dictator was out of earshot. The *puros* (that is, the extreme Jacobin liberals), with the veteran Valentín Gómez Farías again at their head, sought to restore the Constitution of 1824, and General Urrea, who had escaped Santa

246

Anna's firing squad the year before, was on hand to make the indispensable pronunciamiento, on July 15, 1840. For twelve days the forces of Bravo and Urrea were locked in a bloody embrace in the streets of the capital and the unfortunate citizens were cut down by cannon fire, while they had to listen to the proclamations that Gómez Farías and Bustamante hurled at each other. Meanwhile, no word came from Manga de Clavo. How was Santa Anna to know which side was representing the true interests of the fatherland? Stalemate. An arrangement was made between the forces, Gómez Farías again trudged off into exile, and the liberals went back to their holes.

General Anastasio Bustamante was again president, by the grace of Santa Anna and the Poder Conservador. But Bustamante was unlucky in his efforts to get money, and General Gabriel Valencia "pronounced." This time Santa Anna's nose did not fail him, and he warned President Bustamante to hearken "to the penetrating cry of a generous people." Bustamante did not hearken closely enough, so Santa Anna himself "pronounced." His forces moved rapidly from Vera Cruz to Puebla, and from Puebla to Tacabaya. More fighting in the streets, twenty-eight days of it, while dead soldiers rotted in the gutters.

The capital, long inured to pronunciamientos and barracks revolutions, regarded this one with hopeless resignation. Fanny Calderón, who was in the midst of it, saw it as a kind of fiesta, with comic overtones. "September 2, 1841. Mexico looks as if it had got a general holiday. Shops shut up, and all business is at a stand. The people, with the utmost apathy, are collected in groups, talking quietly; the officers are galloping about; generals, in a somewhat partycolored dress, with large gray hats, striped pantaloons, old coats, and generals' belts, fine horses, and crimson-colored velvet saddles. The shopkeepers in the square have been removing their goods and money. An occasional shot is heard, and sometimes a volley, succeeded by a dead silence. The archbishop shows his reverend face now and then upon the opposite balcony of his palace, looks out a while, and then retires. The chief effect, so far, is universal idleness in man and beast—the soldiers and their quadrupeds excepted."

General Bustamante was at his wits' end to outplay the Benemérito de la Patria. Suddenly inspired, he did a back somersault and himself "pronounced" for the liberals and the Constitution of 1824! General Juan Almonte, commanding a division of government troops, had a reasonable doubt of Bustamante's sincerity and "pronounced" on his own account for the same Constitution. This was patently an absurdity, so a military junta from the three forces met and reached an agreement, whereby President Bustamante followed Gómez Farías into exile. But that left the presidency vacant. And who do you think was chosen? Right again!

By this time Santa Anna had thrown off all pretense of ruling by law. There was no law but his caprice. He must have soldiers and more soldiers. His personal bodyguard was made up of twelve hundred men in gorgeous uniforms. Money? The country had demanded a dictator; now it could pay for him. Santa Anna "borrowed" money, hundreds of thousands of pesos, until the country was picked as clean as the bones of a dead Indian boy in Texas. It is only fair to add that the money was not all wasted. Santa Anna's vanity needed monuments with his name on them. A new theater was built; a new market; the city streets were paved—all this in the capital, of course. Dictators have their uses. If there had been any railroads in Mexico the trains would undoubtedly have run on time, or nearly so.

The year 1842 marked the apogee of the glorious dictatorship. Mexico City enjoyed a continual fiesta: holidays to celebrate Santa Anna's birthday, Independence, and what not; parades of the guard; drums and bugles and salvos of artillery; solemn Masses at the cathedral. "His Serene Highness," as Santa Anna was now addressed, had to be amused.

On September 27, 1842, occurred the greatest and most solemn celebration of the year. The corpse of Santa Anna's leg was dug up at Manga de Clavo and brought to the city. His Serene Highness's bodyguard, the cavalry, the artillery, the infantry, and the cadets from the military academy at Chapultepec, all dressed for parade, escorted the urn containing the grisly relic across the city to the magnificent centotaph that had been erected for it in the cemetery of Santa Paula. Ministers and the diplomatic corps attended, hat in hand. Speeches, poems, salvos. A graceful acknowledgement by the

Liberator himself, who solemnized the occasion by wearing a new cork leg, which may still be viewed by the skeptical in the National Museum.

The bill came very high: taxes and more taxes; a twenty per cent duty on imports; a "voluntary" contribution by all the householders of the capital; bottomless depression. Santa Anna, bored by the complaints, retired again to Manga de Clavo and his cockpit, leaving General Bravo to carry on. But Bravo could not cope with the roar of hatred that went up on all sides, and the hero was hastily recalled. The seventh return of Cincinnatus.

The country fell a prey to cynicism and boredom; boredom and a deepening hatred for the little man with the cork leg; hatred of his ceaseless extortions; boredom with his emptiness and vanity. But no boredom exceeded that of His Serene Highness, who seized the first opportunity to retire to the fine new estate of El Encero which a grateful country had given him.

General Valentín Canalizo, who had been left to run the show, satisfied no one. How could he? Another weary cycle of pronunciamientos, and Cincinnatus was sent for again. The eighth return.

Texas, whose independence Mexico refused to recognize, wished to enter the Union. The United States government pressed for the settlement of old claims. By 1844 war threatened. But Santa Anna the patriot would shed every drop of his blood before he would relinquish a foot of the sacred soil of the fatherland. If the gringos wanted war, he would show them. He ordered a levy of 30,000 new troops, and his press gangs rounded up droves of uncomprehending Indian boys. The defense program was to be financed by a forced loan of four million pesos, source unrevealed.

The black despair of the country and the hatred of the government made themselves known in the only way possible: General Mariano Paredes "pronounced" in Jalisco. Santa Anna marched west to meet him, but no sooner had he left the capital than a furious tumulto broke out. The statue of the Benemérito de la Patria was torn from its pedestal, the shiny new cenotaph in the cemetery of Santa Paula was violated, and the Leg was destroyed. The garrison of Mexico City "pronounced." Santa Anna was caught between two fires. That in the city was the more threatening, and he hastened

249

back to put it out. But his troops were fed up and began to desert. By squads, by companies, by regiments, they deserted, while small arms, cannon, and equipment filled the ditches. Within a short week the army of Santa Anna was nothing but a memory. With his cook and two adjutants he fled to the mountains of Vera Cruz, where he was recognized by a party of Indians and captured. At the fortress of El Perote a military tribunal tried to find an excuse to shoot him. He was saved by his stump and limped off into exile. Universal relief. Only one general did him the honor of "pronouncing" in protest, while the clergy and the rich sang Te Deums for their and their goods' delivery.

On March 1, 1845, the United States announced the admission of Texas into the Union. Minister Almonte demanded his passports. The Mexican government promptly declared war on us. War? Surely no country in history was ever less prepared to fight. The army: 20,000 men on the rolls, and 24,000 *officers*. The treasury was empty. The despair of the people flamed up in hatred against the criminal stupidity of their rulers. General Paredes "pronounced" again. Half a dozen generals in various parts of the country "pronounced." The war could take care of itself. General Paredes marched on the capital. General Valencia prepared to defend it. There was really little sense in their fighting each other, so they made an arrangement by which Paredes became president and dictator. Paredes to the country: "I am resolved to make my ideas triumph or perish in the attempt. I am determined to punish no one for his past misdeeds, but I shall shoot anyone who opposes me, be he archbishop, general, minister, or anyone else!" His prose was not up to Santa Anna's.

The garrison of the capital could not stomach the pretensions of Paredes, and "pronounced." The country was without a leader. The country was in danger. Yes, Santa Anna was back from his exile, uninvited. He was received with distrust, but received. The smart Yankees had let him through the blockade at Vera Cruz, and Santa Anna retired to El Encero to await the inevitable call. The factions in the capital were bidding for his support. The liberals looked stronger. The liberals won it. Valentín Gómez Farías, also back from exile and again at the head of his puros, begged Santa Anna not to

250

offend his people by withholding his presence from them. And Santa Anna, now a liberal democrat, clad in decent civvies, was driven in an ordinary hack through the silent streets of the capital to the palace, where he was persuaded to accept the presidency. In the treasury were exactly 1,839 pesos with which to finance the war with the "Colossus of the North."

Whatever his shortcomings, Santa Anna was an incomparable organizer. He announced a new levy and beat together an army of 18,000 men, without money. Gómez Farías, now vice president, moved heaven and earth to raise funds. He slapped a sequestration order on the property of the clergy for four million pesos, none of which got to Santa Anna in time. The generalísimo could not wait. The fatherland really was in danger. Santa Anna drove his starving and freezing troops three hundred miles from San Louis Potosí to Buena Vista to meet Zachary Taylor. On the way he lost 4,000 men from desertion, hunger, and disease. It was an army of desperate and fainting men that faced General Taylor on February 22, 1846. The excellent American artillery, firing from well-prepared positions, chopped through the Mexican ranks, but they came on, taking position after position at the point of the bayonet. They fought magnificently; they fought until they drove Taylor's men to the last ditch; they fought until they dropped from hunger and fatigue. A heavy storm stopped the battle, and Santa Anna retired under cover of darkness. His men could take no more. He had lost 1,500 in killed and wounded. If the American troops had not been fought to a standstill, they could have annihilated their exhausted enemy. As it was, Taylor allowed Santa Anna to withdraw unmolested.

The Retreat from Moscow. The army that entered San Luis Potosí seventeen days later was an army of barefoot skeletons. The news of the defeat was received in Mexico City with the usual pronunciamientos against the government. Deadlock between Gómez Farías and the rebels. The Great Arbiter hastened to the scene. He was the only one who could decide the conflict, *because he was the only one without convictions.* And, of course, he reassumed the presidency.

The army of Winfield Scott landed at Vera Cruz. It would be pointless to repeat the story of Scott's mad invasion of Mexico. He had about 10,000 men. Mexico City alone could have raised a force of several times that many, if it had wished to do so. But the Mexicans were defeated in advance by hatreds, jealousies, poverty, despair, indifference, and apathy. Why fight? What could be worse than the degradation they had already suffered? Many of the "decent people" even welcomed the American invasion as a relief from the intolerable military anarchy. Santa Anna was to prove them correct.

Mexico City was not properly defended. Why? Because Santa Anna refused to share the glory with General Gabriel Valencia, commander of the northern division. There is no other explanation for the easy American victory. The Americans were heavily outnumbered; their line of supplies was three hundred miles long and thinly held; they had no reserves and no way to get any. With the spirit he had shown against Taylor at Buena Vista, Santa Anna should have crushed Scott. Instead, when everything was set for the battle and Valencia was in a strong position, Santa Anna ordered him to retire. Valencia exploded with frustration and fury; he cursed Santa Anna for a coward and refused to obey. Whereupon Santa Anna withdrew his own troops and left Valencia to be cut to pieces. Santa Anna himself marched out of the city with his fresh army without firing a shot, abandoning the scanty defenders of the Castle of Chapultepec to certain destruction, including the boys of the military academy, the famous *Niños Héroes*. He marched past the convent of Churubusco, which was held by a regiment of Irish deserters from Scott's army—misguided men who thought they were fighting for the Church against the Protestants. (Fifty of them were tried later and hanged for desertion, much to Scott's distress.)

The rest is in the textbooks: the Treaty of Guadalupe Hidalgo, by which we took half the territory of Mexico and thereby fulfilled Manifest Destiny; Mexico dismembered and helpless, and condemned for all time to dependence upon us.

The paranoiac Santa Anna led his troops off intact, while he proclaimed, declaimed, and heaped abuse upon the "betrayers of the fatherland." His disgusted army melted away, as it had done once before. By the time it reached Puebla there was only a handful left, and His Serene Highness deserted in his turn and fled to Tehuacán.

A band of wild Texans followed close behind and came within an ace of capturing him. "Remember the Alamo, Santy Anny?" The fugitive tried to take refuge in Oaxaca, but the governor refused him permission. The governor was a Zapotec Indian named Benito Juárez. So Santa Anna decided that the enemy was safer than his own people, and surrendered to Major Kenly at El Perote.

Benemérito de la Patria! What a price for a leg!

Santa Anna, actor to the last, entertained his captors with a banquet at El Encero, dictated an eloquent farewell message to an ungrateful fatherland, and exiled himself to Venezuela, April 6, 1848.

The immense disaster that he and his kind had brought upon Mexico had the immediate effect that the reader has already anticipated: pronunciamientos by all parties and caudillos, denouncing the betrayal of the fatherland, denouncing Santa Anna, and denouncing each other. Death to the monarchists! Death to the liberals! Death to the santanistas! Death!

The provisional government gave way to a "moderate" government under General José Joaquín Herrera, who, with his successor, General Mariano Arista, performed miracles to meet the financial crisis. The fifteen million dollars of conscience money we paid Mexico after the war was soon gone. The moderates suffered the fate of their kind and pleased no one. And then General Arista committed the unpardonable sin: *He reduced the army!*

Pronunciamientos in Guadalajara. Arista resigned. The new provisional president, Juan Bautista Ceballos, dissolved Congress by force and made an arrangement with the rebels. Confusion. The army and the conservatives decided it was time for a strong hand. Their "plan": Religion and property, and the rest, *under the perpetual dictatorship of Antonio López de Santa Anna!* He had not even been consulted.

The conservatives were not without powerful arguments in favor of a dictatorship. The Constitution of 1824 had amply proved the unsuitability of a weak federal system. The disaster of 1848 had destroyed the last vestige of national unity. Mexico had become many Mexicos in fact. The municipal district of Cuernavaca seceded from the state of Mexico, and the district of Yautepec seceded from Cuernavaca. Mexico split into cells, and the cells into more cells, each with its cacique making and interpreting laws, and collecting taxes and import duties as he pleased. Justice was bought and sold at the lowest prices in history. A British agent, one Mr. Falconner, got wholesale rates when he bought thirty-five members of the national legislature for 60,000 pesos. Commerce was at a standstill. The police of the capital gathered up the bodies of those who died of hunger. The soldiers quartered in Mexico City conducted themselves like an invading army, and looted and murdered at will. The situation was intolerable, and men of all persuasions began to look wistfully back on the days of Santa Anna. The conservatives, led by Lucas Alamán, saw no help for Mexico but a monarch, failing which, the best substitute they could think of was the old dictator, whom they hoped to control. They were to sink still lower in the dark years to come.

Santa Anna, now sixty, was brought back from Venezuela and, for the eleventh and last time, limped into office, in April, 1853. The dying Alamán, worshiping order to the last, consented, on his own terms, to head the government of the man he despised and needed. Alamán to Santa Anna: "In your hands, General, lies the happiness of the fatherland." He had no illusions about the man he meant to use merely as a stopgap for a monarchy. But the old aristocrat, probably the only disinterested figure among the conservatives, was past leading any party. He finished his tragic and monumental *Historia de México* and died, June 2, 1853, a month after taking office.

Without the brain and energy of Alamán to restrain them, the conservatives went the whole way back to Oriental despotism. Santa Anna was made Perpetual Dictator and was dressed up to look like royalty. The liberals were suppressed or driven into exile. Benito Juárez made cigarettes for a living in New Orleans. A number of liberals joined old General Juan Alvarez in the south and invited Santa Anna to come and get them. The Perpetual Dictator now had the best military machine he had ever commanded, but somehow it lacked punch. His campaigns were fiascos. The liberals had no army to speak of, but they refused to be crushed. On the contrary, their movement gained strength daily. The dictator was up against a thing he could not control or understand: a war of ideas, a revolt against the whole stupid, suffocating, backward-looking notion that the destiny of a people can forever be directed by a handful of willful men with guns.

Santa Anna reverted to type and went in for lavish and expensive display: uniforms, brass buttons, fancy coaches, and suchlike folderol. Money ran low, and he sold the Mesilla of Arizona to the United States for ten million dollars, with which he was able to buy the loyalty of the generals for another year or so. But the liberal movement would not down. Provincial caciques joined it one after another, until the dictator began to feel besieged. Worst of all, he was beset by his ancient affliction, boredom. The lick-spittle sycophants, the silly titles, the nauseating adulation, the endless round of meaningless functions would have turned the stomach of a hardier man. He discovered that he was hardly more than a prisoner in the hands of the gang that had brought him back from his comfortable hacienda and his fighting cocks in Venezuela. He became acid and irritable. He was lonely in his imitation royalty, and in his loneliness takes on dignity for the first time in his life. The great actor had made one too many last appearances. Then, one day in August, 1855, with a touch of his old audacity, Santa Anna ordered his coach and galloped off to Vera Cruz and exile, and off the stage of Mexico.

Seventeen years later the old man was allowed to hobble back to the fatherland he had served so ill. He spent his last four years in solitude, and died forgotten, on June 21, 1876.

# 21

## HIDALGOS

The conservative elements of Mexico fought (and still fight) with such single-minded fury to preserve at all costs their ancient privileges that it may not be out of place here to insert a note on the phenomenon of Spanish nobility (*hidalguía*) as practiced in America. I have mentioned elsewhere the feudal heritage of the Spanish conquistador, his firm belief that he was somehow noble because his profession was the bearing of arms. The *Poem of the Cid* (twelfth century) is the best document for the reader to consult on the subject, as well as one of the grandest yarns ever spun. By the time of the Conquest of Mexico this tradition had so permeated every stratum of Spanish society, and the numerous privileges and prestige of the noble were so highly prized, that few Spaniards, regardless of origin, did not aspire to that state. The discovery of the New World let down the bars. The constant protest of the early governors of the Indies was that every cobbler, or blacksmith, or mechanic, as soon as he landed, cast aside his tools and set himself up as an hidalgo. Rodrigo de Albornoz, Contador (accountant) of New Spain in the time of Cortés, voiced the general complaint in a letter to Charles V of December 15, 1525.

"If in any of your dominions, Caesarean Majesty, it was ever necessary to prescribe the manner of life of your subjects and vassals, here it is even more necessary, for, since the land is rich in food and in mines of gold and silver, and everyone becomes swollen with the desire to spend and possess, by the end of a year and a half, he who is a miner, or farmer, or swineherd, no longer will be so, but wishes to be given Indians, so he spends everything he has on ornaments and silks, and, if he has a wife, the same thing holds for her. In like fashion other mechanics cease the pursuit of their trades and incur heavy expenses, and do not work or extract gold or silver from the mines, in the belief that they will be given Indians to serve them and support their families in gentility."

Outside the economic consequences of the Conquest—and, of course, intimately linked with them—the tradition of nobility had the most profound effects upon the psychology and social habits of the white men of New Spain, and upon all those who in later centuries aspired to the same privileges. The noble state rested upon two broad assumptions: the right to bear arms and the right to hold land, particularly the right to hold land—the more land the greater nobility. This curious obsession led merchants to abandon their commerce, miners to give up mining, and manufacturers to cease manufacturing, to become country squires and landlords, surrounded by retainers.

*Death to the gachupines! Land and Liberty! Bread and Land!* Such have been the slogans of Mexico's tumultos and social revolutions, from the jacquerie of Miguel Hidalgo in 1810 to Francisco Madero's mild attempt at political reform a hundred years later, and the fierce agrarian revolt of Emiliano Zapata, which left the haciendas of the south charred skeletons of former grandeur. All these movements were essentially revolts against the hereditary nobility's monopoly of land.

One of the most grievous of the ills bequeathed by the Spaniards to the New World was this passion of the white men to grab land and set themselves up as semi-independent feudal lords over vast estates—known as the institution of *latifundismo*. In the century following the Conquest about ten thousand land grants were made in New Spain in the old agricultural lands south of the Chichimec frontier, ranging in size from a single *caballería* of about a hundred acres to huge areas given over to sheep, cattle, and sugar—a total of perhaps 100,000 square miles. Later on, when the north country was opened, some of the grants, like that of the Marquesado de Aguayo, were enormous, veritable principalities. There is nothing peculiarly Spanish about latifundismo. It appears under certain conditions with such unfailing regularity that it seems to obey a universal law. These conditions are, in brief: cheap land; a cheap, abundant, and more or

257

less servile laboring class; ready markets for produce; and an exploiting class either trained in arms or able to hire mercenaries to put down "labor troubles." New Spain had all these elements. When any one of them is missing, the system is likely to collapse, as it did when the police state of Porfirio Díaz weakened and Mexico flamed up in revolution. The cotton empire of the Old South, and the great fruit, cotton, and produce "ranches" of California are examples of modern latifundismo in the United States.

Writers trying to explain the fall of Rome agree on the destructive effects of the huge slave-operated *latifundia* which spread like a blight over Italy, debasing rural life, dislocating the population, and filling the cities with masses of degraded and indigent vagabonds. The sturdy and independent comunidad of Spain gave way before the Roman tax collector and landlord. The Spanish peasant had the choice of becoming a slave or turning bandit, and he bitterly learned to bide his time. The Spanish Republic of 1931–1939 was, among other things, a revolt against latifundismo, and it was crushed by the classes interested in upholding the privileges of a landed nobility.

To understand the psychology of latifundismo in New Spain we must again go back to the Middle Ages, when the Visigothic barbarians overran the Peninsula. The Visigoths were professional warriors. Their power rested upon their ability to fight and upon their possession of land. In time they made it their exclusive privilege to bear arms and possess land. They became a military landed nobility. The reader will at once recognize the essentials of feudalism, which in its simplest terms was a contract between a land-holding and arms-bearing warrior and those who needed his protection. The Visigoths, with the help of the Spanish–Roman bishops (as explained in chapter 15), held on in Spain for three hundred years, without, however, winning the loyalty of the Spaniards whose land they had taken. On the contrary, their tyranny and exactions were such that the Spaniards welcomed the hordes of Arabs and Berbers who paraded through the country in 711 and chased the Gothic nobility into the fastnesses of the Pyrenees and Asturias. In their distant retreat the Gothic knights reverted to their ancient trade of marauding; warfare again became their way of life

258

and their livelihood. As time went on and their marauding took on the dignity of a crusade against the infidel, more and more warriors went into the profession, until it is safe to say that a very considerable part of the free population of Christian Castile became noble, at least in the high privilege of bearing arms and living on spoils.

At the same time, however, true nobility required the cachet of land, and, as the class of warriors grew, the amount of land available became scantier, until Castile became a country of little nobles, and, indeed, got its name from that circumstance. (Castile derives from the Latin *castella,* that is, little forts, or castles.) A great many of these proud barbarians were left without any land at all and had to make a living by hiring themselves out to anyone who could pay the price, to Moslems and Christians indifferently, somewhat like the generals of the period of Santa Anna. They were the men whose descendants, centuries later, became the conquistadores of the New World.

There were, of course, innumerable gradations of nobility, depending upon the value of one's horse and armor, upon the amount of land one held, upon the length of time that one's ancestors had professed the Christian faith, or upon the purity of one's blood—that is to say, the absence of degrading Moorish, Jewish, or peasant strains. *Pureza de sangre* was required in at least one's four grandparents. In any case, the noble was a privileged being and was always superior to the non-noble, however rich or talented, who did things with his hands, or who was soiled by commerce in useful articles, although there were so many exceptions that the rule is a shaky one to follow. The great Cid, for example, was originally a miller, and later acted not unlike a business tycoon. The true noble did recognize that the king was a notch above him in nobility, but beneath the king he was any man's equal and most men's superior— *Del Rey abajo ninguno,* none under the king, as the old saying goes.

The great haciendas created by the ruling class of Mexico became in time, especially after Independence, when government control was removed from private enterprise, little principalities, in which the masters lived in full enjoyment of the traditional privileges of the

259

noble caste. The center of the hacienda was the "big house," walled and fortified like any mediaeval castle. The Indian population of the hacienda, although nominally hired for wages, was, in effect, a body of retainers, tied to their lord by the intangible spiritual and material bonds characteristic of the feudal relationship. The hacendado was the patriarch. He was the godfather of the Indians' children, and not infrequently the father. He gave away their daughters in marriage, or took them as concubines. He was the judge in their quarrels, and their protector against their enemies. In short, he was their *patrón*. In exchange, he lived on their labor, permitted no strikes, and punished slackness and disobedience with greater or less rigor according to his nature, without interference from the civil authorities, and sometimes even with their help. He maintained on the hacienda a church and a school, in which his hired chaplain taught the Indians something of the Christian doctrine, but particularly the virtues of humility and obedience. The hacendado was an irresponsible despot, not necessarily a bad one, and the hacienda was a faithful miniature of the old Hapsburg state, without its law.

The benefits of the feudal contract were not altogether one-sided. If the Indian peón had no real liberty, which he had never known anyway, and if he worked for illusory wages that he never saw, on the other hand his subsistence was usually assured by a patch of ground, his precious *milpa;* he had a permanent abiding place among his own people and familiar surroundings; and his folkways (*costumbre*) were not ordinarily interfered with. He had frequent holidays, in the celebration of which he could get gloriously drunk and escape for a while from reality, and in his old age he might count on a few years of authority as village elder, and spend his dotage in the sun chattering with his cronies. He was, to be sure, kept in ignorance of the white man's cultural adornments and was usually illiterate, but when I look over most of the books he might have read if he had been taught, the atrocity seems overemphasized.

A society based on latifundismo was bound to be static. If the master-and-serf relationship was to endure, neither the upper nor the lower stratum could be allowed to step over the boundaries of accepted conventions. Hence the extraordinary bitterness, or even frenzy, of the conservatives toward the betrayers of their class, such as Valentín Gómez Farías. The late Mexican pundit, José Vasconcelos, who in his last years retreated into the sixteenth century, could hardly find words harsh enough (in his *Breve Historia de México*) to describe Gómez Farías, "the North American agent and disciple of Poinsett, tool of the Yankees," and so on.

The worst features of latifundismo were likely to appear in the second and third generations, when the spoiled offspring of the hacendados got into the habit of going off to Mexico City or Paris to live, and entrusted the hacienda to a *capataz* (overseer), whose duty it was to keep an adequate revenue flowing in. Absentee landlordism meant the driving of the land and workers beyond their capacity; it meant the seizure of the Indians' milpas and the ejidos of the villages; it meant tyranny and hardship, and the eventual ruin of the estate. Landed families rose and fell with such regularity that our old saying about there being three generations from shirtsleeves to shirtsleeves became a proverb in Mexico also.

A Spanish immigrant might be a farrier, a carpenter, or an *arriero*. No matter. By hard work and frugality, or by any means, he would acquire a piece of land. He had taken the first step toward nobility. If he could accumulate enough to save his children from useful and humiliating work, he was well along the way, even though his children despised him for an uncouth gachupín. Succeeding generations became progressively more emancipated, until, if the estate could stand the strain, the family emerged as a useless colony of parasites. This was only possible, of course, because there existed a servile class to support them.

The men of the Creole landed families, by all accounts, had an amusing enough time of it: in their youth some schooling, no discipline, a great deal of lovemaking, riding, gaming, quarreling, and cockfighting. Flirting was a fine art, in both sexes, and obeyed an elaborate code which mystified the priggish Marvin Wheat (in his *Travels in Western Mexico*, 1857): "While the fair sex trip along with downcast eyes and solemn countenances to the sacred shrine, to dip the curved finger in holy water, and cross their

261

foreheads, typic of their faith . . . the sterner sex have taken their position, to behold youth and beauty gracefully glide by them. . . . This habit of gentlemen taking their position outside of the church, who should regard gallantry and the grace which adorn the fair sex, and walk, in like cases, in company with the ladies to show them a due respect and courtesy, I cannot but condemn as mischievous and impertinent."

In later life men of exceptional gifts might have a go at polite letters, or take up a learned profession, especially the law, for the title of licenciado became an essential label for a political career or a government job of the better sort. Others went into the Church, a great many into the army, and some into gentlemanly farming. Able and intelligent men appeared among them in the same ratio as in any other group, but they rarely achieved more than a respectable mediocrity in science or in letters. The burden of nobility was too heavy, and talent faltered and came to a halt in the face of universal indifference and disapproval.

The women of the landed class were condemned to a life the vapidity of which makes us yawn at the very thought. The impressionable Marvin Wheat never tired of praising their graciousness and kindness, "though they may not be able to read and write. The instruction of the female sex is, I am told, most shamefully neglected, for the largest portion of them is far from having the first rudiments of a Spanish education."

Fanny Calderón, although very sympathetic to Mexico in general, gave up when it came to the higher reaches of female society. *"Quant à la morale,"* she wrote to her friend Prescott, in 1840, "they *do nothing* from morning till night. The morning they pass in a most untidy deshabille covered with an old *reboso,* smoking a paper cigar, or rolling along in a carriage, dressed in blonde, velvet, and the most superb diamonds, that is, for a visit of ceremony; dresses *very* short and little white or colored satin shoes. In the evening they do nothing that I could ever find out, not even amusing themselves. I never saw a book in their hands or in their rooms. You may imagine that their ignorance is *total.* They are very amiable and good natured, but I do not wonder that so many become nuns, as I think they amuse themselves quite as well in a convent as at home. Of course there are exceptions, but *not* in the article of ignorance. There are some who sing well, some few who play, a *very* few who draw, but I do not know one who *reads*."

The mores of the landed gentry were singularly unchanging. It may have been pride, or it may have come from an uneasiness that, if any crack should be allowed to appear in the dikes of their scheme of things, the brown flood would seep in and overwhelm them. They walled themselves in and became strangers in their own country. Anyone who has lived in an old-fashioned Mexican family (incidentally the most gracious and hospitable people imaginable) cannot but notice the gulf that separates master and servant. Regardless of the size of the family, which is frequently vast, or of its poverty, which in these days is common, there is no hint of a breakdown in the hierarchy. It is curious to see two mutually exclusive societies living under the same roof. The mistress of the house is often an excellent cook, that is, of certain special dishes, and she spends a good part of her time in the kitchen; but all the fetching and carrying, plucking and peeling, and the like, must be done by the servants, or she will lose face. She may go to the market and haggle over the price of eggs, but she may not carry them. The eldest daughter of such a household said to me one day in complete seriousness: "Yes, I suppose Diego Rivera is a great artist, in spite of his atheistic ideas, but *his wife!* Do you know, I saw her the other day in the market *carrying her own basket like an Indian!*"

This is what might be called psychological latifundismo, and it has not changed since 1840, or since 1540, for that matter, *and it is catching.* It is not confined to the Creoles. It is easily demonstrable that the passion for holding land, with the sweet privilege of ordering one's fellows about, pervades all classes. It is a folkway. The schoolmaster Plutarco Elías Calles was one of the stalwarts of the Revolution for bread and land, but he retired as one of the greatest landholders of Mexico. Luis Morones, the radical labor leader, the same. Revolutionary generals and their hangers-on, the same. All this in spite of the fact that latifundismo, at least in its early form, was unsound. But one mustn't say so. Latifundismo in the Old South, with its base of slave labor, was hysterically defended in the press and in the pulpit, in the face of overwhelming evidence that the

South was going bankrupt. F. L. Olmsted exposed the imminent ruin of the South in two remarkable books, *A Journey in the Back Country* and *A Journey in the Seaboard Slave States,* which are as fine a piece of scientific reporting as could be desired, but he was bitterly denounced as a damned Yankee abolitionist. Psychological latifundismo still hangs on in the South, just as it does in Mexico. The presence of a dark and presumably inferior race, ready to do one's bidding, is, I suspect, one of the chief props of the noble ego. But remember the Alhóndiga!

Thus in Mexico I have rarely talked with a member of the dying aristocracy without being met with a kind of ritual: "The Indians are an inferior race." "They will not work unless coerced." "They were better off under the old system." "They made more real wages, had more leisure, worked more efficiently, and were happier." "Education is bad for them, makes them discontented and 'uppity.' " "The hacienda system is the only one that will produce enough to feed the country." "Look how things have been going since the Revolution." Etc. All this in face of the fact that few haciendas in the old days were solvent. The hacendados had lived on borrowed money for so long that paying off a mortgage was almost unheard of. From the eighteenth century, and probably earlier, they had borrowed money on their lands, first from religious foundations, later from banks and loan sharks, until the country was plastered with mortgages like a billboard. It became a tradition that obligations were sufficiently discharged by occasional payments of interest. A few bad years, and foreclosure made way for another noble family.

Out of this situation arose the tiresome repetition of the statement that the Church owned most of the soil of Mexico. It should be obvious that if it had not been the Church it would have been some other agency. Given the habits of the hacendados, it was inevitable that religious foundations, with their constantly accumulating capital, should come to own numbers of bankrupt haciendas. This is not to argue that the Church should be in the moneylending business, a question which, fortunately, I do not have to decide. The bankruptcy of the hacienda system became clear when José Limantour, Minister of Finance under Díaz, began to call in mortgages held by the Bank of Mexico, whereupon the outraged hacendados threw their support to Francisco Madero, himself a member of a great landholding family, presumably in the hope that he would not betray his class.

The sharp stratification of society in Mexico had several interesting effects. In the old days, the whites, by assuming all the privileges (that is, the better posts in the Church, the government, and the army), by having a better education, by wearing better clothes and eating better food,[1] and by living in better houses, surrounded by servants, were envied, resented, hated, and imitated. The whites are now out as the ruling class, and the mestizo is in, and the mestizo is assuming the same marks of nobility that he formerly envied. On the heavy ground swell of the Revolution the mestizo rode into power, and he now herds the Indians (peasants is probably a more accurate term, for it is hard to find out just what an "Indian" is these days) in the traditional noble fashion—all for their own good, of course, but I have never noticed that the Indians are consulted about the various "plans" for their improvement.

Another effect of the Revolution upon the ex-noble was to make him take shelter more than ever behind his shield of scornful aloofness. "Why do you always address me in French?" I asked a licenciado whose family had been broken in the Revolution. "Why?" he answered. "Because I don't want to be taken for a Mexican!" "The greatest calamity Mexico has suffered," I was assured by an ex-hacendado of Chihuahua, "was the failure of the United States to take over the country in 1848. *You know what to do with the Indians!*" I once addressed a group of very respectable ladies in Mexico City, explaining the techniques of government devised by the Spanish Crown to administer the complicated Indian problem. When I had finished, to my astonishment I was more vigorously applauded than I thought my talk justified. "It was a great privilege to hear you, Dr. Simpson," one of them remarked to me, "and I wish

[1] One of the most curious fetishes of the upper class is its insistence on having wheat bread to eat. Everybody eats maize (tortillas), of course, but having wheat bread on the table is a necessity. It establishes one's superior position. Back in the sixteenth century the Spaniards had to have wheat; it was their traditional food and it distinguished them from the maize-eating Indians, although it cost twice as much to raise and had no greater food value.

more could have heard you. It's time we learned how our ancestors handled things. *They knew what to do with the Indians!*"

Over the dinner table of a little provincial hotel (this was back in 1940) I listened to the local nobility discussing politics and took a few notes.[2] "Have you seen this latest scheme of our government for

[2] These notes were recorded near the end of the Cárdenas régime, when feeling was running very high and armed revolt was openly talked of. This resentment was not confined to the ex-privileged. It is difficult to get an Indian to talk politics, but I did scrape up an acquaintance with a lad of about twenty whom I had engaged to look after my luggage at a way station on the Tehuantepec Railway. The train, as usual, was many hours late, and we got fairly chummy over a bottle of beer and a few cigarettes. He was a bright lad but running over with bitterness. I append a condensed and bowdlerized version of his remarks.

"You ask me what my trade is. I haven't any. I make a little money carrying bags for travelers. There isn't any work here. They wouldn't let me work anyway. Every few days some *cabrón* comes along and tells me to join a union. Why? I say. So you can work and earn some money, he says. You son of the *tiznada*, I say, what do you mean, work? There isn't any work. Never mind, he says, you join up or else. This last *puto cabrón* had a gun. So I say, go ahead and shoot me, you *hideputa*. I'm not afraid to die. I'd as soon get shot as starve to death, anyway. This bastard wanted me to pay a hundred pesos to join his stinking union. You son of the great whore, I say, you know I don't make a hundred pesos in a year. Say, brother, I say to another (a new one comes around from a different union every few weeks), say, brother, who pays you to do this? Why don't you try working for a living? Why don't you go up in the mountains and try organizing the Chamula? But they take good care not to. The Chamula are only Indians, but they have enough to eat and no one is going to take it away from them. They would chop any organizer into dog meat with their machetes.

"And now these sons of dogs are running the government and you can't make a living, because they steal everything in sight. I used to go out in the country and buy maize and bring it to town and sell it cheap. I built up a little trade and I didn't hold people up. Do you think they'd let me go on? Bah! They stuck on a tax when I brought it in, another tax for a license, and Christ knows how much more for freight, and my maize finally cost me so much that I couldn't sell it. We used to sell a lot of maize in this country, but no one bothers any more.

"And now they are taking the land away from the people who know how to work it and giving it to these lazy sons of animals who don't know how to do anything but steal. The land stops producing, of course, and goes to hell. They took over a sugar finca here last year, a little one of 500 hectares. What is left of it now? Nothing.

"Why don't I join an ejido, you ask? Because I don't belong to a union! I don't know about the ejidos in the rest of the country, but those around here are nothing but a lot of *mierda*. What we need is a real revolution to clean these sons-of-whatever out and let us go to work."

communist education? Believe it or not, those swine are now going to teach our youngsters *the scientific truth*. What do they know about scientific truth, or any other kind, I'd like to know?" "What we need is another revolution, a real one this time, to get this revolutionary scum off our necks!" "They are always talking about destroying castes and setting up a classless society. They have made themselves into a privileged class a thousand times worse than anything we ever had before!"

From a gun-toting but otherwise amiable gentleman of Oaxaca, about that same time: "The country is going to the dogs! No one does any work these days. Why should he? Only to have his land taken away from him? In the old days the Indian had work and enough to eat. The hacendado took care of him and gave him land for his milpa. We used to export grain from Oaxaca. Now we have to bring in hundreds of carloads a year. I hope the revolutionaries are satisfied!"

From a banana grower of Vera Cruz: "This country is in a terrible crisis. The Revolution has debauched the workers. Their leaders teach them that they are being exploited if they have to work for a living, and that all they have to do is to reach out and take what they want. Spoil the rich and the foreigner! The people don't know, and the politicians don't care, that at the same time they are destroying Mexico. Expropriation has taken a great deal of land out of production, because the Indian will only work under compulsion. He is now taught that the government will take care of him. So, when he is given land, he sits down and does nothing. Don't take my word for it. Look around you. Look at food prices. Beans up from fifteen to forty-five centavos a kilo in five years; rice up from twenty to sixty, and so on. I tell you the whole population is being debauched by these politicians. They can all be bought. I could shoot you this moment. Your government could send a man to investigate, and I could shoot him. I might have to spend a night in jail, but it wouldn't cost me more than a hundred pesos to go free. The point is that there is no longer any law in Mexico. The law is the whim of the local cacique. I am a Mexican and it hurts me to have to say such things, but I have seen too much and suffered too much at the hands of these brigands. For it is brigandage to steal the work of a man's hands. It is worse; it is stupidity! You are going to Chiapas. It was once a prosperous coffee country, until they began expropriating the plantations. Watch what happens to coffee production in the next two years. I know, because I have seen it happen in sugar and bananas. I can see that you think I am cowardly and unpatriotic not to do something about it. But I know when I am beaten. I keep my mouth shut and pay up."

From an ex-coffee planter of that same state: "Yes, that's all true. They took my land and equipment and didn't know what to do with it, so they wrecked my plant and sold the copper vessels for scrap. Twenty years' work! But I am old and a foreigner. . . ."

From a former landowner of Chiapas, now much reduced: "To get to be governor of a state in this country you don't have to know anything about the job. What you do is to gather up all the loafers and good-for-nothings of the state capital, promise them anything, and let them elect you. Naturally, you will have to pay them off, but you can save something out for yourself. For instance, we have been assessed three times in the past ten years to build a road across this state. To be sure, some of it has been built, enough to connect the capital with the nearest railway junction, but the rest of the state can go hang! Then you make a deal with the gang in Mexico City—a case of you scratch my back and I'll scratch yours—and they will support you if anyone makes trouble. It's damnable! Some day, long after I am dead, Mexico may become a great nation, but it will not be done until we demand of our politicians some standard of civilized conduct."

Now, a great many of these criticisms were, unfortunately, just, but it did not occur to the ex-privileged that they had any responsibility in the matter. The trouble with them, it seems to me, was that they were not willing to fulfill their end of the feudal contract. When, with the rise of the monarchy, the fighting nobles of Spain lost their reason for being, some of the best of them, like the Mendozas, went into the public service and directed the destinies of their country during her most glorious period. I do not say, by any means, that the Creoles of Mexico were the only ones capable of running the country—history proves the contrary—but they had so many initial advantages that logic demanded their participation, even under a government they hated, although it might have been difficult for them to break into the ranks of the Revolution. Most of them, however, in those stormy days were content to stand aside and croak in arm-waving impotence, like the honest men I have quoted, or to wait for some foreign Moses to lead them out of the wilderness.

Back in the 1850's a foreign Moses was the hope and aim of the conservatives. Their native Moses had fled back to the fleshpots of Egypt, and they began to look around for some European prince to reestablish the "principle of authority" and relieve them of the responsibility of looking after themselves.

# 22

# JUÁREZ, THE MAN OF LAW

*It has always been my most ardent desire to reestablish the rule of law and the prestige of authority.*—Governor Benito Juárez of Oaxaca, 1847

The long chapter on the age of Santa Anna was intended to illustrate two major themes: the struggle of the colonial elements for survival against middle-class liberalism, and the rise of military *caudillismo,* which in its worst form was *santanismo,* and which was eventually to triumph with the dictatorship of Porfirio Díaz. The monotonous "plans" and pronunciamientos that confuse the records of half a century were symptomatic of the incurable division of Mexican society. The main lines of cleavage should be apparent by this time, and the reader will be prepared for the desperate showdown between the clerical-minded conservatives and the revolutionary liberals. It should also be apparent that the only possible winners were the military. The opening act of the tragedy was the ferocious "Three Years' War" of 1857–1860; the principal action was the French Intervention and the Empire of Maximilian, 1862–1867; and the denouement was the military dictatorship of 1876–1910. The figures who dominate the scene are a middle-class Indian lawyer, Benito Juárez, and a primitive but brilliant caudillo, Porfirio Díaz.

Santa Anna galloped out of Mexico City on August 9, 1855. The provisional government set up by the "Plan of Ayutla" moved in four days later, after the city garrison had duly "pronounced" for it. Meanwhile, the disgusted population of the capital took things into its own hands and "pronounced" with an old-fashioned tumulto.

The houses of Santa Anna's ministers were looted, and the dictator's expensive carriages were burned in a glorious bonfire. It was a strangely purposeful and orderly tumulto, apparently organized to teach the conservatives that dictatorships were out.

The overthrow of Santa Anna, however, was not accepted by the conservatives as more than a temporary setback in their struggle for power. "All hope of reconciliation between the liberal and conservative parties was chimerical," wrote José Vigil, in his *Historia de la Reforma*. "They were separated by an abyss of hatred; the tendencies of both were perfectly defined, and there was no other prospect but a battle to the death between the two political bodies, which, since they derived from opposing principles, must necessarily arrive at opposite conclusions."

The years from 1855 to 1867 might appropriately be called the period of the religious wars, because, of all the questions involved in the struggle, the position of the Church in a liberal republic was the one that admitted no compromise. The issue was joined. The conservatives could not accept change without destroying the rigid fabric of their ideal commonwealth, and the liberals were just as insistent and unyielding in their position, that is, that the state could not tolerate an institution, the Church, which denied the principle upon which that state was founded, namely, popular sovereignty. It was natural, therefore, that the liberal party should include all colors of anticlericalism, from the small moderado group, represented by Ignacio Comonfort, to the violent Jacobin puros of the extreme left.

Racial and economic issues complicated the picture at the same time. The liberals attracted to their cause ambitious Indians and mestizos, some of whom were high-minded idealists, and others military and political caciques thirsting for power. The presence of Indians and mestizos among the liberals gave the struggle something of the aspect of a race war, although, to be sure, there were Indian generals, such as Ramón Méndez and Tomás Mejía, and whole Indian tribes, the Yaqui, for example, in the ranks of the conservatives. When that stalwart old Indian insurgent, General Juan Alvarez, who had been campaigning on his own ever since 1810, led his ragged army into the capital after the liberal triumph, the nice

271

people thought they were in for another servile revolt. They remembered the Alhóndiga and shuddered. The economic crisis was further complicated by the growing number of foreigners: English, Spanish, American, and French merchants, miners, speculators, and the like, who were always quick to threaten the Mexican government with intervention when they did not receive favored treatment.

General Alvarez was put in as provisional president, and he soon showed the conservatives what to expect by appointing to his cabinet such convinced liberals as Melchor Ocampo, Guillermo Prieto, Miguel Lerdo de Tejada, and Benito Juárez, who had returned from New Orleans to make his first appearance on the national stage. The only moderate was Ignacio Comonfort, Minister of War. The liberal government began its work by passing the mild "Ley Juárez," which restricted the jurisdiction of the ecclesiastical courts to bona fide ecclesiastical cases, for these courts, as has been mentioned above, had long been the refuge of influential laymen who were in some way connected with the Church. Reasonable though it was, the "Ley Juárez" provoked such an unexpectedly violent storm of protest that Alvarez was induced to resign, and Comonfort took his place.

Comonfort has fared badly at the hands of historians. As a moderate he was suspected by both sides and trusted by neither. He made the mistake of trying to be reasonable at a time when reasonableness was out of the question. He put down the pronunciamientos against him with unheard-of gentleness and treated the rebels so amiably that a section of the outraged liberal militia "pronounced" for the restoration of Alvarez. The clergy, on the other hand, were soon disabused of their hope that Comonfort's moderation meant that he was a conservative in disguise, for he strengthened his cabinet with the stoutest of liberals, Don Santos Degollado.

The next gun fired in the campaign was the drastic "Ley Lerdo," which prohibited corporations (that is, religious foundations and civic communities) from holding real property. The purposes of this law were three: (1) to destroy the economic power of the clergy by forcing them to sell Church lands; (2) to finance the government with the proceeds from the heavy transfer tax on the sales of Church

272

lands; and (3) to create a new class of small proprietors by breaking up the communal holdings of the native villages, for the liberals were saturated with laissez-faire doctrine. Morelos had advanced the same proposal forty years before.

The authors of the "Ley Lerdo" have been condemned for thus recklessly destroying a considerable part of the economic resources of the country, for the religious foundations, with all their faults, were superior to most hacendados in efficiency of land management and, most likely, in their treatment of the workers. The income from them supported all the public charities, hospitals, and schools and colleges. As bankers, the religious foundations financed the haciendas and other enterprises at a reasonable rate of interest, usually five per cent, in contrast to the ruinous usury collected by their successors. The conservatives were wild with resentment at this attack on "religion." One unexpected result of their feeling was that the pious wealthy refused to bid for the expropriated Church properties, many of which as a consequence were gobbled up by speculators. There was certainly no discernible gain in this change of ownership. But whether the liberals were concerned with these aspects of the matter or not is of no consequence. They were in a war for survival and they struck where it hurt.

The liberals were also clearly mistaken in thinking that the destruction of community holdings would turn the Indians into small peasant proprietors overnight. The Indians had no capital and could not purchase or operate the land thus released. Besides, they had very little conception of private landed property. Since their comunidades were "corporations" within the definition of the law, their ancient ejidos, which had been inviolable under Spanish rule, were subject to denunciation and were bought up by caciques, speculators, and hacendados, at a fraction of their value. This uncomprehended attack upon their communal life brought whole tribes into the conservative camp. The restoration of the Indian ejidos has been a strong bargaining point with Revolutionary leaders since 1915.

The Constituent Congress called by the liberals worked the entire year of 1856 under a heavy bombardment of criticism, and on February 5, 1857, brought out a new constitution, designed to make of Mexico a liberal, democratic republic. The signing of it was a solemn and moving ceremony. That aged prophet of liberalism, Don Valentín Gómez Farías, was led up to the rostrum on the arms of two deputies and was the first to sign. Then he knelt and swore by the Holy Gospel to recognize and obey the Constitution. The emotion of the deputies exploded in a tremendous ovation. "We swear! We swear!"

The Constitution of 1857 seems mild enough at this distance, but the fury with which it was assailed passed anything yet seen. The liberals had learned little since 1824. The new constitution set up a democratic, representative government of a single house, since the old Senate had shown marked conservative leanings. It continued the federal system, but attempted to correct its weaknesses by giving Congress the power to remove state executives for cause. It abolished military and clerical immunities (the "Ley Juárez"). It allowed nuns and priests to renounce their vows without penalty. It established secular education. And it tacitly recognized freedom of worship by saying nothing about it.

Pronunciamiento in Querétaro: "A handful of men without faith, without religion, without principles, possessed by cruelty and vengeance, breathing death and destruction, have put their heavy foot on the neck of the Mexican Nation! They have reversed the order by which societies should be guided, and for more than a year their heavy chains have bound the fatherland. These impious men would take away our Religion, and their foul lips have blasphemed the name of the Almighty. They have insulted our priests and thrown them into jail; they have destroyed our temples and turned them to profane uses. These sacrilegious men, full of avarice, have seized the goods of the Church and have reduced her ministers to beggary. What is worse, they have impiously mocked at the excommunications and anathemas of the Church. They are preparing mourning, bloodshed, devastation, and rapine for the Mexican Nation, and, finally, they will complete our ruin if Divine Providence does not watch over good Mexicans!"

Pope Pius IX made the issue very clear: "The Chamber of Deputies, among the many insults it has heaped upon our Most

Holy Religion and upon its ministers, as well as upon the Vicar of Christ on Earth, has proposed a new constitution containing many articles, not a few of which conflict with Divine Religion itself, its salutary doctrines, its most holy precepts, and with its rights. . . . For the purpose of more easily corrupting manners and propagating the detestable pest of indifferentism and tearing souls away from our Most Holy Religion, it allows the free exercise of all cults and admits the right of pronouncing in public every kind of thought and opinion. . . . And so that the Faithful who reside there may know, and the Catholic world may understand, that We energetically reprove everything the Mexican government has done against the Catholic Religion, against its Church, its sacred ministers and pastors, and against its laws, rights, and properties, We raise our Pontifical voice in apostolic liberty . . . *to condemn, reprove, and declare null and void everything the said decrees and everything else that the civil authority has done in scorn of ecclesiastical authority and of this Holy See. . . .*" [Italics supplied.]

It seems a bit shocking to us to see the papacy assume the right to nullify the constitution of a nation. We should certainly have resented such an act in this country. Mexico, however, was in a different category. The right of the Church to dictate policies of government, as we have seen, had been accepted by the Spanish Crown ever since the Conquest. The privileges of the Church had the sanction of time, and so it is not surprising that it should make assumptions in Mexico which would not have been tolerated in the United States.

Bishop Clemente de Jesús Munguía of Michoacán was specific. He declared in a pastoral letter that the faithful could not accept Article 3, which established secular education; 5, which allowed members of religious orders to renounce their vows; 6, which recognized freedom of speech; 7, which established freedom of the press; 12, which abolished tithes and privileges of nobility; 13, which suppressed ecclesiastical courts; 27, which prohibited corporations from holding land; 36, which defined the duties of the citizen: registration, service in the militia, the right to vote; 39, which proclaimed popular sovereignty; 72, which gave Congress the power to make laws enforcing these articles; and 123, which established federal authority in matters of worship and religious discipline. It was evident that the Church would accept no government except one of her own making.

The controversy was soon taken out of the field of argument. Even before the Constitution of 1857 was promulgated, a good part of the country was on the march. A conspiracy of nationwide scope was directed by a secret organization in Mexico City calling itself the Directorio Conservador. The first serious uprising occurred at Puebla, which the rebels took and held for several weeks late in 1856. Bishop Antonio Pelagio Labastida y Dávalos of Puebla was exiled for preaching against the Constitution. In his absence the episcopal governor of the diocese, Canon Antonio Reyere y Lugo, took over the leadership of the rebellion. He called upon the people of Puebla to make war by every means possible on "the enemies of Religion, who are attacking the independence and sovereignty of the Church." *Independence and sovereignty.* It would be difficult to define the issue more clearly.

Bishop Labastida, writing from his exile in Havana, was more temperate, although his meaning was no less evident: "I have been resolved, not only from today, but since the day of my consecration, to suffer any sacrifice and to undergo, with the grace of God, every trial, rather than violate in the slightest degree my conscience and the solemn vow I have made to God!"

The terrible bitterness of the religious war is not easy for us to imagine in these relatively tolerant times. The moderate Comonfort was elected president under the new constitution and took office on December 1, 1857. The only possible answer of the conservatives was the inevitable pronunciamiento, and the garrison of Tacubaya "pronounced" on December 17. The ground had been more carefully prepared this time. The conspirators of the Directorio Conservador convinced Comonfort that the constitution would not work, and he consented to become dictator under the "Plan of Tacubaya." At the last moment, however, he weakened and fled the country, leaving in power the tool of the clerical party, the vain and incompetent General Félix Zuloaga, who found himself faced with the grim task of running the government with a discredited party and an empty treasury. The liberal government, which had been forced out of the capital, took refuge with Santos Degollado and Melchor Ocampo in Michoacán.

The ensuing Three Years' War followed the horrible pattern of its predecessors, with sack and arson, the noose and the firing squad, teaching "liberalism" and "conservatism" to one side or the other, while fields went unplowed and hunger stalked. On the conservative side were wealth, the army, the Church, arsenals and supplies, and the machinery of government; on the other, bands of militia under jealous and touchy chieftains, but with the trackless back country behind them, and behind them also the unsmiling figure of one Indian lawyer, Benito Juárez.

Of all the national heroes of Mexico, the one most difficult to see clearly, through the thick foliage of myth that has overgrown him, is Juárez. We are invited to believe in the existence of the illiterate shepherd boy of Guelatao who, like an Indian David, slew almost single-handed the French Goliath, and whose wisdom and vision were such that he anticipated all the thinking of the present revolutionary leaders of Mexico. If we listen to the other side, we are treated to the spectacle of a monster, a kind of Antichrist, whose diabolical genius aimed at the destruction of everything good and holy. He was a "bandit," a "murderer," an "atheist," and the betrayer of the "true" Mexico. The power of these myths, to evoke emotion and confuse thinking, is immense. Too much blood has been spilled to allow either side to treat Juárez as an understandable human being. I attempt it with some trepidation.

One would hardly have picked out Benito Juárez in 1857 as the man destined to lead the liberal government through its mortal crisis. He had neither the learning of Melchor Ocampo nor the fire of Santos Degollado. Thus far he had shown no unmistakable signs of greatness in his fifty-one years. Born in a humble Zapotec family of Oaxaca in 1806, he overcame the handicaps of poverty and ignorance of Spanish, thanks to a kindly protector, who wished to educate him for the priesthood. Discovering, after some years in the Theological Seminary of Oaxaca, that he had no vocation for the Church, Juárez took up the study of law, in which he achieved distinction by his industry alone. He was admitted to practice in

277

1834. He served in the state legislature from 1832 to 1834, and was imprisoned in 1836 for suspected participation in the revolt against the conservatives, then in power. From 1842 to 1845 he served as an official in the state treasury and directed the finances of Oaxaca with honesty and efficiency. He was elected to the short-lived liberal Congress of 1846 and served until it was dissolved by Santa Anna in 1847. He returned to Oaxaca and was elected governor, and during his term of office accomplished two things worthy of note: he balanced the state budget, leaving a surplus in the treasury, and he refused sanctuary to Santa Anna after the disaster of 1848—which is not to be taken as an indication that Juárez had always been opposed to Santa Anna; rather, it was probably the patriot's reaction to the dictator's betrayal of his country. Indeed, up to the outbreak of the Three Years' War, Juárez had been an honest and plodding civil servant, with a marked streak of stubbornness and courage.

Two consistent traits appear throughout the career of Juárez which serve to explain him: a deep piety and a conviction of rightness. His piety (not to be confused with clericalism) is manifest in all his acts, as judge, teacher, governor, and president. The long years he spent as a student of theology were not long years of revolt against religion, as we gather from official textbooks. To postulate an irreligious or atheistic Juárez is to make him a consummate hypocrite, which he most assuredly was not. He believed in God and Order. With the early Jesuits, he believed that government had its sanction in God's will expressed through the will of the people. In thus elevating the popular will he naturally ran afoul of the clerical prejudices of his time, but he did so from religious conviction. He had a puritanical belief in his own rightness, and an unyielding, rock-like constancy in the face of the most appalling circumstances, qualities that give Juárez the grandeur of a medieval saint. He was a Mexican St. Dominic, the Lawgiver. To make of Juárez a popular revolutionary after the Jacobin pattern, a leader of the masses in a raw struggle for power, or a prophet of the present Revolution, is to misread his history. The ferocious attacks of the sinarquistas (see chapter 26) were directed against that mythical Juárez, just as, on the other side, the "cult of Juárez," as it is frankly called, is the cult of a myth.

Once we accept Juárez as a Puritan, his career is not at all mysterious. He was convinced that the Church was corrupt and that in her abuse of wealth and privilege she had betrayed her trust. The "Ley Juárez," therefore, was an act of purification of the Church, as well as a blow against the enemies of the liberal state. He has never been forgiven for the execution of Maximilian, and there seems to be an anomaly here, for the pious Juárez, whose aim it was to become the head of a Christian state, put to death the equally pious Maximilian, who had the same ambition. Their ideal states, however, rested upon opposing principles: that of Juárez upon popular suffrage (God's will acting through the people); whereas that of Maximilian rested upon the modern heresy of divine right. One or the other had to be destroyed. But I anticipate.

When Santa Anna was restored to power by the reactionary coup of 1853, one of the first things he did was to banish Juárez from the country, in revenge for Juárez' unkindness of 1848, and Juárez rejoined the colony of exiles in New Orleans. There he met Melchor Ocampo, the clearest thinker of the liberal party. It may be, as the debunking Francisco Bulnes affirmed (*El Verdadero Juárez*, 1905), that Juárez' education in liberalism began at that time and that Ocampo became his guide and teacher. However it was, when Juárez returned to Mexico he was no longer a country lawyer, but a stubborn warrior in the cause of liberalism. He was called to head the Ministry of Justice in the administration of Comonfort, and there tasted the sweet and heady wine of power. He was the Law. Perhaps it was the effect of the *Pandects* of Justinian, in which he learned that Law is above all persons and above its own makers. The liberal Constitution of 1857 was for him a Mexican *Corpus Juris Civilis*, and he was its instrument. Juárez had the unswerving legalism of a high priest of Israel or a royal visitor of Philip II. In the long and tragic years of the civil war he never yielded or compromised or deviated from the straight path of Law, as he saw it. *It was Juárez' stubborn conviction of right which held his mercurial party together for ten desperate years.*

After the defection of Comonfort, Juárez became constitutional president of a government in exile—in exile, at least, from the capital. He took up the gauntlet thrown down by the conservatives

279

and published a number of decrees implementing the Constitution, thereby banishing all possibility of compromise: (1) the complete separation of Church and state; (2) the secularization of all male religious orders (that is, making their members secular priests); (3) the suppression of all religious corporations; (4) the suppression of novitiates in nunneries; (5) the nationalization of all the real property of the Church; and (6) the abolition of tithes.

These decrees were not merely reprisals for clerical rebellion against the government; they obeyed a statesmanlike perspective of the fundamental nature of the conflict—a conflict in which to yield was to be destroyed. They were body blows against the forces that had made unity under the Republic impossible.

The Three Years' War dragged out its weary length to exhaustion. General Zuloaga as conservative president obeyed his clerical masters and annulled the objectionable legislation of the Juárez government as fast as it appeared, but his notorious incompetence soon got him replaced by the best general among the conservatives, Miguel Miramón. But with all their advantages of good leadership and unity, the conservatives were no better off than they had been with Santa Anna. They were even worse off, because the liberals held the port of Vera Cruz, where all foreign goods entered *and paid duties*. Their armies, under Miramón, Mejía, and Márquez, won most of the engagements, but they could not win the war. The country and the terrain were against them, and in time their enemies learned how to fight. As things got darker and darker for the conservative forces, their chiefs began to waver in their loyalties. By the end of 1860 the conservatives were definitely defeated, and the liberal army, now 28,000 strong, paraded through the capital in triumph on January 1, 1861.

It was only a truce. When Juárez moved into the National Palace his liberal government was just as prostrate as its opponents had been. Commerce was nonexistent; agriculture was almost dead; the customs had been pledged up to eighty-five per cent of receipts; the 28,000 officers and men of the army had not been paid; and the income from the tax on expropriated Church property was much smaller than had been anticipated. The monthly deficit of the treasury was 400,000 pesos. To add to the woes of the Juárez government, the dispersed chieftains of the conservative army continued a dozen little wars of their own in various parts of the country. Then, Melchor Ocampo disagreed with Juárez over policy and retired to his home in Michoacán, where he was seized and shot by General Márquez—the lowest level to which that talented butcher ever descended. Santos Degollado begged for the privilege of avenging the murder of his friend, and was himself caught and shot. The year 1861 was a nightmare. The liberal victory had solved nothing, and foreign and domestic critics blamed Juárez for the plight of Mexico. But by some miracle he stood, while the despairing conservatives continued their quest for a foreign Moses.

The occasion was propitious. The American Civil War had broken out and the liberals were cut off from any possible help across the border. Napoleon III was deluding himself and his country by pretending that he was as great as his uncle and that the manifest destiny of France was to rule the Latin world, including Spanish America. There was an abundance of unemployed princes in Europe, one of whom the Mexican plotters hoped might be induced to take the job of running the country. For many years the civil conflicts had advertised to the world (in the reports of foreign diplomats and investors) that Mexico was a hopelessly barbarous country that needed a Strong Hand. Mexico owed everyone. A growing heap of foreign claims, dating from the "Pastry War" and before, had necessarily been left unpaid. Juárez recognized them to the amount of 80,000,000 pesos and pledged his government to pay them, but Mexico's credit was gone and her debtors accepted the necessity of the great Intervention.

The undertaking between France, England, and Spain was signed in October, 1861, and was duly blessed by the pope. According to its terms, the signing parties had no designs upon the sovereignty of Mexico, but were only to seize the ports of entry and collect the customs until the claims should be satisfied. Napoleon and his Mexican accomplices, however, had other ideas. Without the knowledge of England and Spain, Archduke Maximilian of Austria had been persuaded to accept the imperial throne of Mexico, and Napoleon undertook to make it safe. When the commanders of the British and Spanish forces saw what the game was, they withdrew, leaving the French to embark upon the most fantastic adventure of the nineteenth century. The first French division landed at Vera Cruz on January 7, 1862.

It is outside the province of this volume to retell the incredible story of Maximilian and his empire. No episode in recent decades has been more thoroughly exploited. It had everything to delight the heart of a scenario writer: a beautiful, romantic, and really royal young couple; titles, uniforms, parades, and martial music; brave deeds and lots of shooting; and a heart-rending and truly tragic ending. We must leave all that to the lovers of pageantry and name the affair for what it was: a desperate gamble on the part of the dying colonial elements of Mexico to regain their lost advantages by means of a puppet prince whom they hoped to dominate; a cynical grab of territory by Napoleon the Little; and a novelesque adventure by a foolish young man and his power-mad wife, who saw themselves as exponents of Divine Right in the Western Hemisphere.

And Juárez? From the famous black carriage in which, unescorted, he governed liberal Mexico for ten years, came not a word about shedding the last drop of his blood for the fatherland, and the rest. That stone image of an Indian lawyer to the people of Mexico: "To proclaim, as our adversaries do, that they are not making war upon a country, but upon its government, is to repeat the empty declaration of all those who undertake a war of aggression. Besides, it is clear enough that one offends a nation when one attacks the government which that nation has erected and desires to support. . . . If I were merely a private citizen, or if the authority that I exercise were the result of some shameful mutiny, . . . then I should not hesitate to sacrifice my position, if in that way I could shield my country from the scourge of war. [But] since that authority is not my patrimony, but a trust confided to me by the nation in order to maintain its independence and honor, I have accepted it, I shall keep it for the period prescribed by our fundamental law, and I shall never yield it to the discretion of a foreign enemy. Rather, I shall wage against [that enemy] the war that the whole nation has accepted, until I oblige him to recognize the justice of our cause."

Thus Benito Juárez, facing destruction by the greatest military power of Europe. It is the driest and most formidable declaration of war I have ever read.

The French had their hands full. Instead of the military parade they had expected, they encountered a savage and desperate resistance. At Puebla, on May 5, 1862, General Laurencez was soundly whipped by the Mexican army of Ignacio Zaragoza. (May 5 is justly celebrated as one of the great holidays of Mexico.) Napoleon III had to send more and more troops, until the French had 34,000 regulars in Mexico, without counting the conservative Mexican forces, which numbered another 20,000. The liberals could not hope to stand against such weight, so they retired to their protecting mountains and to the guerrilla warfare they knew so well. The French commander in chief, Marshal Forey, and his successor, Marshal Bazaine, had the same experience that Santa Anna and Miramón had had before them. They chased the liberal troops from place to place; they shot "bandits" by the score; but they could not win an honest victory. They had, in fact, an impossible assignment. To conquer and occupy a mountainous wilderness three times the size of France would have taken an immensely greater force than the one they had. However, after two years' hard campaigning the French had cleared out a living space in the middle of the country; the *mission civilisatrice* was declared to be sufficiently advanced; and Maximilian and Carlotta landed at Vera Cruz on May 28, 1864.

Te Deums, Masses, speeches, fireworks. Even so, the frigidity of their reception in that ancient liberal stronghold was so marked that Carlotta burst into tears. Maximilian to his new subjects: "Mexicans! You have asked for me! Your noble nation, by a spontaneous majority,[1] has designated me to watch over your destinies from this day forward!"

Labastida y Dávalos (now archbishop of Mexico), fresh back from exile in Cuba, with his eye on the main chance: "Let us not forget that we owe this situation of true liberty and well-being, and the opportunity to continue the aggrandizement of our country, to the immortal genius of the Emperor of the French, under the government of our beloved son Maximilian I!"

[1] Maximilian may well have believed this nonsense, for the French and the Mexican conservatives had rigged a plebiscite to that effect.

Giuseppe Garibaldi to the Mexican officers captured by the French at Puebla: "To the brave officers who fought for Mexican liberty their brother sends a message of friendship and hope!"

Old General Juan Alvarez to Maximilian and the world at large: "I still live!"

Maximilian and his court paraded about the "pacified" area of the Plateau and were everywhere entertained with carefully staged spontaneous fiestas, while the godless French openly scoffed at the barbarians whom they were supposed to be defending against the hosts of Satan. The "bandits" continued to annoy the forces of civilization, to Maximilian's distress, and he, puzzled and frightened by their ingratitude, finally listened to his advisers and decided that he would have to exterminate the Juaristas before there could be peace. "From this day forward," ran his edict, "the struggle will be between the honest men of the nation and the gangs of criminals and bandits. There will be no more indulgence for those who burn towns, for those who rob, and for those who murder peaceful citizens, poor old folk, and defenseless women." Death to all bandits taken in arms! Death! But *death to the bandits* also worked both ways, as Maximilian was to discover.

Everything went wrong for the civilizing mission. Contrary to hopes and expectations, the North won the Civil War in the United States, and President Johnson suggested to the French ambassador in Washington that it might be just as well if Bazaine got out of Mexico. Phil Sheridan's army on the Rio Grande lent weight to the suggestion. Napoleon's worries at home were sharpened by Prussia's fast and successful wars against Denmark and Austria. France might well be next on the list, and the French people were already complaining openly about their emperor. In Mexico the liberal "bandits" were as far from extermination as ever, so Napoleon submitted to the inevitable and abandoned his dupes to their fate.

As soon as the French props were pulled out, the whole gaudy card house of the conservatives collapsed. A young mestizo general named Porfirio Díaz moved in from the mountains of Oaxaca and took Puebla. Maximilian, weak-minded or quixotic to the last, joined Miramón at Querétaro to face certain destruction, and watched his army being cut to pieces at Cerro de las Campanas. On that same hill, on June 19, 1867, Maximilian and his two faithful generals, Miramón and Mejía, faced a firing squad, while all the world shuddered. There were no exceptions in the Law of Juárez.

*Death to the bandits? Death?*

The black carriage of Benito Juárez rolled into the capital on the morning of July 15, 1867. General Díaz had spent 20,000 pesos of his scanty funds to decorate the streets for the great event, and his troops were paraded in a glittering array of force, but Juárez sat unsmiling through it all. He knew who the enemy of Law was bound to be. Díaz never forgave him.

Juárez faced the most appalling conditions that any Mexican president ever faced, economic and political chaos, but he faced them confidently, or stoically. He meant to weld all factions into a nation, a nation ruled by Law. One of his first acts after the peace, however, showed how chimerical such an ideal was, for he evidently expected the 60,000 soldiers of the Republic to share his Spartan devotion to the fatherland, and he dismissed 40,000 of them!

His furious generals, each of whom commanded something like a personal army, had the psychology of the conquistador. Had they not saved the fatherland from the foreigner? Was this their reward for ten years of bloodshed and suffering? Were they to be turned out like beggars in a country which was theirs by right of conquest? The answer of some was to organize themselves into a violent opposition party, called the *Constitucionalistas,* who denounced Juárez as a dictator and demanded the election of Porfirio Díaz. A good many of them did not wait for an election, but went back to their old trade of marauding and "pronouncing."

Nevertheless, in the election of October, 1867, Juárez won the presidency by a substantial majority—possibly, as his enemies charged, by manipulating the election machinery. But his party was divided by jealousies and intrigues; the country was overrun by bandits and ex-soldiers, imperialist and republican; Indian tribes in the northwest were in open revolt; the treasury was empty; the people were hungry. To make matters worse, a terrible drought ruined the crops of 1869 and Juárez could do nothing to relieve the famine. But his government survived! That it could do so amidst universal misery, military opposition, and the unsleeping enemies of

285

liberalism is proof that Juárez had with him a large part of the nation. His loyal forces, under that prodigy of drunkenness and energy, General Sóstenes Rocha, smashed disaffected caudillos one after the other. General Díaz retired to Oaxaca to plot and manufacture munitions, and in a year or two there seemed to be some prospect that the government would endure.

With his admirable pertinacity Benito Juárez applied himself to the slow task of rebuilding his country according to the blueprint of 1857. The eternal financial crisis was partly met by the honest and efficient Minister of the Treasury, Don Matías Romero. Industry was encouraged; the building of the Vera Cruz railway, begun in 1850, was resumed; the voracity of local caciques was somewhat controlled; secular schools were opened. Juárez intended to unify the country in fact, and he pursued a policy of conciliation toward the late enemies of the Republic. An amnesty law of 1870 restored all but a few of the ex-imperialists to freedom and citizenship, and Indian communities were mollified by his quietly discouraging further alienation of their ejidos. The blessings of comparative peace brought about a belated flowering of letters, and men like the liberal Ignacio Altamirano and the conservative José María Roa Bárcena wrote novels and verses of some merit, and, much more important, they wrote without fear. In the field of scholarship, distinguished figures like Manuel Orozco y Berra and José Fernando Ramírez contributed works of lasting value in the history of their country. There seemed to be some truth in the statement of Don Justo Sierra, that the Intervention and the empire had made Mexico a nation.

The first hard test of the new peace came with the presidential election of 1871. Of the three candidates, Juárez, Sebastián Lerdo de Tejada, and Porfirio Díaz, none received a majority of the votes, and the election was thrown into Congress. Congress gave Juárez a plurality and he was declared president. Pronunciamiento by Porfirio Díaz: The election was illegal! His "plan": "The Constitution of 1857 and freedom of elections!" To arms! Again Díaz and his confederates were smashed by General Rocha, but it would have taken no prophet to foresee the fate of Mexico when Juárez should be no more. And Benito Juárez, the stern patriot, the Man of Law, the symbol of a Mexico still lost in the distant future, died on July 18, 1872.

# 23

## THE RISE AND FALL OF DON PORFIRIO

The legend of Don Porfirio is full of magic. In all Mexico there is only one Don Porfirio. His name evokes the nostalgic longings of the disinherited who, since the Revolution of 1910, have been looking back on the Age of Don Porfirio much as Lot's wife looked back on Sodom and Gomorrah. The good old days of Don Porfirio have become a kind of cult, not limited by any means to the ex-nobility, for the present devotees of the God of Industrialization recognize in Don Porfirio the prophet who showed them the way to the Promised Land—which makes *porfirismo* a much less prickly subject to attack than *juarismo*. For everyone of late feels kindly toward Don Porfirio, although his most ardent admirers, naturally, continue to be those who hope that some day another Strong Hand will take over and run the country more to their heart's desire. It is one of the many charming inconsistencies of Mexico that Porfirio Díaz, the military caudillo and bitter enemy of Juárez, should have succeeded the Lawgiver of Oaxaca and ruled Mexico for a third of a century as an irresponsible despot, under the cloak of the liberal Constitution that Juárez and his devoted company had fought so long to establish.

Sebastián Lerdo de Tejada, the immediate successor of Juárez, was an able and vigorous man, but he lacked something, and I suspect it was the symbolic value of Juárez: Juárez the Indian, Juárez the high priest of Law and Justice. Who but Don Benito could have gone unguarded through the back country for ten years, alone in his battered black carriage, trusting to the exquisite courtesy of his own people? Lerdo de Tejada continued the policies of his late chief, and he even succeeded in appeasing most of the caudillos who had "pronounced" for Díaz; that is, all but Díaz himself, who retired to a sugar farm in Vera Cruz and bided his time. Lerdo inaugurated the

287

Iron Age in Mexico with the opening of the Vera Cruz railway in 1873, and for a time there was some hope of tranquillity. But Lerdo pleased no faction. The *lerdistas,* the *juaristas,* the *porfiristas,* all felt cheated, for he gave the country to none of them. He kept himself in power by the only means possible: by trickery, fraud, and interference with the "rights" of caudillos. He was denounced as a dictator and the destroyer of liberty.

Porfirio Díaz slipped back into Oaxaca in 1875. His old army friends took heart and "pronounced" against the intolerable tyranny of Lerdo. In January, 1876, they published the necessary "plan," the Plan of Tuxtepec, a hodgepodge of protests, meaning that the military chieftains considered Mexico to be their prey and that they would not be balked. Sympathetic pronunciamientos popped all over the country. The loyal Sóstenes Rocha fought a bitter and losing war for a long year, but in the end he and his chief were beaten. Lerdo fled the country on November 21, 1876.

Juárez and his Law had been rejected in favor of rule by force, and the astonished conservatives suddenly found themselves presented with a dictator, gratis. For the next thirty-four years they were to enjoy the most efficient despotism ever seen in the western hemisphere. Don Porfirio's slogan was "Bread and the Club": bread for the army, bread for the bureaucrats, bread for the foreigners, and even bread for the Church—and the club for the common people of Mexico and those who differed with him. It was the culmination and inevitable last act of the tragedy that began with the mutiny of Agustín de Iturbide.

Porfirio Díaz had the virtues of a great barbarian, and he needed them. The lesser caudillos who had elevated him had to be kept quiet, and they had to be kept harmless. Unlike Juárez, Don Porfirio was not so naïve as to expect his military chieftains to put their country's welfare before their personal fortunes. Their new master had the cunning of a Caesar Borgia. He gave his generals little jobs and restored them to their rightful place at the public trough; he kept them apart and played them off against each other; he split the army into small units and scattered them about the country; but he did not trust it. For his immediate use in terrorizing dissenters he organized a private army of thugs, whom he called his *bravi* and who could be counted on to wreck newspapers and remove suspected opponents in their own way. The police, of course, could never track down the criminals.

The nation was suffering from its endemic plague of banditry. Don Porfirio's solution was to set up a national gendarmerie called the Rurales, recruited from the gunmen of the cities and from among the bandits themselves. They were given showy uniforms, good salaries, and the power to shoot on sight, and no questions asked. Into their capable hands was placed the task of making Mexico safe for Don Porfirio and his friends. Troublesome Indian caciques, striking workmen, indiscreet speakers and writers, and honest bandits disappeared into the noisome dungeons of the fearful old Belén Penitentiary, or were shot "while attempting to escape," an effective device known as the *Ley Fuga*. In the course of a few years Mexico became the best policed country in the world. It was ruled by martial law, without courts, and the Rurales loved to shoot.

As the years rolled by and Mexico lay quiet in her straitjacket, foreign capital was encouraged to come in; manufactures and agriculture flourished; railroads pushed their way south from the border; American miners reopened the ancient *reales de minas* of the Spaniards, and smelters began to belch their yellow fumes into the desert air. Silver, gold, copper, lead, and zinc flowed north to feed the rapidly expanding commerce and industry of the United States; and coffee, sugar, bananas, and henequen found a ready market abroad. In 1893, Don Porfirio's brilliant Minister of Finance, José Ives Limantour, funded the public debt at a reasonable rate of interest and balanced the national budget. Mexico was solvent! This feat was so close to being a miracle that Don Porfirio was hailed everywhere as the "Coming Man." Grumblers were quiet for once, or, if they had anything to say, they said it to themselves. For many years Mexico saw not a single pronunciamiento, and the *Pax Porfiriana* was a blessing that his country could appreciate meaningfully.

Like Santa Anna, Don Porfirio had to have appropriate monuments to his immortality. The capital was cleaned up and modernized; beggars and léperos were kept out of town; electric lights blinked, over the protests, to be sure, of the gas monopoly; streetcars clanged; and a rash of marble palaces broke out, the most hideous example of which is the bastard Palace of Fine Arts.

For the Creole aristocracy the dictatorship of Don Porfirio meant the return of the Silver Age. The hacienda reverted to the pure type of the feudal estate, with the terrible Rurales to call on in the event of trouble. Elegant carriages drawn by high-stepping thoroughbreds again paraded up and down the Paseo on Sundays. The ladies discarded the graceful Spanish mantilla for the *dernier cri* from Paris. Their sons were sent to France for an education and came back pattering the lingo of the *boulevardier* and scoffing at the barbarism of their own country. The best people went in for building houses in the villainous style of the Second Empire. I was shown through one of them by its proud owner, now reduced to taking in boarders. It was a museum piece of velvet draperies, pier glasses, marble tables, gilt, dazzling chandeliers, spindly chairs, artificial flowers, and stuffed birds. "Isn't it beautiful!" she exclaimed. "They don't build houses like this any more. *There is nothing Mexican in it!*" This good lady belonged to the class of which Charles Flandrau makes such kindly fun in his delightful *Viva Mexico!* Their ready hospitality, their reckless good living and charming manners were one of the pleasantest features of Creole life. Happy days were here again, and Don Porfirio would live forever.

The clergy awoke from their long nightmare and discovered that religion and the liberal dictatorship of Don Porfirio were not necessarily incompatible. The offensive laws of Juárez' day were discreetly ignored; religious schools and thinly disguised nunneries appeared; and should there be trouble the pious Doña Carmen Díaz could be counted on to patch things up with Don Porfirio, who was an indulgent husband. The ranks of the clergy were swelled by Spanish, French, and Italian priests, until by the end of the régime they numbered some five thousand, against the pitiful five hundred of the dark days of Juárez. Only the native clergy grumbled.

If the dictatorship of Don Porfirio meant the return of the Silver Age for the Creoles and the clergy, for the foreigner it was the Golden Age. Mexico became "the mother of foreigners and the stepmother of Mexicans." The foreigner soon learned that he could buy justice and favors from the swollen and underpaid bureaucracy, which grew to include a large percentage of the literate population of the country. *Empleomanía,* the government-job mania, infected the whole middle class of Mexico. But the foreigner was king, for the new paradise was made possible by his money and industry, and the sweat of Mexican workmen. His factories and mines were rarely disturbed by strikes or similar unpleasantnesses, and, when they were, the Rurales, the army, and the judiciary saw to it that the malcontents gave no more trouble. Strikers were slaughtered by the score and by the hundred at the Cananea mines and the textile mills of Río Blanco. "You can't make an omelet without breaking eggs." Díaz made Mexico a colony of foreign capitalism, principally American, although Mexican capitalists did not suffer. His amazing success was to a considerable extent a by-product of our post-Civil War prosperity; Mexican economy reflected our booms and panics, and began to show signs of weakness about 1907.

Don Porfirio had the intelligence to surround himself with able men, his *científicos,* a brilliant group of lawyers and economists, headed by Limantour, worshipers at the new and glittering shrine of Science and Progress. They honestly believed that a dictatorship was the only possible government for their backward country, and they did their utmost to force modernity upon it. They resembled the Bourbon administrators of the eighteenth century, those efficient administrators of benevolent despotism, and they made themselves into a tight oligarchy, ruling Mexico for her own good.

The científicos were cultivated men, and along with its material improvements they thought their capital should have its cultural ornaments as well. They encouraged letters of an innocuous kind, mostly perfumed imitations of the French, but no subversive nonsense. Poetry, the novel, the theater, all flourished in Mexico City in Don Porfirio's reign, but they were remote from the life of the country and are now hardly more than literary curiosities. Of much more lasting importance were historical works, for it seems to be characteristic of dictators to encourage historians, in the hope, I imagine, of having their names handed down to posterity. Justo Sierra, Joaquín García Icazbalceta, Vicente Riva Palacio, José Vigil, Alfredo Chavero, Francisco Bulnes, and Carlos Pereyra, among others, working in the new and intoxicating method of positivism, brought Mexican historiography to a height it has not attained since, and their writings are still indispensable to the student of Mexico.

An interesting phenomenon of the dictatorship was the change that took place in Don Porfirio himself. The illiterate guerrillero who had fought the French in the mountains of Oaxaca underwent a subtle metamorphosis as he gained in power and dignity. At fifty-one he married Carmen Rubio, a beautiful girl from a distinguished Creole family. He began to turn white. He dressed like a European banker, when he was not in his gorgeous uniform loaded with metals. His wife taught him table manners. As his régime took on an air of permanence and his machine functioned more and more perfectly, he found himself surrounded by a crowd of place-seekers and yes-men. His claque poured out an ever-thickening stream of flattery, and he loved it. If, as Disraeli said, one applies flattery to royalty with a trowel, on Don Porfirio one used a hose. He was half-smothered with foreign decorations, each with its appropriate scroll. He listened to speeches that would have upset the stomach of a Santa Anna, but none of them surpassed the toast proffered by Elihu Root in 1907: "If I were a poet I should write eulogies; if I were a musician I should compose triumphal marches; if I were a Mexican I should feel that the steadfast loyalty of a lifetime would not be too much to give in return for the blessings he has brought to my country. But as I am neither poet, musician, nor Mexican, but only an American who loves justice and liberty, and hopes to see their reign among mankind progress and strengthen and become perpet-ual, I look to Porfirio Díaz, the President of Mexico, as one of the great men to be held up for the hero worship of mankind!"

Beyond question the material and even the cultural advancement of Mexico during the dictatorship of Don Porfirio was very great: so many miles of railroads, so many millions of dollars invested in this and that, so many years of peace and order, eighty millions of pesos in the treasury. It may even be true that Díaz was a superior kind of benevolent despot. It may also be true that some sort of military dictatorship was inevitable after the frightful chaos of the mid-century, and that if Don Porfirio had not taken over, Mexico would have been torn to pieces by the rival caudillos whom he so effectively checkmated. Otherwise, the price of the *Pax Porfiriana* was too high. It threw Mexico back into the hands of an irresponsible autocracy, without the Laws of the Indies or the salutary fear of a royal visitor to curb it. There was no law but the will of Don Porfirio. The legislature became a mockery, kept to lend the color of legality to his acts. He cynically referred to his lawmakers as *mi caballada*, "my herd of tame horses." Elections were such a farce that hardly anyone took the trouble to vote. All of the offices of the Republic were filled with Don Porfirio's men. Between 1883 and 1894, by a series of colonizing laws passed by his caballada, Díaz gave away, to foreign speculators and personal friends, 134,500,000 acres of the public domain, that is, *about one-fifth of the entire area of the Republic.* Not satisfied with this colossal rape, the land sharks prevailed upon Díaz to throw open for seizure and settlement the remaining lands of the Indian communities—which he could legally do under the "Ley Lerdo." When the Indians objected, as did the Maya and the Yaqui, the army and the Rurales put down the "rebellions," and thousands of prisoners were sold into slave gangs to cultivate henequen in Yucatan and tobacco in the Valle Nacional of Oaxaca. By the end of the Díaz régime not ten per cent of the Indian communities had any land whatever. In short, the Díaz régime was the denial of elementary justice to a large part of the population. The price was blood.

One of the curious things about the dictatorship of Don Porfirio was that its beneficiaries evidently thought, and certainly hoped, that it would never end. But toward the last his feline brain began to thicken and his trigger finger lost its cunning. A handful of revolutionary thinkers, like Felipe Carrillo Puerto and the Flores Magón brothers, Enrique and Ricardo, preached socialist and anarchist doctrines, wrote pamphlets and edited newspapers, and faced death, imprisonment, torture, and exile, but their work went on. In 1908 a mild little man named Francisco Madero published a book entitled *La Sucesión Presidencial en 1910,* in which he brought up the forbidden subject of Don Porfirio's successor. What! Could Don Porfirio die? A year later Andrés Molina Enríquez wrote a shocking book, *Los Grandes Problemas Nacionales,* which somehow got by the censor, although it was later suppressed. Molina's book was a terrifying exposure of the whole hypocritical, stifling miasma of despotism, Porfirian despotism. Books, to be sure, would not have caused anyone's downfall, because most of the reading public was safely tied to government jobs, but they might profitably have been read by the elect and by the foreigners, whose heads were thrust deep in the sand.

The year 1910 was the year of the Great Centennial, celebrating the hundredth anniversary of Miguel Hidalgo's *Grito de Dolores* and the birth of Independence. It was also meant to advertise to the world the triumph of progress and *porfirismo*. The irony of the double program was almost too heavy to be ignored, but it *was* ignored. Like a plant whose roots have been cut off, the Golden Age of Don Porfirio threw out its last spray of blossoms with the Centennial, and died. The century died as it had begun, in bloodshed. No one mentioned that 1910 was also the centennial of the Alhóndiga.

The fall of Don Porfirio was as inevitable as it was unplanned. Up to 1908 all suggestions that the Golden Age might end were rigorously suppressed, and their authors expiated their temerity in exile, prison, or death. In 1908, however, the aging dictator granted an interview to an American newspaper man, James Creelman, which was published in *Pearson's Magazine* under the heading "Thrilling Story of President Díaz, the Greatest Man on the Continent." The greatest man on the continent had told Creelman that the Mexican people were now ready for democracy and that he intended to retire in 1910. The story was probably meant for circulation north of the border, or perhaps it was a trial balloon. If the latter, it was soon bouncing wildly about among the politicians and intellectuals of Mexico. The news was too good to be true, for the truth was that the younger generation was bored with its doddering dictator and his senile government. Not a few men were concerned with the fate of the country when Don Porfirio should retire, for no provision had been made for the succession, and several offered themselves as potential saviors of the fatherland.

The one who first capitalized on the situation was Francisco Madero, whose book has been mentioned. Madero was not a revolutionist. Indeed, a more unlikely leader of a revolution can hardly be imagined. He came from a large and rapacious family of landowners of Coahuila. He was a kindly man with no particular training for anything. Following the mores of his class, he had spent part of his youth in Paris, and had managed to complete a semester's residence at the University of California. His diminutive size (five feet two), squeaky voice, and lack of biceps he compensated for by going in for messianic oddities: teetotalism, vegetarianism, and spiritualism. In one of his séances his Ouija board told him that he was to be president of Mexico, and the Creelman article told him that the time was at hand. His first step was to publish his book, which had nothing remarkable about it, being a few mild suggestions, to the effect that it might be a good idea to restore the Constitution of 1857 and give the people a chance to elect a *vice-president*. That vice-president could easily be Panchito Madero, and Don Porfirio might die. Stranger things had happened.

Don Porfirio was good-natured about the competition of his puny antagonist and allowed him to travel about the country haranguing audiences; but to his astonishment Madero was everywhere received by enthusiastic crowds. Madero invented a slogan that caught on: "Effective Suffrage—No Reelection!" It did not mean much, perhaps, but it was at least a protest against the interminable dictatorship of Don Porfirio. Madero's success was so sensational that Don Porfirio became alarmed and had him jailed in San Luis Potosí. Various other candidates were discouraged in one way or another, and Don Porfirio and his stooge, Ramón Corral, were duly elected president and vice-president on September 30, 1910.

Meanwhile, on Independence Day, September 16, the Great Centennial was inaugurated, with 20,000,000 pesos spent on fireworks, decorations, military parades, banquets, speeches, poems, and carloads of champagne, while Francisco Madero, in his cell at San Luis Potosí was writing the "plan" which was to ignite the glorious bonfire of revolution.

After the election Madero escaped across the border to San Antonio and there "pronounced" in heroic style. Nobody seemed to pay much attention to him and, after a laughable fiasco, he gave up his revolution as a bad job and set out for Europe. But down Chihuahua way a rough storekeeper named Pascual Orozco and a gorilla-like bandit whom he had befriended decided to stage a revolution on their own. The bandit was one Doroteo Arango, better known to history as Francisco Villa. At the news of their uprising Madero abandoned his European trip, hastened back to Chihuahua, and persuaded Orozco and Villa to let him lead their revolution under his "Plan of San Luis Potosí." So, in February, 1911, Madero had a party at last and, what was more important, an army.

Other prospective saviors of the fatherland had taken up arms. Abraham González gathered together a band of cowpunchers and went on the warpath in northern Chihuahua, while down south in the state of Morelos a fierce fighting cock of a man named Emiliano Zapata was exciting the Indians by telling them that the land was theirs and the only way to get it was to take it. His "plan": *Land and Liberty, and Death to the Hacendados!* The price of the Golden Age of Don Porfirio.

Even in Mexico City things were happening. The *caballada* committed the unheard-of lese majesty of calling for Don Porfirio's resignation. Crowds of *maderistas* took to parading before the National Palace. Díaz frantically cabled José Limantour to come back from France and help him out. Limantour stopped in New York, where he held conferences with Madero's agents and got them to agree to an armistice. But things had got out of control. The troops of Villa and Orozco were already besieging Ciudad Juárez, just across the Rio Grande from El Paso, and they pushed Madero aside and took it by storm, on May 10, 1911.

All the world could now see how rotten the federal army was, and *tumultos* broke out with increasing frequency and violence. The situation of Don Porfirio was patently hopeless, and Limantour accepted defeat and agreed to Don Porfirio's resignation, without even consulting him. Under the terms of the agreement a provisional government would be set up, under Francisco de la Barra, until Madero should be elected president—an event that was taken for granted.

On May 23, 1911, the news of the capitulation broke in Mexico City. The next morning huge crowds paraded down the streets to the Zócalo. *Resign! Resign!* Mobs milled before the National Palace. *Resign! Resign!* Don Porfirio's answer: "Fire!" Two hundred dead.

All that evening Don Porfirio, suffering from a raging toothache and the importunities of his family and friends, refused to accept the dreadful fact that his time had come. And then, toward midnight, he retired to his chamber and, in halting and clumsy phrases, penned a long and self-righteous resignation which ended with the prophetic words: "I hope . . . that when the passions which accompany every revolution have been calmed, a more conscientious and substantiated study will cause a more correct judgment to arise in the national conscience which will permit me to die bearing in my heart a just recognition of the esteem which all my life I have consecrated . . . to my fellow citizens."

Congress received the terrifying document in deathlike silence. The *caballada* was free at last!

# 24

## THIS STRANGE, EVENTFUL HISTORY

"Thinkers," muttered the major absently [in Mariano Azuela's novel, *The Flies*], "prepare the Revolution; bandits carry it out. At the moment no one can say with any assurance: 'So-and-so is a revolutionary and What's-his-name is a bandit.' Tomorrow, perhaps, it will be clearer."

"Nonsense!" interrupted the doctor. "It's a problem in elementary arithmetic. Let us suppose that we wish to discover the equivalent value $x$ of a certain hero named So-and-so. Let us also suppose that before the Revolution $x$ equaled zero pesos. After the Revolution, let us say, $x$ equals 100,000 pesos. But, since So-and-so could not have acquired a single peso without taking it from someone else, by cancellation we arrive at the result: $x$ equals a bandit!"

News of the great renunciation of Don Porfirio brought Francisco Madero down from the north, surrounded by a cloud of relatives. Along his way he was cheered by delirious crowds. The new savior of the fatherland had had greatness thrust upon him. True to his promise in the Plan of San Luis Potosí, he called for national elections, to be held in October, 1911. His halo was bright and untarnished, and he was virtually the unanimous choice of the voters.

Madero ruled with sweetness and light and brotherly love: the Constitution of 1857, free speech, a free press, the right of assembly. But behind him was a crowd of self-seeking politicians, headed by members of his own family. The real power of the Madero administration lay in the hands of his brother Gustavo, who was tough and knew what he wanted. Gustavo took a leaf out of Don Porfirio's book and organized a small army of gangsters, whom he called his *porra*, which is to say "club," a *porra* being a heavy, knobbed stick. Other relatives joined up and got on the bandwagon, and Mexico was soon suffering from as corrupt and expensive a régime as that of Díaz, without its saving stability. The Plan of San Luis Potosí had said something about restoring lands to the Indian villages, but the subject was dropped. Emiliano Zapata, disillusioned with the little white man, whom he had never trusted anyway, again called his people to arms and resumed the burning of haciendas and the murder of hacendados. Free speech had the disquieting effect of allowing the discussion of explosive revolutionary doctrine. An able young lawyer named Luis Cabrera brought forward a wicked plan to break up the swollen estates by taxing idle lands. The weak toleration of such heresy proved beyond a doubt that Madero was a dangerous lunatic. The word was passed that Madero must go.

The first to "pronounce" against him was his early backer, Pascual Orozco. Orozco was premature. After one expedition against him had failed, Madero gave the job of running him down to General Victoriano Huerta, although he hesitated because of Huerta's notorious addiction to alcohol. Huerta was a murderous drunkard, to be sure, but he was also a good soldier, and Orozco fled across the border. Then Madero showed his ignorance of Mexican history by asking Huerta to account for the million pesos given him to finance the campaign. Huerta indignantly refused to do so and was retired in more or less disgrace. Two other pronunciamientos, by Generals Bernardo Reyes and Félix Díaz (the latter a nephew of Don Porfirio), were put down without much difficulty, and then Madero committed his second blunder: *He did not shoot his prisoners.*

During his first year in office, Madero did other tactless things, such as neglecting to continue Don Porfirio's policy of protecting foreigners and their property. Zapata and lesser caudillos were on the warpath, and Madero was unable to stop them. The country was ripe for saving and, at two o'clock on a Sunday morning, February 9, 1913, the garrison troops of Tacabaya marched to the prison where General Reyes was confined and released him. Then, with Reyes at their head, they marched to the National Palace. Meanwhile, Gustavo Madero had got wind of the uprising and dashed to the Palace ahead of the conspirators. There he persuaded the guard not to abandon the President, so when Reyes and his men approached the gates they were met by a burst of machine gun fire, which killed Reyes and two hundred people on their way to Mass at the Cathedral. Then it was that Madero embraced his fate: He put Victoriano Huerta, the drunken maniac whom he had insulted, in command of the Palace troops.

Then followed, from February 9 to 18, 1913, the "Tragic Ten Days," which did not shake the world. General Huerta, from the Palace, and General Félix Díaz, commanding the Citadel, cynically sprayed Mexico City with shells, killing and maiming civilians, but never by any chance hitting each other. General Felipe Angeles, the best and most honorable soldier of the Republic, hastened back from Morelos (where he had been trying to control Zapata) to protect Madero, but found himself blocked by United States Ambassador Henry Lane Wilson, who objected to having guns placed near the embassy. The horrible farce was continued by Huerta's sacrificing a company of loyal Rurales to the machine guns of Félix Díaz, just to prove that the show was on the level. The denouement was of a piece with the rest of the business. Madero and his cabinet were arrested by officers of his guard while Huerta was unaccountably absent, and Gustavo Madero was delivered over to the soldiers of the Citadel and tortured to death.

On February 18, 1913, Félix Díaz, Victoriano Huerta, and Henry Lane Wilson drew up, in the United States Embassy, the "Compact of the Citadel," which was a "plan" to reconstruct the Mexican government along safe and sane lines. Ambassador Wilson to the diplomatic corps: "Mexico has been saved! From now on we shall have peace, progress, and prosperity!" Wilson to the State Department at Washington: "A wicked despotism has fallen!"

At midnight, five days later, on February 22, 1913, President Madero and Vice-President Pino Suárez, despite Huerta's guarantee of their personal safety (made to Ambassador Márquez Sterling of Cuba), were shot "while attempting to escape."

General Huerta's triumph over the forces of evil was celebrated

300

with feasting and merrymaking. The good old days of Don Porfirio were back again and prosperity was around the corner. Huerta, however, turned out to be unmanageable. His seventeen months as president were an uninterrupted orgy of drunkenness, robbery, and murder. The cabinet that Ambassador Wilson and the diplomatic corps had picked out for him included some of the best men among the conservatives, but they soon resigned in disgust, and Huerta was left to rule Mexico with his personal gang of thugs. Critics of Mexico's Nero were quietly done away with. In Congress Belisario Domínguez denounced Huerta as a bloody tyrant and accurately prophesied his own assassination. A hundred and ten dissenters in Congress were jailed. Only the members of the Catholic Party remained, and they had to do what they were told. Popular revulsion against the shame of Victoriano Huerta was the real beginning of the Revolution.

Venustiano Carranza, bewhiskered conservative governor of Coahuila, honestly horrified at the murder of Madero, and interested in his own political future, "pronounced" against the usurper. His "Plan of Guadalupe" was pure *maderismo*: overthrow of the dictator and restoration of the Constitution of 1857. There were already three respectable forces in the north, those of Francisco Villa and Pablo González (known as "the general who never won a battle"), and, off in Sonora, that of the remarkable man who was to become the real leader of the Revolution, Alvaro Obregón. Carranza adopted the title of "First Chief of the Revolution," which Villa and González could not stomach. Not trusting them anyway, Carranza trekked across the Sierra Madre Occidental and joined forces with Obregón in Sonora.

The Revolution began its southward sweep. It had become a conquest of Mexico by the Men of the North. It had no ideology as yet beyond the vague program of Carranza: the destruction of plutocracy, praetorianism, and clericalism. For the present its job was to conquer the country. Obregón's terrifying Yaqui troops in the west, and Villa's equally ferocious cavalry, his famous *dorados,* driving down from Chihuahua, had a glorious fiesta of killing and looting. *Death to the federals! Death to the hacendados!* Cities, towns, and haciendas were stripped bare, and prisoners were always

301

shot. Villa and his two blood-thirsty cronies, Tomás Urbina and Rodolfo Fierro, were childishly vain of their marksmanship, and there was an abundance of targets. Martín Luis Guzmán, who served as Villa's secretary, tells (in *The Eagle and the Serpent*) how Villa humored Fierro once when they had captured five hundred federals, by allowing him to shoot the lot. Fierro complained that his pistols got too hot, but he stuck it out and only one man escaped, under cover of darkness.

Alvaro Obregón was the one leader of the North who sensed the vital issues of the great tumulto. He had witnessed the enslavement of the Yaqui Indians and the seizure of their lands. His own life as a mechanic and farmer had made him familiar with the problems of the Mexican worker. He turned out to be a born caudillo and became the most successful general of the Revolutionary forces. Above all, he was intelligent, practical, and hard-minded. Revolutionary theories to him were not a religion, but could be trimmed to fit the occasion. He accepted Carranza as "First Chief," but he meant to make himself ruler of Mexico.

Meanwhile, down in the old liberal haunts of Morelos and Guerrero, Zapata's agrarian movement, now legitimized as the "Plan of Ayala," was given form by an ex-schoolmaster, Don Antonio Díaz Soto y Gama, with a program that aimed at nothing less than a complete restoration of land to the Indians. Huerta's federal army, half of which existed on paper, was no match for the wild men of Zapata, while in the North his garrisons melted before the fire of Villa and Obregón.

Huerta was doomed by another and unforeseen event. Up in the States, an ex-college professor, a kind of strait-laced Presbyterian dominie with a strong urge to impose his tight moral code on the rest of the world, was elected president. Woodrow Wilson looked upon Huerta's murderous career and was not pleased. Nor was he pleased with Ambassador Henry Lane Wilson's part in the "Compact of the Citadel." He recalled the ambassador and sent down a personal envoy to see Huerta and try to persuade him to be civilized and let the Mexican people choose their own president. The envoy, John Lind, was a well-meaning but heavy-handed man, with no Spanish, and contemptuous and arrogant besides. Lind infuriated Huerta and the Mexican Foreign Minister, the able Federico de Gamboa, by repeating Wilson's threat to withhold recognition unless Huerta should step down and call a general election, *in which Huerta should not be a candidate*. The unfortunate result of his insulting interference was that Huerta found himself unexpectedly backed by a strong wave of patriotism. He all but expelled John Lind and made warlike gestures at Washington. Puzzled and angry at such lack of appreciation, President Wilson decided that Huerta would have to be got rid of, by war, if necessary. He opened the border for the shipment of arms to the *constitucionalistas* Carranza, Villa, and Obregón, arms paid for by tens of thousands of head of cattle stolen from the vast empire of the Terrazas family of Chihuahua.

The necessary "incident" was not long in coming. Some American sailors loading gasoline at Tampico were arrested and held in jail for an hour or so. They were released with apologies by the Mexican commandant; but our Admiral Henry T. Mayo, who belonged to the romantic school of Santa Anna and the Prince de Joinville, and who very likely was acting under President Wilson's instructions, held that the United States flag had been insulted and that only a salute of twenty-one guns could wipe out the stain. The Mexican commandant refused; the delighted Huerta refused: he would protect the fatherland against the northern bully. The silly business got beyond reasonable solution—perhaps it was not meant to be solved. Wilson, outraged by Huerta's bombast, which, of course, was meant for Mexican consumption, and hearing that a shipload of German arms was on its way to Huerta at Vera Cruz, ordered Admiral Mayo to occupy the port. The dead: two hundred Mexican soldiers, twenty-one American Marines.

The occupation of Vera Cruz naturally provoked tremendous indignation throughout Mexico. Carranza, stirred in his patriotism, and possibly fearing that Huerta would utilize the occasion to steal the show, denounced the incident as a violation of the Treaty of Guadalupe Hidalgo (which it was) and so shared in the glory of saving the fatherland.

Huerta's hour had struck, however, at the moment our govern-

303

ment put its weight behind Obregón and Villa. The armies of these two caudillos now raced south, with Mexico City as the prize of the winner. Carranza managed to persuade Villa to stop at Zacatecas, and Obregón, after several days of fighting the federals, entered the capital in triumph on August 15, 1914. Huerta fled across the border and drank himself to death in peace.

Carranza was now shakily in the saddle, at the mercy of his obstreperous generals and defied by the indomitable Zapata. He faced a sullen country, which was in a vast depression, its economy disrupted and hunger rampant. Villa, with his formidable Northern Division, broke openly with Carranza and made a bid for United States support. He somehow managed to convince President Wilson and Secretary of State William Jennings Bryan that he was the hope of Mexico. Bryan was even reported to have spoken of him as Mexico's Sir Galahad, and Villa enjoyed a moment of hero worship in both countries. A new government was planned, to be formed by a convention at Aguascalientes in October, 1914. Villa was easily persuaded to consent, since Aguascalientes was in his satrapy. The delegates soon discovered that Villa was boss. The provisional president, General Eulalio Gutiérrez, elected by the convention, was virtually his prisoner. Obregón did not take this highhandedness sitting down, but wisely went over to Carranza, while Villa and his *convencionistas* moved on the capital. Meanwhile, Villa had made a deal with Zapata, and the two famous caudillos rode into the Promised Land side by side, while the best people shuddered prophetically behind barred doors. The difference in the conduct of the two armies was the difference between men of principle and bandits. Zapata's Indians humbly begged their bread at the doors of the rich; Villa and his gang went on a glorious spree of drunkenness, rape, and murder.

Provisional President Gutiérrez of the convencionistas stood it as long as he could, but he soon made his escape to Carranza in Vera Cruz. Obregón bided his time in Puebla, and the disgusted Zapata retired to Morelos and his private war. Obregón, now that Villa was deserted by Zapata and his army demoralized by drink and venery in the capital, struck. The *villistas* abandoned Mexico City, where a wild panic ensued (graphically described by Mariano Azuela in *The*

*Flies*). They retreated to Celaya, where, in April, 1915, occurred the most terrible battle of the civil war. Primitive fury was no match for the cool brain of Obregón, and, after three bloody days, Villa retreated northward in his long trains of freight cars, pulling up the track behind him. Obregón relaid the track and squeezed Villa relentlessly, month after month, until Villa was driven to gamble everything on a last desperate flight across the western mountains to Agua Prieta, Sonora, which was held by a hard-faced mestizo named Plutarco Elías Calles. Villa's wild dorados left their bodies hanging on the barbed wire. After five years in the sun, their chief found himself back at his starting point, banditry.

In the course of the bitter civil war, the support given to Huerta by the clergy, as well as the ancient anticlerical tradition of Mexican liberalism, had given the Revolution a violent anticlerical bent. Obregón demanded a "loan" from the clergy which was, of course, refused. By way of retaliation he drafted a number of priests into his army. Religion was being attacked! The strong interventionist sentiment in the United States was heightened by the agitation of the Catholics, who had little grasp of the history of the Church in Mexico. They put great pressure on President Wilson who, luckily for us, contented himself with writing a series of his famous notes in protest, which did no particular harm beyond infuriating the Mexicans.

In spite of Carranza's resentment over our occupation of Vera Cruz, and in spite of his notorious pigheadedness, he had finally to accept our aid, and Wilson cut off Villa's supply of arms in October, 1915. Villa answered by stopping a train at Santa Ysabel, Chihuahua, and shooting sixteen American engineers. In March, 1916, he led a raid into New Mexico and massacred nineteen people at Columbus. All this barbarity may have been pure vendetta, or it may have obeyed a primitive statesmanship, because it was almost bound to end in intervention, and intervention always creates heroes in Mexico. We had "recognized" Carranza meanwhile, although he was denounced by Catholics as a "modern Nero," and Wilson was forced into an uneasy alliance with him. He could think of nothing better to do than to send Black Jack Pershing across the border to catch Villa. He did not know his geography or the Mexican people.

Pancho Villa instantly became the popular idol of the country, and racy ballads ridiculing the gringos were joyfully sung by every tavern minstrel.

With all its troubles, although Villa and Zapata were still marauding, by 1916 the rule of Carranza showed some promise of stability. His most ticklish problem was to dispose of the five-hundred-odd generals and their shoals of followers who had risen with the Revolution and who were ruling their satrapies quite independently of the "First Chief." They made and applied laws as they saw fit, and most of them carried on a system of more or less legalized thievery, blackmail, and extortion; "x equals a bandit." The conservatives looked to Carranza for protection, and he gained influential friends by repudiating the racial implications of the Revolution, as well as its leaders. But he stubbornly and foolishly refused to take advice or criticism from his staff. His best men, including Obregón, abandoned him, and Mexico suffered one of the most corrupt régimes in her tragic history.

Carranza's personal rule was now bankrupt, and he was obliged to call a constitutional convention at Querétaro in December, 1916; but he soon discovered that he had no voice in it. It was dominated by two men who refused to be cheated, Generals Francisco Múgica and Alvaro Obregón. A new constitution (the present one) was thrown together *in six weeks*. In reality the Constitution of 1917 must be thought of as another "plan," imposed upon the nation by the victorious Men of the North. It was a weapon forged to ensure the success of their Revolution. To a very great extent it was a renovation of the Constitution of 1857, but it contained several articles that departed radically from the laissez-faire liberalism of Ocampo and Degollado. The new state was to be a managed state, and its leaders thought of themselves as a dictatorship of the proletariat. Article 27 denied the ownership of the land in fee simple: the land belonged to the people; it must be restored to the people. The people owned all the subsoil minerals, including petroleum, which might be exploited only by Mexican nationals, or by foreigners willing to obey Mexican laws. Article 27 aimed to reconquer for the Mexican people all the land and the rights to exploit it alienated by Don Porfirio or by the "Ley Lerdo" of 1856.

Article 27 meant the extinction of the hacendado class and the end of foreign rule, and that was its purpose. The uproar that it caused was deafening, as will appear later.

A hardly less shocking article was Article 123, the Magna Charta of Mexican labor. It recognized the workers' right to organize, strike, bargain collectively, to receive adequate compensation, sick benefits, and the like. It was a whole social program.

Strategically, these two articles had the purpose of bringing into the revolutionary camp the peasants and workers of Mexico. It is doubtful that the thinking of their authors went much beyond that point. These were war measures, and the civil war was still raging.

The hottest spot of all in the Constitution of 1917 was probably Article 3, which put teeth into the anticlerical provisions of the Constitution of 1857. It also was a war measure, a declaration of independence from the clergy. The clause most bitterly resented by the Catholics was the one that made *all* public education secular, and the primary grades compulsory.

The Constitution of 1917 was, in short, the blueprint of a managed industrial and agrarian republic, with leanings toward socialism, and its enemies were, of course, the same that we have met all along the way since 1824.

For three years the Constitution hardly emerged from the blueprint stage. Carranza, who was inclining more and more to the Right, was definitely not interested in agrarian and labor reforms. The National Agrarian Commission, which his government had set up in 1916, distributed only half a million acres to the peasants in three years, while the clergy cried robbery, and the disillusioned Zapata went on the warpath again. But Zapata, who was a kind of saint to his followers, but an intolerable menace to everyone else, was treacherously murdered by a certain Colonel Jesús Guajardo, whom the grateful First Chief rewarded with a general's commission.

The practice of employers in the Federal District of paying their men in worthless Carranza scrip brought on a general strike, which Carranza put down with the military, thereby alienating any support he may have had among labor. He tried to quiet the uproar by consenting to a labor convention at Saltillo in May, 1918, but he was

307

outplayed by a young leader named Luis Morones, who organized the first nationwide union, the *Confederación Regional Obrera Mexicana,* better known as the CROM. At the same time Morones created a political wing of the union, the Mexican Labor Party.

Having now lost his revolutionary friends, and having failed to win enough new ones on the Right (he was bitterly hated by the Catholic party, for example), Carranza plodded through to the close of his dull and reactionary régime. Since he was pledged to the Madero principle of "No Reelection," he could not gracefully succeed himself. But he loved power and was unwise enough to try to impose upon the electorate the unknown Ignacio Bonilla, who was not even identified with the Revolution. The only possible choice of the nation was obviously the conqueror of Huerta and leader of the Revolution, Alvaro Obregón. Obregón, quite reasonably fearing arrest or worse, escaped from the capital in disguise and, with the backing of Morones and the new CROM, "pronounced" against Carranza in April, 1920. The nation, heartily sick of mediocrity and corruption, made his march to Mexico City a triumphal parade, while Carranza was murdered in bed by one of his own officers, after a wild train chase over the Vera Cruz railway.

An ex-music teacher, Adolfo de la Huerta (who should not be confused with Victoriano Huerta), was made provisional president, but it goes without saying that Alvaro Obregón was duly "elected." Mexico had a new master, one who knew what he was about and who would stand for no nonsense. Obregón meant to restore peace and prosperity, and he made the Revolution respectable. Everyone became a Revolutionary with a capital R. Ancient Díaz bureaucrats, ex-Huerta generals, and swarms of new caudillos were absorbed into the Obregón System. A new jargon came into being: One talked "revolutionarily well," or one acted in a "revolutionary manner," meaning that one stood in with the Boss.

A great deal of nonsense was talked at the time (particularly by the Catholics, who hated Obregón and his System) about Mexico's "going Bolshevist," because the leaders of the Revolution had adopted the Marxist vocabulary current among left-wing circles of the day. It was the natural reaction of people who had something to lose. But the fact is that Obregón was an able politician and a

308

practical statesman. He had to have a strong party. He encouraged the radical CROM, but he created a check to it by allowing the peasants to organize the *Confederación Nacional Campesina*, the CNC, under Zapata's old mentor, Antonio Díaz Soto y Gama. He kept the state politicos in line by putting his own men in key positions, and he followed Don Porfirio's policy of keeping his generals on the payroll. The expense was enormous, but Obregón could not run the risk of pronunciamientos. Perhaps he did not even wish to get rid of the Revolutionary chieftains, for Obregón had a fondness for his old cronies. His generals were above the law, as generals still are.

For all his agrarian sympathies, Obregón was not eager to attack the complicated and dangerous problem of distributing land on any *zapatista* basis, that is, by outright expropriation. He did allow free villages (i.e., those not in haciendas) to apply to the Agrarian Commission for land, but he left the initiative to the peasants, and they, intimidated by hacendados and caciques, or persuaded by their priests that expropriation was robbery, were modest in their demands. Besides, the villagers had no capital with which to buy tools, seeds, and animals, and their borrowing was checked by the exorbitant interest collected by the loan sharks. Finally, a large part of the population, not necessarily the upper class, was indifferent, if not actively hostile, to the government. It would take long years of indoctrination to teach the oppressed and illiterate masses to see good in any program emanating from Mexico City.

The labor movement, which was essentially urban, had a better start. Luis Morones, its leader, was now one of the most powerful men in the country. He was the czar of labor, a caudillo in the classical pattern. He organized gangs of thugs known as his *palanca*, that is, "lever," with which he pried blackmail from unwilling employers, induced rival unions to join the CROM, or murdered people who got in his way. As the strength of the CROM grew under the protection of Obregón, its little bosses discovered that employers were willing to pay good cash to avoid strikes. Cash and corruption made the union bosses as obnoxious as their military brethren, and their arrogance and rapacity made their destruction merely a matter of time. Still, in spite of its leaders, Mexican labor made some real advances toward a more decent standard of living, although the distressing consequences of corruption among their leaders were that the workers, rendered cynical by the cynicism of their bosses, looked upon the labor movement as a grab for power and easy money.

The most encouraging advance toward the rebuilding of Mexico according to the new blueprint was made in education, in spite of Catholic opposition. Obregón wisely chose as its head a man who had no party affiliations, a scholar and writer, José Vasconcelos. Vasconcelos was not even a revolutionary in the official sense. He had, indeed, a profound contempt for the parvenu barbarians thrown up by the Revolution, but he did have an idea that the Mexican people would accept a new set of values if given the chance. Every village was to have its school where the future citizens were to learn the elements of agriculture, the three Rs, and the doctrines of the Revolution. Vasconcelos was hooted at, and praised, for distributing quantities of cheap editions of the classics translated into Spanish.

The landowners and the oil people could not be expected to swallow Article 27 without protest, and their cries of Bolshevism kept the United States from recognizing Obregón for three years. This did him no harm, rather the contrary, because it has always been popular for a president to protect Mexico from the foreigner, preferably the United States, a device that Santa Anna and Porfirio Díaz had utilized to their profit. But elections were approaching, and Obregón could not afford to provoke a pronunciamiento. So he turned reasonable: Article 27 was declared not to be retroactive; foreign claims for damages incurred during the Revolution were allowed; payments on foreign debts were resumed; and Calvin Coolidge recognized Obregón as the legitimate president of Mexico, on August 23, 1923.

The election of 1923 marked the triumph of the Obregón System. It was marred only by the shortsighted opposition of Adolfo de la Huerta, who had been persuaded to run against Obregón's candidate, Plutarco Elías Calles, and who "pronounced" when it turned out that the election had been thoroughly rigged. De la Huerta was supported by the traditional enemies of the Revolution, as well as by a number of lesser caudillos who felt that Obregón had not rewarded them properly. The revolt was short, but extremely violent. Obregón was saved by his superior military skill and by the loyalty of labor and the peasantry, and De la Huerta retired to Los Angeles, California, to teach music again. One evil effect of the episode, besides the 60,000,000 pesos it cost, was the naming of fifty-four new generals to replace the ousted friends of De la Huerta. The army always wins.

Plutarco Elías Calles was a despot, usually benevolent, but always a despot. He ruled lawfully when it was convenient; otherwise, his enemies "committed suicide," a new euphemism in the Mexican political lexicon. The Obregón System in his hands became perfect and powerful. Calles even put the army to work building roads and policing them afterwards; he supported Vasconcelos' schools; he allowed the agrarian program to go forward, not too rapidly for safety; and some 8,000,000 acres of land were distributed to 1,500 villages in four years.

Calles' strongest support came from organized labor, the CROM, which was a kind of militia by this time. Luis Morones was made Minister of Industry, with the power to settle strikes as he chose. As a result, Morones' lieutenants, who called themselves the *Grupo Acción,* built country houses and traveled about in expensive cars; but the shiniest and most expensive car of all was the bomb-proof Cadillac of the diamond-bedecked leader of Mexico's embattled workers, Luis Morones.

Calles had strong anticlerical opinions, and his more or less open war with the clergy came to a head in 1926, when he was bitterly attacked in the conservative papers of the capital. He retaliated by deporting some hundred-odd foreign priests and nuns, by closing all the religious schools, and by ordering all priests to register with the civil authorities. The reaction was the most violent and dangerous revolt ever faced by the government. It followed much the same pattern as the clerical revolt against Juárez, but the clergy had been modernized, and it struck. All religious services in the Republic ceased on July 31, 1926. The pious majority of the country were horrified. In Jalisco, Michoacán, and Colima the terrible Cristero rebellion broke out, getting its name from its battle cry, *¡Viva Cristo Rey!* "Long live Christ the King!" "Death to the heretics!" In priest-

311

led tumultos government schools were burned, teachers were murdered, and a train from Guadalajara was blown up, killing, it was alleged, a hundred passengers. The local caudillos, all Calles men, took the repression of the revolt into their own hands. They rounded up thousands of rebels and herded them into concentration camps and hanged many on telegraph poles, while the soldiers burned villages and stole everything in sight. The frightful suppression of the Cristeros brought new demands for intervention from the Catholics of the United States, but cautious Calvin Coolidge reckoned that it was none of this country's business. Nevertheless, the appalling reports that continued to come out of Mexico kept Catholic feeling in the United States at the boiling point, and Coolidge was persuaded to mediate, which he did by sending as ambassador Dwight Whitney Morrow.

Morrow, who was branded by the Cristeros as "a partner of Morgan, the famous Jewish banker of Wall Street," had the assistance of Father John J. Burke and the legal adviser of the National Catholic Welfare Council. They met with Calles at San Juan de Ulúa, but got little out of him, for he complained that the Mexican hierarchy had treated him as if he were the devil in person, not the president of the Republic. Father Burke and Bishop Leopoldo Ruiz y Flores of Michoacán were impressed by Calles' sincerity, and Bishop Ruiz set out for Rome to inform the pope that a happy solution was possible. An agreement was, in fact, patched up, with the blessing of the pope, to the anguish of the Cristeros, who felt they had been sold down the river. It included (1) a general amnesty for all Cristeros who would lay down their arms; (2) the restoration of priests' and bishops' houses; (3) civil registration of only those priests who had been appointed by the superior hierarchy; (4) religious teaching to be permitted in public schools; (5) appropriate guarantees of all this.

The agreement was published on June 27, 1929, and on June 30 the churches were opened, to the accompaniment of a wild clangor of bells. Morrow, who was in Cuernavaca at the time, upon hearing the joyful din, is reported to have said to his wife: "Betty! Do you hear that? I have opened the churches of Mexico!"

Calles' friction with the United States was considerably worsened by a new crisis over Article 27. He had decreed that the oil companies would have to exchange their old titles for fifty-year leases, while the companies stood fast on the rights granted them in the days of Don Porfirio. Luckily, the row blew over, thanks to the hasty publication by W. R. Hearst of some clumsy forgeries purporting to prove that Calles had bought up a number of United States senators for a round million dollars. The oil people lost a good deal of public sympathy at the same time when the noisiest of the interventionists, Secretary of the Interior Albert B. Fall and oilman Edward L. Doheny, got themselves into a mess with the Teapot Dome scandal.

Morrow weathered this crisis also. He liked the Mexicans, and a good many Mexicans liked him. He went to bullfights and put himself out to be friendly. He was openhanded in the grand manner, although he did not escape the inevitable charge that he had greased some important palms. He and his wife renovated a graceful old house in Cuernavaca and furnished it with *Mexican* handicrafts. To show his appreciation of the lovely city, Morrow commissioned Diego Rivera to paint a magnificent fresco in the ancient Palace of Cortés, now the Ayuntamiento, for which he paid Rivera $10,000 and thereby got him expelled from the Communist Party as a capitalist. (Rivera told me that he had *not* been expelled, but had resigned in disgust.)

The end of the first Calles term found Mexico at peace with the world. Foreign and domestic capital was edging timidly back into the country; roads were opened, and they could be traveled in safety; a great many schools had been built, although the supply of teachers, at twenty dollars a month, was inadequate, as it still is. The railroads had been repaired, and the first waves of tourists discovered Mexico, the Land of Romance.

Under the protection of her modern benevolent despots, Mexico's latent artistic genius blossomed in an astonishing renaissance. Rivera, Orozco, Siqueiros, Mérida, Tamayo, and a host of followers, touched by the fire of the Revolution, rebelled against the parlor art of the Age of Don Porfirio. They found their inspiration in the tremendous sculptures and wall paintings of pre-Conquest civilizations, in the rude but vigorous murals of the cantinas, and especially

313

in the macabre and thoroughly Mexican woodcuts of José Guadalupe Posada. With religious conviction they set out to teach the Mexican people the blessings of the New Order, interpreting history to suit their need and unmercifully pillorying the former rulers of Mexico on the walls of public buildings. The violence of their murals, even more than the liberties they took with history, horrified the best people and sharpened the class war beyond measure. At the same time the superlative excellence of a great deal of the new art was immediately recognized abroad, and Mexico became the Mecca of western artists.

One of the most heartening signs of the new artistic life was the extraordinary success of the children's open-air art classes. The youngsters were given paints, brushes, and canvas, and were told to paint whatever their fancy dictated. The charming work of the Mexican children, sold in village squares and published by the Ministry of Education, did more to awaken appreciation of Mexico in this country than all the suffocating propaganda of the tourist agencies.

The Revolution could hardly fail to stimulate literary expression, although its turbulence and the lack of a large reading public prevented a flowering comparable with that of the plastic arts. Nevertheless, that gentle and clear-eyed old physician, Dr. Mariano Azuela, portrayed the Revolution, with its violence, contradictions, hypocrisies, pathos, and humor, in several striking novels, the best known of which are *The Underdogs, The Flies,* and *The Bosses.* The more caustic pen of Gregorio López y Fuentes drew the types thrown up by the Revolution with extraordinary fidelity, in *El Indio* and *Mi General.* The more literary Martín Luis Guzmán wrote a masterful first-hand chronicle of the Revolution in his well-known *The Eagle and the Serpent.*

If, along with these advances, Mexico was sodden with the corruption of labor racketeers, thieving generals, and venal judges—well, no people can hope entirely to escape their heritage.

In the election of 1927, Generals Francisco Serrano and Arnulfo Gómez, backed by the smoldering Cristeros, decided to buck the Obregón System and have a go at the presidency. They were very ill-advised. Their plot had hardly got beyond the talking stage when the swift hand of Calles overtook them. The crosses marking the graves of Serrano's party may still be seen on the old Cuernavaca road. Gómez was caught and shot in Vera Cruz.

For some reason no other candidates presented themselves, and Obregón was duly elected president on the skip-stop plan that he and Calles had adopted. Alvaro Obregón was a hard man and an ambitious man, but he was also ambitious for the welfare of his country, which needed his toughness in her time of troubles. So it was a disaster for Mexico when he was murdered by a young religious fanatic, José de León Toral, on July 17, 1928. A great deal of ugly talk circulated at the time about the "responsible authors" of the crime, and the Mother Abbess María Concepción Acevedo y de la Llata (*La Madre Conchita*) was condemned to several years in the penitentiary for "complicity." Toral was shot, of course, with "*¡Viva Cristo Rey!*" on his lips. The Cristeros died uniformly well.

Other "responsible authors" were suggested. Obregón had been hated by Luis Morones, among others, and it was discreetly whispered that his death was not unwelcome to Calles, who, it was said, did not relish the prospect of giving up his power. Nothing came of this chatter, and Calles effectively stopped further talk by announcing that there would be no more military caudillos in the president's chair. Certainly not! He also made a magnificent grandstand play by marching, bareheaded and unescorted, in Obregón's funeral. Santa Anna would have envied him.

# 25

## THE REVOLUTION COMES OF AGE

Calles' statement about the end of caudillo government was, of course, so much eyewash. The interim president, Emilio Portes Gil, was imposed by Calles. Calles men filled all the key positions in the army and in the state governments. A new capitalist class had come into being during the Obregón–Calles régime: generals, provincial caciques, and labor racketeers. Their money was invested in land and industry, but particularly in urban real estate. The revolutionary plutocrats found themselves in the same boat with their ancient enemies, the old hacendado–clergy–foreigner complex of Don Porfirio's day. Like Díaz, Calles was the policeman of the New Order. He was also its principal beneficiary.

The new millionaires, with their riches acquired in the service of the fatherland, had the psychology of the silver aristocracy of colonial times, without their piety. They erected palaces in Cuernavaca and Lomas de Chapultepec which advertised to the world the wealth of the owners. Medieval castles, Gothic cathedrals, Hollywood bungalows, acres of stained glass, tennis courts, swimming pools, imported statuary, stables and garages left no doubt about it. The heroes of the Revolution discovered that it was pleasant to wear tailored clothing, ride in Cadillacs, and consort with honest-to-goodness millionaires from the States.

Calles and his satellites were above the law. One day I was almost run down by a fancy car that was traveling through the crowded streets of the capital at about forty miles an hour. I was badly scared and my language was appropriate. A policeman grinned at me. "Think nothing of it," he said; "he missed you, didn't he?" I had to admit it. "The next time you see a general's car coming," he added, "get out of the way." "But," I protested, "how am I to know a general's car from any other?" *"You just learn to smell 'em!"* was the cryptic answer.

The whispered comments of minor bureaucrats and ordinary citizens about the arrogance and vulgarity of their new overlords were unprintable, but the perfumed rivers of flattery that Calles soaked up made the efforts of former claques seem amateurish. The machine of Calles–Portes Gil was now called the National Revolutionary Party, the PNR, and it was supported by a huge war chest, kept filled by a device invented by Morones, of taking a percentage of the salaries of all government employees, except, of course, the army. The CROM, however, was out of power. It had served its purpose and was now a hindrance to Mexico's new capitalists.

The presidential election of 1929 was controlled by the PNR. Elections became as dismal a farce as they had been under Don Porfirio. One wonders why they were held at all, for no candidate had the ghost of a chance of election unless he was backed by the Party. Calles and his PNR nominated Pascual Ortiz Rubio, a mild and ineffectual party hack, familiarly known as Don Pascualito or, by the scalding Mexican humorists, as "Don Nopalitos," from his fancied resemblance to the thick green leaves of the prickly pear. An abortive pronunciamiento was easily suppressed by Calles. The independent candidacy of José Vasconcelos, however, was another matter. The bitter philosopher toured the country and spoke to great crowds of disillusioned revolutionaries, Cristeros, and eager Catholics, exposing at the risk of his life the corruption of the government and the betrayal of the Revolution by Calles. Calles' answer was to send truckloads of gunmen to Vasconcelos meetings and spray them with machine guns. Vasconcelos fled the country and continued his campaign among the Catholics of the United States. Ortiz Rubio was elected by a handsome majority.

Calles' country house in Cuernavaca, on the "Street of the Forty Thieves," as the humorists had it, was now the capital of Mexico. The unhappy Ortiz Rubio ran the government as best he could, with one ear glued to the telephone. The grateful PNR voted Calles the title of *Jefe Máximo de la Revolution,* "Supreme Chief of the Revolution," and when he spoke, no dog barked.

Calles went to Europe in 1930 and came back with a brand-new message. He had discovered that small peasant proprietorship, as practiced in France, was a failure. The distribution of ejidos to Mexican families was, therefore, a mistake, the obvious remedy being to encourage large plantations. Although there was considerable justification for this solution, as was to become evident during World War II, it was suspected that Calles was not disinterested, for he was now a great landlord. The distribution of ejidos almost ceased.

The Jefe Máximo continued to undercut the CROM by encouraging independent unions and by keeping its *líderes* away from the public trough. Membership in the union dropped in a few years from a claimed million and more to a small fraction of that number, and its leaders drifted away to more profitable fields, that is, all but Morones, who managed to keep his armored Cadillac and his diamonds.

At the same time Calles, the bitter anticlerical, whose persecution of the Catholics in 1926 had brought on the bloody Cristero rebellion, made overtures to the Church. After all, religion and the Strong Hand had always got on nicely together. But his provincial caudillos did not lose their prejudices so easily, and a new persecution of the Church occurred in 1931 and 1932. The Constitution of 1917 allowed the individual states to limit the ratio of priests to the population to one in a hundred thousand. For no well-explained reason, the state governors took to applying the law, and within a year or so there was only a handful of priests left in the Republic. It was rumored, not without plausibility, that Calles was behind the persecution and was using it to persuade the Church to listen to reason. The expulsion was accompanied by the expected riots, and reprisals by state troops. The noise of battle became so loud by 1932 that Ortiz Rubio could not make himself heard, and Calles announced that the president had resigned. It was significant that Ortiz Rubio sent his resignation to Calles in Cuernavaca, rather than to Congress. That body had sunk to the level of Don Porfirio's *caballada*.

The next *pelele*, or front man for Calles, was the wealthy gambling-house owner and business partner of Calles, Abelardo

Rodríguez, hailed as "the friend of the protelariat." His adminis-tration was marked by the appearance of gangs of toughs who called themselves the Gold Shirts, and whose function was to beat up Communists (read opponents of Calles, some of whom really were Communists) and Jews. These thugs were a recrudescence of the *bravi* of Díaz, the *porra* of Gustavo Madero, and the *palanca* of Morones. It had a fascist stench about it.

Calles' betrayal of the Revolution was countered by labor groups and agrarians. They were strong enough to capture a sizable block of Calles' own PNR, and they pushed through a measure to resume the distribution of land to the peasants. To rescue the villages from local caciques, land distribution was made the responsibility of the federal government. A new bank was established to finance the ejidos. A young instructor of philosophy at the National University, Vicente Lombardo Toledano, undertook the reorganization of labor which was to result in a new and leftward orientation of the workers and peasants.

Another power in the anti-Calles movement within the PNR was the Minister of Education, Narciso Bassols, who began the program of "socialized education," to emancipate Mexican youth from clerical influence by teaching the "scientific truth," as revealed by Karl Marx, in the public schools. The clergy and the pious generally were very bitter about this "atheistic" education, and still are. In a market place of Michoacán I overheard two women talking about it. First woman: "Sister, they say we shall have to send our children to the atheist schools. What are we going to do?" Second woman: "You may do what you like, but as for me, they can kill me if they wish, but I will not send my boy to be taught mortal sin. Death rather than that!"

In the remote state of Chiapas I managed to obtain an interview with Bishop Gerardo Anaya, recently returned from exile. I: "Do you mind telling me how they are taking the new educational program in your diocese?" Bishop: "I really have nothing to say about it." I: "But surely you can tell me something. People have been talking about little else ever since I came to this town [San Cristóbal]. How do the teachers go about it?" Bishop: "My son, you are evidently new in these parts. How should the teachers know what is expected of them? You see, this is *Mexican* socialism, which means that, whatever it is today, tomorrow it will be something else. So it is quite idle to try to find out what it is."

The doctrinaire handling of the religious question by the leaders of the Revolution was understandable in the light of the history of the Republic, but it always meant that in time of crisis the government had to face a fanatical opposition. Perhaps a whipping boy—the Church—was necessary to keep the Revolution alive; but political wisdom, to say nothing of ordinary humanity, demanded some kind of conciliation in an overwhelmingly Catholic country.

The six-year presidential term, filled by the three *peleles* of Calles, ended in 1934. The Jefe Máximo had to find a new president. The growing radical group in the PNR was getting restless and would have to be appeased. The Great Depression had knocked the props out from under laissez-faire liberalism. "Plans" were in the air. Even the United States had its New Deal. So the PNR got up a Six-Year Plan to put the Revolution back on its feet. It included a renewed agrarian program, the protection of the rights of labor, the conquest of illiteracy, the "economic independence" of Mexico. A little-known veteran of the Revolution, General Lázaro Cárdenas, was selected as the Party candidate. Several independents were allowed to run, for the sake of appearances, but Cárdenas was elected by the expected overwhelming majority.

The Jefe Máximo had made a bad mistake. The mild-spoken man from Michoacán really believed that the Six-Year Plan was good and that it could be made to work. Not only that, but he turned out to have as keen a nose for politics as Calles himself. He recognized from the beginning that the greatest obstacle in the way of any effective reform was Calles and the whole corrupt set of military and political millionaires who had wrecked the Revolution. Cárdenas had the shrewd instinct of Benito Juárez and took his program directly to the people, traveling without military escort to remote villages, by car and horseback, and even on foot, and he convinced the people that he was one of them.

For two years after his election Cárdenas campaigned against the Jefe Máximo. He made himself solid with labor by allowing strikes. He suppressed the gambling houses by which some of Calles' friends had made their fortunes. He threw out the Calles cabinet and installed one of his own. He even courted favor among the Catholics by protecting them from the state bosses. On the other hand, he showed the new plutocrats that he could be broad-minded by including one of the most notorious of them, General Saturnino Cedillo, of San Luis Potosí, in his cabinet—possibly, also, because he wanted to keep an eye on him. By the end of two years Cárdenas was ready for a showdown with the Jefe Máximo. There was talk, and some probability, of a pronunciamiento by Calles men, but for some reason it did not materialize, and one day the Supreme Chief of the Revolution and his former strong-arm man, Luis Morones, found themselves unceremoniously dumped across the border. The ousting of Calles was the most spectacular feat of political engineering that Mexico had ever seen, and it was thoroughly enjoyed by all hands.

For the next four years (1936–1940) the young master was free to devote himself to an honest (on his part) and not unsuccessful effort to make the Six-Year Plan work. He took over the PNR, purged it of unrepentant *callistas,* and eventually renamed it the Party of the Mexican Revolution, the PRM. (These frequent changes of name are confusing to an outsider, but it cannot be helped. By whatever name it is known, there is only one real party in Mexico, the party in power.) He boldly drove a wedge into the army hierarchy by giving the enlisted men an increase in pay, so that "Juan Soldado" could now look upon the president as his patrón. Cárdenas continued the Obregón tactic of encouraging the labor unions and agrarians to form bodies of militia, to be called on at need, but he took care to see that they remained balanced.

During the four effective years of his term Cárdenas distributed more land to the peasants than had been distributed in all the years since the beginning of the Revolution. In the Laguna district of Durango and Coahuila a strike among the cotton workers gave Cárdenas the opportunity to put his "democratic socialism" into practice. This he did by condemning 600,000 acres of rich land, compensating the owners by offering them agrarian bonds, which most of them refused to accept, not unreasonably, because the bonds were virtually worthless. Cárdenas settled 30,000 families in the Laguna and organized them into a multitude of interlocking units, to form the first great state-operated farm. The project required large-scale financing, and a new bank was created for the purpose, the Banco Nacional de Crédito Ejidal, with a capital of 30,000,000 pesos. To provide water, always in short supply, a great dam at El Palmito on the Nazas River was begun, with a capacity of three billion cubic meters (metric tons). It was completed in 1946 and justly named the Lázaro Cárdenas Dam. This was benevolent despotism with imagination.

By the end of 1936 the new bank reported: "In the Laguna region credits were granted to 29,690 families organized in ejidos, for the cultivation of 247,000 acres. The total of these loans was 8,124,692 pesos, guaranteed by crops of an estimated value of more than 50,000,-000 pesos. . . . During the last week in January [1937] investment by the National Bank of Ejidal Credit in the Laguna region reached a new weekly high of more than a million pesos, . . . the largest part of which is to be used for purchasing cotton seed." [1]

The obvious danger in such a program was that the peasant might become a serf of the bank, as critics pointed out. I have not heard any concrete complaints on this score from the Laguna region, but a sugar man from Los Mochis, Sinaloa, another vast communal project, made some pertinent observations on the new system, from the manufacturer's point of view. "The sugar people at Los Mochis

[1] The Laguna project was hailed abroad as the solution to Mexico's land problem. The sociologist Clarence Senior wrote an enthusiastic account of it entitled *Democracy Comes to the Cotton Kingdom* (Mexico, 1940), following closely what Cárdenas had said in his "Message to the Mexican Nation on the Solution of the Agrarian Problem of La Laguna," delivered at Torreón on December 1, 1936, when he handed out land titles to *ejidatarios* in person, a very effective piece of propaganda. The millennium was here again, and Cárdenas was the new Messiah. Unfortunately, the weather refused to cooperate, and a long drought soon forced a large part of the ejidatarios to emigrate. The endemic water shortage reached a crisis in 1963 (reported by Saul Landau in the San Francisco *Chronicle* of September 8, 1963), and the government attempted to relieve the pressure by sending 500 heads of families to virgin lands in the jungle of Campeche, in the hope that others would follow. "When I asked the ejidatarios about the possible migration," wrote Landau, "they were evasive. Since the land division started in 1936 two additional generations have grown up on Laguna land, on the same four hectares, with a mystic attachment to their dusty plots. 'Today the charity came,' said an old peasant. 'But it's borrowed time. Today we get something. Tomorrow we might die.' "

322

are sitting pretty with the ejido system. Once upon a time they had all the bother of payrolls, labor disputes, medical care, housing, and the general responsibility for field hands. Now they are rid of all that. The whole business is reduced to a matter of bookkeeping, and the bank holds the bag."

What the peasants of Los Mochis thought of the new setup, I have no way of knowing. It was probably good for them. They could no longer lay off when they felt like it without incurring the displeasure of their community leaders, who were not inclined to be tolerant of slackness when the ejido had to pay for it. They could not strike.[2] What? Strike against themselves? Apparently they had to work as hard as ever, possibly harder, and their big boss was the distant and impersonal bank. The bank seemed to be caught in the same dilemma as the ancient encomendero: It had to make a living with Indian labor, but it must not use coercion. It was unlikely that the bank, operating through its own bureaucracy, would prove to be a more humane taskmaster than the hacendado, whom one could argue with, or take a shot at, as the occasion demanded. The bank became, in fact, the administrator of a huge estate, and it had to make good. At least it had to make enough profit to cover overhead expenses and replace its capital. Sugar cane can be sold at a profit only if the market allows it; but cheap production requires cheap labor, so the bank must drive a hard bargain, or close up. The ejidatarios of Los Mochis, like those of any other state-operated ejido, are not paid wages, but receive a share of the proceeds from the sale of products, after the bank has deducted interest, carrying charges, and capital payments. In the end the ejidatario's income must depend upon the wholesale price of whatever he produces. With all its flaws, however, the communal ejido is a challenging experiment in education, and a great many peasants are learning to live with it and to appreciate the advantages it undoubtedly gives them.

The most powerful support of the Cárdenas program came from the new, militant, and left-wing *Confederación de Trabajadores de*

[2] One of the enduring headaches of the Avila Camacho administration (1941–1946) was a series of labor disturbances at Los Mochis; but they were a symptom of the depression in living conditions, rather than a protest against the ejido system.

*México,* the CTM, organized in 1936 by Vicente Lombardo Toledano, to replace the discredited CROM. It became, as it was intended to become, a working-class militia, like its predecessor. With the backing of Cárdenas, it reached into every field of activity, from the federal white-collar workers and schoolteachers, to the boys who snatched one's luggage, willy-nilly, at the railway stations. The quasi-military nature of the CTM brought along with it the ancient curse of caciquismo, and pistol-toting líderes became an unmitigated nuisance. It was as hard to convict a líder of a crime as it was to convict a general. And yet, in spite of this hereditary incubus, Mexican labor made some real gains during its league with Cárdenas. Its twenty years of betrayals and sellouts had been a tough education, and it was not likely that future líderes would meet with a passive acceptance of treachery.

The civil war in Spain found Cárdenas and the CTM vigorously supporting the Spanish Republican government, while the rest of the democratic world seemed to be doing its best to ensure the victory of General Franco's weird assortment of Italians, Moors, Germans, Carlists, and Falangists. President Cárdenas had a clearer vision of the essentials of the conflict than our own government, which at the time was aligned with Chamberlain's appeasers of Hitler and Mussolini. The arrival of 500 refugee Spanish children at Vera Cruz in 1937 was one of the most moving events in the history of the generous Mexican people, who took them in and cared for them. Cárdenas was also the first to seize the opportunity of inviting an unlimited number of Spanish Republicans to Mexico in 1939 and giving them Mexican citizenship, for he recognized the great value to the Mexican economy of those hardy peasants and mechanics. He did the same thing for the exiled intellectuals of Spain. At the urging of the philosopher Alfonso Reyes, he established the Colegio de México and staffed it equally with Mexican and Spanish professors. By these enlightened measures Mexico was enriched by the cream of Spanish workers, scholars, scientists, writers, and artists.

Cárdenas was, of course, condemned as a Red. He was polluting the holy soil of Mexico with the atheistic scum who had been run out of Spain by that paladin of the Faith, Francisco Franco. Shirt organizations, German and Spanish, joined the traditional conservative elements of Mexico in fighting the whole Cárdenas program. They were soon reinforced by the most formidable enemy that Cárdenas had challenged, the foreign oil companies.

A strike of refinery and oil field workers had dragged on for two years, with each side making charges so diametrically opposed that compromise was out of the question. A Supreme Court decision favored the workers. Most of the companies refused to obey it and were declared to be "in a state of rebellion." On March 18, 1938, President Cárdenas signed his famous order expropriating the oil properties.

In the ensuing dispute an immense amount of literature was circulated by both sides, and epithets such as "Communist" and "imperialist" were freely exchanged. To the oil workers, who were saturated with the xenophobia of the Revolution, the expropriation meant the emancipation of Mexico from the foreign yoke. A monster mass meeting was organized by Lombardo Toledano on March 23, 1938, to celebrate Mexico's new Independence Day. The *Mexican Labor News* became lyrical: "At nine o'clock in the morning the demonstrators began their march toward the central Zócalo, and the last contingents had not passed by the main balcony of the Palace, where President Cárdenas, with several members of his administration, reviewed the parade, until four in the afternoon. At the height of the demonstration the tremendous square was solidly packed with a mass of wildly cheering humanity celebrating the dawn of what thousands of placards and standards hailed as the economic independence of Mexico."

March 18 was declared a national holiday. Two years later I watched the somewhat stereotyped celebration. Mexico had been through a lot of trouble with her new baby, but I could not help admiring the spirit, kept alive by cheer leaders, of the crowd. The faithful *Mexican Labor News* repeated its shopworn tribute: "All over the country, in cities and towns and villages, workers, peasants, soldiers, and all of the people paraded through the streets with cheers and music and banners that proclaimed: 'The Wealth of Mexico Must Be Possessed by Mexico!' In Mexico City more than a hundred thousand men, women, and children crowded into the great

Plaza of the Constitution. . . . Flags were hung from the Palace windows, and flags and enormous pictures of Cárdenas and Camacho . . . were hung from the cathedral towers. Bells rang; the uniformed drum and bugle corps of the CTM workers played the marches of the Mexican Revolution; and when the plaza was full to overflowing, the thousands there began to sing the National Anthem with all the strength of their voices. This was Mexico's reiteration of her declaration of independence from foreign imperialism."

The demonstration, even though it was as unmercifully mechanized as the rooting section of an American college, was an impressive and moving performance, but I could not help wondering whether the expropriation was good statesmanship at that time. The Mexican government had made no preparations for carrying on the oil business and was in no position to meet the economic pressures that the affected interests were certain to apply. There was as yet no native technical staff capable of handling the complicated problems of the production and distribution of oil. Mexico had to assume a very large but undetermined debt to pay for the expropriated properties. The cutting off of income from oil brought an immediate and violent drop in the exchange value of the peso, and, since a great many manufactured articles and a considerable amount of prime necessities had to be purchased abroad, the cost of living began to soar. Strikes and threats of strikes, protesting against the pinch, kept the country in a turmoil, and poverty struck hard.

The oil properties had been turned over to the unions to administer, and here the utopians received another shock, for they discovered that the unions were just as avid to make money at the public's expense as the corporations had been, and they were less easily controlled. The number of employees on the payrolls steadily increased, despite the falling demand for oil, and overhead charges tended to eat up what little profit could be made in a restricted market. Cárdenas was accused of playing fast and loose with the national economy.

The railroads, which had also been put under union management, were in a state of collapse. The unions' excuse was that the lines were worn out, that there was insufficient working capital, and that the rolling stock was falling to pieces—all of which was true. But things got steadily worse and wrecks became so frequent that the public was alarmed. The Mexican humorists got to work on the situation and circulated the story that one particularly frightful wreck near Zacatecas had been caused by the engine crew's habit of playing poker during runs. The story was indignantly denied. The disease of the railroads was apparent in the irresponsibility of the trainmen. Featherbedding reached an all-time high. Every man on a crew had a "helper," but the service could not have been worse. The emancipated rail workers seemed to have caught the manners of their bosses and treated the public with contempt.

The trouble with the theory of workers' administration, it seems to me, was the assumption that if the men were given the responsibility of running their own business they would somehow acquire public spirit and pride in their work. But that would have taken a training that the men had never had. Meanwhile, the workers' administration ran their business with an eye on immediate returns. By 1940 President Cárdenas was threatening to take over the railroads and the oil industry if the workers did not behave themselves. "Independence from foreign imperialism" was a soul-satisfying slogan, although no one had a clear idea of what it meant. As long as Mexico needed goods and food from abroad, and as long as she had to exchange her own products for imports, "economic independence" was impossible, just as it is impossible for all the rest of us. Expropriation and workers' administrations did not solve the matter, and Cárdenas was intelligent enough to recognize it.

Lázaro Cárdenas was the last of the great caudillos of the Revolution to make himself president. By the end of his term, 1940, the Revolutionary Party was a smooth-running machine, sure of its power and firmly controlled by its leaders, of whom the acknowledged head was now President Cárdenas. Its aim was to bid for wide public support. The military were kept in the background, and since that time the presidents have not been identified with the violent period of the Revolution. President Cárdenas announced that the election of 1940 would be entirely free, and he probably meant it, although he certainly knew that no candidate opposing the Party had the slightest chance of winning. He allowed complete freedom of criticism during the campaign. All the sins of the ruling machine were pitilessly exposed and a great deal of mud was slung. General Juan Andreu Almazán, who had become many times a millionaire through government contracts and other means peculiar to generals, toured the country in a vigorous campaign against the "Reds" (meaning Cárdenas), the atheists, the godless public schools, the Spanish refugees, and a great many real abuses of the Cárdenas régime. Foreign and Mexican capitalists, the clergy, the wealthy (or ex-wealthy) Creole nobility, the Cristeros, the fascists, unorganized labor, and unconverted peasants listened and believed. That unpredictable genius, Diego Rivera, still sore at his expulsion from the Communist Party and at Cárdenas' "betrayal" of the Revolution, became Almazán's secretary.

In spite of Almazán's lack of a constructive program, there was unquestionably a heavy backing for him throughout the country. During the heat of the campaign I traveled through the states of Jalisco, Michoacán, Mexico, Puebla, Vera Cruz, Oaxaca, and Chiapas, and everywhere I saw demonstrations for Almazán and heard talk of a rebellion against the Revolutionary Party. On the Party's side there was not much talking, although the usual organized demonstrations paraded about the capital, rather listlessly, I thought. There was no enthusiasm for the official Party candidate, Manuel Avila Camacho, even among his supporters. The humorists dubbed him the "Unknown Soldier," with considerable truth. But the efficient Party machine functioned well and quietly. Local caciques could be counted on to protect their jobs; government employees, the same. There was a good deal of sporadic assassination of *almazanistas*, mostly chargeable to local feuds, and the perpetrators were never caught. The "free" election went the way it had to go: for Almazán, 100,000-odd votes; for Avila Camacho, 2,000,000-odd.

There were the expected shrieks of fraud. Almazán made a spectacular flight to the United States, although he was in no particular danger. His action looked like a bid for our support in the coming revolution against the "Red" government of Mexico. Meanwhile, however, the Second World War had taken a serious turn. Our State Department suddenly and belatedly awoke to the fascist threat to all American republics and talked about "hemispheric solidarity." The Cárdenas government became respectable. Almazán was quietly discouraged and, just as quietly, went home to face charges of "betrayal" flung at him by his disillusioned supporters.

Lázaro Cárdenas ended his term as one of the most controversial figures in Latin America, but it must be acknowledged that he rescued Mexico from the dismal corruption of Calles and the spoiled caudillos of the Revolution. He was a builder. Roads, public works, dams, irrigation and power projects, and the like went forward with his full support. Thousands of schools were built. He inaugurated the change in peasant land use toward larger and more efficient communal ejidos. Indeed, he never forgot his own peasant origin, and his constant preoccupation with the good of the small farmer made him the best loved of all revolutionary presidents. After the smoke of the election of 1940 had blown away, I was talking with an Indian farmer of Michoacán. "What do you think of President Avila Camacho?" I asked. "He is a great man," he answered. "I helped elect him." "Naturally," I said, "but in what way is he great?" "Why, he is a friend of Don Lázaro!" With which I began to understand why Cárdenas has continued to be one of the most powerful figures in the Republic.[3]

By the end of the Cárdenas régime in 1940, the term "revolution" had been wrenched out of its ordinary context. *The* Revolution was now a glittering edifice fashioned out of all the notions of the Party planners. The Party had become the Revolution, and, as its spokesmen said quite openly, if not altogether accurately: "The Revolution *is* Mexico." The Party of the Revolution, renamed the Institutional Revolutionary Party (the PRI), has become a vast bureaucracy with endless proliferations, and each cell is presided

[3] One gets used to surprises in Mexican politics. For example, Lázaro Cárdenas, now a considerable capitalist in his own right and undisputed boss of Michoacán, embraced the cause of Fidel Castro, who had proclaimed the independence of Latin America from Yankee imperialism. Cárdenas' action has several possible explanations: his early left-wing sympathies; his resentment against the United States, dating from the expropriation of the oil companies, when he was freely labeled a Red by his opponents here; and he could also have been smarting over our unexplained refusal to grant his son a visa to come to this country and study engineering at one of our universities.

329

over by a functionary who owes the Party his loyalty and his livelihood. The president is the titular head of the official family and is bound by the same discipline as the other members. He is the front man of a monolithic hierarchy and he has to obey its mandates. For better or for worse, Mexico has become a corporate state under the direction of the Party, and it is the president's job to make its program work and to see that the Party gets the credit. He is given flattering titles, and his name and picture are never absent from official publications, but whatever he does must be "revolutionary" (in the Pickwickian sense). The busy Party propagandists see to it that everything, from the completion of a new dam or the opening of a new factory to the discovery of the bones of Cuauhtémoc, is turned into a Party triumph. This unfailing self-praise makes Party literature singularly dull reading and, rightly or wrongly, awakens a feeling of wariness in the reader. This wariness applies particularly to statistics.

The first of the purely Party presidents was Manuel Avila Camacho, at his back the towering figure of Lázaro Cárdenas, his Minister of Defense, high in the Party councils. In the nature of things such presidents can rarely be men of heroic stature, bound as they are to implement the official program. The Party's the thing, and the rest of my space will be taken up with the formidable situations it has had to deal with as, with vast energy and talent, her managers made Mexico in the next twenty years the leading industrial nation of Latin America.

# 26

## THE WELFARE STATE
## MAINLY POLITICAL

In times of crisis the strength and weaknesses of a nation are exposed for all to see. Thus it was with Mexico during the Second World War and after, when the Revolutionary Party (that is, the government), invented by Obregón, corrupted by Calles, and purged and perfected by Cárdenas, was tested in a series of severe shocks, and survived. These shocks and stresses were caused partly by the impact of war, partly by the weather, and partly by the very nature of the ruling group, which suffers from the rigidity inherent in all quasi-military governments. To understand the causes and implications of the recurring crisis that beset the new welfare state,[1] a short review of its structure will be of some value.

When, in 1920, the Revolutionary Party definitely took over the management of the country, General Obregón's immediate and imperative task was to rescue Mexico from the political and economic chaos left by the civil war. The Revolution had made a clean sweep of the old ruling class: the hacendado, the industrialist, the banker, the merchant, the bureaucrat, of Don Porfirio's dictatorship. An entirely new ruling class had to be created. It had to be strong and it had to be effective. It was forged out of the four large groups that had joined forces during the Revolution: the new army,

---

[1] The term "welfare state" is debatable, but it is preferable, possibly, to "corporate state," although the PRI bears a marked resemblance to, say, the organization of General Motors, with its myriad agencies and experts, and its management and policies securely fixed in the hands of a Board of Directors. This, indeed, was the ideal cherished by the Científicos of Don Porfirio's time.

the state political bosses (caciques), the labor unions (the CROM of Morones and, later, the CTM of Lombardo Toledano), and peasant organizations (principally the Confederación Nacional Campesina, the CNC).

All these groups had a heavy interest in keeping the Party going, and the Party had to keep them all reasonably happy. The result was a system of linked privilege now deified as The Revolution, and no government could hope to control any part of it beyond a certain point. In its formative years it was obliged to countenance a great deal of irregularity among its constituents, because it could not do otherwise and hope to survive. Of all these groups the army, of course, was the one which must never be challenged. Indeed, since Independence no government had existed except with its consent. Frank Tannenbaum, an old and staunch friend of Revolutionary Mexico, wrote, in his thoughtful *Mexico: The Struggle for Peace and Bread* (1950): "It is still true . . . that the Army is the chief source of the government's power. As Cárdenas once expressed it, 'When the land belongs to the villages, the government will also belong to them, but . . . now the government depends upon the Army.'" In other words, the government would stand precisely so long as the army chieftains were kept happy, and any government that forgot that elementary fact of life would vanish without a trace.[2]

In order to give the régime a wide popular base, Obregón and his successors encouraged the formation of agrarian leagues, which were tied to the government by the powerful motive of free land expropriated from the haciendas. "For all practical purposes," observed Tannenbaum, "they are creatures of the State, created,

[2] Of late years the PRI has made a persistent and successful effort to create in the public mind the "image" of a civilian government. Since 1946 all four presidents have been civilians; generals, except in the Department of Defense, have been conspicuously absent from it. The obstreperous caudillos of the stormy days of the Revolution and civil war have long since disappeared, and their place has been taken by a proud new professional army, which carefully avoids any suggestion of political involvement. It is, nevertheless, inescapably political, for it is the supreme police force of the nation, an effective deterrent to disorders and pronunciamientos, and a guarantee of the stability of the present system. As in Cárdenas' day, the army is still the main prop of the government in times of trouble.

supported, and financed by the State. They are not merely beholden to the State, they are dependent upon it."

The same held true for the more highly organized and militant urban labor movement. To quote Tannenbaum again: "What is true of these peasant organizations is still more true of the labor unions and the labor movement. . . . They are essentially creatures and instruments of the government; they are strong with the strength of the administration that breathes the breath of life into them. There is no independent trade-union movement of any consequence in Mexico. . . . The government has protected, financed, and nurtured the trade-union movement as a stick to lean upon or to be used against its political enemies in and out of the country. . . . The unions and *ejidos* serve one important function: they give the President a seeming and, in a measure, a real support among the people."

The *quid pro quo* exacted by labor was the surrender of the government in all issues in which the interests of labor were involved. The seizure of the oil fields and the railroads was forced upon Cárdenas by the unions. The government abdicated its function as arbiter in labor disputes. All labor legislation, as Daniel Cosío Villegas observed in his melancholy *La Crisis de México* (1947), had only one purpose: to favor the worker; with few exceptions the courts always decided for him; and, thus protected by the state and the courts, the worker lost all sense of responsibility and perspective, and looked upon the public as a source of spoils, while the employer came to feel that the courts were merely instruments of vengeance and coercion, and that he could not hope for justice from them. Hence, concluded Cosío, the employer was forced to protect himself by bribery and the payment of blackmail (the *mordida*).

The vast edifice of the Revolution was cemented together by the common interests of these groups. They became crystallized into an impenetrable monolith, and the government had to face the charge (made by disillusioned idealists, such as the late Luis Cabrera, Daniel Cosío Villegas, and Frank Tannenbaum) that the Revolution had abandoned the democratic base upon which it had been erected; that it had turned away from the spiritual and civic betterment of the people and gone in for physical and tangible improvements: highways, dams and irrigation systems, factories, school buildings, and public services. But, they maintained, these undeniably great achievements had failed to transform the country or make it happier. There was no longer a flaming conviction of faith in the hearts of the men of the Revolution. Its leaders, chosen from an ever-shrinking inside group, thought that democracy was something that could be imposed on the country by edict from the National Palace, "although," observed Cosío, "to create in Mexico a democracy with any traces of authenticity is a task that would dismay any reasonable man." For a democracy must rest upon an informed and educated public, but in Mexico the sparse and frequently illiterate population, scattered in remote places without adequate communications, had no opportunity to participate in the government, or the training to do so even if the opportunity existed.

In Cosío's opinion, the members of the national Congress were, therefore, in effect appointed by local Party caciques, and their generally low caliber was notorious. Further, a national legislature in a democracy had the double function of acting as critic and censor of the executive, and of expressing public opinion; but the Mexican Congress did neither; it was a rubber stamp for the Party bosses; it was as servile as it was under Don Porfirio, and in the eyes of the public a deputy or a senator "has become the standard by which all human baseness is measured. . . . Any notion of restoring [to respectability] this organ of government, which is as essential to democracy as it is to progress, is hopeless."

While admitting the justice of this grim indictment, I think that Cosío and other critics expected too much. The Revolution, as I pointed out in a former chapter, was a conquest of Mexico by the Men of the North. They were a small minority of the nation. They had to make themselves strong by bargaining, by allowing elements like the workers and peasants to share in the spoils of conquest. Their vigorous propaganda convinced a great many people, in Mexico and abroad, that the Revolution was a democratic movement. So it was, of course, in part, but the invited guests attended on a permissive basis; those who got out of line were got rid of. In such an atmosphere anything that we should recognize as democracy

334

could not exist, and the lip service paid to it in Party publications should not be taken literally.

In answer to the sinking of two of her tankers by German submarines, Mexico declared war on the Axis powers on May 28, 1942, and, in spite of bitter internal opposition, with admirable spirit and generosity strove to carry her end of the heavy burden laid upon her. The opposition came, naturally, from the conservative Catholic elements, which always and necessarily disapproved of the actions of the revolutionary government. They were particularly wrought up over the declaration of war, because those same elements had been opposed to the Allies in the First World War, when Austria was still the favorite daughter of the Church. Their traditional sympathies made them very susceptible to Axis propaganda, and the Axis took full advantage of the situation. Out of that situation the old Cristero movement was reborn under the name of *sinarquismo*, a phenomenon of such deep historical roots and so symptomatic of the maladjustments inherent in a one-party system, that it deserves our attention.

An organization calling itself the "Anti-Communist Center," founded in Guanajuato in 1936 by a Nazi propagandist, Oscar Hellmuth Schreiter, attracted a good many supporters in that strongly Catholic region. It disappeared when Mexico entered the war, but its functions were continued by the Unión Nacional Sinarquista, founded in 1939 by José Antonio Urquiza and Salvador Abascal. Its ideology was the familiar one of the Spanish Falange: God, Church, and family; direction from above and obedience from below; every man a soldier of the Cross; unquestioning acceptance of the decisions of the leader; *hispanidad*, that is, the essential unity of the Spanish world as it had been in the time of Philip II; a Catholic, corporate state under a hierarchical, authoritarian government. Such a program could hardly fail to have an immense appeal for large numbers of unregenerate Mexican Catholics and the still smoldering Cristeros.

The sinarquista tub-thumpers taught that Mexico was reaping the bitter fruit of her folly in abandoning the old tried ways of Catholic leadership. They denounced the government, particularly Ezequiel

Padilla, the Secretary of Foreign Relations, for getting Mexico into a ruinous war without her consent. They denounced it for sending agricultural workers to the United States and allowing Mexican lands to lie idle; for sending food abroad and letting the Mexican people starve; for imposing Party men on the country and making a mockery of elections; for tolerating universal corruption and racketeering among public servants, army officers, and labor unions. They reached across the border and, through an elaborate system of cells in the United States, got a wide and profitable following here among Spanish-speaking communities and uninformed Catholics. The disgraceful zoot-suit riots in Los Angeles, California, in the spring of 1943, which culminated when a mob of sailors, unhindered by the police, dragged Mexicans from movie theaters and beat them up, served to crystallize the common feeling of Mexicans in this country and bring them into the sinarquista camp. Vociferous criticism of the "pluto-democracies" and unstinted praise of the Franco régime left little doubt of the source of sinarquista inspiration.

Although there was a good deal of fantastic nonsense in the sinarquista bill of complaints (such as the charge that Mexico was shipping food to the United States, when precisely the opposite was true, and that sending agricultural workers to this country meant the abandonment of Mexican lands—rural Mexico was teeming with idle men, as usual), nevertheless there was enough truth in it, and the sinarquistas were desperate enough, to give them a formidable strength. Demonstrations, seditious speeches, riots, and bloodshed became so frequent and threatening that the government had to act to head off what looked like another Cristero rebellion. The sinarquistas and their newspapers were suppressed (temporarily) and the movement was driven underground, where it continued to thrive on persecution.

Sinarquismo, like the Cristero movement, was a kind of Mexican Carlist crusade, essentially romantic, rooted in tradition, and feeding on the myth of ancient Spanish glory, with which its adherents identified themselves. Its romanticism was manifest in many ways. The ideals to which its young men were dedicated were poverty, obedience, and loyalty—loyalty to the Catholic Church and to the "true" Mexico, not to the "spurious" Mexico of the Revolution, which they confidently told themselves they would destroy. The new Mexico was to be an Augustinian City of God on earth, born in blood and suffering; indeed, the City must be watered and fertilized by the blood of martyrs. The soldiers of the Cross must expect and court martyrdom. This quixotic frenzy led to the establishment, in 1942, of two agricultural colonies in the most discouraging parts of the country. Five hundred families of enthusiasts, untrained, unequipped, and unprepared for pioneering in the desert, were settled in an arid waste, characteristically named "María Auxiliadora," in Lower California near Magdalena Bay, thereby causing a mild international flurry, because it was noised about that the sinarquistas were plotting to deliver that naval base to the Japanese. The second colony, named "Villa Kino" after the famous Jesuit missionary, was planted in the wilderness of the Sonora Desert. Neither of the sites had any water. The colonies lasted for two tortured years, living entirely on the scanty alms of the faithful, but finally had to yield before the inexorable landscape. The sinarquistas were held up to the ridicule of the Party, of course; but the implications of this irrational outburst of primitive mysticism should not be taken lightly. Mass immolation is not funny, and it is certainly as dangerous as TNT.

Several years later, for example, in León, Guanajuato, the sinarquistas waged a vigorous campaign against the local Party government. *La Voz de León,* edited by the sinarquista leader, José Trueba Olivares, openly called for violence. "One of these days," he wrote, "this democratic farce in Mexico will have to end!" A mass demonstration was staged on January 2, 1946, in the public square of León, and rapidly got out of hand. The military were jeered and pelted with stones. Colonel Luis Olvera Barrón, the local commandant, irritated and trigger-happy, gave the order "Fire at will!" and the City of God was fertilized with the blood of 274 martyrs (27 dead and 247 wounded). The "León Massacre" caused such intense excitement that President Alemán had to intervene and call off the troops. The sinarquistas were even allowed to win the state election, and Guanajuato had the first antirevolutionary government in the Republic.

A further illustration of this madness was a demonstration before

337

the Juárez monument in the Alameda of Mexico City, on December 19, 1948. It was devoted to vilification of the "Antichrist," Benito Juárez, and the face of his statue was covered with a black cloth. The sentiment of the meeting was expressed in a speech by Dr. Rubén Mangas Alfaro, head of the sinarquistas of the Federal District. One sentence will serve to summarize the matter: "The period of the so-called Reform and Revolution [of 1857] was the period of shame and ignominy, and this great thief [Juárez] was the one responsible for every filthy thing done at that time, for he devoted himself to robbing churches!"

For a few days there seemed to be some likelihood that the sinarquistas would achieve the martyrdom they hopefully awaited, but President Alemán refused to intervene, thereby bringing down on his head the wrath of a group of old heroes of the Revolution, including Generals Rodolfo Sánchez Taboada and Francisco Múgica, who roared: "If the citizens of 1949 are afraid to fight, we old ones are still alive!" An organized counter-demonstration of 100,000 embattled revolutionaries did homage before the statue of Juárez on February 5, 1949, the thirty-second anniversary of the signing of the Constitution of 1917, and the government was obliged to suppress the new political arm of the sinarquistas, the Popular Force Party.

In spite of official efforts to play down the significance of sinarquismo, it seems to me that it illustrates a grave failure of the revolutionary régime. Sinarquismo was plainly the result of frustration. The Revolution virtually disfranchised a large and vigorous part of the population, the intransigent Catholics, who had no voice in the government unless they accepted doctrines repugnant to their faith. "Effective suffrage" did not apply to them, because only the PRI candidates had any hope of winning. In the by-election of 1949, for example, of the 147 deputies elected, 146 were PRI men, as well as all seven state governors. The only recourse of the disfranchised was violence, as in the tragic Cristero rebellion, and their suppression raised their despair to pathological intensity. It is difficult to see how the Revolutionary Party can absorb or conciliate the extreme Catholic group, given the bloody history of the past century. Nevertheless, if the Party's claim to "democracy" means anything, it must somehow make room for the participation of minorities, or it will surely have to suppress them by force and accept the dismal consequences.[3]

Along with sinarquismo came an irruption of religious fanaticism. Religious movements in Mexico, as the reader may have observed, do not confine themselves to exhortations. In June, 1944, a hungry lad out of a job stole the jewels from an image of the Virgin in the village of Tlacotepec, Mexico, whereupon the true believers seized him from the constable and quite literally tore him limb from limb. About the same time a furious mob in Jalapa de Díaz, Oaxaca, destroyed the local Protestant chapel and chased its congregation into the mountains. In Santiago Yeche, an Otomí village in the state of Mexico, only thirty miles from Mexico City, in April, 1945, two members of the Church of God were chopped to pieces with machetes. In January, 1947, an octogenarian member of that same sect was stoned to death as he went to place flowers on his wife's grave. Well-meaning Protestant missionaries have a rugged time in most parts of rural Mexico, although there are exceptions, like the Quaker mission school near Toluca, which is rather an experiment in international education.

Now, Protestantism, although its adherents number only about 300,000 in an overwhelmingly Catholic country, has always been linked in the minds of the faithful with Freemasonry, liberalism, and similar deviltry, and it is violently resented. In November, 1944, following a country-wide agitation that had been going on since the

[3] Since this was written, increasing prosperity and a more conciliatory policy by the government have taken much of the bitterness out of the conflict. "The PRI is now so secure," writes Howard F. Cline, in his *Mexico: Revolution to Evolution* (1962), "that it can afford to relax and does not need many of the repressive measures it earlier took in dealing with the opposition. This in large part accounts for the peaceful nature of political campaigns and elections. In sharp contrast with earlier days, armed clashes between partisans simply do not now occur. Under the most extreme provocations in 1958, PRI followers and leaders used restraint; obvious efforts by the Party of National Action (PAN) to harvest a useful crop of martyrs were frustrated. One of their members was unfortunately killed, the sole fatality to mar the record. In the more relaxed atmosphere, the opposition parties go on campaigning, certain of defeat long before the ballots are counted" (p. 167).

beginning of World War II, Archbishop Luis María Martínez of Mexico City called upon all good Catholics to defend the Faith against the menace of Protestantism. A pastoral letter circulated by the bishops of Durango, Sinaloa, and Chihuahua said in part: "In these latter years we have observed a great activity on the part of several North American sects, which are attempting to uproot the Catholic faith from the hearts of Mexicans and drag them down into heresy." In answer to the archbishop's appeal a flurry of placards appeared in the windows of Mexico City: "This is a Catholic family. We reject Protestant propaganda!" A lively boycott was organized against such subversive elements as the Palmolive Soap Corporation, the Radio Continental, and the YMCA. No one knows to what lengths the crusade might have gone if a group of old Freemasons of the Revolution, including a solid phalanx of former presidents, had not denounced the archbishop and the boycott as unpatriotic and inimical to the war effort. So he publicly, and wisely, deplored the boycott as contrary to the precepts of religion, and the excitement blew over for the time being.

The conservative Catholic National Action Party (the PAN—the initials spell "bread" in Spanish) tried its wings in the 1944 campaign for the governorship of Aguascalientes. Its candidate, the moderate and colorful Don Aquiles Elorduy, preached reform and took over most of the stock sinarquista complaints. His opponent, Don Jesús Rodríguez, stood on the firm platform of the eternal principles of the Revolution. Elorduy was widely supported, not only by the extreme right, for one of his chief props was that stalwart old liberal, the late Don Luis Cabrera, a Founding Father of the Revolution.[4] Elorduy lost, of course. He protested the election as fraudulent and demanded a recount, but his protest was disallowed by the courts. Indeed, as Cabrera said, there had been no free election since 1912. An opposition candidate could hardly hope to

[4] Cabrera, one of the most incisive minds of Mexico, made it clear that he was supporting Elorduy as a protest against the corruption of the Revolutionary Party and its monopoly of Mexico's civic life. He had some hope that the moderate PAN might develop into an effective and needed opposition party. Two years later the PAN invited him to run as its candidate against Miguel Alemán. Cabrera declined, possibly because the PAN had identified itself too closely with reactionary elements.

prevail except by the classical pronunciamiento of disaffected military chieftains.

There was little probability of such an occurrence. During the heat of the sinarquista agitation in 1943, President Avila Camacho addressed a group of 480 generals who had rallied round the flag. "The Mexican Army," he said, "is ready to act!" And it undoubtedly was. About that same time a disordered young captain was caught red-handed in a schoolboy plot to overthrow the government. He was tried by court-martial and sentenced to be hanged for treason; but the president commuted the sentence, "in order," as he wrote to General Cárdenas, Secretary of Defense, "to keep the army free from such a stain on its honor."

A formidable obstacle in the way of reforming the Revolutionary Party was the local boss, the cacique, who controlled his district by patronage, corruption, and violence. "With few exceptions," reported the *Inter-American Monthly* for April, 1944, commenting on the bumping off of two state governors, "the states which form the Mexican Federation are still governed according to a semi-feudal system, in which the governor is the great *cacique,* or political boss. As such he personally controls the best businesses, the confiscation and distribution of land, for his own profit or that of his followers and friends. Political opponents are generally severely treated. . . . Such an atmosphere of violence and favoritism naturally breeds hatred and a desire for revenge, which at times culminates in murder."

Since caciquismo relied heavily on violence, it was in large measure responsible for the calamitous disease of pistol-toting (*pistolerismo*). Several years ago I was talking with one of the excellent agricultural workers (*braceros*) who have done such a useful job in harvesting crops in the United States. "What," I asked him, "struck you most forcibly about this country?" "Sir," was his polite but unexpected answer, "what seemed to me most rare at first was that no one was carrying a gun." He was making unwittingly a profound observation on caciquismo, for everyone in the hierarchy of the cacique packed a gun, so everyone else had to pack one also, just in case. In a very real sense postwar Mexico was ruled by gun-toters. The leaders of the caciques' private armies were generally immune from legal action. After one particularly cynical slaughter at Tlalnepantla, Mexico, in 1942, the pistolero Saturnino Osorio, accompanied by an armed guard of ten, "called" on Isidoro Fabela, governor of the state, and offered in his defense the following: "I am innocent. It was not I who killed Suárez Ocaña and Posada. Juan García [member of the National Chamber of Deputies] merely asked me for my war machinery and I gave it to him. That's all there was to it." Osorio's "war machinery" consisted of several automobile loads of gangsters armed with tommy guns and .45s. He and his army of two hundred were at the time in the employ of the governor of Quéretaro.

In 1947 the federal government attempted, with no great success, to abate this nuisance and embarked on a campaign of "depistolizing" the country. Unfortunately, the job was left to the local state authorities, who, I suspect, were not always enthusiastic about it. General César Lara, governor of Chiapas, seems to have taken it seriously and reported to President Alemán that his state had been completely "depistolized," for he had totally forbidden the use of firearms, and he and his adjutants had set the example. Other districts were not so lucky. In 1949, in the Costa Grande region of Guerrero, "white guards" in the employ of caciques and landlords were reported to have murdered forty-eight men, mostly ejidatarios, in spite of the "depistolization" order by the military authorities. For four years southern Puebla was terrorized by gangs of pistoleros, to such an extent that the citizens of Izúcar de Matamoros appealed to President Alemán to "take pity on this unlucky town" and save it from the brutality of its cacique. In the neighboring city of Acatlán sixty murders were reported, and when the distracted mayor called on the military for help, he was shot for his meddling. In July, 1950, the whole section was put under martial law and patrolled by federal troops.

Caciquismo had a close tie-in with the operations of monopolists and black marketeers during the war, and with the age-old system of irregular taxation known as the *mordida,* or squeeze. The government found it next to impossible to control the rapacity of market-riggers, or "hunger merchants," who operated under the protection of caciques—necessarily, for without it they could hardly have stayed out of jail, or even alive. The first requirement for a successful deal was to stand in with the boss. If you didn't, things were likely to happen. Down near Tuxpan, Vera Cruz, for example, there was a large banana plantation worked by the farmers through their ejidos. For some time they marketed their crops through a broker, who paid them 130 pesos a ton for their produce delivered at the dockside. But 130 pesos a ton hardly covered the cost of production; so the farmers complained to President Avila Camacho and got an order authorizing the National Bank of Ejidal Credit to handle the marketing, and the farmers received twice as much for their bananas. Just what happened then was never clearly explained, but when the 1944 crop was harvested and shipped to Tampico, it was discovered that no provision had been made to carry it farther. No one could do a thing about it, and the bananas rotted on the dock. Is that evidence that something dubious was going on? Possibly not, but the pattern was very familiar.

Take the case of the coffee and banana growers of Tapachula, Chiapas, just this side of the Guatemalan frontier. Around Tapachula lies a fine stretch of land, and the plantations looked very prosperous. Someone else must have thought so too, for in 1944 the growers complained that they had to pay a squeeze of 250 to 1,000 pesos a carload before they could move a sack of coffee or a bunch of bananas. The governor of the state was unable to help them. Caciquismo? I don't know. Nobody knows positively, but of this you may be sure: Nothing of the kind could very well go on without the knowledge of the boss, and if he wouldn't help you, then God help you!

The mordida was generally accepted as just one of those things. Civil servants in a position to put on the squeeze were expected to collect a percentage from their clients to augment their inadequate salaries. While traveling through Oaxaca in the winter of 1949–1950 I was distressed to see the many charcoal burners' fires glowing like candles in the vanishing forests, this in spite of the federal law prohibiting unlicensed cutting. "How do they get by with that?" I asked a friendly and loquacious engineer. "It's simple," he answered. "The city of Oaxaca has no other fuel. Each one of those fires means that an Indian and his boy work about two weeks burning two

343

donkey-loads of charcoal, which they sell here for two pesos a load. On their way down from the mountains they are met by an official who collects one peso a load. So the Indian gets two pesos for his two weeks' work. It's rough, but we have to have fuel."

In the Federal District the mordida seemed to be more highly organized, as befitted the growing industrialization. An ingenuous paint manufacturer explained the system to me. "Business is pretty good in my line. People will buy paint for their houses even if they can't afford an extra pair of pants. But the mordida is worse than it used to be. Formerly I doled out a hundred pesos each to a number of inspectors. The money circulated; they could buy paint and pants with it. Now I have to give the money to a diputado or his friends, and it goes into new Cadillacs or out of the country. We are back in the days of Don Porfirio. A diputado gets a salary of 12,000 pesos [1,400 dollars in 1950] a year for three years, but by the end of his term he usually owns an apartment house and a couple of big cars. Well, I guess the answer is that we all take what we can get."

So standardized did the mordida become that no complaint was made when the port captain of Manzanillo, Colima, demanded a mordida of 5,000 pesos before he would allow the completion of a new wharf. The gouge was evidently considered legitimate, for the metropolitan papers merely commented: "The obstacles were finally overcome and the work was completed." The wharf was opened in December, 1948.[5]

The war brought sharply home to the government the perennial threat of food shortage. For half a century Mexico had been importing staples to make up her deficit. Anticipating a reduction in foreign sources of supply, the government encouraged planting by pegging the price of maize. In 1942 a heavy planting yielded an adequate crop of 2,350,000 tons. The 1943 crop, however, which was to have yielded 2,500,000 tons, was reduced by drought to about 1,700,000 tons. Other crops suffered in proportion, until the country

[5] In the years that have passed since I took these notes, the federal government has made vigorous efforts to control caciquismo and the mordida. The marked decrease of complaints is evidence of its success, although I suspect that these folkways are too deep-rooted to disappear entirely in our time.

was faced with famine conditions, with the usual plagues of black markets, rocketing prices, and general misery. The pinch was felt as early as May, 1943, when bread riots were of daily occurrence in the industrial city of Monterrey. There was no grain coming in, and the merchants said they could not afford to handle it at the prices fixed by the government. By June of that year greenstuff had all but disappeared from the markets of Mexico City. By September, 1943, in Nuevo Laredo on the banks of the Rio Grande, there was no maize in the public market. The scanty grain which was brought in by the farmers sold at fifty centavos a kilo on the black market, against the fixed price of seventeen centavos, and by December, 1943, it was bringing ninety-five centavos. A laconic news story from Nuevo Laredo reported "acute distress among the poor." In Guanajuato people stood in line all night in the hope of getting a handful of maize for the day's tortillas. In Tulancingo, Hidalgo, and in Celaya, Guanajuato, panic and bread riots became routine. Coatepec, Mexico, and Jalapa, Vera Cruz, made urgent appeals for relief to the federal government. Such normally well-provided centers as Puebla, Pachuca, Morelia, and Cuautla were out of essential staples. Throughout the spring and summer of 1944 starvation and rioting in cities and towns became such commonplaces that they hardly made news. Oaxaca, Río Verde, San Luis Potosí, Culiacán, San Blas, Torreón, and Durango joined the hunger march. Even Mexicali, just across the border from our fabulously rich Imperial Valley, was without bread for days on end.

The food crisis, of course, became a political issue, and there was a lot of irresponsible name-calling and blaming the government. The sinarquistas said it was a judgment of God brought on the country by the atheists. President Avila Camacho threw the whole weight of the government into relief measures and bought enormous quantities of food in this country, approximately a million tons; but the decrepit transportation system, already overtaxed by the huge war traffic, was unequal to the task of distribution, and the people had to tighten their belts for many months. The crisis, however, did have the beneficial effect of demonstrating the danger of having to depend on foreign sources for food. An intensive program of developing land and water resources was undertaken. Hundreds of millions of pesos went into vast irrigation systems, millions of acres were brought into production, and by 1948 President Alemán was able to report that Mexico was producing all her basic foodstuffs except wheat.

The war brought to Mexico the ugly and familiar specter of inflation. Our heavy buying of war materials opened long-abandoned mines and encouraged the planting of considerable areas in guayule (for rubber), fibers, and oil seeds. When German submarines threatened to close the seas to our merchant marine, we countered by spending $30,000,000 on the rehabilitation of Mexican railroads. Mexico was fairly flooded with money. Fugitive capital, running away from chaos in Europe, or from the Bureau of Internal Revenue in this country, bought Mexican real estate and generally took a flier in anything that looked reasonably safe. Mexico, for the first time in generations, was a creditor nation with money in the bank. War buying began to cut into the traditional trade deficit in 1939–1940. By 1942 there was a favorable balance of 80,000,000 pesos, and it went up to 127,000,000 pesos in 1943. The government celebrated its solvency by paying off 284,448,000 pesos of the public debt in 1944. The ancient oil claims were settled, and the first check for $3,796,391 was delivered on September 30, 1943. Immense sums were put into highways, dams, and other public works, and the payrolls helped to swell the inflation. European refugees and war-rich tourists brought in an estimated 500,000,000 pesos a year between 1942 and 1945, while agricultural workers sent home from this country 300,000,000 pesos a year. With one thing and another the amount of money in circulation increased during the war at the rate of 90,000,000 pesos a month, until by the end of 1944 some three and a quarter billions were in circulation, or between four and five times the amount in 1934. It is interesting to note that the price indices followed the same track with startling fidelity.

The war-rich of Mexico City had to be noticed, and they had to be amused. They went on a spending binge of impressive size, described by Verna Carleton Millan in *The Inter-American Monthly* for April, 1944: "Overnight, Mexico has acquired dozens of new millionaires, thousands with lesser fortunes. The new-rich, aided by the largest foreign colony in Mexico's history, are generally trying to make as much money as possible before inflation builds up to an economic collapse. . . . While the front pages speak of food shortages and actual hunger among the people, the inside society pages print lavish descriptions of the most elaborate parties Mexico has ever seen." Pandering to the tastes of the excitement-hungry, shoals of expensive hotels, cabarets, and honky-tonks were opened; their perfumed patrons were driven up to the doors in bootlegged cars, and flashy women with odd accents offended the respectable. It was great fun while it lasted, but in the near-famine of 1943–1944 the general run of Mexicans, regardless of party, were not amused, while the sinarquistas indulged in Old Testament prophecies about the fate of Sodom and Gomorrah.

Meanwhile, competition for food and for the scanty goods that appeared in the markets boosted prices until the peso bought only about a fifth as many beans and tortillas as it had in 1934, and real wages (based on buying power) dropped to less than half their level in 1934, and to almost half that of 1890, in the bad old days of Don Porfirio.

In an unexpected way the war relieved this situation somewhat and gave rise to one of the most interesting and, I think, most significant movements of modern times, the migration of agricultural workers (braceros) to the United States. When the draft put some millions of our young men into uniform, we were suddenly faced with a dangerous shortage of farm labor, and we sensibly turned to Mexico for help. On August 4, 1942, we contracted with the Mexican government for 50,000 braceros, who were brought here to work on farms, and who were paid in dollars at the prevailing wage of our own farm workers. This meant that the bracero could earn *fifteen to twenty times* as much as he could earn at home. The tremendous news caused something like a gold rush. Farmers abandoned their fields, and schoolteachers their desks, and swarmed into the recruiting offices. In the first week 7,000 men passed the severe medical examination in Mexico City alone. In a single day of June, 1944, the exciting rumor of a new demand sent 13,000 men boiling into the town of Irapuato, thereby causing a food panic in the exhausted market. The competition for permits was so keen that several members of the National Congress were indicted for selling them, and the smuggling of men across the Rio Grande (hence the

347

term "wetback") became big business. Thousands of men were dammed up at the border by Mexican troops and were fleeced by smugglers (*coyotes*) who got them across for a price, and who robbed and sometimes murdered them on their way out. Bodies of unlucky wetbacks were collected from the muddy waters of the Rio Grande, nine in a single day of February, 1949.

Our Border Patrol had to set up detention centers for captured wetbacks. We had started an avalanche and could do little to stop it. A commission appointed by President Truman reported, in August, 1951, that in the first six months of that year more than 150,000 wetbacks had been deported from the California-Arizona sector alone. At the same time the United States Embassy in Mexico City announced that in the remaining months of 1951 we would need 300,000 more braceros. It was all very confusing. Against the 74,600 braceros contracted for in 1947–1949, for example, 142,600 wetbacks had been gathered up and legitimized, instead of being deported, and it is a safe guess that as many more escaped detection.[6]

An extremely ugly situation arose out of the smuggling of wetbacks. Unscrupulous employers on our side of the border preferred wetbacks to legitimate braceros, because the wetbacks were not protected by the international agreement, and could be hired more cheaply and housed and fed as the employer pleased. Stories of the brutality practiced against these unfortunates were widely circulated in Mexico and tended to cancel out the generally favorable reports of returning braceros. The use of this coolie labor by Imperial Valley farmers alarmed our agricultural labor unions. Resentment on both sides of the border was so hot by the end of 1951 that the Mexican government threatened to stop all labor migration to this country unless the matter was corrected. It seems doubtful, however, that the wetback movement can be halted, for the wage differential is so great that large numbers of pauper

[6] A professional wetback class was created, the numbers of which are not known. No shame at all is attached to them. I talked with one well-dressed, proud young wetback in Oaxaca, who showed me a sheaf of nine driver's licenses from Pennsylvania to California. Another, whom I met in Mendocino County, California, was supporting his wife and children in Oaxaca. He gave me their address and invited me to call.

workers will slip across the border so long as they can find work. A sharp reminder of the real nature of the trouble was issued by the Mexican Department of Agriculture in May, 1950. It warned the country that a great many ejidos along the border were being abandoned; that in the district of Nuevo Laredo alone, 296 out of 390 ejidatarios had given up their land and gone to the United States as braceros, and, I venture to add, as wetbacks.

The unforeseen wetback complication was unfortunate, for the bracero movement was full of hopeful implications both for Mexico and for us. For one thing, it was the most effective program in international education that could well be devised. The braceros were not only excellent workmen, but their natural courtesy tended to dispel the dense cloud of ignorance and prejudice all too common in this country. Some of them, to be sure, got drunk on payday and landed in jail, but that was a small matter compared with the respect and even affection which they won among us. There was some abuse of braceros reported, particularly in Texas, where the barbarous color line was applied to them, with the result that a number of Texas counties were blacklisted by the Mexican government for discrimination. But even Texas had come to depend upon the bracero to work its vast agricultural empire and might in time learn that pigmentation was not so important after all.

South of the border the great migration could have been the yeast —and may still be—of a salutary fermentation. Thousands of returning braceros brought to all parts of Mexico new ideas, new techniques, new habits. One bracero I talked with in the Sacramento Valley had saved more than a thousand dollars, with which he was going to buy a tractor for the use of his village in Michoacán. Braceros remember the good food and the abundant markets they found here. Each goes home with as many large bundles of clothing as he can carry. Those I talked with had nothing but praise for the treatment they had received. At a road patrol station in the mountains of Oaxaca, the sergeant in command discovered that I was from California. "I worked in California for two seasons," he informed me with obvious pride. "It was wonderful. I got to be a pruner in the orange groves of Anaheim, the best job they had. You've got to be good to be a pruner, for the crop depends upon good pruning. They paid me seventy cents American an hour! Say, do you think you could get me back there?"

This attitude among returning braceros was general enough to worry the professional patriots. Admiration for this country (*pochismo*) had a dangerously weakening effect upon Party propaganda, which formerly could fall back on xenophobia in times of embarrassment; but a poll of the braceros elicited the comforting information that the great majority were interested only in high wages and that their patriotism was unimpaired. The poll was unnecessary. Braceros, at least those I have known, are exceedingly proud of being Mexican. At the same time, and I think this is the crux of the matter, patriotism does not *have* to be nourished by hatred of the foreigner, and one of these days we could have a million humble friends in Mexico, just as they could have as many among us, and that, I submit, is a heartwarming thing to contemplate.[7]

Popular education has been since Obregón's time one of the most publicized aims of the Revolution. The Constitution of 1917 made all elementary education secular and compulsory. Federal support of the program has been generous—355,680,000 pesos in 1951, a great deal of it spent in the erection of school buildings, many thousands of which dot the landscape from one end of the country to the other, in marked contrast to prerevolutionary times.

But buildings, it was soon discovered, do not educate. In 1945, Jaime Torres Bodet, Secretary of Education, informed a shocked nation that half the population of school age and over could neither read nor write—this after twenty-five years of effort. Even without the usual handicaps of undernourishment (Torres Bodet reported

[7] As I write this (1965), our Congress has passed a law abolishing the bracero program, on the ground that the braceros are taking jobs away from our unemployed. How our unemployed are to be induced to do the backbreaking work of the braceros is a question that no one has answered. The effect of the law on Mexican economy is bound to be grave. If I may venture a guess, the flood of wetbacks will increase, as well as the number of legitimate emigrants, who will find ready employment here. The emigration, indeed, has already attained startling dimensions. In California alone it is estimated that there are a million and a half Latins, mostly Mexicans. From Brownsville to San Francisco a creeping reconquest of the territory lost in 1848 is discernible.

350

that 135,000 out of the 193,000 children attending school in the Federal District did not get enough to eat), indifference, inertia, and religious antagonism, one tremendous factor by itself explained a good part of the failure: Teachers could not make a living at teaching.

In the early days of the program some thousands of young and enthusiastic men and women were encouraged to go into the profession. They were the missionaries of the New Order, and not a few of them suffered martyrdom during the Cristero trouble. They were given tenure and salaries which, although not glittering, at least assured them a modest competence. Following the fashion of the time, they formed themselves in an Educational Workers Union and made their opinions felt in politics. But, as teachers everywhere have learned, their union had no real power to protect them. In 1932 the late unlamented General Saturnino Cedillo, governor of the state of San Luis Potosí, was jailing teachers without trial and withholding their pay for months at a stretch for "communistic activities," which meant that they were demanding more money. Finally a desperate and penniless band of teachers walked the two hundred miles to Mexico City to lay their grievances before the president. Cedillo was liquidated shortly afterward for straying from the Party fold, and the teachers presumably got their back pay.

The San Luis Potosí case was extreme, but it illustrated the helplessness of teachers in the face of caciquismo and public indifference. Their salaries were always the last to be raised, and they could not apply the mordida to fill the gap, having nothing marketable to sell. Their long misery sapped the vitality of the profession to a critical degree. In the fall of 1944 several hundred schools in the state of Durango did not open because their teachers failed to show up, many of them having enlisted as braceros. A mass demonstration of teachers in front of the National Palace in Mexico threatened: "We must have more pay or we will close the schools!" In 1945 the Department of Education calculated that the minimum salary necessary to support a teacher and a normal family of five was 317.60 pesos a month. At that time the federal schools of Coahuila were paying 126.20 pesos a month, and the teachers were making up the difference by working as day laborers.

351

Strikes, demonstrations, violence, and repression advertised the plight of the teachers, and tardy and inadequate increases eased the strain somewhat. In 1950 the salaries of uncertified teachers in Jalisco were advanced from 90 to 150 pesos a month; those of certified teachers, from 120 to 200. Meanwhile, inflation and the devaluation of the peso had reduced its purchasing power to a little more than a fourth of what it had been in 1939. A Zapotec schoolmaster of Miahuatlán, Oaxaca, a dignified and self-respecting young man, told me ruefully that his salary of 200 pesos a month (about 25 dollars in 1950) hardly sufficed to support him and his family—a heroic understatement.[8]

The magnitude of the school housing problem is enough to make one despair of its solution. The vast building program is defeated in advance by the birth rate. The *annual* increase in the number of schoolchildren was estimated to be 171,200 in 1960, while in 1965 it is expected to reach the staggering total of 226,900. The result was that in 1960 only half the youngsters advanced beyond the second grade. In the circumstances one wonders why the rate of illiteracy is as low as it is, an estimated 45 per cent in 1960.

Higher education in the provincial universities suffered from lack of funds and languished because they could not attract superior men to their faculties. The ancient University of San Nicolás de Hidalgo (now the University of Michoacán) reported in 1946 that 180 of its 800 students had dropped out because of poor instruction. By 1949 conditions were so bad that the students, led by the rector, demonstrated before the governor's palace. They complained that the university could not function because the professors were paid only two pesos a day; moreover, they had no library and no laboratory. Their resentment against the governor was very hot because he had just spent a million pesos on an outdoor theater. The row took on political coloring and the governor interpreted it as an attack on the

[8] Meanwhile, the federal government has been striving to encourage education at all levels; the state governments likewise. The national budget for education rose from 314,000,000 pesos in 1950 to 1,900,000,000 in 1960, while the school population in the primary grades rose from 3,000,000 to 5,100,000; but the number of teachers rose from 72,000 to 105,000, an actual decline in ratio from one-to-forty to one-to-fifty.

Party. He called out the troops. Luckily, only two students were killed and a few dozen wounded. President Alemán transferred the commandant and promised that justice would be done.

The situation of the professor in a provincial university at that time is best illustrated by two quotations. The first is an extract from the report of Don José María Ibarra, president of the state legislature of Jalisco, made in February, 1950: "The Technological Institute [of Guadalajara] began its second trial year with magnificent results. The technical courses were entirely completed by young men who, in the future of Jalisco, will play a very important part in the many industries that are being installed here. . . . The state will assume the burden of this noble task."

The second is from a conversation I had at that time with a seedy, frayed, but gentle and intelligent-looking man, whom I rightly spotted for a professor—at that same school, as it turned out. "Yes," he said, "I am a teacher. I am too old to do anything else. I teach physics and mechanics—out of books, for we have no laboratory where the student might verify his book knowledge, which, of course, he loses.

"What are we doing to educate our people? I'm sorry to say that our school system is failing. How can we teachers teach properly if we have to hold down three jobs, as I do, merely to get enough to eat? . . . There is really no longer any incentive for a young man to dedicate himself to learning. Most of our students, when they see there is no reward in it, go into politics or commerce. And that is true of all our professions: medicine, law, and the rest. The result is that we lack the trained intelligence to help ourselves. We are like ignorant savages sitting on a treasure. . . .

"The latest bit of bureaucratic efficiency they have put in is enough to make one give up the ghost. I do not receive a salary any more; I have a time card. At the door of my classroom I present my card to a clerk, who punches it, and at the end of the month the holes are added up and I am paid off like any laborer. Dignity, pride in one's work, security, and time for study—all those old dreams of the scholar are gone. Have I said enough?"

Since I took these lugubrious notes, in 1950, notable changes have taken place in the provinces, where new "universities," and technical

353

and normal schools, have sprung up everywhere, and are supported on an unprecedented scale, even including better salaries for the professors. But all these institutions together cannot compare in influence and resources with the National University, which in the past thirty-five years has had its own ups and downs.

Back in 1929, in a wave of enthusiasm for democratic processes, President Portes Gil reincorporated the National University of Mexico as the National Autonomous University, and its government was entrusted to a mixed directorate, half of whose members were elected by the faculty, half by the student body, with the power of hiring and firing all personnel. The result, which should have been anticipated, was that the university became a training school for politicians. The professor who failed a student had to be prepared to defend himself, and a professor who wanted a job had first to electioneer among the student caciques. University politics took on all the excitement of national politics: the same cleavages appeared, and rival caciques used the same methods as their betters. In 1944, for example, the rector, Don Rodulfo Brito Foucher, who stood with the right wing, appointed Don Antonio Díaz Soto y Gama (whom the reader first met as Zapata's brain trust) director of the National Preparatory School. The left wing was annoyed, and on July 26 a battle was fought between those who liked the rector and those who did not. Students climbed to the roofs of buildings and dropped bricks on the heads of their enemies, two of whom were killed. That was all it cost to procure the resignations of Don Rodulfo Brito Foucher and Don Antonio Díaz Soto y Gama.

A new director, approved by the left wing, was elected, Don Alfonso Caso, the distinguished archaeologist, who would be an ornament to any faculty, in Mexico or anywhere else. But this time the right wing was unhappy and raised a row. A self-styled "Committee for the Defense of the University" staged a noisy demonstration against Don Alfonso Caso, whom they accused of communism. The evidence? He was the brother-in-law of Vicente Lombardo Toledano, the labor leader.

Student "revolutions" became endemic. Political unrest kept the university in a turmoil, and one wondered when the studying got done. In April, 1948, left-wing students issued an ultimatum to Don

Alfonso's successor, Don Salvador Zurbirán, demanding more lenient examinations. He refused to yield, and they threw him bodily into the street. Properly called hoodlums by the metropolitan press, 4,000 of them marched in protest against this insult to their honor. President Alemán wearily intervened and managed to quiet the storm before any blood was spilled.

A good deal of this turbulence was the natural blowing off of steam common to university students everywhere, and there has been much less of it since the opening in 1950 of the dazzling new University City, where the gymnasium, athletic fields, space, and fresh air have siphoned off their surplus energy. Moreover, a growing pride in the university and its achievements, and a new spirit of loyalty to it among its 27,000 students make it unlikely that they will tolerate such disturbances, especially since a university degree is the best guarantee of a job in the federal bureaucracy or in industry.

# 27

## THE WELFARE STATE
## MAINLY ECONOMIC

The greatest and most urgent problem that Mexico's new managers had to face was the stark need of survival. The endemic shortage of foodstuffs, aggravated by the tendency of the population always to press beyond the limits of subsistence, gave them plenty to think about. From the first two chapters of this volume the reader may have got the notion that the situation was hopeless, but human ingenuity has contrived to overcome, for the time being at least, some of the more formidable handicaps.

The gravity of the problem is evident. Mexico is relatively poor in exploitable agricultural land. Of her 494 million acres, only about 59 million can be put to work producing food, or, say, an area the size of Illinois and Indiana combined. The implied comparison is misleading, because the fertility of Mississippi Valley bottom land is vastly greater than that of Mexican soil generally. Indeed, in all Mexico there are only 25 million acres of grade A land, and it has to be irrigated. The remaining 34 million acres are what is called *temporal,* that is, land depending upon the erratic rainfall, and it can be counted on to produce a full crop only once in three to five years.

To this sobering picture of agricultural poverty must be added the exploding population, which, as we have seen in chapter 2, threatens to touch 100,000,000 by the end of this century. This is the specter that haunts Mexico. The ultimate impossibility of feeding the country is the strongest motive behind the new program of industrialization, which has had such a spectacular growth in the past two decades. In the words of Adolfo Orive Alba, the able Secretary of

Hydraulic Resources under President Alemán: "Mexico is not, and can never be, an essentially agricultural country, and she will therefore have to orient her destiny toward industrialization." His view of agriculture, on the other hand, was unexpectedly optimistic: "The complete exploitation of the 10 million hectares [25 million acres] of irrigable land, the sanitation of the tropical areas, and the cultivation of the 14 million hectares of temporal land will satisfy the needs of the future population and leave a surplus of certain products for export."

Ten years later (1960), Orive Alba, in his *Política de Irrigación en México,* reported that the state- and federal-operated ejido systems numbered sixty-five, the area affected was 1,628,800 hectares (about 4 million acres), and that production between 1925 and 1960 had risen by about 350 per cent. As early as 1951, for the first time in half a century, Mexico was balancing her maize budget. Other food crops, except wheat,[1] followed the same pattern, an accomplishment that occasioned understandable rejoicing and pointing-with-pride; but it was a kind of war measure, adopted in a desperate battle with a sleepless enemy, the population growth—over a million new mouths to feed every year! No sacrifice was too great, no cost too heavy, to win a victory, however temporary it might prove to be. How the soil of Mexico can support the 76-odd millions of the 1980's hence is a question, *the* question, which would dismay the heart of the most enthusiastic devotee of industrialization.

Mexican engineers have had to work against time. They could not always make the long study necessary to plan the most effective use of land and water resources. They lacked reliable data on precipitation, which in any case would be uncertain ("normal" and

---

[1] Wheat is the despair of Mexican agronomists. As the population becomes more urbanized, the consumption of wheat becomes more general. In 1951 its consumption reached a record high of 35 million bushels, of which 15 million had to be imported from the United States. The yield in Mexico is one of the lowest in the world, about nine bushels to the acre. Marte R. Gómez, Secretary of Agriculture, said in 1946: "If present conditions are accepted as irremediable, Mexico will have to continue being, eternally, a wheat-importing country." Since then considerable progress has been made in the development of hybrids and rust-resistant strains, with a corresponding increase in production.

"average" precipitation are only figures of speech in Mexico), and the engineers sometimes built dams and then suffered the mortification of seeing them lie empty for years.[2] Señor Orive Alba, reporting in November, 1951, on the disastrous four-year drought on the Plateau, said that the situation could not be charged to the inadequacy of the dams, but to the failure of the rains! By that time the water storage of the whole country was down to nineteen per cent of capacity; but, as he justly pointed out, even so the dams assured the production from a million acres which otherwise would have been lost. A dry cycle, however, may last twenty-five years, as did that of 1900–1925. What then? It may be that the engineers will come up with a method of utilizing sea water economically, which will again push away the specter.

Quite aware of these grim implications, the engineers looked longingly at the stupendous rainfall of the Gulf Coast and dreamed of ways to bring it to the Plateau, or at least to put it to work producing food. Covering some 20,000 square miles of the states of Vera Cruz, Oaxaca, and Puebla, lies the great basin of the Papaloapan River. The main stream and its tributaries flow down from the highlands through steep and rugged barrancas, typical of the escarpment, and here and there they have built up fertile plains of debris on the valley bottoms. They join forces at the base of the escarpment, forming the Mississippi-like lower Papaloapan, which meanders for a hundred-odd miles over the flat coastal plain before flowing into the Gulf. The Papaloapan basin is in the area of very heavy precipitation, and the river discharges an estimated thirty billion tons of water a year. This vast runoff is, indeed, the greatest hazard to life in the basin, for the summer floods are extremely violent (the drop from the top to the bottom of the basin being more than a mile vertically), besides which they cover the hot flats of the basin and make it one of the worst malarial spots in the Republic.

Nevertheless, here was water, and the engineers dreamed of a Mexican TVA: dams, flood control, sanitation, hydroelectric plants, canals to drain the swamps and bring water to the drier regions,

[2] The Rodríguez Dam, in Lower California near Tijuana, was completed in 1944, and in the next seven years stored not a drop of water.

358

dikes to protect the cities, roads and railroads for communication, and factories in which to process the abundant new produce and give employment to thousands. A million acres of new land would be brought into production, and 600,000 people would have a new place to live in. It would cost only a billion pesos or so. A Papaloapan Commission was created and given charge of the work, and within three years (in 1950) it was able to make a very encouraging progress report: The great Miguel Alemán Dam on the Río Tonto had been completed; the lower channel of the Papaloapan had been straightened to expedite the runoff; the swamps had been drained and the mosquitoes brought under control; a dike protecting the city of Cosamaloapan had been built and had already paid for itself by saving the city from destruction in the hurricane of 1950. The Commission concluded with the hopeful statement that the Papaloapan basin was potentially the richest piece of land in Mexico. Ten years later, the Commission reported substantial progress in all directions: 300,000 acres of land under irrigation; 250,000 kilowatts of electricity piped to all parts of the Valley; 400 new schools; 1,000 miles of new roads. Only the peopling of the district is slower than expected, for the Plateau inhabitants are very reluctant to move to the hot country. Nevertheless, the Papaloapan project is an imaginative and courageous attempt to harness the truly terrifying power of the river. It has been successful to a degree, and it would be mere carping to doubt the enthusiasm of the planners. I wish, however, that they had given more consideration to what in my opinion is the greatest hazard the project has to face, namely, the Caribbean hurricanes (described in chapter 1), which are passed over in silence in the literature. It is doubtful, in the mind of this amateur at least, that any man-made structure could stand against another such hurricane as that of 1944.

Vast agglomerations of people must have water, and they will do anything to get it, even if it means creating deserts in the process. This observation is pertinent to a consideration of one of the most interesting spots in the western hemisphere, a thirsty city once surrounded by water.

Mexico City is an historical accident. It was built in the middle of a lake because the jealous nations of the Plateau would not let the Aztecs settle any place else. Certainly, no modern planner in his right mind would build a vast industrial capital on a spongy lake bed, a mile and a half above sea level, cut off from access to markets and sources of supply by mountain ranges, at least on three sides, without fuel or an adequate supply of sweet water. It doesn't make sense; but there it is, with about five million people and a huge industrial plant, and there is not the slightest chance that it will consent to be removed to a better site.

It all happened because Cortés and his companions were enchanted with the place. It takes imagination to visualize the Valley of Mexico as it was four hundred years ago. Instead of a noisy city lying in an arid salt waste, begrimed with smoke and choked with dust, the conquistadores beheld a smiling green valley and a New World Venice, villages hugging the shores of the lakes, hills thickly wooded, and plains covered with maize. Fifty years after his first sight of it, Bernal Díaz was still relatively speechless with wonder. "And when we saw the many cities and towns built over the water, and other large towns on the mainland, and the straight and level causeway and how it led to Mexico, we were astonished and said that it was like the things of enchantment related in the book of Amadís, because of the great towers and pyramids, and buildings in the midst of the water, and all of stone and mortar. Some of our soldiers wondered whether they might not be dreaming, and it is not surprising that I should write about it now in this fashion, because there was so much to astonish us that I do not know how to describe the unheard-of and never-before-seen, or even dreamed-of, things that we saw."

But the Castilians were strictly land animals and, once the novelty of their new capital had worn off, they set to work to make it resemble as closely as possible the parched cities of their beloved Castile. They were dismayed to discover that the beautiful lake in which it lay had the habit of rising during the rainy season and running them out of town. They could not take to the water in canoes, as the lake people did. The ancient Mexicans had adapted their way of living to nature; the Spaniards, like us, insisted on making nature adapt herself to them, and they spent the next four centuries in an unintelligent effort to get rid of the water. The battle with the lakes was not definitely won until 1900, when the canal and tunnel of Tequixquiac were opened. The new drainage system was disastrously efficient. The lakes nearest the outlet, San Cristóbal and Xaltocan, were the first to dry up. Lake Zumpango and Lake Texcoco took longer, but eventually achieved complete aridity. The last to go were Lakes Chalco and Xochimilco, once the playground of Mexico, as well as its perpetual source of flowers and greenstuff, now reduced to stinking and unsightly bogs. The famous lacustrine towns of Tlahuac, Mixquic, and Xochimilco, whose "floating gardens" (*chinampas*) were a delight to the eye and nostrils, are sorry anachronisms, their trees withering and their boats cracking. The last solemn act of their demise was celebrated in 1949, when the federal government agreed to spend a thousand pesos a month pumping water *into* the canals, to keep the tourists happy.[3]

It would almost seem that the ancient gods of the lakes are angry at this vandalism and have marked the city for destruction. As the life-giving waters disappear, the floor of the valley sinks, and the city sinks with it. At first the sinking was imperceptible, but as the water receded and the silt had to bear the crushing weight of skyscrapers and factories, the sinking accelerated, until now the city is subsiding at the rate of *more than a foot a year*. Mexico City is already so low that it has to be drained by pumping, and, within a few more years, unless the sinking can be arrested, it will be at the bottom of a sump, and the drainage of the valley will then be *toward* the city. Add to this the lugubrious prospect of a season of heavy precipitation, say, of thirty to forty inches, and the gods of the lakes will surely have their revenge.

Meanwhile, the bulging population of the valley and the new industrial plants drank more and more water, and, until 1951, there was a perpetual and dangerous shortage of it. The Aztecs had got along with the water they piped in from the springs of Chapultepec. The Spaniards and the modern Mexicans found other sources, like the beautiful spring at Xochimilco, and also got along pretty well

---

[3] In 1957 Lake Xochimilco was four feet below its "normal" level, so the Churubusco River was diverted into the canals.

until a few years ago. Industrialization changed all that. The new factories offered jobs, and hundreds of thousands of people moved in to take them. The city rapidly outgrew its water supply and looked around frantically for new sources. The nearest one was the Lerma River, which wanders across the Plateau and supplies the life blood of the rich farming country known as the Bajío. No matter. The city must have water, and the construction of the Lerma Aqueduct was begun, in 1941. Ten years later, on September 4, 1951, it was opened with appropriate and patriotic ceremonies. The indispensable Diego Rivera had been commissioned to decorate the outlet, which he did with his customary skill, save that he saw fit to put a colossal recumbent figure of Cuauhtémoc at the bottom of the pool, the symbolism of which is not apparent to the uninitiated.[4]

The great Lerma Aqueduct is another of those stupendous feats of modern mechanics which make engineers glow with satisfaction and citizens swell with pride. It really *is* stupendous. It was cut through the western mountains, thirty-five miles to its intake at Almoloya del Río, in the state of Mexico. Its most challenging obstacle was the high range of Las Cruces, which was tunneled for nine miles. Works were built in the valley of Toluca to capture the water from riparian springs. On its way to the city the water is put to work generating electricity, 16,000 horsepower. It delivers to the city 1,650 gallons of water a second, with which and with the old sources, there was enough water for a while. But the city has doubled its population since 1951. What then? Well, we'll dig a canal around the rim of Popocatépetl, just below the snow line. Never mind the rich agriculture of Morelos that depends upon it. Or we'll dig a 200-mile canal and tap the headwaters of the Papaloapan. Never mind the thirsty state of Oaxaca that needs the water. Engineers are poets at heart.

In the abundant and lyrical descriptions of the Lerma Aqueduct I

[4] The reader will have noted the parallel between Mexico City and Los Angeles, California. The Owens River Aqueduct made a desert of the lovely Owens River Valley, and the Colorado River Aqueduct threatens to dry up the fertile bottom lands of the Colorado. What the Feather River Aqueduct will do to northern California is a constant source of anxiety.

have looked in vain for a discussion of a fundamental question, that is, what effect this heavy withdrawal will have on the economy and ecology of the Lerma basin. Even before the aqueduct was opened, there was a growing concern about the shrinking of Lake Chapala, the beautiful natural reservoir which is fed by the Lerma River, and upon which the agriculture and industry of Jalisco depend. What could happen, to take the dimmest possible view of the matter, is illustrated by the fate of Lake Cuitzeo, in Guanajuato. Around that ancient lake there were, not long ago, nine Tarascan villages, of some 6,000 families in all, living by fishing, agriculture, and weaving mats (*petates*) from the rushes that grew in the marshes. Lake Cuitzeo was fed by two rivers flowing north from Michoacán. It was a pleasant place, and its people were healthy and fairly prosperous, although not very important. Anyway, the engineers looked at the two rivers and shook their heads over the waste. So the rivers were dammed up, and Lake Cuitzeo dried up; the fish died, swarms of mosquitoes took over the sickly puddles, and malaria and unemployment killed the nine villages quite dead.

Or take Valle de Bravo, one of the prettiest valleys in all Mexico, with abundant water, a mild climate, and about 12,000 acres of rich bottom land, supporting a dense population—at least it did before 1949. But Mexico City needed electricity, and the engineers considered Valle de Bravo and dreamed their maniac dream. Now the Santa Barbara Dam supplies a thrilling number of kilowatts to light the city's neon signs and turn the wheels of its factories, and the old valley is a beautiful blue lake where lovers of nature may swim and fish. The nonchalance with which the promoters of progress view their handiwork is sometimes startling. "What became of the Indians?" I asked of one of them. "Don't worry about them," he answered. "Most of them moved away. Anyway, they were paid 600 to 800 pesos a hectare [30 to 40 dollars an acre] for their land, and those who stayed behind make a living guiding tourists."

Nor can Mexico City be sure that the Lerma River will always have water in it. Deforestation is still a serious problem in its basin, although the government is making vigorous and intelligent efforts to stop it. The technicians of the Lerma Aqueduct warned that unless deforestation was arrested, the springs of the Lerma would dry up.[5] In 1950 the governor of the state of Mexico predicted that, at the present rate of cutting, the state would be a desert in another twenty years. A series of wet years have proved him wrong, but the threat is still there. What a lot of fellow conspirators the old gods of the lakes seem to have!

Whenever you confront a planner with such questions, the chances are very good that you will hear a sermon on the miracles of industrialization. "Fuel? That's easy. We have just brought a 200-mile gas line from the Gulf oil fields. Who uses the gas? Why, the new industries at Tlalnepantla, who else? Sure, the people still cook with charcoal, but we'll fix all that. Oil stoves and kerosene are better and more economical, in the long run." "Wait a minute," you say; "I was going to ask about that long-run business. A workman (not a schoolteacher, of course) earns, say, ten to fifteen pesos a day. He has a wife and four kids. They all have to be fed and clothed. He pays rent, union dues, carfare, medical bills, social insurance, maybe a little income tax, takes the kids to a movie once a month, and sends a few pesos home to his old parents now and then. Take your pencil and figure out how much his wife will have left to buy oil stoves with, to say nothing of kerosene. Anyway, I can see why she goes to the market every day and buys a handful of charcoal instead. Isn't that about it?" [6] "True enough, but don't be in such a hurry. Give us time. Once our industrial program gets going at full speed, we'll create enough wealth for everybody, and to spare!"

The mythology of industrialization, for which we are largely responsible, is very puzzling to a layman. In my quest for enlightenment I had a conversation with a charmingly frank manufacturer of Mexico City. "Please excuse my ignorance," I said, "but how do you make a go of your business? How, for example, do you manage

[5] An engineer protested to me that forests have nothing to do with precipitation. Probably not, but they have everything to do with preventing runoff, erosion, and desiccation of the soil, as we are slowly learning.

[6] Oscar Lewis, in his studies of what he calls "the culture of poverty," draws a convincing and quite horrible picture of life in the working class quarters of Mexico City, in his *Five Families* (1959) and *The Children of Sánchez* (1961).

to compete with foreign products?" "Well," he answered, "for one thing my goods are just as high in quality as you can buy anywhere; for another, the government protects me with a tariff." "But doesn't that mean that your products cost more to manufacture?" "Not at all. I can turn out articles cheaper than they can make them in the States, tariff or no tariff." "How is that?" "Well, most of my ingredients are made right here in Mexico, and they're good, make no mistake about that." "And cheaper, of course?" "Naturally." "That's what I'm getting at. Why are they cheaper? Let me suggest an answer and you correct me if I'm wrong. All your products are cheaper, aren't they, because you pay your workmen only a fraction of what we have to pay ours? Could you compete if you paid your men, say, fifty pesos [six dollars] a day? And, if that is generally true, isn't the whole industrial structure of Mexico built upon a premise of low wages?" "I guess you're right," admitted my honest friend; "I hadn't thought of it that way." [7]

The financial structure of the modern welfare state, with its managed economy, is a towering mystery to most of us. These latter-day Aladdins are apparently able to evoke benevolent genii at will. Doubters are confounded by the very solid and very impressive accomplishments on every hand: roads, dams, aqueducts, the government-owned oil industry and railroads, factories, school buildings, sanitation projects, the conquest of the tropics (the Papaloapan Project), old debts paid and new ones made—a genuinely awe-inspiring record, possible only in a managed economy. The managers call the tune and the people dance. I suspect also that the people pay the piper.

In 1950 the Census Bureau let fall a hint of who is paying the bill, when it published figures on the wage and salary trend for the preceding decade. It noted that between 1941 and 1949 the peso had lost 70 per cent of its purchasing power. At the same time nominal wages (the Census Bureau lumps wages and salaries together) had

[7] In the fifteen years that have passed since I took these notes, some of the promises of industrialization have been fulfilled: Goods are more plentiful, employment has increased, and there is a decided improvement in the dress and appearance of the urban population, that is, outside the pullulating slums.

risen from a base of 100 in 1941 to 277.5 in 1949; that is, the average real wages had dropped by 16.75 per cent, a substantial but not intolerable loss. But "average" wages (and salaries) in Mexico are as meaningless as "average" rainfall. For example, a bank executive's salary of 50,000 pesos a year and a schoolteacher's salary of 2,400 would make an "average" salary of 26,200 for the two classes. Averages are the Jabberwocks of statisticians and should be regarded with a healthy respect for the jaws that bite, the claws that catch.

A consideration of three other groups may clarify the picture. Between 1939 and 1947 the salaries of government clerks rose from an "average" of 340 to 429 pesos a month, a decline in real wages of 52 per cent. The judiciary is not included among them. It sounds odd to us, but Mexican judges have a "Judicial Workers' Union," which complained in 1950 that judges' salaries had risen in twenty years from 900 to 1,150 pesos a month, a decline in real wages of more than 60 per cent. They added that the corruption of the bench had no other cause. The nominal wages of a much better protected group, the steelworkers of Monterrey, rose between 1939 and 1947 from 8.51 to 19.18 pesos a day, a decline in real wages of only 28 per cent. In the words of Frank Tannenbaum: "What is clear is that business activity was increasing, investments in business were growing, a middle class was developing, and the country was showing evidence of industrial progress. But it was doing so at the expense of those who could least afford it—the industrial and agricultural laboring population."

But industrialization depended upon customers, and Mexican industry could hardly hope to capture foreign markets. Therefore it had to depend upon the domestic market, upon those very people whose purchasing power was declining year by year. Artificially supported prices, "overproduction," and lack of sufficient customers produced a continual crisis, which was reflected in periodical panics and the flight of jittery capital. These crises were met by "stabilizing" the currency, a modern euphemism for coin-clipping. The peso was "stabilized" in 1933 at 3.60 to the dollar; in 1941, at 4.85; in 1948, at 8.65; and in the past ten years has found its floor (it is hoped) at about 12.50 to the dollar. That meant that you could sell your oil, silver, fibers, bananas, coffee, and so on, for more and more pesos, with which you could pay your help. On the other hand, you had to pay more and more for your machinery and other imported goods; but, if you could keep your foreign purchases down and your exports up, things did not look so bad, until the next crisis. No matter what you did, however, you had to have customers in the long run or close up shop. Here I should like to turn the discussion over to my learned and generous colleague, the late Professor Sanford Mosk, whose *Industrial Revolution in Mexico*, although it is now somewhat out of date, should be prayerfully read by all planners.

"For many years we can expect Mexican industry to confine itself to producing almost entirely for the domestic market. If the expansion of the internal market does not parallel the expansion of the industrial capacity, serious problems will be created in the economic and social life of the country. . . . For most kinds of manufactured goods, Mexico is a market of 5 to 6 million persons. . . .[8] If the number of consumers for some manufactured products exceed six million, there are many articles that are purchased by fewer people yet. For every small refinement in the taste being catered to, there is a sharp drop in the number of persons entering the market.

"It is obvious that markets like these—or, putting them all together, a market like Mexico—cannot support a large and ramified industrial structure. The market must grow as new industrial plant is built, and it must grow rapidly as long as industrialization proceeds rapidly. What, then, are the possibilities for a speedy expansion of the Mexican market for manufactured goods?

"As industry expands, the industrial wage earners tend to become consumers of more and varied manufactured products. This tendency, however, may be curbed by inflation. . . . Inflation has already wiped out the gains in earnings made by the Mexican industrial workers as a group, and the average real wage in industry has fallen in recent years. With further industrialization, the inflationary potential in Mexico is great. . . . But even if industrial wages should increase rather than decline in purchasing power, the

---

[8] That was in 1950. For 1965 the number should be substantially increased, say, to 8 million, out of a total population (est.) of 40,000,000.

working force in industry is too small to provide a mass market for an expanding industrial output. . . . The potential market for Mexican industry must be sought in the agricultural population, as those engaged in farming, together with their families, comprise approximately 70 per cent of all the inhabitants of the country. . . .[9] The outstanding characteristic of this market is low purchasing power."

This staggering fact has, of course, been in the minds of the leaders of the Revolution from the beginning. At first they accepted the naïve notion of the zapatistas that the poverty of rural Mexico was exclusively chargeable to the inequitable distribution of land (the hacienda system) and its inefficient use, and that it could be cured by dividing the land among the peasants (the ejido system) and starting all over again. The confiscation and redistribution of land on a grand scale was one of the most spectacular features of the Revolution, and, while it alienated forever those who lost their land, it attracted to the support of the Party large numbers of land-hungry peasants. By 1960 some 100,000,000 acres had been distributed in ejidos, and there was no safe way to stop it, for free land to the peasants had become an article of faith, or an implied contract. They had been taught that the land was theirs, and it was sometimes difficult to get them to wait for legal possession. Impatient peasants, humorously called "paratroopers," moved into land which they thought should be theirs and defied the owners to eject them. A great deal of blood was shed in the inevitable clashes between ejidatarios and landowners, and certain sections, like Sinaloa and Guerrero, were kept in a state amounting to civil war.

Whatever the merits of the land program may have been in theory, after twenty years of it the food shortage could no longer be ignored, and Eduardo Villaseñor, Director of the Bank of Mexico, risked his political neck by calling for a cessation of the redistribution of land. "If," he said in 1945, "in order to save the Mexican people from hunger, it should be necessary to call a halt to the program of social reform, the state and the people must choose

---

[9] Since Mosk wrote this (1950), there has been a heavy displacement of the rural population to the cities, until now something less than half lives in the country.

between the blind application of our present [land] law . . . and the solution of the food problem even at the cost of arresting the process of reform." He was, of course, blasted as a reactionary, and hotheads called for his scalp; but there can be little doubt that he was right, and the "Plan Alemán" undertook to raise the food production by any means that promised results.

The government's course was plainly indicated by the record of the 200,000 "small proprietors" who, in 1947, were producing on their 5,700,000 acres 70 per cent of all the crops in the country. The immense discrepancy between their record and that of the ejidos was owing to several well-understood factors. The average holding of the 1,222,910 ejidatarios in 1940 was 14.3 acres,[10] only a fraction of which was good land. Most of them had very primitive notions about farming and used their ejidos only for subsistence. It became plain that, until and unless the ejidatarios could be induced to abandon subsistence farming and produce a surplus for the hungry cities, they could not be entrusted with that vital responsibility. The "small proprietors," on the other hand, with more skill, capital, and superior and larger tracts, were commercial farmers, interested in producing for profit, and the Alemán government encouraged them in every way, mostly by loans, subsidies, and guaranteed prices. The plan paid off, at least in the very important matter of producing enough food to go around.[11]

In conclusion, Mexico's future well-being depends upon agriculture and, in the end, upon a wise adjustment of population to agricultural resources, and of industry to all factors. Her planners should recognize the fallacy in the popular belief that she can support an indefinitely expanding population, along with an indefinitely expanding industrial economy, by exchanging her manufactured goods for food which, they hope, will be supplied by the rest of the world, also indefinitely. Unfortunately, as Japan and England

[10] In 1960 the ejidatarios numbered 2,276,000 (estimated), and the average holding was 40 acres. Their share of the national production had risen to about 50 per cent, a large part of it from the huge government operated "ejidos," already mentioned.

[11] For a detailed and authoritative discussion of the ejido and related topics, the reader should consult Nathan Whetten's *Rural Mexico*.

have both discovered, modern technology has made every nation potentially an industrial nation; their foreign markets are invaded by hungry rivals, and they are faced with the terrifying problem of feeding huge populations on an inadequate and rebellious soil.

No. Mexico (like all the rest of us) must cut her coat to fit her cloth. I keep worrying about those 76 million Mexicans of twenty years hence. Have Mexico's planners asked themselves how many people can live decently on her resources? Have our own, for that matter, asked such questions? Did not William Vogt some years ago startle us into angry denials, in his *Road to Survival,* by suggesting that the ideal population of the United States might be about a hundred million? The advice that I humbly offer to all planners is to tack up on the wall the Aztec prayer with which I began this book: *Grant me, Lord, a little light!*

# GLOSSARY

Agiotista (Sp. *agio,* premium). A money changer.

Aguacate (Az. *ahuacatl*). "Avocado" (U.S.).

Alcabala (Sp.). An excise or sales tax.

Alcalde (Sp.). A mayor. *Alcalde mayor,* the chief magistrate of a province (*alcaldía mayor*). Cf. *corregidor.*

Alguacil (Sp.). A constable.

Alhóndiga (Sp.). A public granary.

Arriero (Sp.). A driver of pack animals.

Arroba (Sp.). A measure of 25 pounds.

Atole (Az. *atolli*). A beverage of maize flour and water.

Audiencia (Sp.). The Audiencia of Mexico was the supreme court; composed of a *presidente* and four justices (*oidores*); in the absence of the viceroy it became the chief executive of New Spain.

Auto de fe (Sp.). A public trial of those condemned by the Inquisition.

Bachiller (Sp.). The lowest academic degree, followed by *licenciado* and *doctor.*

Barranca (Sp.). A ravine or canyon.

Bracero (Sp.). A field hand.

Caballo (Sp.). A horse. *Caballería,* a piece of land granted to a mounted soldier (*caballero*).

Cabecera (Sp.). The head town of a district.

Cabildo (Sp.). A town council. Cf. *regimiento.*

Cacique (Arawak). A chieftain; later applied to the political boss of a town or district.

Carga (Sp.). A load. *Carga de indio,* the load carried by an Indian and weighing two *arrobas,* or fifty pounds; *carga de mula,* 200 pounds; *cargador,* a carrier. Cf. *tameme.*

Carro (Sp.). A two-wheeled cart. Cf. *chirrión.*

Casa de comunidad (Sp.). A building housing the officers of a town.

Caudillo (Sp.). A military chieftain.

Cédula (Sp.). A royal decree.

Chahuixtle (Az. *chiauiztli?*). A fungus that attacks wheat; rust.

Chinampa (Az. *chinamitl?*). Artificial island built up in the fresh-water lakes of Mexico, sometimes (mistakenly) referred to as "floating garden."

Chirrión (Sp.). A huge two-wheeled cart drawn by as many as ten or twelve mules or oxen. From *chirriar*, to squeak.

Científico (Sp.). A name applied to a member of Porfirio Díaz' cabinet.

Cimarrón (Sp.). As an adjective, applied to stray animals gone wild; specifically, a runaway Negro slave.

Cofradía (Sp.). A confraternity or sodality.

Comal (Az. *comalli*). An earthenware griddle for baking tortillas and other food.

Comendador (Sp.). Commander of a military order, such as that of Santiago or Calatrava.

Comunero (Sp.). A member of a *comunidad*; specifically, a rebel or a troublemaker. From the War of the Comuneros of 1522, in Castile. Cf. *Comunidad*.

Comunidad (Sp.). Any organized town; specifically, one of the free towns of Castile that rebelled against Charles V in 1522.

Congregación (Sp.). A congregation or religious order; specifically, an Indian town organized by the government in the late sixteenth century, or early seventeenth.

Corregidor (Sp.). A Crown officer governing a district (*corregimiento*). His functions were essentially the same as those of an *alcalde mayor* (q. v.).

Costumbre (Sp.). As here used applies to Indian custom, which was recognized as common law by the Spanish Crown.

Coyote (Az. *coyotl*). A coyote; specifically, a smuggler of wetbacks.

Creole (Sp. *criollo*). A person born in America of Spanish parents, or of Spanish ancestry.

Curandero (Sp.). A popular physician, uncertified; a quack.

Doctrina (Sp.). Doctrine; specifically, a mission school for Indians.

Dorado (Sp.). Gilded, as in *el dorado*, the gilded man; specifically, one of Francisco Villa's troopers.

Ejido (Sp.). A common allotted to a village for crops or grazing; specifically, in Mexico, land allotted to a peasant for farming; also, a state-operated, cooperative farm. *Ejidatario*, such a peasant, or member of such a farm.

Encomienda (Sp.). An allotment of Indians given in trust to a Spaniard (sixteenth century), with the duty of looking after their spiritual and material welfare. *Encomendero*, the holder of an *encomienda*.

Entrada (Sp.). An expedition or raid.

Estancia (Sp.). A grant of land for running cattle (*ganado mayor*), or sheep and goats (*ganado menor*).

Faenero (Sp. *faena,* a work stint). A pieceworker.

Familiar (Sp.). The lowest rank of Inquisition official; a catchpole.

Fanega (Sp.). A dry measure of 100 pounds; also (as *fanega de sembradura*) the amount of land needed to sow a *fanega* of grain, generally a piece 400 fathoms square.

Flota (Sp.). A fleet; specifically, the regular fleet crossing between Spain and the Indies.

Fuero. (Sp.). A privilege; specifically, the privilege of the clergy and the army to be tried in their own courts.

Gachupín (etymology uncertain). A term of opprobrium applied to Spaniards in Mexico.

Gringo (etymology uncertain). A term of opprobrium applied to non-Spanish foreigners in Mexico.

Grito (Sp.). A shout; specifically, the *Grito de Dolores* which Father Hidalgo raised at the beginning of the War of Independence.

Guacamole (Az. *ahuacamulli*). A paste made of *aguacate,* onions, and chili.

Hacienda (Sp.). The treasury, as *real hacienda;* in Mexico, a large quasi-feudal estate. *Hacendado,* the proprietor of such.

Hermandad (Sp.). A brotherhood; specifically, a local militia serving a Spanish town (fifteenth century); also, an alliance of several such towns.

Juez (Sp.). A judge; but in Spanish usage, a *juez* could also be a magistrate or administrator, as *juez de congregación*).

Licenciado (Sp.). A licenciate, the second rank (after *bachiller*) in the academic hierarchy.

Líder (Eng. *leader*). A labor leader.

Macehual (Az. *macehualli*). A peasant or field hand.

Maguey (Az.). The *Agave americana,* from which *pulque* is extracted; also valuable as a source for cordage (*ixtle* fiber) and paper.

Malacate (Az. *malacatl,* a spindle). A vertical winch powered by horses or mules, used in the mines.

Malpaís (Sp.). Badlands.

Mano (Sp.). A hand; specifically, the roller used for crushing maize.

Manta (Sp.). A piece of cloth (cotton in the early days), widely used as an article of trade and tribute.

Maravedí (Sp.). A fictitious coin, 278 to the silver peso. See *peso.*

Marrano (Sp.). A pig; specifically, a poor Jew (Spain).

Masa (Sp.). Dough made of maize flour.

Mestizo (Sp.). A person of mixed Indian and Spanish ancestry.

Metate (Az. *metlatl*). A curved stone used (with the *mano*) for grinding maize.

Milpa (Az. *milli* and *pa*). A maize field.

Moderado (Sp.). A moderate; specifically, a member of the *moderado* party, as opposed to the *puro* or Jacobin party, and to the clerical party (early nineteenth century).

Monte (Sp.). A hill or wood; specifically, the wood allotted to a village for common use.

Mordida (Sp.). A bite; specifically, graft or squeeze.

Obraje (Sp.). A textile mill.

Oidor (Sp.). A justice of the Audiencia.

Paso (Sp.). A pass; also, a linear measure of about five feet.

Patrón (Sp.). A patron; specifically, a chief or boss.

Peón (Sp.). A foot soldier; also, a manual laborer. *Peonería,* a piece of land allotted to a foot soldier during the Conquest.

Peso (Sp.). The ordinary silver peso, or piece of eight (which became our dollar), was divided into eight *reales* (bits), or two *tostones.*

Petaca (Az. *petlacalli*). A container, usually of wickerwork and covered with leather; a trunk.

Petate (Az. *petlatl*). A mat.

Posada (Sp.). A stopping place, or inn.

Probanza (Sp.). An affidavit of a man's services, usually presented to the Crown in support of a claim for remuneration.

Procurador (Sp.). An attorney; in the Church, a procurator.

Pueblo (Sp.). A town. *Pueblo de realengo,* a town administered by the Crown, as opposed to an *encomienda* or mission town.

Pulque (etymology uncertain). The alcoholic drink made from the juice of the maguey.

Puro (Sp.). As used in the text, a member of the left-wing or Jacobin party (early nineteenth century).

Quemadero (Sp.). A burning place; specifically, for the execution of those convicted by the Inquisition.

Real de minas (Sp.). A mining community.

Real patronazgo (Sp.). The right granted to the Spanish Crown by Pope Leo X to nominate all members of the clergy.

Regidor (Sp.). A member of a town council (*regimiento*).

Repartimiento (Sp.). A distribution, of land, Indians, or whatever; frequently used as a synonym for *encomienda.*

Residencia (Sp.). A trial or investigation to which all public officers had to submit upon the termination of their service, or even during tenure.

Sambenito (Sp.). A special garb worn by those condemned by the Inquisition.

Sinarquista (Mex.). A member of the *Unión Nacional Sinarquista,* a right-wing political party.

Tameme (Az. *tlameme*). A carrier or bearer.

Tenatero (Az. *tanatl,* a cylindrical basket). A carrier in the mines.

Teocentili (Az. *teoxintli*). Maize.

**374**

Tortilla (Sp.). A maize cake.

Vara (Sp.). The Spanish yard of about 33 inches; also, a yardstick.

Vecino (Sp.). A citizen of a community; neighbor.

Venta (Sp.). An inn.

Visita (Sp.). An official visit of inspection. *Visitador,* the officer undertaking such a visit.

Zócalo (Sp.). A marketplace; specifically, the great square of Mexico City, officially known as the *Plaza de la Constitución.*

# SELECTED READING LIST
# OF STANDARD WORKS IN ENGLISH

The steadily growing volume of books on Mexico, even in English, is quite overwhelming. The brief bibliography offered below is hardly more than recommended reading. Luckily, the field has been well covered by R. A. Humphreys, in his indispensable *Latin American History: A Guide to the Literature in English* (London, 1958). For those who read Spanish and other languages the list would have to be immeasurably longer. H. B. Parkes, *A History of Mexico* (1960) lists the more important works. The vast *Handbook of Latin American Studies,* published yearly by the Library of Congress since 1936, reviews all current literature. Howard F. Cline's *Mexico: Revolution to Evolution* (1962) has a valuable bibliography covering contemporary developments in all fields.

Beals, Carleton. *Porfirio Díaz, Dictator of Mexico* (Philadelphia, 1932).

Bolton, Herbert E. *Rim of Christendom: A Biography of Eusebio Francisco Kino, Pacific Coast Pioneer* (New York, 1936).

————. *Outposts of Empire* (New York, 1931).

Brenner, Anita. *The Wind That Swept Mexico* (New York, 1943).

Calderón de la Barca, Madame (Frances Erskine Inglis) *Life in Mexico.* 2 vols. (Boston, 1843; many reprints).

Chamberlain, Robert S. *The Conquest and Colonization of Yucatan* (Washington, D.C., 1948).

————. *The Conquest and Colonization of Honduras* (Washington, D.C., 1953).

Chevalier, François. *Land and Society in Colonial Mexico: The Great Hacienda,* transl. by Alvin Eustis, ed. by Lesley Byrd Simpson (Berkeley and Los Angeles, 1963).

Cline, Howard F. *The United States and Mexico* (Cambridge, Mass., 1953).

————. *Mexico: Revolution to Evolution, 1940–1960* (New York, 1962).

Cortés, Hernán. *Letters,* transl. by F. A. MacNutt, 2 vols. (New York, 1908).

Covarrubias, Miguel. *Mexico South: The Isthmus of Tehuantepec* (New York, 1946).

Díaz del Castillo, Bernal. *The True History of the Conquest of Mexico,* transl. by A. P. Maudslay, 5 vols. (London, 1908–1916; abridged edition by Irving A. Leonard, New York, 1956).

Flandrau, Charles. *Viva Mexico!* (New York, 1908; many reprints).

Gage, Thomas. *A New Survey of the West Indies* (London, 1648; many reprints).

Gibson, Charles. *Tlaxcala in the Sixteenth Century* (New Haven, Conn., 1952).

————. *The Aztecs Under Spanish Rule: A History of the Indians of the Valley of Mexico, 1519–1810* (Stanford, Calif., 1964).

Gómara, Francisco López de. *Cortés: The Life of the Conqueror, by His Secretary,* transl. by Lesley Byrd Simpson (Berkeley and Los Angeles, 1964).

Gruening, Ernest. *Mexico and Its Heritage* (New York, 1928).

Haring, Clarence. *The Spanish Empire in America* (New York, 1947).

Herring, Hubert. *A History of Latin America* (New York, 1956).

Humboldt, Alexander von. *Political Essay on the Kingdom of New Spain,* transl. by John Black, 4 vols. (London, 1811).

Kubler, George. *Mexican Architecture in the Sixteenth Century,* 2 vols. (New Haven, Conn., 1948).

Lanning, John Tate. *Academic Culture in the Spanish Colonies* (New York, 1940).

Lea, Henry Charles. *The Inquisition in the Spanish Dependencies* (New York, 1908).

Leonard, Irving A. *Don Carlos de Sigüenza: A Mexican Savant of the Seventeenth Century* (Berkeley, 1929).

Lewis, Oscar. *Five Families: Mexican Case Studies in the Culture of Poverty* (New York, 1959).

————. *The Children of Sánchez: Autobiography of a Mexican Family* (New York, 1961).

McAlister, Lyle N. *The "Fuero Militar" in New Spain, 1764–1800* (Gainesville, Fla., 1957).

Mosk, Sanford A. *Industrial Revolution in Mexico* (Berkeley and Los Angeles, 1950; 2d edition, 1954).

Parkes, Henry B. *A History of Mexico* (Boston, 1960).

Parry, John H. *The Audiencia of New Galicia in the Sixteenth Century* (Cambridge, England, 1948).

————. *The Age of Reconnaissance* (London, 1963).

Phelan, John L. *The Millennial Kingdom of the Franciscans in the New World: A Study of the Writings of Gerónimo de Mendieta (1525–1604)* (Berkeley and Los Angeles, 1956).

Powell, Philip W. *Soldiers, Indians, and Silver: The Northward Advance of New Spain, 1550–1600* (Berkeley and Los Angeles, 1952).

Prescott, William H. *The Conquest of Mexico*, 3 vols. (New York, 1843; many reprints).

Priestley, Herbert I. *José de Gálvez, Visitor-General of New Spain, 1765–1771* (Berkeley, 1916).

Quirk, Robert E. *The Mexican Revolution, 1914–1915: The Convention of Aguascalientes* (Bloomington, Ind., 1960).

Ricard, Robert. *The Spiritual Conquest of Mexico* transl. by Lesley Byrd Simpson (Berkeley and Los Angeles, 1966).

Roeder, Ralph. *Juárez and His Mexico, a Biographical History*, 2 vols. (New York, 1947).

Senior, Clarence. *Democracy Comes to a Cotton Kingdom: The Story of Mexico's La Laguna* (Mexico, 1940).

———. *Land Reform and Democracy* (Gainesville, Fla., 1958).

Simpson, Eyler N. *The Ejido, Mexico's Way Out* (Chapel Hill, N.C., 1937).

Simpson, Lesley Byrd. *The Encomienda in New Spain: The Beginning of Spanish Mexico*, 3d ed. (Berkeley and Los Angeles, 1966).

Smith, Justin H. *The War with Mexico*, 2 vols. (New York, 1919).

Spratling, William. *A Small Mexican World* (Boston, 1964). Original title: *Little Mexico* (New York, 1932).

Stephens, John L. *Incidents of Travel in Central America, Chiapas, and Yucatan*, 2 vols. (New York, 1841; many reprints).

Tannenbaum, Frank. *Mexico: The Struggle for Peace and Bread* (New York, 1950).

Thompson, J. Eric. *Mexico Before Cortez* (New York, 1933).

Timmons, Wilbert H. *Morelos of Mexico: Priest, Soldier, Statesman* (El Paso, Tex., 1963).

Toor, Frances. *A Treasury of Mexican Folkways* (New York, 1947).

Torres-Ríoseco, Arturo. *New World Literature: Tradition and Revolt in Latin America* (Berkeley and Los Angeles, 1949).

Vaillant, George C. *Aztecs of Mexicos* (New York, 1941).

Vogt, William. *Road to Survival* (New York, 1948).

Whetten, Nathan L. *Rural Mexico* (Chicago, 1948).

Zorita, Alonso de. *Life and Labor in Ancient Mexico*, a translation of Zorita's *Breve Relación de los Señores de la Nueva España* [ca. 1590] by Benjamin Keen (New Brunswick, N.J., 1963).

# INDEX